Student Workboo

Exploring Economics
THIRD EDITION

Robert L. Sexton

Pepperdine University

Prepared by

Stephen L. Jackstadt
University of Alaska, Anchorage

Lee Huskey
University of Alaska, Anchorage

THOMSON
™
SOUTH-WESTERN

Australia · Canada · Mexico · Singapore · Spain · United Kingdom · United States

THOMSON

SOUTH-WESTERN

Student Workbook to accompany Exploring Microeconomics, 3e

Robert L. Sexton

VP/Editorial Director:
Jack W. Calhoun

VP/Editor-in-Chief:
Michael P. Roche

Publisher of Economics:
Michael B. Mercier

Acquisitions Editor:
Michael Worls

Developmental Editor:
Andrew McGuire

Executive Marketing Manager:
Lisa Lysne

Senior Production Editor:
Kara ZumBahlen

Media Developmental Editor:
Peggy Buskey

Media Production Editor:
Pam Wallace

Manufacturing Coordinator:
Sandee Milewski

Printer:
Von Hoffman Graphics, Frederick, MD

Senior Design Project Manager:
Michelle Kunkler

For permission to use material from this text or product, contact us by
Tel (800) 730-2214
Fax (800) 730-2215
http://www.thomsonrights.com

For more information
contact South-Western,
5191 Natorp Boulevard,
Mason, Ohio 45040.
Or you can visit our Internet site at:
http://www.swlearning.com

Table of Contents

CHAPTER 1
THE ROLE AND METHOD OF ECONOMICS

SECTION 1.1
ECONOMICS: A BRIEF INTRODUCTION

KEY POINTS

- Economics is a unique way of analyzing human behavior over a broad range of topics.

- **Economics** is the study of the allocation of limited resources to satisfy our unlimited wants.

- **Resources** are inputs that are used to produce goods and services.

- Our wants exceed what our resources can produce. This is what we call **scarcity.** Scarcity forces us to make choices on how to best use our limited resources.

- **The economic problem:** Scarcity forces us to choose and choices are costly because we must give up other opportunities that we value. This economizing problem is evident in every aspect of our lives.

- Economics concerns anything that is considered worthwhile to some human being. Virtually everything we decide to do, then, has an economic dimension.

- Living in a world of scarcity means facing trade-offs. It is important that we know what these trade-offs are so we can make better choices about the options available to us.

Chapter 1: The Role and Method of Economics

I   REVIEW

A student of economics learns that much of life involves making a _____ between conflicting wants in a world of scarcity. Students develop an economic way of _____ about their options, which is a valuable problem-solving tool.

_____ is defined as the study of the allocation of our _____ resources to satisfy our unlimited wants.

The factors like machinery, labor, water, and land that are used to make goods and services are called _____.

The problem of _____ results because our wants are greater than the goods and services our resources can produce.

We are forced to make _____ about the best use of our limited resources. The cost of choosing to use a resource one way is the lost _____ to use the resource in another way.

Making costly choices about the use of scarce resources is known as the _____ problem.

II   TRUE/FALSE

_____1. The Mayor's Crime Commission has recommended increased spending on midnight basketball programs, which are intended to reduce the city's crime rate. The Crime Commission is making choices with regard to scarce resources.

_____2. Economic resources are only those things produced by nature.

_____3. We have to make choices about the use of resources because they are scarce.

_____4. Since a steel company owns its trucks, there is no cost involved when they are used to ship steel.

_____5. Economics is only useful for analyzing decisions about goods and services that are bought and sold in stores.

_____6. When you stay up late to watch the *David Letterman Show*, you have made an economic decision.

III   MULTIPLE CHOICE

1. Which of the following is not an example of a resource?
   A) rubber trees
   B) paint sprayers
   C) toys
   D) hammers

2. What are the two parts of the economic problem?
   A) Economics explains many things, but some things it doesn't.
   B) Natural resources are scarce, but man-made resources aren't.
   C) Scarcity makes us choose, and choices are costly.
   D) We have unlimited wants and unlimited resources.

3. Which answer best describes why the choice of how much time to sleep is an economic problem?
   A) The amount of time you sleep determines the type of bed you buy and buying a bed is an economic decision.
   B) Time is a scarce resource and an hour of sleep costs since you have to give up other uses of time.
   C) If you sleep in a hotel, you must pay for the room.
   D) Sleep helps you become a more productive worker.

4. Which of the following does not involve a trade-off?
   A) deciding what to do on a Friday night
   B) choosing the best way to get to your best friend's house
   C) depositing your paycheck in the bank
   D) winning the lottery after you have purchased your ticket

IV   APPLICATION AND DISCUSSION

1. In most countries the birth rate has fallen as incomes and the economic opportunities for women have increased. Use economics to explain this pattern.

2. Explain why each of the following is an economic problem.
   A) going on a date
   B) a basketball coach awards one of 10 available scholarships to a point guard
   C) the university's admission policy

3. Write your own definition of economics. What are the main elements of the definition?

SECTION 1.2
ECONOMICS AS A SCIENCE

KEY POINTS

- Economics, like the other social sciences, is concerned with reaching generalizations about human behavior. It is the social science that studies the choices people make in a world of limited resources.

- Conventionally, we distinguish between two main branches of economics: macroeconomics and microeconomics.

- **Macroeconomics** is the study of the aggregate, or total, economy. It looks at economic problems as they influence the whole of society, including the topics of inflation, unemployment, business cycles, and economic growth.

- **Microeconomics** deals with the smaller units within the economy, attempting to understand the decision-making behavior of firms and households and their interaction in markets for particular goods or services.

Chapter 1: The Role and Method of Economics

I   REVIEW

Like other social sciences, the central concern of economics is _____ _____ . It is the social science that studies people's _____ .

Of the two main branches of economics, _____ examines the effects of human behavior on the total economy, while _____ deals with human behavior in smaller units like the household or the firm. Economic problems affecting the whole of society such as inflation and unemployment are topics of _____ . Microeconomics examines the choice making behavior of firms and households and their interaction in _____ .

II   TRUE/FALSE

_____1. The various social sciences—psychology, sociology, anthropology, political science, and economics—examine special questions and very rarely overlap or complement each other.

_____2. When economists study the economics of the avocado industry they are doing microeconomics.

_____3. Since the two branches of economics, microeconomics and macroeconomics, deal with different levels of aggregation, they have nothing in common.

_____4. An economist forecasting the change in the general price level is doing microeconomics.

III   MULTIPLE CHOICE

1. Which of the following is not a social science?
   A) Psychology
   B) Sociology
   C) Economics
   D) Biology

2. Which of the following is the best example of a microeconomics study?
   A) a study of the determinants of the business cycle
   B) a study of the relation between the price level and unemployment
   C) a study of the factors that can lower a firm's production costs
   D) a study of the factors that determine the rate of inflation

3. Which of the following is *not* an example of the use of the problem solving perspective provided by economics?
   A) An investor looks at the tax consequences of selling stocks to buy bonds, which he believes offer a better return.
   B) A rancher recognizes that raising more cattle this year will damage his pasture and limit next year's herd size.
   C) The Archer family takes its vacation at Lake Arrowhead this year because they have done this for as long as anyone can remember.
   D) An economic student thinks about the other subjects that she should be studying before she decides to study economics tonight.

4. Economist Kenneth Boulding said that knowledge is always gained by the systematic loss of information and the elimination of the "great buzzing confusion of information" that the world provides. What did he mean?
   A) Economists can't understand how things work by concentrating on the particulars so we must generalize about human behavior.
   B) Economics can't do everything so it must only concentrate on certain aspects of society, like making money.
   C) Economics can't begin to explain the complex world so economists must concentrate on creating theories and not worry about the real world.
   D) Since there are so many countries in the world, economists must concentrate only on the particular country they know about, like the United States.

5. Which of the following is not a true statement?
   A) The study of unemployment is a topic of macroeconomics.
   B) The study of the effects of unemployment on the demand for fig bars is a topic of microeconomics.
   C) The study of health consequences of unemployment is a topic of social science.
   D) The study of a community's support of the unemployed is a topic of social science.

IV   APPLICATION AND DISCUSSION

1. Identify which of the following headlines represents a microeconomic topic and which represents a macroeconomic topic.

Topic	Microeconomics	Macroeconomics
A. "U.S. Unemployment Rate Reaches Historic Lows"	_____	_____
B. "General Motors Closes Auto Plant in St. Louis"	_____	_____
C. "OPEC Action Result in a General Increase in Prices"	_____	_____
D. "Companies Cut the Cost of Health Care for Employees"	_____	_____
E. "Lawmakers Worry about the Possibility of a US Recession"	_____	_____
F. "Colorado Rockies Make Outfielder Highest Paid Ballplayer"	_____	_____

SECTION 1.3
ECONOMIC BEHAVIOR

KEY POINTS

- Economists assume that individuals act as if they are motivated by self-interest and respond in predictable ways to changing circumstances.

- Most economists believe that it is rational for people to try and anticipate the possible consequences of their behavior before making a decision.

- Actions have consequences. Even inaction, which is a choice not to do something or not to make changes, has consequences.

I   REVIEW

Economists assume that people act _____ _____ they were motivated by self-interest. Since people are also assumed to respond to changes in _____ ways, self-interest is a good predictor of behavior.

Self-interest _____ people to produce more and may also encourage _____. Pursuing self-interest is not the same as being _____.

Choices will have both positive and negative _____. Economists believe that it is rational for people to _____ consequences of their actions before they make a decision.

II   TRUE/FALSE

_____1. Economists believe that people who commit crimes are not considering the consequences.

_____2. Economists assume that we are motivated primarily by our concern for others.

_____3. Economists assume that a person who has decided to take up smoking after the reading the warning label is wrong.

_____4. Economists believe that not much of human behavior can be predicted by assuming that people pursue their own self-interest.

_____5. Economics cannot explain the actions of people who donate their time and money to helping others.

_____6. Friends describe Chandler as "clueless." Even Chandler recognizes that he always seems to do things without the slightest thought about the consequences. Economists would consider Chandler's behavior irrational.

III   MULTIPLE CHOICE

1. Which one of the following scientists observes how people will respond in predictable ways to changing incentives, especially changes in price and costs?
   A) psychiatrist
   B) journalist
   C) biologist
   D) economist

2. Which of the following is not consistent with economists' assumption that individuals generally consider the consequences of their actions?
   A) Robert, the father of two, smokes but takes out extra life insurance.
   B) Marlene, a middle-aged accountant, saves regularly each month toward her retirement.
   C) Mr. Haviland invites Tony and his bull, "Tornado" into his china shop.
   D) Claudia decides to forego studying and settle for a "D" on her physics exam in order to see the Dave Matthews Band in concert the night before her midterm.

3. Most economists assume that peoples' actions are
   A) motivated by submerged emotional needs.
   B) driven by magnetic forces generated by planetary movements.
   C) undertaken in an attempt to improve the well-being of others.
   D) motivated by self-interest.

4. Suppose the general manager of the Kansas City Chiefs football team has negotiated a new contract with star quarterback, Bobby Thompson. The contract pays Bobby a bonus of $1,000 for every pass he completes during the season. Which of the following is most likely to describe Bobby's actions?
   A) Bobby trains less in the off-season since he already has a contract.
   B) Bobby will take risks during the season, throwing long passes that are less likely to be caught but more likely to result in touchdowns.
   C) Bobby will run the ball more than last year.
   D) Bobby will throw mostly short passes, which are most likely to be caught but less likely to result in touchdowns.

IV   APPLICATION AND DISCUSSION

1. Psychologist Kenneth Lux says that economists are wrong in assuming that people are motivated primarily by self-interest. Furthermore, he laments economists' success at selling this view of human behavior to politicians, business leaders, journalists, and people in general, since he believes that self-interest leads to social strife, pollution, and other ills. Lux says that the pursuit of self-interest encourages cheating. According to Lux, "from the standpoint of self-interest it would be irrational for someone not to cheat if they could be reasonably sure of getting away with it." (Kenneth Lux, *Adam Smith's Mistake,* Shambala Publications, 1990, p. 83.)

   What do you think? Are economists wrong to assume that self-interest is the motivation behind economic behavior? Do people other than economists agree with this view? Does self-interest lead to cheating?

SECTION 1.4

ECONOMIC THEORY

KEY POINTS

- A **theory** is an established explanation that accounts for known facts or phenomena. Economic theories are statements or propositions about patterns of human behavior that are expected to take place under certain circumstances.

- Economic theories help us to sort out and understand the complexities of economic behavior. We expect a good theory to explain and predict well. A good economic theory, then, should help explain and predict human economic behavior.

- Economic theories must abstract from many of the particular details of situations to better focus on the behavior to be explained (like a road map). An economic theory provides a broad view, not a detailed examination, of human economic behavior.

- The beginning of any theory is a **hypothesis,** a testable proposition that makes some type of prediction about behavior in response to certain changed conditions. A hypothesis in economic theory is a testable prediction about how people will behave or react to a change in economic circumstances.

- **Empirical analysis**, the use of data to test hypotheses, is applied to determine whether or not a hypothesis fits well with the facts.

- Determining whether an economic hypothesis is acceptable is more difficult than is the case in the natural or physical sciences. The laboratory of economists is usually the real world, and economists cannot control all the variables that might influence human behavior.

- If an economic hypothesis is supported by the data, it can then be tentatively accepted as an economic theory.

I   REVIEW

A _____ is an explanation that is supported by the facts of the real world. Economic theories are propositions used to _____ and _____ human behavior in different circumstances.

Economic theories cannot account for every event; to be useful theories must _____ or focus on only the essential factors.

A _____ is a prediction about how people will behave in certain economic circumstances and can be tested to see how well the prediction fits the _____

Economists engage in _____ analysis to test hypotheses by seeing if they are consistent with the real world observations.

II   TRUE/FALSE

_____1. We expect a good theory will describe everything about a particular economic behavior.

_____2. The statement "incentives matter" is an example of an economic theory.

_____3. A good hypothesis is "Living on Mars would increase the amount of coffee people drink."

_____4. A hypothesis is not the same as a theory.

_____5. Lee McKenzie has an idea that the natural tendency for stock prices is to rise. He promotes this hypothesis as "the Helium Market Strategy to Riches." As a hypothesis, this strategy offers a good way to make money in the stock market.

III   MULTIPLE CHOICE

1. What is the difference between a hypothesis and a theory?
    A) A hypothesis is the prediction made using a theory.
    B) A hypothesis has not been tested, but empirical analysis has shown that a theory is supported by the facts.
    C) A hypothesis makes a prediction about human behavior but a theory does not makes a prediction.
    D) A hypothesis abstracts from reality while a theory describes reality.

2. In her new book "Women Play the Infield but Men are from Leftfield," Marion Knott presents the proposition that women and men react in different but predictable ways in sports and recreation. How can we decide whether her proposition is a good theory?
    A) The theory is a good one if Marion sells a lot of books.
    B) The theory is a good one if many scientists agree with the proposition.
    C) The theory is a good one if it explains and predicts well human behavior.
    D) The theory is a good one since the publisher agreed to print it.

3. William Hanks owns country music station, KQED, in Boise. He would like to predict how changes in the community and in his radio format would affect KQED's share of the Boise radio market. Which of the following do you think is important for a theory that would help Hanks predict his share of the radio audience?
    A) The theory includes a log of every song the station has played for the last ten years.
    B) The theory describes the number and type of cars and car radios everyone in Boise owns.
    C) The theory includes predictions by the fortuneteller, Madam Ouzinke.
    D) The theory isolates only the most important factors Hanks thinks affect his audience share.

4. An economist has been asked to explain why coffee bean production has declined in Brazil during the 1990s. Which of the following would not be an important step in the development of a theory of coffee bean production?
    A) Develop a hypothesis, such as producers reduce coffee production when the price falls.
    B) Do empirical analysis and see whether coffee production has fallen when prices have fallen in the past.
    C) Go "back to the drawing board" and develop a new hypothesis if this one does not fit the facts.
    D) Drink only three cups of coffee a day when he conducts the study.

IV   APPLICATION AND DISCUSSION

1. In the United States, the average woman's annual earnings is less than 75 percent of the average man's earnings. Develop a hypothesis that would help to explain this fact.

2. The Environmental Protection Agency asks you to help them understand the causes of urban pollution. Air pollution problems are worse the higher the Air Quality Index. You develop the following two hypotheses.

    Hypothesis I: Air pollution will be a greater problem the higher the average temperature in the urban area.

Hypothesis II: Air pollution will be a greater problem, the greater the population of the urban area.

Test each hypothesis with the facts given below. Which hypothesis fits the facts better? Have you developed a theory?

Metropolitan Statistical Area	Days with Polluted Air*	Average Maximum Temperature	Population (thousands)
Cincinnati, OH	30	64	1,979
El Paso, TX	13	77.1	680
Milwaukee, WI	12	55.9	1,690
Atlanta, GA	24	72.0	4,112
Philadelphia, PA	33	63.2	5,101
Albany, NY	8	57.6	876
San Diego, CA	20	70.8	2,814
Los Angeles, CA	80	70.6	9,519

*Air Quality Index greater than 100 (2002)

Source: U.S. Dept. of Commerce, Bureau of Census, 2002 Statistical Abstract of the United States, Tables Nos. 30, and 363; U.S. EPA, Airtrends Report, 2002, EPA.Gov/airtrends/Factbook.

SECTION 1.5
PROBLEMS TO AVOID IN SCIENTIFIC THINKING

KEY POINTS

- Virtually all theories in economics are expressed using a *ceteris paribus* ("let everything else be equal" or "holding everything else constant") assumption. In trying to assess the effect of one variable on another, we must isolate their relationship from other events that might also influence the situation that the theory is trying to explain or predict.

- Without a theory of causation, no scientist could sort out and understand the enormous complexity that occurs in the real world. But one must always be careful not to confuse **correlation** with **causation.** The fact that two sets of phenomena are related does not necessarily mean that one caused the other to occur.

- One must be careful with problems associated with aggregation, particularly the **fallacy of composition.** That is, even if something is true for an individual, it is not necessarily true for many individuals as a group.

I   REVIEW

The Latin expression for "let everything else be equal" is _____ _____.

Without a theory of _____, scientists cannot understand the complexity that occurs in the real world.

In seeking to find causes for events, people sometimes mistake _____ for causation.

If someone observes that new car sales and auto accidents rise at the same time and concludes that new car sales cause auto accidents, they are mistaking _____ for causation.

When someone assumes that what is true of an individual is also true of a group, they are committing the fallacy of

_____.

II   TRUE/FALSE

_____1. The Latin term *ceteris paribus* means "the bus stops here."

_____2. Scientists studying the relationship between two variables try to hold other variables constant.

_____3. If two phenomena occur together one must be the cause of the other.

_____4. The fallacy of composition is committed when someone believes that what is true for an individual is also true of the individuals in a group.

III   MULTIPLE CHOICE

1. A scientist trying to test a theory about the relationship between peoples' consumption of alcohol and their longevity would want to hold all of the following variables constant except
    A)   the number of cigarettes that people in the experimental group smoke.
    B)   the amount of alcohol that people in the experimental group consume.
    C)   past histories of heart and lung disease among people in the experimental group.
    D)   the amount of animal fat that people in the experimental group consume each day.

2. Five-year-old Dimitri observes that people who play basketball are taller than normal and tells his mom that he's going to play basketball because it will make him tall. Dimitri is
    A)   committing the fallacy of composition.
    B)   violating the *ceteris paribus* assumption.
    C)   mistaking correlation for causation.
    D)   confusing the direction of causation.

3. Many people have heard that the stock market rises when a team from the National Football Conference (NFC) wins the Super Bowl and falls when a team from the American Football Conference (AFC) is victorious. If Veronica concludes that there is a causal relationship between which team wins the Super Bowl and the direction of stock prices, she is probably
    A)   confusing correlation with causation.
    B)   violating the *ceteris paribus* assumption.
    C)   committing the fallacy of composition.
    D)   confusing the direction of causality, since everyone knows that stock market prices determine which team wins the Super Bowl.

4. "When one major league baseball team spends more money acquiring better players it is better off, but if all other teams do the same thing in order to compete, none of them is better off." This statement demonstrates
   A) the confusion of association with causation.
   B) the *ceteris paribus* assumption.
   C) the problem associated with the misspecification of the direction of causality.
   D) the fallacy of composition.

IV   APPLICATION AND DISCUSSION

1. In the 1940s, Dr. Melvin Page, a Florida dentist and head of the Biochemical Research Foundation, conducted a national campaign to stop people other than infants from drinking milk. According to Page, milk was a dangerous food and a leading cause of cancer. He pointed to the fact that more people died of cancer in Wisconsin, the nation's leading milk producer, than any other state as proof of his claim. (Cited in Martin Gardner, *Fads & Fallacies in the Name of Science,* Dover Publications, 1957, pp. 222–223.)

   From what you know about scientific thinking, the importance of *ceteris paribus,* and the danger of mistaking association for causation, how would you evaluate Dr. Page's claim?

SECTION 1.6
POSITIVE AND NORMATIVE ANALYSIS

KEY POINTS

- In the role of scientist, an economist tries to objectively observe patterns of behavior without reference to the appropriateness or inappropriateness of that behavior. This objective, value-free approach utilizing the scientific method is called **positive analysis.**

- In positive analysis, we want to know the impact of Variable A on Variable B. A positive statement does not have to be a true statement, but it does have to be a testable statement.

- A good economist/scientist strives to be as fair and objective as possible in evaluating evidence and in stating conclusions based on the evidence.

- Opinions expressed about the desirability of various actions are called **normative analysis.** Normative statements, such as incomes should be more equally distributed, involve judgments about what should be or what ought to happen. Normative statements are subjective, non-testable statements.

- It is important to distinguish between positive and normative analysis because many controversies in economics revolve around policy considerations that contain both.

- Disagreement is common in most disciplines. The majority of disagreements in economics stem from normative issues as differences in values or policy beliefs result in conflict.

- Economists may disagree as to the validity of a given economic theory for the policy in question because the empirical evidence appears somewhat conflicting.

- Most economists agree on a wide range of issues, including the effects of rent control, import tariffs, export restrictions, the use of wage and price controls to curb inflation, and the minimum wage. Often, economists argue that if market forces are allowed to work freely, economic analysis can predict certain phenomena with a high degree of success.

I   REVIEW

When economists study human behavior, they emphasize how people behave, not how they should behave. This objective approach is called _____ analysis.

When economists comment on the desirability of particular actions they are making _____ statements. Normative statements involve judgements about what _____ to happen.

It is especially important to be able to _____ between normative and positive analysis when policy considerations contain both. The majority of _____ among economists involve normative issues.

A second important reason economists disagree is disagreement on the _____ of the economic _____ in a particular policy application.

II   TRUE/FALSE

_____1. The following statement is a normative statement: If the tax on cigarettes is increased, people will smoke fewer cigarettes.

_____2. When economists make normative statements they are stating their opinions.

_____3. Since economics is a science, economists never disagree.

_____4. We would expect more agreement among economists with the statement, "Raising the fine the library charges for overdue books will reduce the number of overdue books" than we would expect to find with the statement, "We don't want to discourage the use of the library with fines on overdue books because people ought to read more."

_____5. If an economics professor presents her opinions about policy issues in class, she is still teaching economics.

III   MULTIPLE CHOICE

1. In the recent congressional debate about agricultural price supports, senators, congress women and men, and experts made the following four statements. Which of these statements is a normative statement?
   A) Price supports are important because America should preserve the small family farm.
   B) Without price supports the price of wheat and corn will fall by over twenty percent.
   C) The decline in commodity prices caused by the removal of price supports will result in fewer, larger farms.
   D) The decline in commodity prices caused by the removal of price supports will reduce the number of tractors sold in the United States.

2. Your mother tells you, "Watching ten hours of TV a day will make you stupid." Why is this a positive statement?
   A) She says it with a positive tone in her voice.
   B) It is a proposition that can be tested.
   C) She really means that she doesn't think you should watch so much TV.
   D) Your father agrees with her.

3. Economists sometimes run for public office. Why is it important to be able to distinguish their positive from their normative statements about economic policy?
   A) Economists are always making assumptions and policy should not be based on assumptions.
   B) We really don't have to worry, since trained economists never make normative statements.
   C) Their positive statements will help us predict the consequences of a particular policy while their normative statements will only tell us their opinions.
   D) Their positive statements help us understand the good results of a policy change and their normative statements help us understand the negative results.

4. Which of the following is *not* a reason the textbook gives for disagreement among economists over policy issues?
   A) differences in values, opinions, and beliefs among economists
   B) some economists value freedom while others value fairness
   C) conflicting empirical evidence supporting various theories
   D) economists, like most people, just like to argue with their friends

IV   APPLICATION AND DISCUSSION

1. In the debate about clean air standards we have often heard the statement, "A nation as rich as the United States should have no pollution." Why is this a normative statement? Would it help you make a decision on the national air quality standards? Describe two positive statements that might be useful in determining the air quality standards.

THE LOWELLS

Questions

1.   Mr. Lowell has a theory. What is it?
2.   What information do you think Mr. Lowell used to develop his theory?

C H A P T E R 2
THE ECONOMIC WAY OF THINKING

SECTION 2.1 IDEA 1: SCARCITY

SECTION 2.2 IDEA 2: OPPORTUNITY COST

SECTION 2.3 IDEA 3: MARGINAL THINKING

SECTION 2.4 IDEA 4: INCENTIVES MATTER

SECTION 2.5 IDEA 5: SPECIALIZATION AND TRADE

SECTION 2.6 IDEA 6: MARKET PRICES COORDINATE ECONOMIC ACTIVITY

S E C T I O N 2 . 1
IDEA 1: SCARCITY

KEY POINTS

- Most of economics is knowing certain principles well and when and how to apply them.

- Economics is primarily concerned with **scarcity**—how well we satisfy our unlimited wants in a world of limited resources. People are not able to fulfill all of their wants—material desires and nonmaterial desires. As long as human wants exceed available resources, scarcity will exist.

- The scarce resources that are used in the production of goods and services can be grouped into four categories: labor, land, capital, and entrepreneurship.

- **Labor** is the total of both physical and mental effort expended by people in the production of goods and services.

- **Land** is the natural resources used in the production of goods and services.

- **Capital** are goods that are used to produce other goods. It also includes **human capital**, the productive knowledge and skill people receive from education and on-the-job training.

- **Entrepreneurship** is the process of combining the labor, land, and capital together to produce goods and services. The entrepreneur is the one who makes the tough and risky decisions about what to produce and how to produce it. Entrepreneurs are always looking for new ways to improve production techniques or to create new products. They are lured by the chance to make a profit.

- All economies, regardless of political structure, must decide between several possib ays to prod e goods and services that they want. When digging a ditch, a contractor must decide between m orkers usi ir hands, a few workers with shovels, or one person with a backhoe. A decision must be made which me s appropriate. The best method is the least-cost method.

- The best or "optimal" form of production will vary from one economy to the next. y? Each n ends to use the production processes that conserve its relatively scarce (and thus relatively more nsive) resc s and use more of its relatively abundant resources. **Labor-intensive** methods will be used where ital is rela scarce and **capital-intensive** methods will be used where labor is relatively scarce.

- In every society, some mechanism must exist to determine how goods and servi re to be d ited among the population. (Who gets what?) The question of distribution is an issue that alway uses stro notional responses.

- In a market economy, with private ownership and control of the means of prod n, the an of output one is able to obtain depends on one's income, which in turn, depends on the quantit quality scarce resources the individual controls.

I   REVIEW

Scarcity forces all societies from the richest to the poorest to answer three fundamen uestion
1) _____ do we produce?
2) _____ do we produce these goods and services?
3) For _____ do we produce the goods and services?

In market economies, individuals control the production decisions by "voting" wit ir _____ for the goods and services they want. This consumer control is called consumer _____.

Societies organize in two major ways to answer these economic questions. Econo s are c _____ economies when government officials make decisions in a highly centralized syst

When many individual producers and consumers make economic decisions in a ntrali anner the economy is a _____ economy.

Since there are several ways to produce any good or service, all economies mu cide _____ to produce the goods and services they want. If an economy uses lots of labor to uce and services, economists would say production is _____ intensive.

Countries tend to use production processes that conserve its relatively _____ resources and use more of their relatively _____ resources.

"Who gets what?" is an economic question that _____ forces all societies to answer. This question is about the _____ of output.

In a market economy, the amount of output any one person can secure dep on _____, which depends on the amount and quality of scarce _____ co

II   TRUE/FALSE

_____1. Decisions about what to produce are difficult because it's hard r hat people want.

_____2. Even in market economies the decisions about what goods an r to provide are made by a few industrialists and corporate executives.

_____3. Production methods in high-wage countries likes the United States tend to be more capital intensive than in low-wage countries like Mexico.

_____4. Once a society has chosen what to produce there are no more economic decisions to be made.

_____5. The basketball star LeBron James consumes more goods and services than the average college student does because he is taller and taller people need more.

III   MULTIPLE CHOICE

1. The last two decades have witnessed the transition from command toward market economies in many countries around the world. Which of the following changes would we expect to see in the countries making this shift?
    A) More decisions are being made by individual producers and consumers and fewer made by central planning organizations.
    B) Fewer decisions are being made by individual producers and consumers and more made by central planning organizations.
    C) The importance of government begins increasing in the economy.
    D) More decisions are being made using government sovereignty and fewer made using consumer sovereignty.

2. Barry Henley is running for the Senate on the "Consumer is King" platform. Barry says that as a senator he will stop companies from producing goods consumers don't want and force them to produce those goods that will improve consumers' lives. Barry has a list of the products he will promote. What is wrong with Barry's platform?
    A) Barry is forgetting that in a market economy consumers already do this.
    B) Barry's list of products is too short.
    C) Barry's list should include some goods that let people have a good time.
    D) Barry is forgetting that the government already takes care of this.

3. Which of the following is an example of a capital resource?
    A) an unskilled worker
    B) a large coal deposit
    C) a fishing boat
    D) a yellow-fin tuna

4. Which of the following best illustrates how economists view the problem of how to produce goods and services?
    A) "A bird in the hand is worth two in the bush."
    B) "There is more than one way to brew green tea."
    C) "Once burned, twice shy."
    D) "What's sauce for the goose is sauce for the gander."

5. In the United States, who has the greatest claim on the economy's output?
    A) the thirty homeless families with a combined yearly income of $90,000
    B) the thirty college students with a combined yearly income of $600,000
    C) the thirty school teachers with a combined yearly income of $900,000
    D) the thirty-year-old ballplayer with a yearly income of $1,000,000

IV   APPLICATION AND DISCUSSION

1. Recently the American Film Institute selected *Citizen Kane* as the best movie of all time. *Citizen Kane* is a fictional psychological biography of one of the most powerful newspaper publishers in history, William Randolph Hearst. *Titanic,* an epic romance about the sinking of the Titanic, has made the most money of any film in history. Unlike *Titanic, Citizen Kane* was not a box office success. Do you think Hollywood will make more movies like *Titanic* or like *Citizen Kane?* Why?

2. As women's wages and employment opportunities have expanded over the past 50 years, Americans have purchased more and more labor-saving home appliances like automatic washers and dryers, dishwashers, and microwave ovens.

   Do you think these phenomena are related? Could higher wages and better job opportunities lead to a more capital-intensive way of performing household chores? Explain.

SECTION 3.2
THE CIRCULAR FLOW MODEL

KEY POINTS

- **Product markets** are the markets for consumer goods and services. Households are buyers and firms are seller.

- **Factor markets** are markets where households sell their resources to firms. Firms are the buyers and households are sellers.

- Firms receive payments from households for the purchase of goods and services in the product market.

- Households receive payments from firms as compensation for the resources needed to produce goods and services.

- The **circular flow model** illustrates the interaction between households and firms where income flows from firms to households and spending flows from households to firms.

I   REVIEW

Households make payments to firms for goods and services in the _____ market. _____ flows to the firms in exchange for the goods and services that flow to households.

Firms buy _____ from households in the factor market. Firms use households' labor, land, capital, and entrepreneurship to produce _____ and _____.

Money flows from the firms to the households as _____ for the use of these inputs. The households receive payments in the form of _____, _____, _____, and _____.

The simple _____ flow model illustrates the continuous flow of payments, income, inputs, and goods and services between households and firms. This model shows how product and factor markets are _____.

II   TRUE/FALSE

_____1. In the simple circular flow model money moves in the same direction as the flow of goods and services.

_____2. Resources like labor, land, and capital are purchased in factor markets.

_____3. Payments for resources in the factor markets create the income of households.

III   MULTIPLE CHOICE

1. According to the circular flow model of an economy, the money firms pay households for inputs:
    A) leaves the economy as soon as it is paid.
    B) is used by the households to buy the goods and services produced by the firms.
    C) is less than the amount of money paid to the firms for goods and services.
    D) is mostly saved and not used in the economy.

2. Which of the following is a true statement about what occurs in the product market?
    A) Inputs are purchased by households in this market.
    B) Household consumption spending becomes revenue for firms.
    C) Capital, labor and land are turned into consumer products.
    D) Goods and services are exchanged for inputs.

3. Which of the following is not a type of payment found in the factor market?
    A) Wage
    B) Interest
    C) Retail price
    D) Profit

IV.   APPLICATION AND DISCUSSION

Identify the appropriate market where each of the following transactions takes place by placing an X in the appropriate box.

Transaction	Factor Market	Product Market
Billy buys a sofa from Home Time Furniture for his new home.		
Home Time Furniture pays its manager her weekly salary.		
The manager buys dinner at Billy's Café.		
After he pays all of his employees their wages and pays his other bills, the owner of Billy's Café takes his profit.		

SECTION 3.3
THE PRODUCTION POSSIBILITIES CURVE

KEY POINTS

- The economic concepts of scarcity, choice, and trade-offs can be illustrated by the use of a **production possibilities curve**, which represents the potential total output combinations of any two goods for an economy. That is, it illustrates an economy's potential for allocating its limited resources for producing various combinations of goods in a given time period.

- On a production possibilities curve, we assume that the economy has a given quantity and quality of resources and technology available to use for production.

- The economy cannot produce beyond the levels indicated by the production possibilities curve during a given time period because there are not enough resources to produce that output. However, it is possible to operate inside the production possibilities curve.

- If an economy is operating inside its production possibilities curve, it is not at full capacity and is operating inefficiently. The economy is not getting the most it can from its scarce resources; as a result, actual output is less than potential output.

- Most modern economies have resources that are idle, at least for some period of time. If those resources were not idle, people would have more scarce goods and services available for their use.

- Unemployed resources create a serious problem, not just for labor, but for all resources entering into production. All resources must be used effectively for efficient production.

- Underutilized resources or those not being put to their best uses are illustrated by output combinations inside the production possibilities curve. By putting unemployed resources to work or by putting already employed resources to better uses, we could expand output.

- **Efficiency** requires society to use its resources to the fullest extent—getting the most we can out of our scarce resources.

- If resources are being used efficiently, that is at a point along a production possibilities curve, the cost for more of one good or service is the sacrifice of another good or service.

- The production possibilities curve is not a straight line. It is concave from below (that is, bowed outward from the origin), reflecting **increasing opportunity costs** of producing additional amounts of a good.

- The basic reason for increasing opportunity cost is that some resources and skills cannot be easily adapted from their current uses to alternative uses. Easily adaptable resources are soon exhausted and resources and workers that are less well-suited or appropriate (those with a relatively greater opportunity cost) must then be employed to increase output further.

I   REVIEW

The problem of making choices regarding what to produce and in what quantities can be illustrated with a _____ possibilities curve.

Most economies have resources that are _____ for at least some period of time.

Efficiency requires society to use its resources to the fullest extent and get the _____ output from its scarce resources.

If an economy is operating at a point off and below its production possibilities curve, it means that resources are not being utilized _____.

When a production possibilities curve is bowed outward from the origin it is because of the law of _____ cost.

II   TRUE/FALSE

_____1. The production possibilities curve represents the various amounts of a good a country can produce using different amounts of labor and capital.

_____2. A production possibilities curve might be used to represent the total output combinations of rice and soybeans in South Korea.

_____3. Increasing opportunity cost occurs because some productive resources cannot be easily adapted from production of one good or service, like farming, to another, like manufacturing.

_____4. Idle factories represent unemployed land resources.

_____5. If an economy has lots of unemployed workers and idle factories, it is not operating efficiently.

III   MULTIPLE CHOICE

1. In Exhibit 1, South Korea's production possibilities curve for rice and soybeans is shown. Point A represents total output of
    A) 500 million bushels of rice and 350 million bushels of soybeans.
    B) 850 million bushels of rice.
    C) 350 million bushels of rice and 500 million bushels of corn.
    D) 800 million bushels of soybeans.

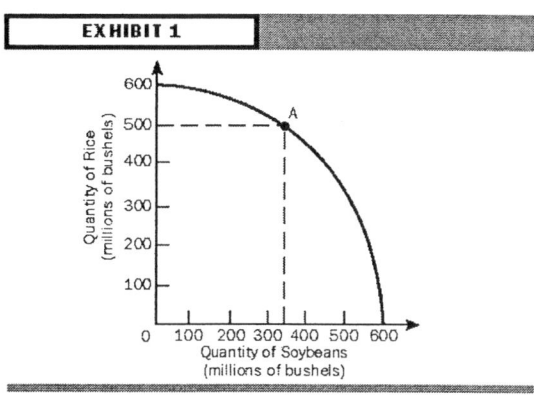

EXHIBIT 1

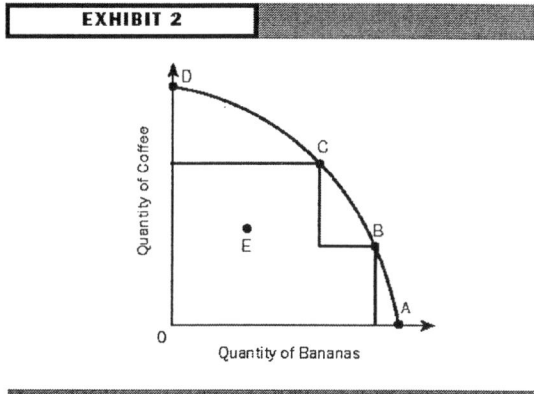

EXHIBIT 2

Refer to Exhibit 2, which represents Costa Rica's production possibilities for coffee and bananas, to answer questions 2, 3, and 4 below.

2. If Costa Rica produces no coffee and devotes all of its resources to growing bananas, it will be operating at point
   A) A.
   B) B.
   C) D.
   D) E.

3. If Costa Rica's economy is not operating efficiently, it will be at point
   A) A.
   B) C.
   C) D.
   D) E.

4. As Costa Rica moves from point A to point D on its production possibilities curve, the opportunity cost of producing coffee, in terms of bananas
   A) does not change.
   B) decreases.
   C) increases.
   D) increases to point C, then decreases to point E.

5. What is the main reason economists are concerned about the problem of idle resources?
    A) Government benefits paid to unemployed workers put stress on the federal budget.
    B) Unemployed resources mean less production and lower standard of living for the nation.
    C) High rates of crime are correlated with high rates of unemployment.
    D) We want to avoid high rates of inflation that are caused by idle resources.

6. Exhibit 3 represents the production possibilities for a country that can use its resources to produce guns, butter, or a combination of both. Which of the following concepts is *not* illustrated by this production possibilities curve?
    A) scarcity
    B) opportunity cost
    C) increasing opportunity cost
    D) economic growth

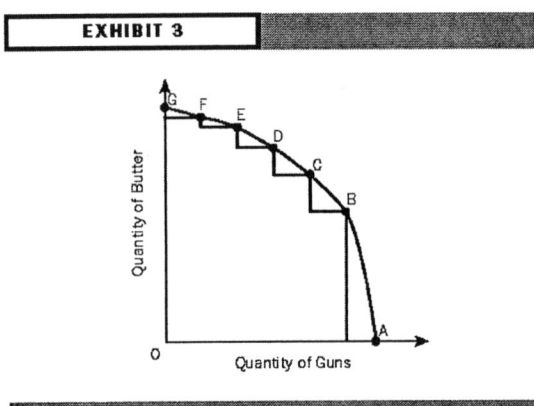

EXHIBIT 3

IV   APPLICATION AND DISCUSSION

1. During wartime, countries shift production from civilian goods, like automobiles and clothing, to military goods, like tanks and military uniforms. When the United States entered World War I in April 1917, for example, the federal government created the War Industries Board and charged it with determining production priorities and converting plants to meet war needs. In the following year, automobile production fell 43 percent as output of military vehicles soared. When the war ended, 19 months later, in November 1918, the government cancelled $2.5 billion in military contracts and the nation resumed normal production. Assuming that in 1917 the United States was at point A on the production possibilities curves shown in Exhibit 4, show what happened between April 1917 and November 1918. Show what happened once the war ended.

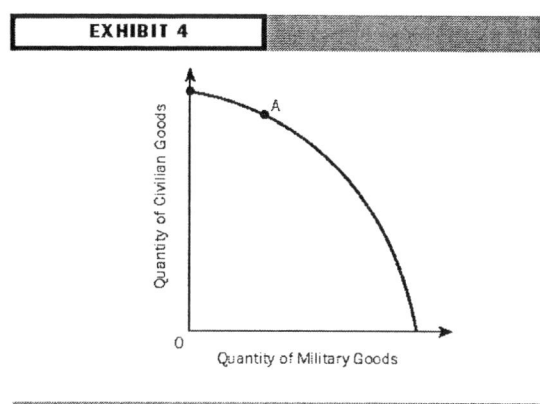

EXHIBIT 4

2. In Exhibit 5, read the examples of idle or unemployed resources and indicate which resource, Capital, Labor, or Land, is involved by putting a check (□) in the appropriate column.

EXHIBIT 5

	Unemployed Capital	Unemployed Labor	Unemployed Land
A) During the 1981–1982 recession, unemployment reached a post–World War II high of 9.7 percent of the labor force. Over 10 million workers were unemployed and output of goods and services fell 2.1 percent.	_____	_____	_____
B) During the same recession, the capacity utilization rate, which shows the percentage of factory capacity being used in production, fell from 81 percent in 1981 to 75 percent in 1982.	_____	_____	_____
C) Between 1929 and 1933, during the Great Depression, unemployment soared to 25 percent of the labor force. Output of goods and services fell by 30 percent.	_____	_____	_____
D) In the mid-1990s, millions of acres of farm land in countries that used to be part of the Soviet Union lay fallow because no one knew who owned them and therefore no one had any incentive to farm them.	_____	_____	_____

3. Is it possible for a country to have unemployed or idle entrepreneurs? In his book *A Bend in the River,* Nobel prize winner V. S. Naipaul describes an underdeveloped country in which the government's constantly changing tax policies and vague laws regarding ownership of property cause entrepreneurs to become demoralized and unresponsive to economic opportunities.

    Is this actually a case of idle or unemployed entrepreneurs? How can tax laws and rules governing property affect entrepreneurs willingness to start new businesses or improve existing enterprises?

SECTION 3.4

ECONOMIC GROWTH AND THE PRODUCTION POSSIBILITIES CURVE

KEY POINTS

- Some nations have been able to rapidly expand their output of goods and services over time, while others have been unable to increase their standard of living at all.

- Investing in capital goods will increase the future production capacity of the economy, so an economy that invests more now (consumes less now) will be able to produce, and therefore consume, more in the future.

- An economy can grow with qualitative or quantitative changes in the factors of production—land, labor, capital, and entrepreneurship. Advancements in technology, improvements in labor productivity, or new natural resource finds could all lead to outward shifts of the production possibilities curve.

- Economic growth means an outward shift in the production possibilities curve. With growth comes the possibility to have more of both goods than were previously available.

- It is important to remember that increases in a society's output do not make scarcity disappear. Even when output has grown more rapidly than population, so that people are made better off, they still face trade-offs. At any point along the production possibilities curve, in order to get more of one thing, you must give up something else.

- The production possibilities curve can be used to illustrate the economic concepts of scarcity, choice, opportunity costs, efficiency, and economic growth. Scarcity is represented by the fact that resource combinations outside the production possibility curve are unattainable. Choice is the fact that one must choose among the alternative bundles available along the production possibilities curve. Opportunity costs are how much of one good you give up to get another unit of the second good as you move along the production possibilities curve. Efficiency would mean being on the production possibilities curve rather than inside it. And economic growth is represented by shifting out the production possibilities curve.

I   REVIEW

A country's economic growth depends on the _____ made today. To grow we have to give up _____ goods and produce more _____ goods.

An increase in an economy's capital stock will allow it to increase its future _____ capacity and consume more in the future. The effect of the increase in a country's capital stock is represented by a(n) _____ shift in its production possibilities curve.

Investment can be more than building new physical capital stock. Upgrading the _____ and _____ of a country's workforce has a similar effect on economic growth.

While today's sacrifices allow a country to produce more in the future, growth will not eliminate _____. Even with more resources, countries must still make _____ among the ways these resources will be used.

II   TRUE/FALSE

_____1. Economic growth just happens. For any country, growth is determined by factors like climate, which it cannot influence.

_____2. B. G. Song wants to be President of Discovakia. He campaigns on the theme "Economic Growth is Always Good." A country will always be better off pursuing economic growth.

_____3. The best economic growth strategy a country can pursue is to produce the most consumer goods it can to keep its workers happy and productive.

_____4. Economic growth is represented by a shift to the right in the production possibilities curve.

_____5. Economic growth will eventually eliminate the problem of scarcity.

III   MULTIPLE CHOICE

1. Which of the following is not an example of an investment in human capital?
    A) Bulgaria builds more classrooms to educate more children.
    B) Uganda increases healthcare spending to reduce the incidence of AIDS.
    C) Chile invests in facilities and equipment to start a salmon industry.
    D) The United States creates a new program to train workers who lost their jobs because of foreign competition.

2. A new economic consulting firm, Growfast Consultants, promotes sacrifice-free economic growth. If they do truly offer growth without sacrifices, their program must include which of the following elements?
    A) reducing consumption today to increase future consumption
    B) receiving gifts of capital from other countries
    C) reducing food production to increase the production of hydroelectric dams
    D) increasing current consumption and reducing the capital goods produced

3. Consider the production possibilities curve in Exhibit 6. Which of the following movements is *not* economic growth?
    A) from A to C
    B) from C to D
    C) from C to B
    D) from B to D

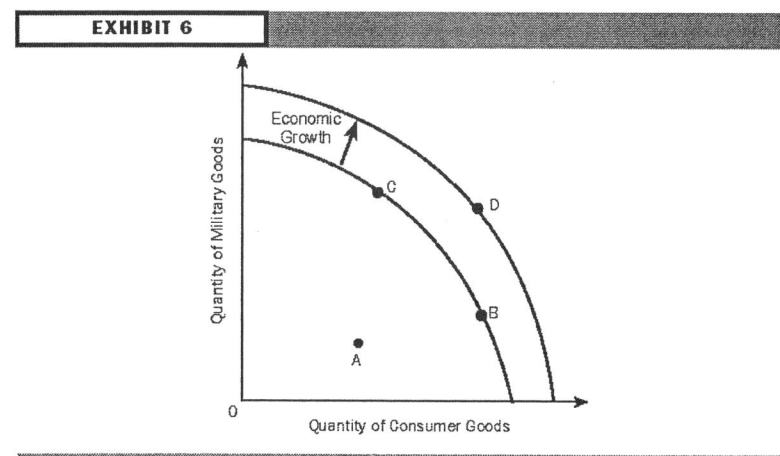

IV   APPLICATION AND DISCUSSION

Chapter 3: Scarcity, Trade-Offs, and Economic Growth

1. Why one nation experiences economic growth and another doesn't is a question that has intrigued economists since Adam Smith wrote *An Inquiry into the Nature and Causes of the Wealth of Nations* in 1776. Explain why each of the following would limit economic growth.

   A) The politically connected elite secure a large share of a country's output and put the proceeds in Swiss banks.

   B) A country has a very low output per person.

   C) The national philosophy is live for the moment and forget about tomorrow.

   D) The government closes all of the schools so more people will be available for work.

   E) The country fears military invasion and spends half of its income on military goods.

Questions

1. If you drew Julie Lowell's production possibilities curve, what would you put on each axis?

2. Why isn't Julie *on* her production possibilities curve?

CHAPTER 4
SUPPLY AND DEMAND

SECTION 4.1
MARKETS

KEY POINTS

- A market is the process of buyers and sellers exchanging goods services.

- The conditions under which exchange occurs between buyers and sellers can vary incredibly, and these varying conditions make it difficult to precisely define a market.

- Goods being priced and traded at various locations by various kinds of buyers and sellers further compound the problem of defining a market. Some markets are local but numerous, others are global.

- The important point about a market is not what it looks like, but what it does—it facilitates trade.

- Buyers, as a group, determine the demand side of the market, whether it is consumers purchasing goods or firms purchasing inputs. Sellers, as a group, determine the supply side of the market, whether it is firms selling their goods or resource owners selling their inputs.

Chapter 4: Supply and Demand

A _____ is the process of buyers and sellers exchanging goods.

The term "market" is hard to define because an incredible variety of _____ arrangements exist in the world.

For some goods, like housing and cement, markets are numerous but _____ limited. For other goods, like gold and automobiles, markets are _____.

The _____ determine the demand side of the market, while _____ determine the supply side.

A _____ market is one characterized by lots of buyers and sellers and in which no single buyer or seller can influence the market price.

II   TRUE/FALSE

_____1. A bookstore is an example of a market.

_____2. A doctor's office is an example of a market.

_____3. A market is always a place.

_____4. Baseball fans determine the supply side of the market for baseball.

III   MULTIPLE CHOICE

1. Which of the following is *not* an example of a market?
   A) a drugstore
   B) the New York Stock Exchange
   C) a factory
   D) a barbershop

2. *Ceteris paribus,* when transportation costs are high relative to the selling price, markets are _____ and _____.
   A) numerous; geographically isolated
   B) numerous; concentrated in a few areas
   C) few; geographically isolated
   D) few; concentrated in a few areas

3. The market for automobiles is
   A) local.
   B) national.
   C) global.
   D) intergalactic.

IV   APPLICATION AND DISCUSSION

1. Is the market for laptop computers local, national, or global?

SECTION 4.2
DEMAND

KEY POINTS

- According to the law of demand, the quantity of a good or service demanded varies inversely with its price, ceteris paribus. More directly, other things equal, when the price of a good or service falls, the quantity demanded increases.

- The law of demand reflects the fact that the price of a good reflects the sacrifice a buyer must make to buy it. A higher price implies a greater sacrifice or opportunity cost. Other things equal, people would want less of a good or service as the necessary sacrifice increases.

- One reason for the inverse relationship between price and quantity demanded is diminishing marginal utility. Since people derive less satisfaction from successive units of the things they consume, they will buy additional units only if the price is reduced.

- Another reason for the inverse relationship between price and quantity demanded is the substitution effect. At higher prices, buyers have an incentive to substitute other goods for the good that now has a higher relative price.

- An individual demand schedule reveals the different amounts of a particular good a person would be willing and able to buy at various possible prices in a particular time interval, other things equal.

- An individual demand curve for a particular good illustrates the same information as the individual demand schedule. It reveals the relationship between the price and the quantity demanded, showing that when the price is higher, the quantity demanded is lower.

- Economists usually speak of the demand curve in terms of large groups of people. The horizontal summing of the demand curves of many individuals is called the market demand curve for a product. It reflects the fact that the total quantity purchased in the market at a price is the sum of the quantities purchased by each demander.

- The market demand curve shows the amounts that all the buyers in the market would be willing to buy at various prices.

- The relative price of a good is its price relative to (or in terms of) other goods. In a world where virtually all prices are changing, relative prices are crucial to economic decisions because changing relative prices alters the trade-offs decision makers face among various goods and services.

- The money price of a good can be higher than in the past and yet have a lower relative price than in the past. (For example: gasoline prices are higher than in the past in money terms, yet they are cheaper relative to other goods and services than they have been in the past.)

I   REVIEW

According to the law of demand, other things being equal, the quantity of a good or service demanded goes up when its price goes _____. The primary reason for the inverse relationship between price and quantity demanded is the _____ effect.

Chapter 4: Supply and Demand

A(n) _____ demand curve is a graphical representation of the relationship between the price of a good and the _____ demanded. The horizontal summing of the demand curves of all the buyers in the market is called the _____ demand curve.

II   TRUE/FALSE

_____1. According to the law of demand, the quantity of a good that people will buy rises as the price of that item rises.

_____2. If the price of bananas falls, we would expect banana consumption to go up.

_____3. The concept of demand is really just an imaginary notion based on what people might want but really can't afford.

_____4. Economists believe that the concept of need is extremely powerful in helping them understand human behavior.

_____5. An individual's demand schedule shows the amount of a good that a person would like to buy whether or not he or she can afford it.

_____6. An individual's demand curve is a graphical representation of that person's demand schedule.

_____7. A market demand curve is constructed by the horizontal summing of many individuals' demand curves.

III   MULTIPLE CHOICE

1. The law of demand says that
    A) as the price of a good rises, people will buy more of it.
    B) as the price of a good rises, people will buy less of it.
    C) as the price of a good falls, people will buy less of it.
    D) demand is related to human needs and has nothing to do with price.

2. According to the law of demand, the relationship between the price of a good and the quantity purchased is a(n) _____ relationship.
    A) positive
    B) unnatural
    C) inverse
    D) legal

3. If Nike were to reduce the price of Air Jordan basketball shoes, what do you predict would happen to the quantity of shoes people will want to buy?
    A) It would stay the same because everyone likes Air Jordans.
    B) It would fall because no one likes cheap shoes.
    C) It would increase because price and quantity are inversely related.
    D) There would never be a reason to reduce the price of Air Jordans.

4. When discussing the law of demand, what do we mean when we say *ceteris paribus*?
    A) It is a Latin term that means the other non-price factors that affect the amount we consume do not change.
    B) It is a Latin term that means "gnarly dude."
    C) It is a Latin term that means there is an inverse relationship.
    D) It is a Latin term that means goods are for sale.

5. An individual's demand curve for a good
   A) shows the amounts of a good that person will buy at various prices.
   B) indicates the market price of an individual good.
   C) is determined by the cost of producing an individual good.
   D) reveals the amounts of a good an individual needs to survive.

6. A market demand curve is
   A) a graphical represenation of the actual demand for markets.
   B) a line that shows the positive relationship between the price of a product and the amount people will buy.
   C) the result of the horizontal summing of many individual demand curves.
   D) a line that shows the amount of a good that will be produced in a given market in a given period of time.

7. A demand curve slopes
   A) up and to the right.
   B) up and to the left.
   C) down and to the left.
   D) down and to the right.

IV   APPLICATION AND DISCUSSION

1. Sid moves from New York City, where he lived in a small condominium, to rural Minnesota, where he buys a big house on five acres of land. Using the law of demand, what do you think is true of land prices in New York relative to those in rural Minnesota?

2. Shown below is Hillary's demand schedule for Cherry Blossom Makeup. Plot Hillary's demand curve on the first graph below.

Price (dollars per ounce)	Quantity Demanded (ounces per week)
$15	5 oz.
12	10
9	15
6	20
3	25

3. Below are Cherry Blossom Makeup demand schedules for Hillary's friends, Barbara and Nancy. If Hillary, Barbara, and Nancy constitute the whole market for Cherry Blossom Makeup, complete the market demand schedule and draw the market demand curve on the second graph below.

Price (dollars per ounce)	Quantity Demanded (ounces per week)			
	Hillary	Barbara	Nancy	Market
$15	5	0	15	
12	10	5	20	
9	15	10	25	
6	20	15	30	
3	25	20	35	

49

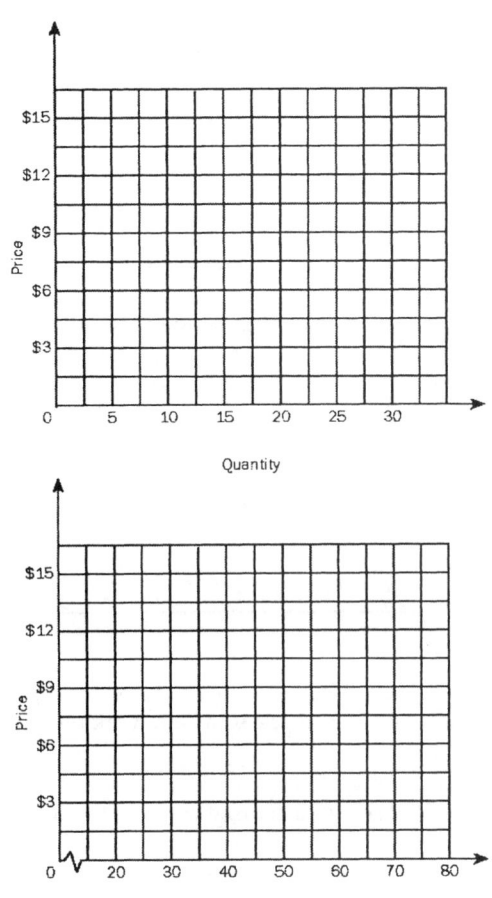

SECTION 4.3

SHIFTS IN THE DEMAND CURVE

KEY POINTS

- Consumers are influenced by the prices of goods when they make their purchasing decisions. At lower prices, people prefer to buy more of a good than at higher prices, holding other factors constant, primarily because many goods are substitutes for one another.

- A change in a good's price leads to a change in quantity demanded, illustrated by moving along a given demand curve. A change in a good's price does not change its demand.

- A change in demand, illustrated by a shift in the entire demand curve, is caused by changes in any of the other five factors (besides the good's own price) that would affect how much of the good is purchased: the prices of closely related goods, the incomes of demanders, the number of demanders, the tastes of demanders, and the expectations of demanders. An increase in demand is represented by a rightward shift in the demand curve; a decrease in demand is represented by a leftward shift in the demand curve.

- The *ceteris paribus* assumption (holding constant the shifters of the demand curve as the price of the good itself changes) allows us to isolate the effect of the price of a good on the quantity of that good demanded from other possible determinants.

- The major variables that shift the demand curve are: the prices of closely related goods; income; number of buyers; tastes of buyers; expectations of buyers.

- Two goods are called substitutes if an increase (a decrease) in the price of one causes a decrease (an increase) in the demand for the other good. Because personal tastes differ, what are substitutes for one person may not be so for another person. Further, some substitutes are better than others (i.e., butter and margarine; economics textbooks and T-shirts).

- Two goods are complements if an increase (a decrease) in the price of one good causes a decrease (an increase) in the demand for the other good. Complements are goods that "go together," often consumed or used simultaneously, i.e., skis and bindings; hot dogs and mustard).

- Generally the consumption of goods and services is positively related to the income available to consumers. As individuals receive more income, they tend to increase their purchases of most goods and services. Other things equal, an increase in income usually leads to an increase in demand for goods (rightward shift), and decreasing income usually leads to a decrease in the demand for goods (leftward shift). Such goods are called normal goods, i.e., CDs, movie tickets).

- Some goods exist for which rising (falling) income leads to reduced (increased) demand. These are called inferior goods, which tend to be lower-quality substitutes for more preferred, higher-quality goods, i.e., thrift shop clothes, store-brand products, bus rides).

- The demand for a good or service will vary with the size of the potential consumer population. An increase in the potential consumer population will increase (shift right) the demand for a good or service.

- Changes in fashions, fads, advertising, etc. can change tastes or preferences. An increase in tastes or preferences for a good or service will increase (shift right) the demand for a good or service.

- While changes in preferences lead to shifts in demand, much of the predictive power of economic theory stems from the assumption that tastes are relatively stable over a substantial period of time (because we cannot precisely and accurately measure taste changes).

- Sometimes the demand for a good or service in a given time period will dramatically increase or decrease because consumers expect the good to change in price or availability at some future date. An increase in the expected future price of a good or a decrease in its expected future availability will increase (shift right) the current demand for it; a decrease in the expected future price of a good or an increase in its expected future availability will decrease (shift left) the current demand for it. However, what is important in terms of demand is what people expected to happen, rather than what actually happened.

- Changes in demand versus changes in quantity demanded revisited: If the price of a good changes, we say this leads to a change in quantity demanded. If one of the five other factors influencing consumer behavior changes, we say there is a change in demand.

I   REVIEW

A change in a good's price leads to a change in _____ demanded, while a change in one of the _____ of demand will lead to a shift in the entire demand curve.

Chapter 4: Supply and Demand

Determinants of demand are called demand _____ and they lead to a change in _____. Some possible demand shifters are: the prices of closely _____ goods; income; number of _____; _____ of buyers; and _____ of buyers.

Two goods are substitutes if an increase in the price of one good causes an _____ in the demand for the other. Two goods are complements if an increase in the price of one good causes a _____ in the demand for the other.

As their incomes rise, consumers generally buy _____ of most goods. When higher income leads to an increase in demand for a good, the good is called a _____ good. If higher income leads to a reduction in demand for a good, it is called _____ good.

The vital statistics of the potential consumer population, including size, income, and age characteristics, are referred to as the _____ of a product.

When demand changes with changes in fashion, the cause of the change is referred to as a change in _____.

_____ about the future, such as fear of shortages or concern over future price rises, may affect consumer _____.

If the price of a good changes, it leads to a change in quantity _____, but if one of the other factors influencing consumer behavior changes, it leads to a change in _____.

II   TRUE/FALSE

_____1. A change in a good's price will lead to a change in demand for that good.

_____2. *Ceteris paribus,* a fall in the price of a good will result in a decrease in demand for its substitutes.

_____3. A fall in the price of CDs will result in a reduction in the demand for tapes.

_____4. An increase in the price of a complementary good will increase the demand for the product in question.

_____5. If the price of tennis racquets falls, the demand for tennis balls is likely to increase.

_____6. If watermelons and mangos are normal goods, demand for them will fall as consumers' incomes rise.

_____7. If duct tape is an inferior good, demand for it will fall as consumers' incomes rise.

_____8. As the U.S. population becomes older on average, we are likely to see an increase in the demand for items like playpens and stuffed animals.

III   MULTIPLE CHOICE

1. The difference between a change in quantity demanded and a change in demand is that
    A) a change in quantity demanded is caused by a change in a good's price, while a change in demand is caused by a change in a variable such as income, tastes, or expectations.

B) a change in demand is caused by a change in a good's price, while a change in quantity demanded is caused by a change in a variable such as income, tastes, or expectations.

C) a change in quantity demanded is a change in the amount people actually buy, while a change in demand is a change in the amount they want to buy.

D) This is a trick question. A change in demand and a change in quantity demanded are the same thing!

2. Which of the following will not cause a change in the demand for a product?
    A) a change in consumers' income
    B) a change in consumers' tastes
    C) a change in the price of the product
    D) a change in the price of a substitute for the product

3. News that eating jelly beans makes you better looking will likely cause
    A) the demand curve for jelly beans to shift to the left.
    B) the demand curve for jelly beans to shift to the right.
    C) a decrease in the quantity of jelly beans demanded.
    D) a decrease in the quantity of jelly beans supplied.

4. If an increase in consumers' incomes causes a decrease in the demand for video rentals, then video rentals are
    A) a luxury.
    B) a normal good.
    C) a necessity.
    D) an inferior good.

5. Suppose the demand for fish tacos increases as the result of an increase in consumers' incomes. Fish tacos must be
    A) a luxury.
    B) a normal good.
    C) an inferior good.
    D) an incredible good.

6. Which of the following is most likely to cause an increase in the demand for disposable diapers?
    A) a decrease in peoples' incomes
    B) a decrease in the price of cloth diapers
    C) an increase in the number of newborn babies
    D) a decrease in the price of disposable diapers

7. If fewer people get tattoos as a result of an increase in tattoo prices, then there has been
    A) an increase in the demand for tattoos.
    B) a decrease in the demand for tattoos.
    C) an increase in the quantity of tattoos demanded.
    D) a decrease in the quantity of tattoos demanded.

8. In the three months before a new $1 per pack cigarette tax took effect in Alaska, smokers in the 49th state bought 175 million more cigarettes than they had during the same period a year earlier. This represents an increase
    A) in the quantity of cigarettes demanded due to an increase in price.
    B) in demand caused by a change in consumers' expectations about the future.
    C) in demand due to a change in consumers' tastes.
    D) in demand due to a change in the number of demanders.

IV   DISCUSSION AND APPLICATION

1. On the graphs below, show the effects of each of the following on the demand for hamburger in Hilo, Hawaii. Identify the responsible determinant of demand in the space provided.

Chapter 4: Supply and Demand

A.   The price of chicken falls.

Determinant: _____

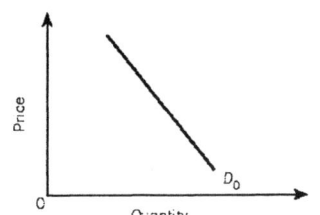

B.   The price of hamburger buns doubles.

Determinant: _____

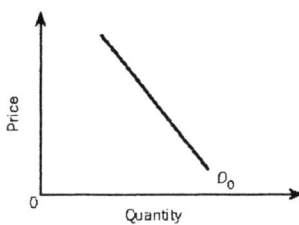

C.   Scientists find that eating hamburger prolongs life.

Determinant: _____

D.   The population of Hilo doubles.

Determinant: _____

2.   On the graphs below, show the effects of each of the following on the demand for Chevrolets in the United States.

A.The price of Fords plummets.

Determinant: _____

B.   Consumers believe that the price of Chevrolets will rise next year.

Determinant: _____

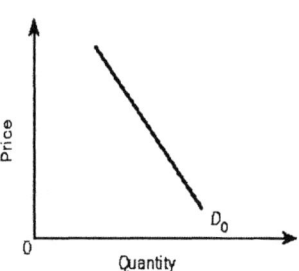

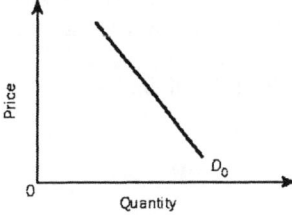

C. The incomes of Americans rise.

Determinant: _____

D.   The price of gasoline falls dramatically.

Determinant: _____

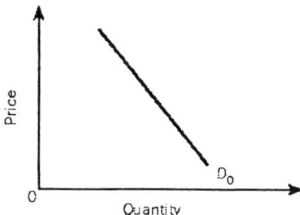

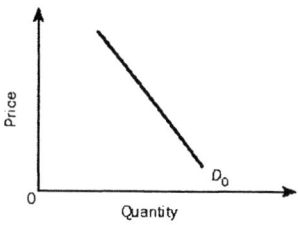

3. The graph shows three market demand curves for cantaloupe. Starting at point A,

A. which point represents an increase in quantity demanded?

B. which point represents an increase in demand?

C. which point represents a decrease in demand?

D. which point represents a decrease in quantity demanded?

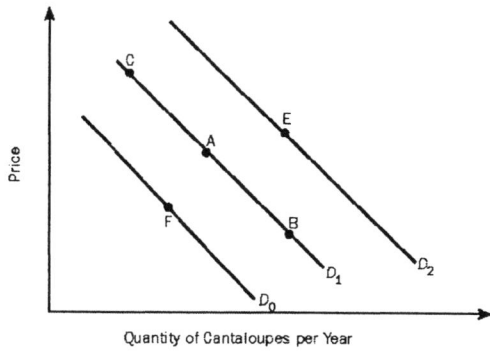

SECTION 4.4
SUPPLY

KEY POINTS

- The law of supply states that, other things equal, the quantity supplied will vary directly with the price of the good. According to the law of supply, the higher the price of the good, the greater the quantity supplied, and the lower the price of the good, the smaller the quantity supplied.

- The quantity supplied is positively related to the price because firms supplying goods and services want to increase their profits, and the higher the price per unit, the greater the profitability generated by supplying more of that good or service. Also, if costs are rising for producers as they produce more units, they must receive a higher price to compensate them for their higher costs.

- An individual supply schedule reveals the different amounts of a product a person would be willing to produce and sell at various possible prices in a particular time interval, other things equal. An individual supply curve illustrates that information graphically.

- The individual supply curve is upward sloping. At higher prices, it will be more attractive to increase production. Existing firms will produce more at higher prices than at lower price in a particular time interval, other things equal.

- The market supply curve for a product is the horizontal summation of the supply curves for individual firms. It reflects the fact that the total quantity sold in the market at a price is the sum of the quantities sold by each supplier.

I   REVIEW

The answer to the questions, "What do we produce and in what quantities?" depends on the interaction of both _____ and _____.

The law of supply states that, other things being equal, quantity supplied varies _____ with price.

A producer requires a higher price to produce additional units of the good because of the law of _____ opportunity costs.

The individual supply curve is _____ sloping as you move from left to right.

Adding the amount each individual producer would supply at each price will give us the _____ supply curve.

II   TRUE/FALSE

_____1. Once we know the demand for a product we can predict how much will be produced.

_____2. A direct relationship between two variables means they move in opposite directions.

_____3. Without a change in technology or input prices, the opportunity costs of production increase as more is produced.

_____4. Individual supply curves usually slope upward and to the right.

_____5. *Ceteris paribus,* a change in a good's price will result in a change in the quantity supplied of the good.

III   MULTIPLE CHOICE

1. In a market economy, the amount of a good that is produced is decided by the interaction of
   A) buyers and sellers.
   B) all consumers.
   C) producers and input suppliers.
   D) all producers.

2. According to the law of supply, when the price of a good increases, we would predict that
   A) more will be consumed.
   B) less will be produced.
   C) more will be produced.
   D) less will be consumed.

3. When the price people are willing to pay for oil decreases, what would we predict would happen to the amount of oil produced in any oil field?
   A) It would decline.
   B) It would stay the same.
   C) It would increase.
   D) It would fluctuate up and down.

4. To produce more wheat, Farmer Jones has to use fields that are on a mountain slope, where it costs $500 more to grow each ton of wheat. Farmer Jones would only produce from these fields when
   A) the price of wheat increases.
   B) the price of wheat decreases.
   C) the cost of wheat increases.
   D) the cost of wheat decreases.

5. When we add up all of the individual firm supply curves, what do we have?
   A) nothing important
   B) the market supply curve
   C) the individual supply curve
   D) the amount produced

IV   APPLICATION AND DISCUSSION

1. Felix is a wheat farmer who has two fields he can use to grow wheat. The first field is right next to his house and the topsoil is rich and thick. The second field is 10 miles away in the mountains and the soil is rocky. On which field do you think the opportunity cost of producing wheat is the highest? Why?

2. At current wheat prices, Felix just produces from the field next to his house because the market price for wheat is just high enough to cover his costs of production including a reasonable profit. What would have to happen to the market price of wheat for Felix to have the incentive to produce from the second field?

3. Below is the supply schedule for Rolling Rock Oil Co. Plot Rolling Rock's supply curve on the first graph below.

Price (dollars per barrel)	Quantity Supplied (barrels per month)
$ 5	10,000
10	15,000
15	20,000
20	25,000
25	30,000

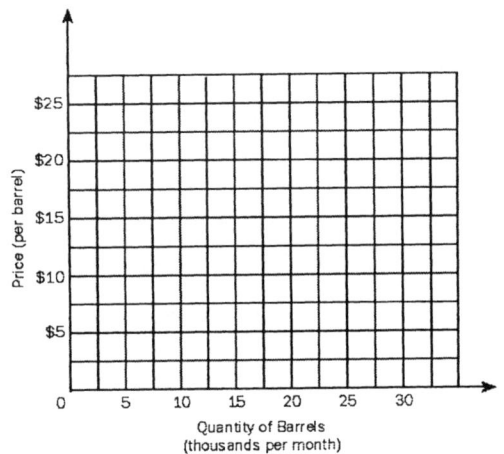

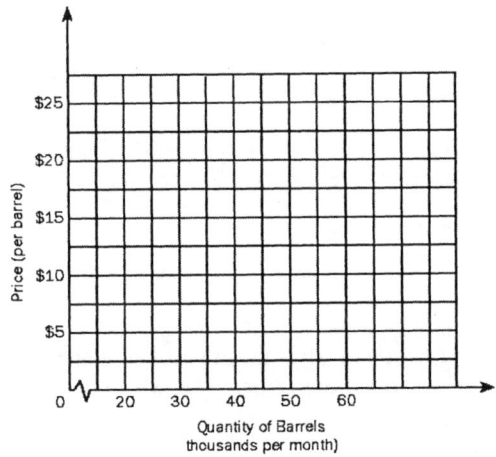

4. Below are the supply schedules for Rolling Rock and two other petroleum companies, Armadillo Oil and Pecos Petroleum. Assuming these three companies make up the entire supply side of the oil market, complete the market supply schedule and draw the market supply curve on the second graph above.

Price (DOLLARS PER BARREL)	ROLLING ROCK	ARMADILLO	PECOS	MARKET
$ 5	10,000	8,000	2,000	_____
10	15,000	10,000	5,000	_____

Quantity Supplied (barrels per month)

15	20,000	12,000	8,000	_____
20	25,000	14,000	11,000	_____
25	30,000	16,000	14,000	_____

SECTION 4.5
SHIFTS IN THE SUPPLY CURVE

KEY POINTS

- Changes in the price of a good lead to changes in quantity supplied, which are shown as movements along a given supply curve. Changes in supply occur for other reasons than changes in the price of the product itself. A change in any other factor that can affect supplier behavior results in a shift of the entire supply curve. These factors include: supplier input prices; the price of related goods, expectations; number of suppliers; and technology, regulation, taxes, subsidies and weather. An increase in supply shifts the supply curve to the right; a decrease in supply shifts the supply curve to the left.

- Higher input prices increase the cost of production, reducing the per-unit profit potential at existing prices, causing the supply of a good to decline. Lower input prices decrease the cost of production, which increases the per-unit profit potential at existing prices. This, in turn, causes the supply of a good to increase.

- The supply of a good can be influenced by the price of related goods. Firms producing a product can sometimes use their resources to produce alternative goods. Suppose a farmer's land can be used to grow either barley or cotton. If the farmer is currently growing barley and the price of barley falls, then this provides an incentive for the farmer to shift acreage out of barley and into cotton. Thus a decrease in the price of barley will increase the supply of cotton.

- If producers expect a higher price in the future, they will supply less now, preferring to wait and sell when their goods will be more valuable. If producers expect a lower price for their products in the future, they will supply more today, rather than waiting to sell when their goods will be worth less.

- Since the market supply curve is the horizontal summation of the individual supply curves, an increase in the number of suppliers will increase market supply. A decrease in the number of suppliers will decrease market supply.

- Technological progress can lower the cost of production and increase supply.

- Supply may also change because of changes in the legal and regulatory environment in which firms operate, such as safety and pollution regulations, minimum wages, taxes, etc. If these changes increase costs, they will decrease supply. If they decrease costs, they will increase supply. An increase in costly government regulations, taxes or adverse production conditions will increase the cost of production, decreasing supply. Subsidies, the opposite of a tax can lower the cost of production and shift the supply curve to the right. In addition, weather can affect the supply of certain commodities.

- If the price of a good changes, it leads to a change in its quantity supplied, but not its supply. If one of the other factors influences sellers' behavior, it leads to a change in supply.

Chapter 4: Supply and Demand

I   REVIEW

When other factors remain the same, price change results in a movement along the supply curve; this is called a change in _____ supplied. When the other important factors that affect supplier behavior change, the entire supply curve shifts; this is called a change in _____.

Labor, materials, and energy are examples of supplier _____. Higher input prices increase the _____ of production and shift the supply curve to the left. Lower input prices _____ the costs of production and shift the supply curve to the _____.

When two goods can be produced using the same resources they are called _____ in production. Producers tend to substitute the production of _____ profitable goods for that of _____ profitable goods.

If suppliers expect the price of a good will be higher in the future, they will sell _____ now so that they will have _____ to sell in the future. If they expect prices to fall in the future they will supply _____ now rather than wait for their goods to be worth less.

An increase in the number of suppliers leads to an _____ in supply, while a decrease in the number of suppliers will lead to a _____ in supply.

Improvements in _____ lead to lower costs and increase in supply.

Government regulations that increase production costs cause _____ in the supply of goods.

Weather can also affect the supply of certain goods, especially _____ products.

If the price of a good changes it will lead to a change in the _____ supplied. If one of the determinants of supply, such as supplier input prices or technology, changes, it will lead to a change in _____ and to a shift in the _____ curve.

II   TRUE/FALSE

_____1. *Ceteris paribus,* if the price of timber increases, we would expect an increase in the supply of lumber.

_____2. When the price of cotton falls, the supply of barley, which can be grown using the same land, will increase.

_____3. Midge sells Persian carpets in the United States. If she expects the price of these carpets will rise next year, she will increase this year's supply and sell more now rather than waiting to sell her stock next year.

_____4. An increase in the number of suppliers selling a product will result in a decrease in the supply of the product.

_____5. Improving technology in an industry usually lowers the cost of producing the product and results in a leftward shift in the supply curve.

_____6. Government can decrease the supply of a product by imposing taxes or regulations that increase the cost of production.

III   MULTIPLE CHOICE

1. John and Kate decide that coffee would be a good business to be in, so they form J & K Coffee Co. What will happen to the market supply of coffee as a result?
   A) It will decrease.
   B) It won't change.
   C) It will increase.
   D) It only changes the price.

2. The difference between a change in quantity supplied and a change in supply is that a change in
   A) the quantity supplied is caused by a change in a good's price, while a change in supply is caused by a change in a variable such as input prices, prices of related goods, expectations, or taxes.
   B) supply is caused by a change in a good's price, while a change in the quantity supplied is caused by a change in a variable such as input prices, prices of related goods, expectations, or taxes.
   C) the quantity supplied is a change in the amount people want to sell. A change in supply is a change in the amount they actually sell.
   D) supply and a change in the quantity supplied are the same thing.

3. Which of the following will *not* cause a change in the supply of a product?
   A) a change in the price of suppliers' inputs
   B) a change in the price of related products
   C) a change in the price of the product
   D) a change in the expected future price of the product

4. El Niño has caused both drought and flood-producing rains in various wheat-growing regions. What would be the likely affect of El Niño on the wheat market?
   A) an increase in supply
   B) a decrease in supply
   C) El Niño will not affect supply.
   D) a decrease in demand

5. Which of the following actions of government would not result in a decrease in the supply of fast-food meals?
   A) an increase in the minimum wage that raises the wages of most workers in the fast-food industry
   B) increased health standards governing fast-food kitchens
   C) decreased property taxes on fast-food outlets
   D) worker safety regulations requiring that lettuce be chopped with a dull knife

6. Pan Am Airlines went bankrupt in 1998 and left the airline industry. What was the likely effect of this change on the airline market?
   A) an increase in supply
   B) a decrease in supply
   C) no change in supply
   D) an increase in demand

7. Steel producers offer to sell sheet steel to U.S. auto producers for a lower price than in the past. With all other factors remaining constant, what would you expect to happen in the auto market?
   A) an increase in supply
   B) a decrease in supply
   C) no change in supply
   D) an increase in demand

Chapter 4: Supply and Demand

IV   APPLICATION AND DISCUSSION

1. On the following graphs show the effects of each of the following on the supply of salsa in the United States. Identify the responsible determinant of supply in the space provided.

    A. Tomato prices skyrocket!

        Determinant: _____

    B. Congress places a 26 percent tax on salsa.

        Determinant: _____

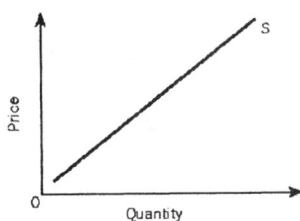

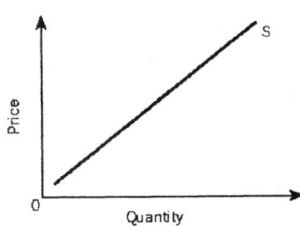

    C. Ed Scissorhands introduces a new, faster vegetable chopper.

        Determinant: _____

    D. Elton John, Madonna, and Paul Newman each introduce a new brand of salsa.

        Determinant: _____

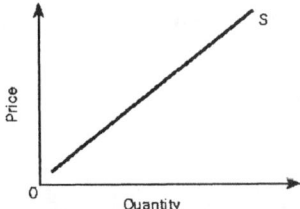

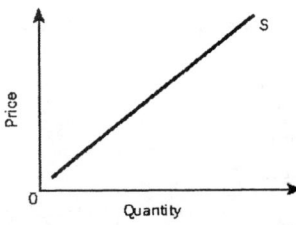

2. On the graphs below, show the effects of each of the following on the supply of coffee worldwide. Identify the responsible determinant of supply in the space provided.

    A. Freezing temperatures wipe out half of Brazil's coffee crop.

        Determinant: _____

    B. Wages of coffee workers in Latin America rise as unionization efforts succeed.

        Determinant: _____

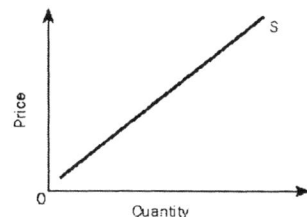

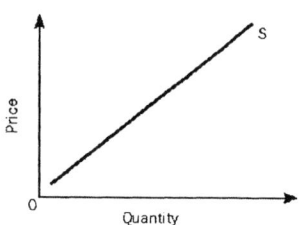

C. Indonesia offers big subsidies to its coffee producers.

Determinant: _____

D. Genetic engineering produces a super coffee bean that grows faster and needs less care.

Determinant: _____

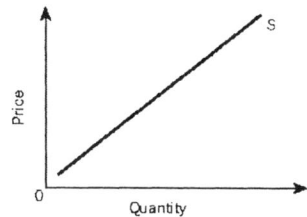

E. Coffee suppliers expect prices to be higher in the future.

Determinant: _____

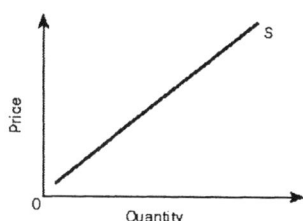

3. Below are three market supply curves for cantaloupe. Compared to point A, which point represents

    A) an increase in quantity supplied?

    B) an increase in supply?

    C) a decrease in quantity supplied?

    D) a decrease in supply?

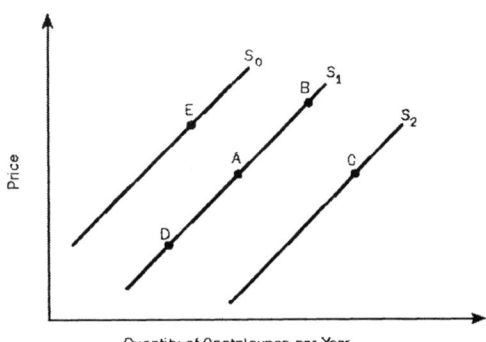

CHAPTER 5
BRINGING SUPPLY AND DEMAND TOGETHER

SECTION 5.1
MARKET EQUILIBRIUM PRICE AND QUANTITY

KEY POINTS

- The price at the intersection of the market demand curve and the market supply curve is called the equilibrium price and the quantity is called the equilibrium quantity.

- At the equilibrium market price, the amount that buyers are willing and able to buy is exactly equal to the amount that sellers are willing and able to produce. If the price is set above or below the equilibrium price, there will be shortages or surpluses. However, the actions of many buyers and sellers will move the price back to the equilibrium level.

- At the equilibrium price, both buyers and sellers are able to carry out their purchase and sales plans. However, at any other price, either suppliers or demanders would be unable to trade as much as they would like.

- At a price greater than the equilibrium price, a surplus, or excess quantity supplied, would exist. Sellers would be willing to sell more than demanders would be willing to buy. Frustrated suppliers would cut their price and cut back on production, and consumers would buy more, eliminating the unsold surplus and returning the market to equilibrium.

- At a price less than the equilibrium price, a shortage, or excess quantity demanded, would exist. Buyers would be willing to buy more than sellers would be willing to sell. Frustrated buyers would compete for the existing supply, causing the price to rise, which would make producers willing to increase the quantity supplied and decrease the quantity demanded, eliminating the shortage, and returning the market to equilibrium.

Chapter 5: Bringing Supply and Demand Together

I   REVIEW

The price at the intersection of the market demand curve and the market supply curve is called the _____ price.

If the price of a good or service is below the equilibrium price, a _____ will result.

If the price is above equilibrium, a _____ will result.

If there is a shortage of a good, the price of that good will _____. If there is a surplus of a good, the price will _____.

II   TRUE/FALSE

_____1. The actual price of a good or service is identical to the equilibrium price.

_____2. If the market for bing cherries is in equilibrium, the quantity of bing cherries demanded will be equal to the quantity of bing cherries supplied.

_____3. A shortage of housing in Columbus, Ohio, will cause the price of housing there to rise.

_____4. Surpluses are the result of too much demand and too little supply.

_____5. As people leave Forlorn, Saskatchewan, the resulting surplus of housing will put upward pressure on housing prices.

III   MULTIPLE CHOICE

Refer to Exhibit 1, the hypothetical monthly demand and supply schedules for cans of macadamia nuts in Kapaa, Hawaii, in order to answer questions 1, 2, and 3.

EXHIBIT 1

Price	Quantity Demanded	Quantity Supplied
$6	700 cans	100 cans
7	600	200
8	500	300
9	400	400
10	300	500

1. The equilibrium price of macadamia nuts in Kapaa is
    A) $6.00.
    B) $7.50.
    C) $8.00.
    D) $9.00.

2. At a price of $7.00 per can, there is a
    A) shortage of 300 cans.
    B) #shortage of 400 cans.
    C) market equilibrium.
    D) surplus of 400 cans.

3. At a price of $10.00, there is a
   A) shortage of 200 cans.
   B) surplus of 200 cans.
   C) market equilibrium.
   D) surplus of 400 cans.

Refer to Exhibit 2, the hypothetical demand and supply curves for donuts in Chicken, Alaska, to answer questions 4, 5, and 6.

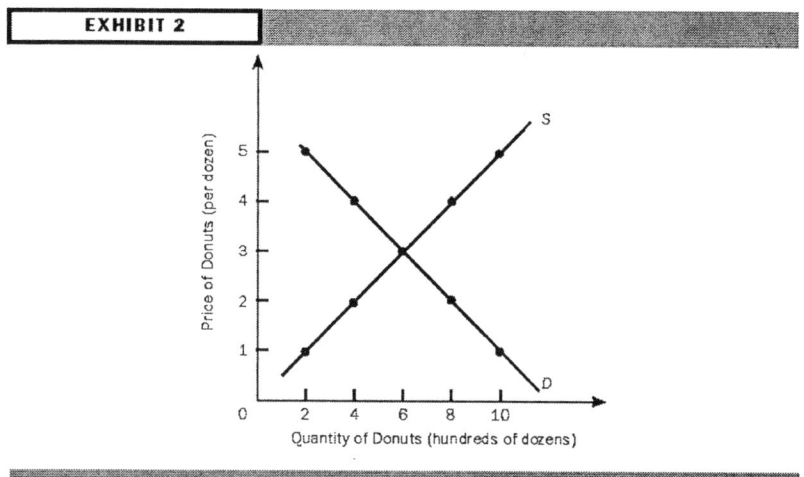

4. At a price of $5.00 per dozen,
   A) a surplus of donuts will exist.
   B) a shortage of donuts will exist.
   C) the market will be in equilibrium.
   D) This is a trick question because no one would pay $5.00 for a dozen donuts in Chicken.

5. At a price of $3.00,
   A) a surplus of donuts will exist.
   B) a shortage of donuts will exist.
   C) the market will be in equilibrium.
   D) Both (A) and (B) are co#rrect.

6. If the price of donuts in Chicken was $2.00 per dozen,
   A) quantity demanded would be less than quantity supplied and prices would rise.
   B) quantity demanded would be less than quantity supplied and prices would fall.
   C) quantity demanded would be greater than quantity supplied and prices would rise.
   D) quantity demanded would equal quantity supplied and prices would remain constant.

IV   APPLICATION AND DISCUSSION

When asked about the reason for a lifeguard shortage that threatened to keep one-third of the city's beaches closed for the summer, the Deputy Parks Commissioner of New York responded that "Kids seem to want to do work that's more in tune with a career. Maybe they prefer carpal tunnel syndrome to sunburn." (*Newsweek,* July 6, 1998)

As someone who knows about the causes of shortages, what do you think is causing the shortage? What would you advise the Deputy Parks Commissioner to do in order to alleviate the shortage?

SECTION 5.2
CHANGES IN EQUILIBRIUM PRICE AND QUANTITY

KEY POINTS

- As discussed earlier, demand curves shift when any of the other factors that affect buyers' behavior change (but not the price of the good itself), and supply curves shift when any of the other factors that affect sellers' behavior change (but not the price of the good itself). These changes (shifts) in the demand and supply curves will lead to changes in the equilibrium price and equilibrium quantity.

- An increase in demand results in a greater equilibrium price and a greater equilibrium quantity. Conversely, a decrease in demand results in a lower equilibrium price and a lower equilibrium quantity.

- A decrease in supply results in a higher equilibrium price and a lower equilibrium quantity. Conversely, an increase in supply results in a lower equilibrium price and a higher equilibrium quantity.

- Very often, supply and demand will both shift in the same time period. That is, supply and demand will shift simultaneously.

- When supply and demand move at the same time, we can predict the change in one variable (price or quantity), but we are unable to predict the direction of effect on the other variable. This change in the second variable, then, is said to be indeterminate because it cannot be determined without additional information about the relative changes in supply and demand.

- We can predict what will happen to equilibrium prices and equilibrium quantities in situations where both supply and demand change by breaking them down into their individual effects, then putting together the price and quantity effects that each of the shifts would have separately.

- An increase in supply decreases the equilibrium price and increases the equilibrium quantity. A decrease in demand decreases both the equilibrium price and quantity. Taken together, they will decrease the equilibrium price, but result in an indeterminate change in the equilibrium quantity. The change in quantity will depend on the relative changes in supply and demand. If the decrease in demand is greater than the increase in supply, the equilibrium quantity will decrease. If the increase in supply is greater than the decrease in demand, the equilibrium quantity will increase.

- An increase in demand increases the equilibrium price and equilibrium quantity. An increase in supply decreases the equilibrium price and increases the equilibrium quantity. Together, they increase the equilibrium quantity, but the change in equilibrium price depends on the relative sizes of the demand and supply shifts. If supply shifted more than demand, the equilibrium price would drop.

- The eight possible changes in demand and/or supply are presented, along with the resulting changes in equilibrium price and equilibrium quantity.

I   REVIEW

A shift in either the supply or demand curves for a good will result in a change in both its _____ price and quantity.

An increase in the demand for a good or service is represented by a shift of the demand curve to the _____ and results in an _____ in the equilibrium price and quantity.

If the supply curve does not change, an increase in demand causes a _____ along the supply curve and an increase in the _____ of the good supplied.

A(n) _____ in the supply of a good or service is represented by a shift in the supply curve to the left. If demand does not change, the decrease in supply will cause a decrease #in the quantity _____ of the good and an _____ in the equilibrium price.

Chapter 5: Bringing Supply and Demand Together

If supply increases at the same time that demand decreases, equilibrium price will _____ while the change in quantity will be _____.

If both supply and demand increase, the equilibrium quantity will _____, while the change in equilibrium price will be _____.

An increase in either demand or supply is shown by shifting the curve to the _____. A decrease in either demand or supply is shown by shifting the curve to the _____.

II   TRUE/FALSE

_____1. If the bing cherry market is in equilibrium at a price of $1 per quart, an increase in the demand for bing cherries will cause a shortage at the existing price.

_____2. Unless there are other changes, when there is a decrease in the price of compact disc players, the equilibrium price of compact discs will also fall.

_____3. While the demand for chicken has not changed, the price of chicken has risen because of an increase in the number of farmers producing chicken.

_____4. At a given equilibrium price, a surplus can be created by either an increase in supply or a decrease in demand.

_____5. Doctors announce that eating chocolate reduces a person's cholesterol, a major cause of heart disease. Barring other changes, the quantity of chocolate consumed will increase.

_____6. If the demand for apples increases at the same time supply of apples falls, the price of apples will tend to fall.

_____7. If the population of Fallbrook, Ohio, decreases dramatically while contractors are busy building more houses, the price of housing in Fallbrook will tend to decrease.

_____8. When both the supply and demand curves shift at the same time, we can determine the direction of both equilibrium price and quantity.

III   MULTIPLE CHOICE

1. Troy Oz, the movie star, is a trendsetter. His promotion of ostrich steaks changes peoples' ta#stes and increases the demand for ostrich meat. What would be the expected effect of this change in the ostrich meat market?
    A) A shortage will occur at the original price, resulting in an increase in the price and the quantity produced.
    B) A shortage will occur at the original price, resulting in a decrease in the price and the quantity produced.
    C) A surplus will occur at the original price, resulting in an increase in the price and a decrease in the quantity produced.
    D) A surplus will occur at the original price, resulting in a decrease in the price and an increase in the quantity produced.

2. What will happen in the market for Broadway shows after unions win a 14 percent wage increase for actors and stage crews?
    A) Ticket prices will rise and the number of shows will increase.
    B) Ticket prices will rise and the number of shows will decline.
    C) Ticket prices will fall and the number of shows will decline.
    D) Ticket prices will fall and the number of shows will increase.

3. How do chicken farmers react to the news of medical research findings that eating chicken makes a person smarter?
   A) They increase the supply of chickens.
   B) They increase the quantity of chickens supplied.
   C) They decrease the supply of chickens.
   D) They decrease the quantity of chickens they supply.

4. Geneticists have discovered a way to increase the average weight of beef cattle by 20 pounds using no more feed than is used today. What effect will this technological improvement have on the beef market?
   A) The price per pound of beef will fall and the quantity consumed will increase.
   B) The price per pound of beef will fall and the quantity consumed will decrease.
   C) The price per pound of beef will rise and the quantity consumed will increase.
   D) The price per pound of beef will rise and the quantity consumed will decrease.

5. The gasoline market is in equilibrium at a price of $1.19 per gallon. Which of the following will not be a result of an increase in the dem##and for gasoline?
   A) A shortage will occur at a price of $1.19.
   B) The new equilibrium price will be more than $1.19.
   C) The gasoline supply curve will shift to the right.
   D) There will be an increase in the quantity of gasoline supplied.

6. Hurricane Andrew caused over $15 billion in damage when it swept through southern Florida in 1992. One result was an increased local demand for plywood to replace broken windows. At the pre-hurricane equilibrium price of plywood, we woul#d expect to see
   A) a surplus caused by excess supply.
   B) a shortage caused by excess demand.
   C) the quantity demand equal to the quantity supplied.
   D) an increase in the supply of plywood.

7. Which of the following could be responsible for an increase in the price of wheat?
   A) an increase in the supply of wheat
   B) an increase in the demand for wheat
   C) a decrease in the demand for wheat
   D) a simultaneous increase in supply and decrease in demand for wheat

8. Nora is delighted to see that the price of her favorite food, artichokes, has fallen. Which of the following could be responsible?
   A) an increase in the demand for artichokes
   B) a decrease in the supply of artichokes
   C) a simultaneous increase in demand and decrease in supply of artichokes
   D) a simultaneous decrease in demand and increase in supply

9. When the demand and the supply of oranges increase at the same time, we can safely predict that
   A) the price of oranges will fall.
   B) the price of oranges will rise.
   C) the quantity of oranges bought and sold will fall.
   D) the quantity of oranges bought and s#old will rise.

10. If the price of cellular telephones went down after simultaneous increases in the supply and demand for cellular telephones, we know that
    A) the supply curve for cellular phones shifted more than the demand curve.
    B) the demand curve for cellular phones shifted more than the supply curve.
    C) the supply and demand curves shifted by the same amount.
    D) the supply and demand curves actually shifted leftward.

IV   APPLICATION AND DISCUSSION

1. Show the effects of the changes listed below on the relevant supply and demand curves. Label the new equilibrium price, P_1, and the new equilibrium quantity, Q_1.

    A) An increase in the price of hot dogs on the hamburger market.

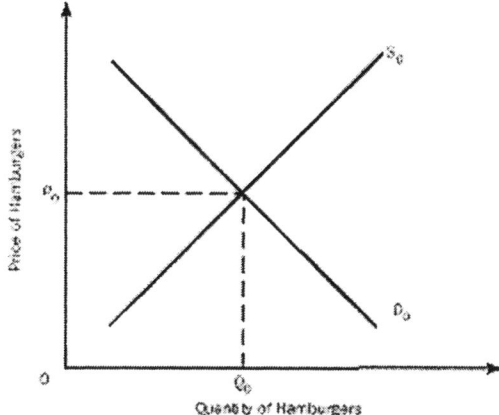

    B) A decrease in the number of taxicab companies in New York City on cab trips.

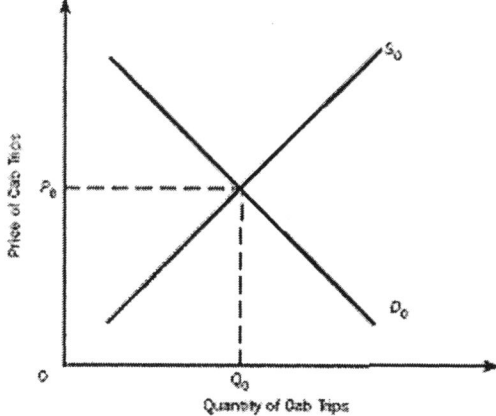

71

C) El Niño rain storms destroys the broccoli crop in two California counties.

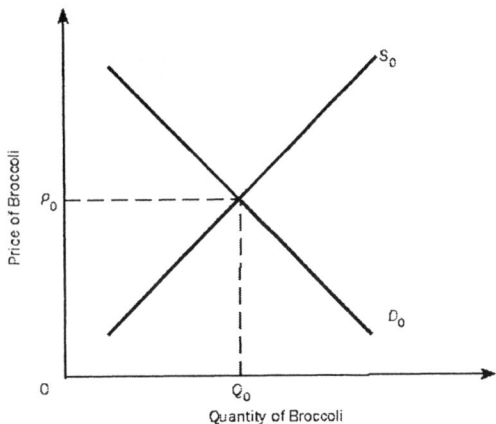

2. Use the supply and demand curves below to show:

A. simultaneous increases in supply and demand, with a large increase in supply and a small increase in demand.

B. simultaneous increases in supply and demand with a small increase in supply and a large increase in demand.

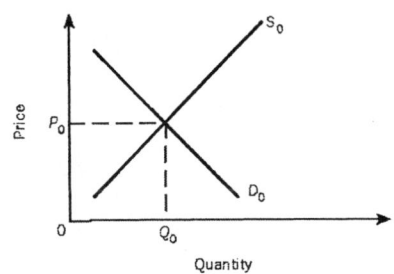
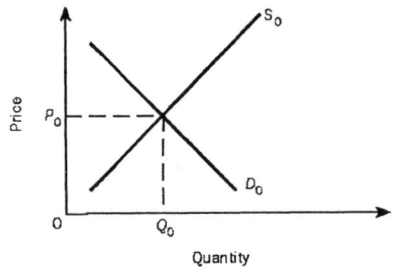

C. simultaneous decreases in supply and demand, with a large decrease in supply and a small decrease in demand

D. simultaneous decrease in supply and demand, with a small decrease in supply and a large decrease in demand

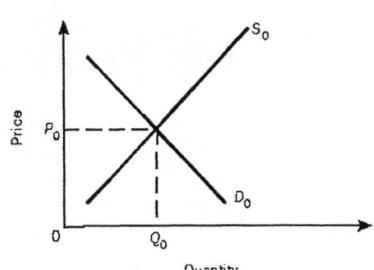
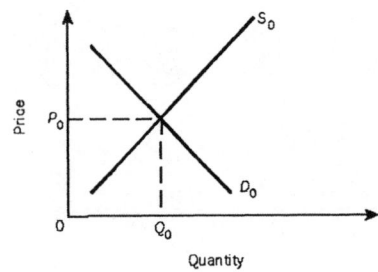

SECTION 5.3
PRICE CONTROLS

KEY POINTS

- While non-equilibrium prices can crop up in the private sector, reflecting uncertainty, they seldom last for long. Governments, however, often impose non-equilibrium prices for significant time periods.

- Price controls involve the use of the power of the state to establish prices different from the equilibrium prices that would otherwise prevail.

- The motivations for price controls vary with the market under consideration. A price ceiling, or maximum price, is often set for goods deemed "important," like housing. A price floor, or minimum price, may be set on wages because wages are the primary source of income for most people.

- Price ceiling example: rent control. Under rent control the price (or rent) of an apartment is held below market rental rates over the tenure of an occupant. When an occupant moves out, the owner can usually, but not always, raise the rent to a near-market level for the next occupant.

- Some results of rent controls:

  Because living in rent-controlled apartments is a good deal, one which would be lost by moving, tenants are very reluctant to move and give up their governmentally granted right to a below-market-rent apartment.

  Because the rents received by landlords are constrained at below market levels, the rate of return on housing investments falls compared to that on other forms of real estate not subject to rent controls, reducing the incentives to construct new rental housing. Where rent controls are truly effective, there is generally little new construction going on and a shortage of apartments persists and grows over time.

  Since landlords are limited in what rent they can charge, there is little incentive to improve or upgrade rental apartments in order to get more rent. In fact, there is some incentive to avoid routine maintenance, thereby lowering the cost of apartment ownership to a figure approximating the controlled rental price.

  Rent controls promote housing discrimination. With rent controls, there are likely to be many families wanting to rent a controlled apartment, some desirable and some undesirable, as seen by the landlord, because the rent is at a below-equilibrium price. The landlord can indulge in his "taste" for discrimination in favor of "desirable" renters without any additional financial loss beyond that required by the controls.

- Price floor example: the minimum wage. Since 1938, the federal government has, by legislation, made it illegal to pay most workers an amount below a legislated minimum wage (price for labor services).

- Some results of the minimum wage:

  Because it would produce willing workers who will be unable to find jobs, an increase in the minimum wage would create additional unemployment for low skill workers.

  The unemployment impact of the minimum wage falls mainly on the least-experienced, least-skilled persons, often teenagers and minorities, holding the lowest paying jobs. They lose their jobs or are unable to get them in the first place and suffer a decline in earnings, not a gain.

  Those who continue to hold jobs with the same hours and working conditions after the minimum wage is increased gain substantially, and therefore are supporters of efforts to increase the minimum wage.

- The analysis does not "prove" minimum wages are "bad." There is an empirical question of how much unemployment is caused by minimum wages, and some might believe that the cost of unemployment resulting from a minimum wage is a reasonable price to pay for assuring that those with jobs get a decent wage. But it does impose a cost, and it falls not only on unskilled workers and employers, but also on consumers of products that were made more costly by the minimum wage.

Chapter 5: Bringing Supply and Demand Together

- When markets are altered for policy reasons, it is wise to remember that the actual results of actions are not always as intended, as we have seen in the cases of rent control and the minimum wage. We must always look for unintended consequences, the secondary effects of an action that may occur along with the intended effects. The unintended effects may sometimes completely undermine the intended effects.

I REVIEW

Price controls involve the use of government power to impose _____ prices.

A maximum price imposed by government is called a _____ price. A minimum price is called a price _____.

Rent controls are laws that# set rental prices _____ the equilibrium price. Rent controls have several effects. First, people living in rent-controlled apartments are _____ to move; second, the incentive to build new rental housing is _____; third, the stock of rental housing tends to _____ over time; and fourth, rent control promotes _____ against people that landlords deem undesirable.

Minimum-wage laws set wages for unskilled workers _____ the equilibrium wage. Minimum wage laws result in a(n) _____ in the quantity of labor demanded and a(n) _____ in the quantity of labor supplied. Minimum wage laws may also result in a _____ of fringe benefits to employees.

II TRUE/FALSE

_____1. The main purpose of government price controls is to keep prices at equilibrium levels.

_____2. Price "ceilings" get their name from the fact that they are set above equilibrium.

_____3. Price "floors" get their name from the fact that they represent a "floor" below which the legal price cannot fall.

_____4. The rent control law in Berkeley, California, is an example of a price ceiling.

_____5. Price floors cause surpluses.

III   MULTIPLE CHOICE

Please refer to Exhibit 1 to answer questions 1, 2, and 3.

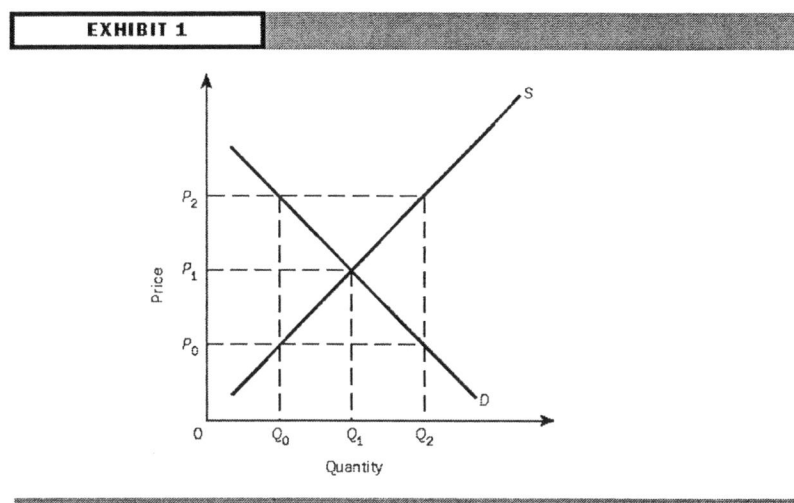

EXHIBIT 1

1. In the market shown in Exhibit 1, the equilibrium price is
    A) P_2.
    B) P_1.
    C) P_0.
    D) not shown.

2. If the government establishes a price ceiling at P_0 in the market shown in Exhibit 1, the result will be
    A) a surplus in the amount $Q_2 - Q_0$.
    B) a shortage in the amount $Q_1 - Q_0$.
    C) a shortage in the amount $Q_2 - Q_0$.
    D) market equilibrium at Q_1.

3. If the government establishes a price floor at P_2, the result will be
    A) a surplus in the amount $Q_2 - Q_0$.
    B) a shortage in the amount $Q_2 - Q_0$.
    C) a shortage in the amount $Q_0 - Q_1$.
    D) market equilibrium at Q_2.

4. Which of the following is *not* an effect of rent controls?
    A) reduced incentives to build new rental housing
    B) reduced incentives for landlords to keep rental units in good repair
    C) discrimination against people# deemed undesirable on the part of landlords
    D) increased turnover as tenants move more frequently from one rental unit to another

5. Which of the following is not likely to be an effect of an increase in the federal minimum wage?
    A)   an increase in the quantity of low-skilled labor supplied
    B)   a decrease in the quantity of low-skilled labor demanded
    C)   a decrease in teenage unemployment
    D)   an increase in teenage unemployment

IV   APPLICATION AND DISCUSSION

Giving in to pressure from voters who charge that local theater owners are gouging their customers with ticket prices as high as $10.00 per movie, the city council of a Midwestern city imposes a price ceiling of $2.00 on all movies. What effect is this likely to have on the market for movies in this particular city? What will happen to the quantity of tickets demanded? What will happen to the quantity supplied? Who gains? Who loses?

Questions

1.   When the price was $3.00, was there a surplus or a shortage of autographs?

2.   What happened to the quantity of autographs demanded when the price rose to $10.00?

CHAPTER 6
ELASTICITIES

SECTION 6.1

PRICE ELASTICITY OF DEMAND

KEY POINTS

- The law of demand establishes that quantity demanded changes inversely with changes in price, *ceteris paribus*. But how much does quantity demanded change? This is very important to understand for many economic issues. This is what the **price elasticity of demand** is designed to answer.

- The price elasticity of demand measures how responsive consumer behavior (quantity demanded) is to an incentive (price) change.

  The price elasticity of demand is defined as the percentage change in quantity demanded divided by the percentage change in price.

  Price elasticity of demand (E_D) = $\dfrac{\text{Percentage change in quantity demanded}}{\text{Percentage change in price}}$

- Following the law of demand, there is an inverse relationship between price and quantity demanded. For this reason, in theory price elasticity of demand is always negative. In practice, however, this quantity is always expressed in absolute value terms or as a positive number for simplicity.

- The percentage changes in the elasticity of demand formula are measured using the average price and average quantity, so that we do not get different values for the elasticity of demand depending on whether we moved up or down the demand curve. We are actually calculating the midpoint elasticity.

Chapter 6: Elasticities

- The basic intuition behind elasticities is straightforward if you use an analogy to a rubber band. If the quantity demanded (or length) is very responsive to even a small change in price (or pressure), we call it elastic. If even a huge change in price (or pressure) results in only a small change in quantity demanded (or length), then demand is said to be inelastic.

- A demand curve or a portion of a demand curve can be relatively elastic, unit elastic, or relatively inelastic.

- A segment of a demand curve is **elastic** ($E_D > 1$) if the percentage change in quantity demanded is greater than the percentage change in price that caused it (a perfectly elastic demand curve is the limiting case).

- A segment of a demand curve is **inelastic** ($E_D < 1$) if the percentage change in quantity demanded is less than the percentage change in price that caused it (a perfectly elastic demand curve is the limiting case).

- A segment of a demand curve is **unit elastic** ($E_D = 1$) if the percentage change in quantity demanded equals the percentage change in the price that caused it.

- At a given point, quantity demanded is much more responsive to a given change in price on a flatter, more elastic demand curve. Therefore, when a demand curve is relatively steep, *ceteris paribus,* its price elasticity of demand is relatively low (more inelastic), and when the demand curve is relatively flat, its price elasticity of demand is relatively high (more elastic).

- For the most part, the price elasticity of demand depends on the availability of close substitutes, the proportion of income spent on the good, and the amount of time people have to adapt to a price change.

- Goods with close substitutes tend to have more elastic demands, while goods without close substitutes tend to have less elastic demand. For example, the elasticity of demand for a Ford, Toyota, or a Honda is more elastic than the demand for a car because there are more and better substitutes for a certain type of car than for a car itself. The fewer close substitutes, the less elastic the demand curve, such as insulin for diabetics, heroin for an addict, and emergency medical care.

- The smaller the proportion of income spent on a good, the lower its elasticity of demand. If the amount spent on a good relative to income is small (such as salt), then the impact of a change in its price on one's budget will also be small. As a result, consumers will respond less to price changes for these goods than for similar percentage changes in large-ticket items (such as textbooks), where a price change could have a potentially large impact on the consumer's budget.

- The more time that people have to adapt to a new price change, the greater the elasticity of demand. The more time that passes, the more time consumers have to find or develop suitable substitutes and to plan and implement changes in their patterns of consumption. Hence, the short-run demand curve is generally less elastic than the long-run demand curve.

I   REVIEW

The price elasticity of demand measures the _____ of quantity demanded to changes in the price.

Price elasticity of demand is defined as the _____ change in quantity demanded divided by the _____ change in price.

Demand is _____ when the quantity demanded is very responsive to changes in price. In this case the price elasticity is _____ than one and the percentage change in quantity is _____ than the percentage change in price.

When demand is inelastic, the price elasticity is _____ than one and the quantity demanded is _____ very responsive to price changes.

If the demand is perfectly _____, consumers will buy the same amount regardless of the price.

Chapter 6: Elasticities

Demand for a good will be more elastic the greater is the number of close _____ available for the good. Elasticity of demand will also be greater for goods that take up a _____ proportion of a household's budget.

The price elasticity of demand will be greater the _____ the time period consumers have to adjust to price changes.

II   TRUE/FALSE

_____1. The price elasticity of demand equals the change in quantity demanded divided by the change in price.

_____2. The widespread availability of e-mail has increased the elasticity of demand for the service of the U.S. Postal Service.

_____3. Tim and Becky Tew have a business that organizes tours to exotic locations. They know that after raising their prices by ten percent, the quantity of tours they sell will fall by six percent. The demand for their services is inelastic.

_____4. Since auto wax is a product used to maintain a car, the elasticity of demand for auto wax is similar to the elasticity of demand for cars.

III   MULTIPLE CHOICE

1. Marge and Al Costa own a steel mill and know that a seven percent increase in the price of the steel they sell will result in a twenty percent reduction in the quantity of steel they sell. The demand curve facing their firm is
    A) elastic.
    B) inelastic.
    C) unit elastic.
    D) unit inelastic.

2. The Up and Down Garage Door Co. knows that a five percent increase in the price they charge for doors results in a fifteen percent decrease in the number of doors they sell. What is the elasticity of demand facing the Up and Down Company?
    A) 0.05
    B) 0.33
    C) 3.0
    D) 0.15

3. In America's War on Drugs, dramatic increases in the price of heroin have had little effect on the use of the drug by heroin users. The demand for heroin among users is
    A) elastic.
    B) inelastic.
    C) unit elastic.
    D) unit inelastic.

4. The demand for petroleum products over a year is more elastic than the demand over a month. What will be the difference in the response in each of these time periods to a twenty-percent increase in price?
    A) The percentage change in quantity demanded will be greater over the year than over a month.
    B) The percentage change in quantity demanded will be less over the year than over a month.
    C) The percentage change in quantity demanded will be the same over the year than over a month.
    D) The percentage change in quantity demanded over the year will be in the opposite direction of the change over the month.

IV   APPLICATION AND DISCUSSION

Complete the following table by circling the good that you think has a relatively *more* price elastic demand and then identify the most likely reason by putting a check in the appropriate box.

	More Substitutes	Greater Share of Budget	More Time
1. Cars or Chevrolets	☐	☐	☐
2. Salt or Housing	☐	☐	☐
3. New York Mets or Cleveland Indians	☐	☐	☐
4. Natural Gas this month or over the year	☐	☐	☐

S E C T I O N   6 . 2
TOTAL REVENUE AND PRICE ELASTICITY OF DEMAND

KEY POINTS

- When demand is relatively price elastic ($E_D > 1$), **total revenues** will rise as the price declines because the percentage increase in the quantity demanded is greater than the percentage reduction in price. If the price rises and the quantity demanded falls, then total revenue falls because the percentage decrease in the quantity demanded is greater than the percentage increase in price.

- When demand is relatively price inelastic ($E_D < 1$), total revenues will fall as the price declines because the percentage increase in the quantity demanded is less than the percentage reduction in price. If the price rises and the quantity demanded falls, then total revenue rises because the percentage decrease in the quantity demanded is less than the percentage increase in price.

- A straight-line demand curve (having a constant slope) will change price elasticity continuously as you move up or down it. When the price falls on the upper half of the demand curve, there is a negative relationship between price and total revenue, so demand is relatively price elastic. When the price falls on the lower half of the demand curve, there is a positive relationship between price and total revenue, so demand is relatively price inelastic.

I   REVIEW

Total revenue is equal to the price of a good times the _____ of the good sold.

If the demand for a good is elastic, total revenues will _____ as price declines. On the other hand, if the demand for a good is inelastic, total revenues will _____ as the price declines.

If the demand for wheat is inelastic, farmers as a group will become _____ off as a result of a reduction in the supply of wheat.

The steeper one demand curve is relative to another, the more _____ it is relative to the other, although the elasticity of demand _____ along a linear demand curve.

Chapter 6: Elasticities

As you move along a linear demand curve from a high price to a low price, the demand changes from relatively _____ at high prices to relatively _____ at low prices.

II   TRUE/FALSE

_____1. If Guillermo sells 100 dozen donuts at $3.60 per dozen, the total revenue he receives is $360.00

_____2. If Guillermo increases the price of his donuts and the total revenue he receives goes down, the demand for donuts is elastic.

_____3. When the demand for a good is relatively elastic, price and total revenue vary in the same direction.

III   MULTIPLE CHOICE

1. When the demand for a good is relatively *elastic,* total revenues will rise as the price declines because the
   A) percentage increase in the quantity demanded is greater than the percentage decrease in price.
   B) percentage increase in quantity demanded is less than the percentage decrease in price.
   C) quantity demanded remains the same as price decreases.
   D) decline in price is offset by a decline in quantity demanded.

2. If the demand for a good is relatively *inelastic,* total revenues will rise as price rises because the
   A) percentage increase in price is offset exactly by the percentage decrease in quantity demanded.
   B) increase in price is accompanied by an equal increase in quantity demanded.
   C) percentage increase in price is greater than the percentage decrease in quantity demanded.
   D) percentage increase in price is less than the percentage decrease in quantity demanded.

Use the weekly demand schedule for Sunshine Video Rentals in Cloverdale, Minnesota, shown in Exhibit 1 to answer questions 3 and 4.

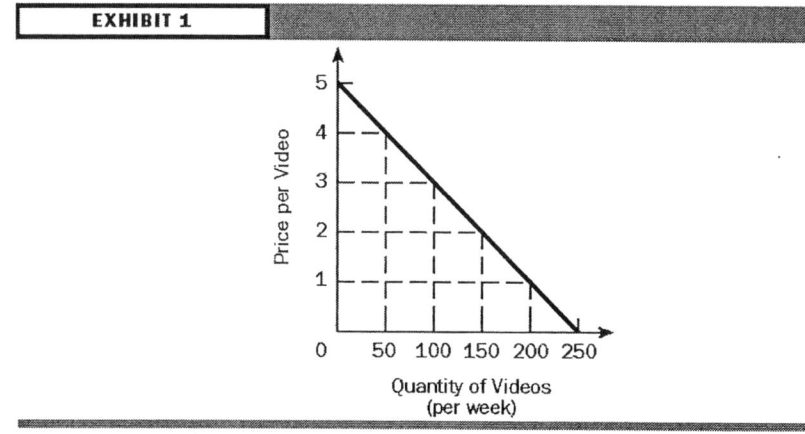

3. When Sunshine Video Rentals lowers their rental price from $4 to $3, total revenue
   A) goes from $200 per week to $300 per week.
   B) goes up from $250 per week to $400 per week.
   C) goes down from $300 per week to $200 per week.
   D) remains the same.

4. Between a price of $2 and a price of $1, demand is
   A) elastic.
   B) inelastic.
   C) unitary elastic.
   D) multielastic.

IV   APPLICATION AND DISCUSSION

1. The Cowtown Hotel is the only first-class hotel in Fort Worth. The hotel owners were concerned by an increase in the hotel's vacancy rates. Wayne Bruce, the manager of the hotel, hired Lastic and Associates, an economics consulting group, to offer advice about improving the hotel's profitability. Dr. Lastic suggested they could increase this year's revenue by raising prices.

   "What's going on?" thought Wayne. He asked Dr. Lastic, "Won't raising prices reduce the quantity of hotel rooms demanded and increase vacancies?"

   What was Lastic's reply? Explain why Lastic would suggest increasing prices.

SECTION 6.3
PRICE ELASTICITY OF SUPPLY

KEY POINTS

- According to the law of supply, there is a positive relationship between price and quantity supplied, *ceteris paribus*. But by how much does quantity supplied change as price changes?

- The **price elasticity of supply** measures how responsive the quantity sellers are willing to sell is to changes in the price. In other words, it measures the relative change in the quantity supplied that results from a change in price.

- The price elasticity of supply (E_S) is defined as the percentage change in the quantity supplied divided by the percentage change in price.

   $E_S = \dfrac{\text{Percentage change in quantity supplied}}{\text{Percentage change in price}}$

- Goods with a supply elasticity that is greater than 1 ($E_S > 1$) are relatively elastic in supply. With that, a 1 percent change in price will result in a greater than 1 percent change in quantity supplied. (The extreme case is perfectly elastic supply, where E_S = infinity.)

- Goods with a supply elasticity that is less than 1 ($E_S < 1$) are relatively inelastic in supply. This means that a 1 percent change in the price of these goods will induce a proportionately smaller change in the quantity supplied. (The extreme case is perfectly inelastic supply, where $E_S = 0$.)

- Time is usually critical in supply elasticities because it is more costly for producers to bring forth and release resources in shorter periods of time. Hence, supply tends to be more elastic in the long run than the short run.

Chapter 6: Elasticities

- The relative elasticity of supply and demand determines the distribution of the tax burden for a good. If demand has a lower elasticity than supply in the relevant tax region, the largest portion of the tax is paid by the consumer. However, if demand is relatively more elastic than supply in the relevant tax region, the largest portion of the tax is paid by the producer. In general, the tax burden falls on the side of the market that is less elastic, which has nothing to do with who actually pays the tax at the time of the purchase.

I   REVIEW

The price elasticity of _____ is defined as the percentage change in the quantity supplied divided by the percentage change in the price. It measures how _____ the quantity sellers are willing to sell is to changes in price.

When supply is perfectly _____, a change in the price will not change the amount supplied. When supply is perfectly _____, no goods will be sold below a certain price, but at higher prices, as much as buyers want will be supplied.

Supply is more elastic in the _____ run than in the _____ run.

The relative supply and demand elasticities determine the _____ of the burden of a tax imposed on a good or service. If the demand is relatively _____ elastic than supply, the producer pays the greater proportion of the tax. If demand is relatively _____ elastic than supply, the consumer pays the greater proportion of the tax.

II   TRUE/FALSE

_____1. While the price elasticity of demand increases with time, the price elasticity of supply for all goods and services is constant over time.

_____2. If the supply elasticity of electricity in California is less than the supply elasticity in New York, the prices in California must be higher.

_____3. If the supply of corn is perfectly inelastic, there is no price increase that will result in an increase in the quantity supplied.

III   MULTIPLE CHOICE

1. An increase in the price elasticity of the supply of cement since 2001 means that a given percentage increase in the price of cement will result in
   A) a smaller percentage increase in the quantity of cement supplied than prior to 2001.
   B) a larger percentage increase in the quantity of cement supplied than prior to 2001.
   C) a smaller percentage increase in the quantity of cement demanded than prior to 2001.
   D) a larger percentage decrease in the quantity of cement supplied than prior to 2001.

2. When the supply of a good is perfectly inelastic, an increase in the price will result in
   A) an increase in the quantity of the good supplied.
   B) a decrease in the quantity of the good supplied.
   C) no change in the quantity of the good supplied.
   D) an increase in the quantity of the good demanded.

3. Past studies have shown that a 10 percent increase in the price of men's shoes results in a 23 percent increase in the quantity producers will supply. What is the price elasticity of supply in this case?
    A) 23.0
    B) 2.30
    C) 0.43
    D) 0.23

4. Suppose that government programs to discourage smoking, like ad campaigns and warning labels, have the effect of changing elasticity of demand for smoking from inelastic to elastic. How will this change the distribution of the burden of the cigarette sales tax?
    A) Smokers' share of the burden will increase.
    B) Producers' share of the burden will increase.
    C) The share of the burden will not change.
    D) The share of the burden will increase for both consumers and producers.

IV   APPLICATION AND DISCUSSION

Mayor George Henry has a problem. He doesn't want to anger voters by taxing them because he wants to be reelected, but the town of Gapville needs more revenue for its schools. He has a choice between taxing tickets to professional basketball games or food.

If the demand for food is relatively inelastic while the supply is relatively elastic, and if the demand for professional basketball games is relatively elastic while the supply is relatively inelastic, in which case would the tax burden fall primarily on consumers? In which case would the tax burden fall primarily on producers?

SECTION 6.4
OTHER TYPES OF ELASTICITIES

KEY POINTS

- The **cross price elasticity of demand** measures both the direction and magnitude of the impact that a price change for one good will have on the quantity of another good demanded at a given price.

- The cross price elasticity of demand is defined as the percentage change in quantity demanded of one good at a given price divided by the percentage change in price of another good.

    Cross price elasticity of demand = Percentage change in quantity demanded of one good at a given price

    Percentage change in price

- If the cross price elasticity of demand between two goods is positive, they are substitutes because the price of one good and the demand for the other move in the same direction. If the cross price elasticity of demand between two goods is negative, they are complements because the price of one good and the demand for the other move in opposite directions.

- The **income elasticity of demand** is a measure of the relationship between a relative change in income and the consequent relative change in quantity demanded, *ceteris paribus*. The income elasticity of demand coefficient not only expresses the degree of the connection between the two variables, but it also indicates whether the good in question is normal or inferior.

- The income elasticity of demand is defined as the percentage change in quantity demanded at a given price divided by the percentage change in income.

Income elasticity of demand = Percentage change in quantity demanded at a given price
Percentage change in income

- If the income elasticity is positive, then the good in question is a normal good because the change in income and the change in quantity demanded move in the same direction. If the income elasticity is negative, then the good in question in an inferior good because the change in income and the change in quantity demanded move in opposite directions.

I REVIEW

The cross elasticity of demand measures the effect on the quantity demanded of one good of a change in the price of _____ good. It is equal to the percentage change in the quantity demanded of one good at a given _____ divided by the percentage change in the price of a second good.

The _____ as well as the magnitude of the change is measured by the cross elasticity.

In general, a positive cross elasticity means the two goods are _____ and a negative cross price elasticity means the two goods are _____.

An elasticity that measures the percentage change in the quantity demanded of a good, *ceteris paribus,* given a1-percent change in income is called the _____ elasticity of demand.

The good is a normal good when demand and income move in the _____ direction and it will have a positive income elasticity. If the income elasticity of demand is negative, the good is an _____ good.

II TRUE/FALSE

_____1. The cross elasticity of demand of cars made by Ford and Toyota is negative.

_____2. If bus travel in the United States is an inferior good, a five percent increase in per capita incomes will result in an increased number of bus trips per person in the United States.

_____3. Last year the consumption of melons increased by about four percent. While prices and many other factors affecting melon consumption remained the same, per capita income increased by about four percent. The income elasticity of melon demand is four.

_____4. The income elasticity of food is less than 1, so as a country's income grows it will spend a decreasing share of its national income on food products.

III MULTIPLE CHOICE

1. A study commissioned by the Santa Fe Zephyrs baseball team found that, *ceteris paribus,* when incomes in Santa Fe increased by 40 percent, ticket sales went up by 20 percent. What is the income elasticity of demand for Zephyrs tickets?
   A) 20
   B) 40
   C) 2.0
   D) 0.5

2. If the cross elasticity of demand between football ticket prices and baseball ticket sales was negative, football and baseball games are
   A) substitutes.
   B) complements.
   C) inferior.
   D) superior.

3. A study of the housing market in Anchorage, Alaska, found the income elasticity of demand for mobile homes was negative. This shows that mobile homes in Anchorage are
   A) substitute goods.
   B) complementary goods.
   C) inferior goods.
   D) normal goods.

4. Which of the following identifies a pair of goods that are substitutes?
   A) Food and water: the income elasticity of food is less than the income elasticity of water.
   B) Frozen food and gasoline: the cross price elasticity of demand is greater than zero.
   C) Lawn mowers and electric saws: the price elasticity of demand for mowers is less than the elasticity of saws.
   D) Cigarettes and coffee: the cross price elasticity of demand is negative.

IV APPLICATION AND DISCUSSION

You have the following observations on U.S. intercity rail travel:

Between 1990 and 1993 rail travel increased from 17.5 passenger miles per person to 19 passenger miles per person. At the same time neither per mile railroad price or incomes changed but the per mile price of intercity airline travel increased by 7.5 percent.

Between 1995 and 1998 per capita incomes rose by approximately 13 percent while the price of travel by rail and plane stayed constant. Intercity rail travel was 20 passenger miles per person in 1995 and 19.5 in 1998.

Assuming the demand for travel didn't change between these periods:

1. Calculate the income elasticity of demand for intercity rail travel.

2. Calculate the cross price elasticity of demand for intercity rail travel.

3. What type of good is intercity rail travel?

THE LOWELLS

Questions

1. Why did Mr. Lowell choose chicken rather than steak for his barbecue?

2. In the comic strip, the price of chicken has fallen. Cite two things that could have made the price of chicken fall.

CHAPTER 7
MARKET EFFICIENCY AND WELFARE

SECTION 7.1 CONSUMER SURPLUS AND PRODUCER SURPLUS

SECTION 7.2 THE WELFARE EFFECTS OF TAXES AND SUBSIDIES

SECTION 7.1
CONSUMER SURPLUS AND PRODUCER SURPLUS

KEY POINTS

- What a consumer actually pays for a good is usually less than what she is willing to pay. The monetary difference between what the consumer is willing to pay and what the consumer actually pays is called **consumer surplus.**

- Consumer surplus is shown graphically as the area under the demand curve (willingness to pay for the units consumed) and above the market price (what must be paid for those units).

- If the consumer is a buyer of several units of a good, the earlier units will have greater marginal value and therefore create more consumer surplus because marginal willingness to pay falls as greater quantities are consumed in any period.

- An increase in supply will lower the price and increase your consumer surplus for each of the units you were already consuming, and will also increase consumer surplus from increased purchases at the lower price. Conversely, a decrease in supply will increase the price and lower the amount of consumer surplus.

- **Producer surplus** is the difference between what a producer is paid for a good and the seller's cost for producing each unit of the good. Because some units can be produced at a cost that is lower than the market price, the seller receives a surplus, or net benefit, from producing those units.

- Producer surplus for a particular unit is the difference between the market price and the seller's cost of producing that unit. Total producer surplus is shown graphically as the area under the market price (what was paid for those units) and above the supply curve (the total cost, or sum of marginal costs, of producing those units).

- A higher market price due to an increase in demand will increase total producer surplus. Part of the added surplus is due to a higher price for the quantity already being produced, and part is due to the expansion of output made profitable by the higher price.

- With the tools of consumer and producer surplus, we can better analyze the total gains from exchange. The demand curve represents a collection of maximum prices that consumers are willing and able to pay for additional quantities of a good or service, while the supply curve represents a collection of minimum prices that suppliers require to be willing to supply additional quantities of that good or service.

- At the market equilibrium, consumers receive consumer surplus and producers receive producer surplus. Both consumers and producers benefit from trading every unit up to the market equilibrium output. Buyers purchase each good, except for the very last unit, for less than the maximum amount that they would have been willing to pay; sellers receive more than the minimum amount they would have been willing to accept to supply the good.

- Once the equilibrium output is reached at the equilibrium price, all of the mutually beneficial trade opportunities between the suppliers and the demanders will have taken place, and the sum of consumer and producer surplus is maximized.

- The **total welfare gain** to the economy from trade in a good is the sum of the consumer and producer surplus created. Consumers benefit from additional amounts of consumer surplus and producers benefit from additional amounts of producer surplus.

- A deadweight loss is the net loss of total surplus that results from the misallocation of resources.

I   REVIEW

The difference between what a consumer *actually* pays for a good and what they are *willing* to pay is called consumer

_____.

A consumer's willingness to pay _____ for each additional unit of the good he consumes. Earlier units purchased add _____ to consumer surplus for later ones.

When price falls consumer surplus increases because you buy _____ of the good and because you get _____ consumer surplus from those units you would have purchased at the original price.

As the price of a product falls, the consumer surplus derived from consumption of the product _____.

The difference between the price a seller is paid for a good and her cost of providing it is _____ surplus.

The welfare gain from trade of a product equals the _____ of the consumer surplus and the producer surplus created by each unit traded. Both buyer and seller are _____ _____ from each of the units traded than they would have been without trade.

Once the equilibrium output is reached, all _____ _____ trade opportunities between suppliers and demanders will have taken place.

A deadweight loss is a reduction in total surplus that results from the _____ of resources.

II   TRUE/FALSE

_____1. In an efficient market, the prices that consumers pay for goods and services are equal to the value that they derive from those goods and services.

_____2. If Choon would be willing to pay $30 to attend a Dodger game but actually pays $20, he receives a consumer surplus of $10.

_____3. During the winter of 2000–2001, regulations prevented California electric utilities from raising the price per kilowatt hour they charged customers. When the cost of producing electricity rose, the utilities' producer surplus declined.

III   MULTIPLE CHOICE

1. When Roy buys one more apple because of a decrease in the price of apples, the marginal willingness to pay for the extra apple is
    A) greater than that of previous apples and his consumer surplus goes up.
    B) less than that of previous apples but his consumer surplus is larger.
    C) less than that of previous apples and his consumer surplus goes down.
    D) the same as that of previous apples and there is no change in his consumer surplus.

To answer questions 2 and 3 please refer to Exhibit 2.

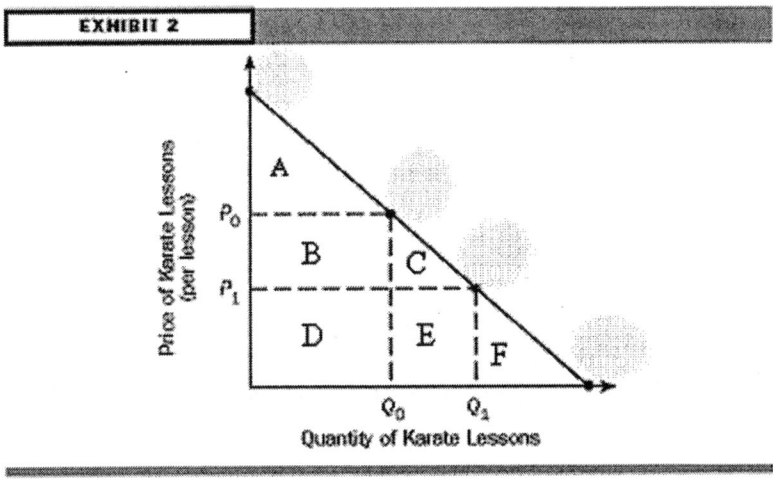

2. Carmine thinks he should be more assertive and believes that karate lessons would help. If the price of each karate lesson is P_0, his consumer surplus is equal to the area
    A) $a + b + c + d + e + f$
    B) $d + e + f$
    C) a
    D) $b + c + d + e$

3. If the price falls from P_0 to P_1, the change in Carmine's consumer surplus is equal to the area
    A) $a + b + c$
    B) $b + c$
    C) $d + e$
    D) $c + e + f$

4. The group, Doctors of Optometry Protest Exchange in Sunglasses, wants to stop international trade in sunglasses. These D.O.P.E.S. argue that because producing countries earn a producer surplus, free, unregulated trade is bad because producers are exploiting consumers. What do the D.O.P.E.S. ignore about trade?

A) Consumers will be better off as long as the consumer surplus is greater than the producer surplus.
B) Consumers will be better off as long as the consumer surplus plus the producer surplus is greater than one.
C) Consumers will be better off as long as the consumer surplus is greater than zero.
D) Consumers will be better off as long as the producer surplus is less than zero.

IV   APPLICATION AND DISCUSSION

Steve loves potato chips. His weekly demand curve is shown in Exhibit 3.

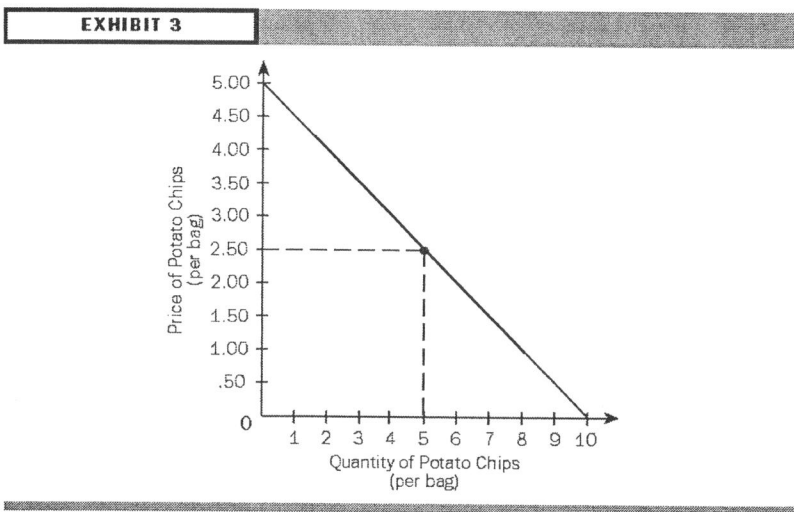

EXHIBIT 3

A) How much is Steve willing to pay for one bag of potato chips?

B) How much is Steve willing to pay for a second bag of potato chips?

C) If the actual market price of potato chips is $2.50, and Steve buys five bags as shown, what is the value of his consumer surplus?

D) What is Steve's total willingness to pay when he buys five bags?

SECTION 7.2
THE WELFARE EFFECTS OF TAXES AND SUBSIDIES

KEY POINTS

- We can use consumer and producer surplus to measure the welfare effects of various government programs, such as taxes, subsidies, and price controls.

Chapter 7: Market Efficiency and Welfare

- **Welfare effects** refer to the gains and losses associated with government intervention.

- After a tax is imposed, consumers pay a higher price and lose the corresponding amount of consumer surplus as a result. Producers receive a lower price after tax and lose the corresponding amount of producer surplus as a result. The government gains the amount of the tax revenue generated, which is transferred to others in society.

- The deadweight loss of a tax occurs because the tax reduces the quantity exchanged below the original output level, reducing the size of the total surplus realized from trade. The tax distorts market incentives: the price to buyers is higher than before the tax, so they consume less, and the price to sellers is lower than before the tax, so they produce less. This leads to deadweight loss, or market inefficiencies—the waste associated with not producing the efficient output.

- The size of the deadweight loss from a tax, as well as how the burdens are shared between buyers and sellers, depends on the elasticities of supply and demand. Other things equal, the less elastic the demand curve, the smaller the deadweight loss. Similarly, the less elastic the supply curve, the smaller the deadweight loss. The more elastic the curves the greater the change in output and the larger the deadweight loss.

- Elasticity differences can help us understand tax policy. Those goods that are heavily taxed often have a relatively inelastic demand curve in the short run. This means that the burden falls mainly on the buyer. It also means that the deadweight loss to society is smaller than if the demand curve was more elastic.

- A government subsidy also produces a deadweight loss. This welfare loss results from production that is greater than competitive equilibrium.

- We can see the welfare effects of a price ceiling by observing the change in consumer and producer surplus from the implementation of the price ceiling. Consumers can now buy at a lower price, but cannot buy as much as before (since suppliers will not supply as much). Producers lose producer surplus from the lower imposed ceiling price. The net loss is a deadweight loss triangle.

- We can also use consumer and producer surplus to see the welfare effects of a price floor, where the government buys up the surplus. Consumers lose consumer surplus due to the higher price floor, and must also pay taxes to pay for the buying and storing of the unsold (to consumers) output. Producers gain producer surplus from the higher prices and greater output (since the government buys up what is not sold on the market). On net, there is a deadweight loss from the price floor because consumers are buying less than the market equilibrium output and producers are producing more.

I   REVIEW

The efficient output occurs at the market-clearing price, which is where the sum of consumer and producer surplus is _____. Economists refer to the gains and losses associated with government intervention in the economy as _____ effects.

The net loss in consumer and producer surplus from government intervention in the economy is called a _____ loss. This loss results because government intervention distorts market _____, like price.

Taxes result in consumers buying _____ because they pay a higher price and suppliers selling less because they receive a _____ price. The net loss results because the _____ output is not produced.

The size of the deadweight loss from a tax on a good depends on the _____ _____ of supply and demand.

The deadweight loss from a price ceiling results from production that is _____ than the efficient output. The loss from a price floor results from consumers buying _____than the efficient output and producers producing _____.

II   TRUE/FALSE

92

_____1. While deadweight loss from a tax is smaller the less elastic the demand for a product, it is greater the less elastic the supply.

_____2. If the governor of the Misty Isles imposes a $75 tax on tourists coming for day visits, only the tourists will suffer the deadweight loss.

_____3. Rent control is a price ceiling that imposes losses on consumers.

_____4. Economists don't worry much about the losses imposed by taxes because we are only losing deadweight.

III   MULTIPLE CHOICE

1. In which of the following cases will there be no deadweight loss from a tax increase?
    A) The demand for the product is perfectly elastic.
    B) The demand for the product is perfectly inelastic.
    C) The demand for the product is more elastic than supply.
    D) The demand for the product is less elastic than supply.

2. Mayor Lexion needs to raise public revenues to balance the budget before this year's election. He doesn't want to impose much of a welfare loss on his community. Mayor Lexion should probably *not* tax which of the following goods?
    A) salt
    B) used cars
    C) cigarettes
    D) matches

3. When the government introduced agricultural price supports, it ususally also became the buyer of last resort, purchasing the surplus created by the price floor. Which of the following is *not* a likely outcome of a price support program for cheese?
    A) Consumer surplus declines because consumers pay a higher price and consume less.
    B) Consumers' tax bills go up as they pay to buy the surplus cheese surplused.
    C) Producer surplus declines because they receive less and produce more.
    D) Producers sell less to consumers and more to the government.

IV   APPLICATION AND DISCUSSION

The 2000–2001 California energy crisis produced brownouts, utility company bankruptcies, and worries about high prices. The California electric power regulatory program imposed price ceilings on electricity sold to consumers. Exhibit 4 describes the California situation with P_S as the price ceiling. Answer the following referring to this exhibit.

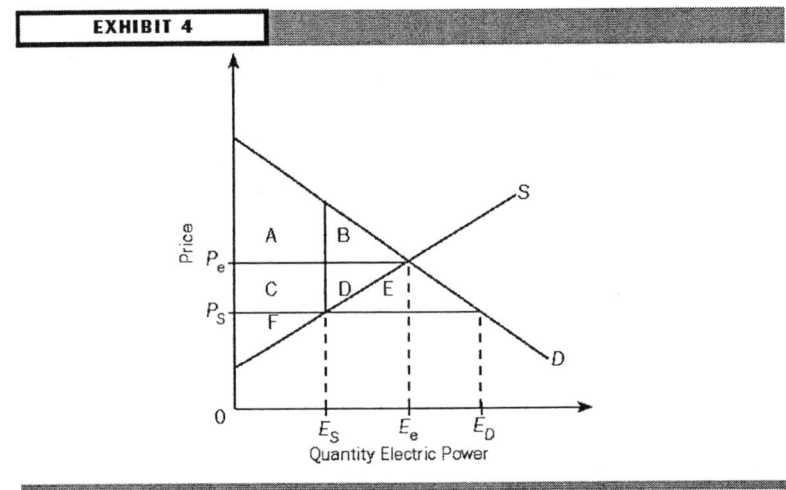

A) What was the loss imposed on consumers by this price ceiling?

B) What was the loss imposed on producers by this price ceiling?

C) What was the loss imposed on California by this price ceiling?

D) Use this exhibit to explain the brownouts in California.

E) What would have to be true for consumers to support market set prices? Use the exhibit to explain why there might not be support among consumers for raising prices.

CHAPTER 8
MARKET FAILURE AND PUBLIC CHOICE

SECTION 8.1 MARKET FAILURE AND EXTERNALITIES

SECTION 8.2 PUBLIC GOODS

SECTION 8.3 IMPERFECT INFORMATION

SECTION 8.4 PUBLIC CHOICE

SECTION 8.1
MARKET FAILURE AND EXTERNALITIES

KEY POINTS

- Sometimes the market system fails to produce efficient outcomes because of a lack of competition or the side effects of what economists call **externalities**.

- An **externality** is said to occur whenever there are physical impacts (benefits or costs) of an activity on individuals not directly involved in the activity. If the impact on the outside party is negative, it is called a **negative externality**; if the impact is positive, it is called a **positive externality**.

- The classic example of a negative externality is the air used by a polluting factory. The polluted air "spills over" to outside parties. Such damages are real costs. Unlike the other resources the firm uses in production, no one owns the air, so the firm does not have to pay for its use.

- If a firm can avoid paying the cost it imposes on others—the external costs—it lowers its own costs of production, but not the true cost to society. As a result, it will tend to produce too much from society's standpoint, causing an efficiency loss due to an overallocation of scarce resources to the production of the good.

- The government can intervene in market decisions in an attempt to take account of negative externalities. It may do this by estimating the amount of those external costs and then taxing the manufacturer by that amount, forcing the manufacturer to bear the costs. If government could impose a pollution tax equal to the cost of the negative externality, then the firm would produce at a socially desired level of output. Tax revenues could be used to compensate those who had suffered damages from the pollution or in some other productive way.

- As an alternative to pollution taxes, the government might simply prohibit certain types of activities causing pollution, or might force firms to clean up their emissions.

- For some goods, the individual consumer does not receive all of the benefits. The benefits not received by the consumer are called positive externalities. (Examples include landscaping and education.)

- Because the decision makers involved ignore some of the real social benefits, the private market does not provide enough of goods that generate external benefits. This often results in the government subsidizing or producing many goods, such as subsidized education and "free" inoculations against communicable diseases.

- At the market equilibrium for goods providing external benefits, output is less than the efficient level because many people that benefit do not have to pay for those benefits. If we could add the benefits that are derived by nonpaying consumers, the demand curve would shift to the right, increasing output.

- Because producers are unable to collect payments from all of those that are benefiting from the good or service, the market has a tendency to underproduce goods with external benefits, causing an efficiency loss. A subsidy equal to external benefits would shift the demand curve to the right and result in an efficient level of output. The government could also use regulation in such situations.

- In either the case of external benefits or external costs, buyers and sellers are receiving the wrong signals: The apparent benefits or costs of some action differ from the true social benefits or costs.

- Sometimes externality problems can be handled by individuals without the intervention of government. People may decide to take steps to minimize their own negative externalities or to contribute to the production of goods with positive externalities. (Examples include choosing not to drive a gas guzzling car, or choosing to donate time or money to schools because of the positive externality associated with education.)

I   REVIEW

When the costs or benefits of an activity impact people outside the market mechanism, economists say a(n) _____ exists.

If production or exchange harms outside parties, it is called a(n) _____ externality. If production or exchange benefits outside parties, it is called a(n) _____ externality.

Air pollution is an example of a(n) _____ externality.

If the education of a person benefits not only that person, but others as well, economists say that education generates _____ externalities.

When producers are unable to collect payments from all those who benefit from a good, the market has a tendency to produce too _____ of the good.

When producers shift the costs of producing a good onto others who are not involved in production or consumption of the good, the market tends to produce too _____ of the good.

II   TRUE/FALSE

_____1. Litter is an example of a positive externality.

_____2. Economists believe that producers pollute because they are evil.

_____3. Cigarette smoke is an example of a negative externality.

_____4. The aroma from a neighbor's lilac bush is an example of a positive externality.

_____5. If fertilizer producers are able to shift some of their production costs onto outside parties, the actual output of fertilizer is likely to fall short of society's ideal.

_____6. When production of a good generates significant positive externalities, the government can improve economic efficiency by subsidizing it.

III   MULTIPLE CHOICE

1. Mae likes to go to bed early while Vinnie, who lives in the apartment next door, likes to stay up late and play the drums. Vinnie is probably
   A) a thoughtful and considerate neighbor.
   B) providing Mae with a positive externality.
   C) inflicting a negative externality on Mae.
   D) "rocking" Mae to sleep.

2. In a market where firms are able to cut their private costs by shifting costs onto others, which of the following will *not* be found?
   A) Negative externalities will occur.
   B) Output of the good being produced will be too low.
   C) The prices of products produced by the firms will be too low.
   D) Inefficiencies will occur.

3. If Carl spends thousands of dollars beautifying his front yard, he is probably
   A) inflicting a negative externality on his neighbors.
   B) providing his neighbors with a positive externality.
   C) reducing the value of his own home.
   D) reducing the value of his neighbors' homes.

4. Mayor Casterbridge believes that education benefits everyone and urges the City Council to provide the school district with more money. An economist would say that the Mayor believes that
   A) there are nontrivial external costs associated with education.
   B) there are positive external benefits associated with education.
   C) teachers are overpaid.
   D) teachers promote ideas that undermine family values.

5. To correct a negative externality like pollution, government may properly consider all but which of the following?
   A) impose special taxes on activities that cause pollution
   B) prohibit activities that cause pollution
   C) force polluting firms to clean up emissions
   D) provide special subsidies for activities that cause pollution

6. To promote activities that generate positive externalities like a healthier, more beautiful environment, government may properly consider all but which of the following?
   A) special taxes on the activities that generate positive externalities
   B) provide subsidies to producers who produce goods that provide positive externalities
   C) provide subsidies to consumers who consume goods that provide positive externalities
   D) pass laws that require people to consume goods that provide positive externalities like education and inoculations for communicable diseases

IV   APPLICATION AND DISCUSSION

In the town of Appleton, where apple growing is the primary industry, Mayor Singleton has asked the City Council to provide parcels of free public land to beekeepers for the establishment of apiaries (places where honey bees are kept). From what you know about bees, externalities, and opportunity costs, evaluate the Mayor's proposal.

SECTION 8.2
PUBLIC GOODS

KEY POINTS

- **Public goods** are another source of market failure. Unlike private goods, the consumption of public goods is neither **rival** nor **excludable**. (National defense and flood control are examples—all those affected benefit simultaneously and it is prohibitively costly to exclude anyone from consuming it.)

- Public goods and externalities can lead to the **free-rider problem**. It might well be advantageous from society's perspective to provide a public good, such as cleaner air, but people have little incentive to pay for the benefits they will receive because they know that they cannot be prevented from receiving the benefits.

- We are likely to get too little of public goods without some intervention. The fact that people who do not pay for public goods cannot be excluded from consuming them precludes charging consumers for benefits received, encouraging beneficiaries to act as free riders, so that some goods with benefits greater than costs will not be produced.

- Because non-payers cannot be excluded from enjoying the benefits of public goods the free-rider problem prevents the private market from supplying the efficient amount of public goods. The government may be able to overcome the free-rider problem by providing or financing the public good and imposing taxes to pay for it.

I   REVIEW

A good that is yours and yours alone is called a _____ good. Goods that are both not rival and not excludable are called _____ goods.

Someone who receives benefits that they don't pay for is called a _____ rider.

Because non-payers can't be excluded from consumption and because of the free-rider problem, the market tends to produce too _____ public goods.

I   TRUE/FALSE

_____1. National defense is an example of a public good.

_____2. A Ford Expedition is an example of a public good.

_____3. The difference between private and public goods is whether or not a private party or a public agency owns them.

_____4. Since the free market tends to overproduce public goods, governments often undertake policies to discourage their production.

III   MULTIPLE CHOICE

1. Leanne pays $5.00 to attend a Fourth of July fireworks display at Prospect Park, while Crystal watches the fireworks from the parking lot next to the park. Crystal is
   A) a free rider.
   B) a rivalrous consumer.
   C) an excludable consumer.
   D) unpatriotic.

2. Talk radio programs like "Rush Limbaugh" and "Dr. Laura" are
   A) rival in consumption.
   B) not excludable.
   C) excludable.
   D) positive externalities.

3. Public goods are
   A) cheap to produce, but expensive to buy.
   B) exclusive in consumption and rival in consumption.
   C) nonrival in consumption and nonexclusive.
   D) impossible for free riders to consume.

4. Where a free-rider problem exists, goods tend to be
   A) underproduced and overconsumed.
   B) underconsumed and overproduced.
   C) high priced and available only to the rich.
   D) low priced and available only to the poor.

IV   APPLICATION AND DISCUSSION

Review the list of goods below and determine whether they are private or public goods by indicating whether or not they are nonrival and/or nonexclusive. Remember public goods are both nonrival in consumption (one person's consumption doesn't diminish another's) and nonexclusive (you can't keep nonpayers out).

Good	Nonrival Consumption	Nonexclusive	Private Good	Public Good
1. Hot Dogs	☐	☐	☐	☐
2. Cable TV	☐	☐	☐	☐
3. Broadcast TV	☐	☐	☐	☐
4. Automobiles	☐	☐	☐	☐
5. National Defense	☐	☐	☐	☐
6. Pollution Control	☐	☐	☐	☐
7. Parking in a Parking Structure	☐	☐	☐	☐

8. A Sunset	☐	☐	☐	☐
9. Admission to a Theme Park	☐	☐	☐	☐

SECTION 8.3
IMPERFECT INFORMATION

KEY POINTS

- Information can be treated like most other scarce goods: It is desirable and limited, and people are willing to pay a positive price to obtain it. Just as in any other cost–benefit evaluation, however, individuals will stop searching for information prior to making decisions when the cost of obtaining that additional information outweighs the benefit they expect to gain from it.

- When information costs to consumers are greater than the perceived benefits, consumers will make less informed decisions. As George Stigler pointed out, "It is perfectly rational for people to make 'poor' decisions if the cost of information necessary to make good decisions exceeds the benefits."

- Much legislation passed at the federal as well as the state and local levels in the past 50 years seems directed towards reducing information costs and keeping consumers from making dangerous or worthless purchases. (Examples include food inspection, occupational licensing, and requiring provision of certain information.)

- Few quarrel with the objective of reducing information costs to consumers and suppliers, which permits more intelligent market decisions and leads to greater satisfaction. However, there is opposition to certain types of governmental action in this area on the grounds that the costs of providing the information is too high, that the government is disseminating inaccurate or misleading information, or that special interest groups have managed to manipulate the regulation to their own advantage, which may not be in the public interest. (An example is occupational licensing laws, which supposedly protect misinformed consumers from getting shoddy services, but may also restrict competition, reducing the supply of workers providing these services, and leading to higher prices. FDA testing requirements are another example.)

- Government-provided information can be an efficient mechanism for reducing market failure from information costs. But excessive government information policies can actually worsen the allocation of resources when the information provided is costly, relatively useless, and/or creates other market imperfections, such as monopoly due to licensing.

- **Caveat Emptor**, or "let the buyer beware," is less comforting as products become more sophisticated and numerous and consumers have a more difficult time getting objective information to evaluate products. Information costs are very high. But product liability laws can make it unprofitable to sell shoddy merchandise, providing a substantial incentive to provide safe products independent of government regulations.

- **Asymmetric information** exists when the available information is initially distributed in favor of one party relative to another. Examples include sellers of defective used cars (lemons).

- If quality-detection costs are sufficiently high, high quality products will tend to be withdrawn from the market and the average quality will fall. The phenomenon where one party enters into an exchange with another who has more information is called **adverse selection**.

- In adverse selection situations, the least-cost solution would have the seller reveal his superior information to a potential buyer. The problem is that it's not individually rational for the seller to provide a truthful and complete disclosure, and this is known by a potential buyer. Only if the seller is punished for not truthfully revealing exchange-relevant information will a potential buyer perceive the sellers disclosure as truthful.

- The existence of asymmetric information gives rise to **signaling** behavior on the part of sellers, such as demonstrating the ability to complete a college degree. Signaling cuts employers' hiring costs.

- Another information problem associated with the insurance market is **moral hazard**. If an individual is insured against a cost, they have reduced incentives to take precautions against those costs, which can result in higher costs and therefore higher insurance rates. Moral hazard arises from the fact that it is costly for the insurer to monitor the behaviors of the insured party. Warranty agreements that limit the responsibility of the insurer in those situations are one method of controlling a user's potential abuse.

I   REVIEW

Since information is scarce like other goods, people will stop searching for it when the _____ of obtaining additional information outweighs the _____ they expect to gain from it.

Government often acts to reduce _____ costs for consumers.

Occupational _____ laws are intended to insure consumers that certain standards will be met by providers of goods and services.

Occupational licensing laws often restrict the _____ of services and lead to _____ prices to consumers.

Governmental information policies can actually reduce efficiency when the costs of providing the information exceed the _____ of the information.

Asymmetric _____ exists when one party to a trade has better information than the other. In the used car market this may result in "_____ cars driving good cars from the market."

Obtaining a college degree may be considered a form of _____ behavior that indicates intelligence and perseverance.

_____ hazard is an information problem in the insurance market that results from the high cost of monitoring the insured. Insurance against risks changes a person's _____ to take precautions against risk.

II   TRUE/FALSE

_____1. A rational person will get all the information she possibly can before making any decision.

_____2. Information supplied to consumers by the government helps them make better decisions.

_____3. Warning labels on cigarette packages are a form of information provided to consumers by government.

_____4. Climbers on North America's highest peak, Mt. McKinley take more risks because current National Park Service policy insures that they will be rescued if they get into trouble.

_____5. Signaling behavior on the part of job-seekers is futile because employers know it has nothing to do with real job performance or productivity.

III   MULTIPLE CHOICE

1. The City Council of a northeastern city has recently voted to eliminate their requirement that taxis have special licenses in order to operate. Henceforth anyone with a valid driver's license can carry passengers for a fee. The likely effect of this program will be
    A) higher cab fares.
    B) fewer taxis.
    C) higher cab fares and fewer taxis.
    D) lower cab fares and more taxis.

2. Which of the following statements is false?
    A) Information can be useful.
    B) Gathering information is costly.
    C) You can't have too much information.
    D) Rational people will gather information as long as the marginal benefits of information are greater than the marginal costs.

3. Which of the following is *not* an objection to the provision of government information services?
    A) The costs to government of providing some types of information is too high.
    B) Government sometimes disseminates inaccurate information.
    C) Government often provides consumers with valuable information about potentially dangerous products.
    D) Special interest groups often manage to manipulate regulations to their own advantage.

4. Good apples cost more to produce than bad apples because good apples are harvested later and with more care. Consumers, however, can't tell the difference between the two before they bite into them. Why will the good apples be driven from the market?
    A) Producers will always concentrate on the lowest cost goods and would never produce good apples.
    B) Consumers don't know enough to identify a really good apple until after they've tasted it, and would prefer to pay less.
    C) Consumers would not be willing to pay more than the cost of a bad apple for any apple, so good apples growers would lose money and leave the business.
    D) Producers wouldn't sell bad apples unless consumers preferred them to good apples.

IV   APPLICATION AND DISCUSSION

In order to get a license to practice in the United States, foreign-trained veterinarians must take an exam given by the American Veterinary Association. Only 48 people per year are allowed to take the exam, which is administered at only two universities. The fee for the exam, which must be booked at least 18 months in advance, was recently raised from $2,500 to $6,000. ("Checkbooks Ready?" *Wall Street Journal,* July 7, 1998, p. 1.)

What effects does this clinical competency exam have on the number of veterinarians practicing in the United States? Do you think it improves the quality of veterinary services?

SECTION 8.4
PUBLIC CHOICE

KEY POINTS

- When the market fails, as in the externality or the public good case, it may be necessary for government to intervene and make public choices. However, just because markets have failed to generate efficient results doesn't necessarily mean that government can do a better job.

- **Public choice analysis** is the application of economic principles to politics. Public choice economists believe that government actions are an outgrowth of individual behavior. Specifically, they assume that the behavior of individuals in politics, like those in the marketplace, will be influenced by self-interest. Bureaucrats, politicians, and voters make choices that they believe will yield them expected marginal benefits that are greater than their expected marginal costs.

- There are differences between the private sector and the public sector in the "rules of the game." But the self-interest assumption is central to the analysis of behavior in both arenas.

- Scarcity and competition are present in the public sector, as well as in the private sector.

- In private markets, there is an **individual-consumption-payment link,** where the goods one gets reflects what one is willing to pay for. The link breaks down when goods are decided on by majority rule. If the majority decides that certain goods will be provided, people will have to purchase the goods through higher taxes, whether they value the goods or not.

- In a two-party political system successful candidates will seek to please **median voters**, those in the middle of the distribution of voter preferences.

- There are both costs and benefits to being politically informed.

- For most people, the costs of becoming politically informed are substantial, while the benefits are negligible. As a result, most people assume a state of **rational ignorance**.

- Individuals often come together with others that have similar political goals to form **special interest groups**. The activities of these groups are usually aimed at getting substantial benefits for a relatively few individuals while spreading the costs over such a large number of taxpayers that the amount any one person will have to pay is negligible.

I   REVIEW

The application of economic principles to politics is called public _____ theory.

Economists assume that people are influenced by self-_____ in both the private and public arenas.

In the public sector the presence of _____ forces politicians and voters to make choices.

Unlike the private sector, choices made in the public sector by majority rule break the individual-consumption-_____ link. When the majority decides what to purchase, individuals pay for goods through higher _____, independent of the value they attach to the goods.

II TRUE/FALSE

_____1. Public choice theory is the study of how people make decisions in their private lives.

_____2. Public choice economists believe that politicians and voters are motivated primarily by their concern for the welfare of others.

_____3. Making efficient decisions in the public sector is more difficult than in the private sector because efficient public decisions would require information on the desires of all of the many people affected.

III MULTIPLE CHOICE

1. Public choice analysis of government behavior shares each of the following principles with economic analysis of market behavior *except* which one?
   A) the assumption that people act out of self-interest
   B) that scarcity is present in both the public and private sectors
   C) the assumption that people in the private sector act out of self-interest while those in the public sector are motivated by concern for the good of all
   D) the belief that competition is present in both the public and private sectors

2. Clinton's Supermarket has established a new policy. Consumers no longer shop for individual items, filling their grocery carts and paying for the total purchased. They are now assigned carts that are already filled and must pay the price assigned to the cart. This approach to shopping is inefficient because it
   A) breaks the individual-consumption-payment link.
   B) lowers the information costs involved in shopping.
   C) causes more wear and tear on the carts since they are used more often.
   D) saves consumers precious time spent shopping.

3. Most independent studies of sports facilities like major league ball parks have found that they
   A) provide no significant economic benefits to the community.
   B) actually reduce overall income in the community.
   C) usually boost overall employment in the community.
   D) are particularly good investments because they generate significant benefits without costing the community anything.

4. Surveys reveal that most citizens are not well-informed about political issues. According to public choice theory, this is due to the fact that
   A) most TV and radio news shows are of poor quality.
   B) most people tend to identify themselves as either Republicans or Democrats and mindlessly follow the recommendations of party leaders.
   C) schools tend to do a poor job teaching students about political issues.
   D) for most people, the costs of being politically informed exceed the benefits.

IV APPLICATION AND DISCUSSION

As you have learned, economists assume that individuals respond in predictable ways to incentives. Public choice theorists assume that this is true in both the private *and* public sectors. Examine the lists below and match each individual with the incentive to which they are likely to respond.

Individual

1) Grocery Shopper
2) U.S. Senator
3) Business Owner
4) U.S. Federal Agency Director
5) Factory Worker
6) Voter

Incentive

a) re-election
b) higher salary
c) low food prices
d) high profits
e) a bigger budget
f) more government services

THE LOWELLS

Questions

1. How do helmet laws affect the costs of motorcycle riding?

2. How do they affect the benefits of motorcycle riding?

CHAPTER 9
CONSUMER CHOICE

SECTION 9.1 CONSUMER BEHAVIOR

SECTION 9.2 THE CONSUMER'S CHOICE

SECTION 9.1
CONSUMER BEHAVIOR

KEY POINTS

- Individuals take action in response to recognized opportunities to advance their goals. This assumption that individuals act to advance their goals—known as **the rule of rational choice**—merely implies that whatever individuals do is done with a purpose. In economics we assume that each individual seeks to maximize his or her own well-being or satisfaction.

- Economists developed the concept of **utility** to allow them to study the relative levels of satisfaction that consumers get from the consumption of goods and services.

- Utility varies from individual to individual depending on specific preferences. Therefore, it is not possible to compare the relative satisfactions of different persons.

- **Total utility** is the total amount of satisfaction derived from the consumption of a certain number of units of a good or service. **Marginal utility** is the additional satisfaction generated by the last unit of a good that is consumed.

- Total utility increases with additional consumption, but the incremental satisfaction—the marginal utility—that results from the consumption of additional units tends to decline as consumption increases.

- This **law of diminishing marginal utility** means that each successive unit of a good that is consumed generates less additional satisfaction than did the previous unit.

- It follows from the law of diminishing marginal utility that as a person uses more and more units of a good to satisfy a given want, the intensity of the want, and the utility derived from further satisfying that want diminishes.

I REVIEW

The assumption that individuals act to advance their goals is known as the rule of _____ choice.

A _____ is a hypothetical unit of satisfaction derived from consumption.

Economist believe that it is _____ to make interpersonal utility comparisons.

The total amount of satisfaction derived from the consumption of a certain number of units of a good is called _____ utility.

The _____ utility is the additional satisfaction generated by the last unit of a good consumed.

The law of diminishing marginal utility states that the incremental satisfaction from the consumption of additional units of a good _____ as consumption increases.

II TRUE/FALSE

_____1. In economics we assume that people often act on whims or "just for the heck of it."

_____2. A "util" is a hypothetical measure of the amount of satisfaction a person gets from consuming one additional unit of a good or service.

_____3. Economists do *not* think it is possible to compare the relative utility that two people get from consuming an additional unit of a particular good.

_____4. As a pizza lover consumes more and more pizza, the extra satisfaction she gets from each additional slice decreases.

III MULTIPLE CHOICE

1. The increase in total utility that Shigeo gets from eating an additional piece of sushi is called
   A) marginal utility.
   B) interpersonal utility.
   C) disutility.
   D) continuing utility.

2. As Vicki eats more and more french fries, her
   A) total utility falls, but the marginal utility of each fry rises.
   B) marginal utility rises as long as the total utility derived from the fries remains positive.
   C) total utility rises, as does the marginal utility of each additional fry.
   D) total utility rises, but the marginal utility of each additional fry falls.

3. When one of the ugly stepsisters argues that she, rather than Cinderella, should go to the ball because she will derive more utility from it than Cinderella, an economist would
   A) probably agree.
   B) demand to see, in writing, how much utility each woman will receive from attending the ball.
   C) point out that making interpersonal utility comparisons isn't possible.
   D) ask how many balls each woman has attended so she can calculate the marginal utility that each would gain.

4. Bananas are Victor's favorite food. In a world where marginal utility increased with consumption, Victor would
    A) eat only bananas.
    B) eat bananas until he got tired of them, then switch to eating something else.
    C) eat bananas until his total utility became negative.
    D) never eat bananas.

IV   APPLICATION AND DISCUSSION

The following table shows Rene's total utility from eating escargot.

1. Fill in the blanks that show the marginal utility that Rene derives from eating escargot.

Escargot Per Day	Total Utility	Marginal Utility
1	10	_____
2	18	_____
3	24	_____
4	28	_____
5	30	_____
6	30	_____

2. Plot Rene's total and marginal utility curves on the graphs in Exhibit 1.

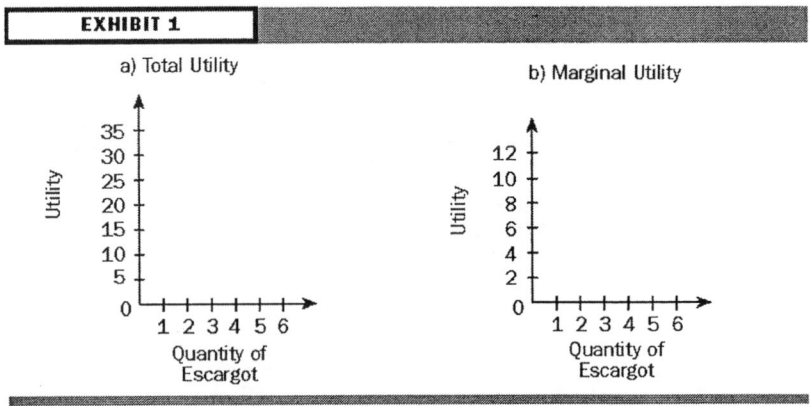

SECTION 9.2
THE CONSUMER'S CHOICE

KEY POINTS

*   A rational consumer will avoid making purchases of any one good beyond the point at which other goods will yield greater satisfaction for the amount spent.

- Marginal utility is an important concept in understanding and predicting consumer behavior. By comparing the marginal utilities generated by units of the goods that he or she desires as well as their prices, a rational consumer seeks the combination of goods that maximizes his or her satisfaction.

- In order to reach consumer equilibrium, consumers must allocate their income in such a way that the ratio of the marginal utility to the price of the good is equal for all goods purchased. When this goal is realized, $1 worth of additional gasoline will yield the same marginal utility as $1 worth of additional bread or apples or movie tickets or soap.

- Given a fixed budget, if the marginal utilities per dollar spent on additional units of two goods are not the same, the consumer can increase total satisfaction by buying more of a good with a higher marginal utility per dollar and less of another good with a lower marginal utility per dollar.

- Consumers will continue to alter their purchases to increase their satisfaction until the ratio of the marginal utility to the price of each good is equal for all goods purchased. When the optimum, utility-maximizing level of each good has been purchased, consumers are said to have reached the point of **consumer equilibrium**.

- The law of demand—buying more of a good as its price is reduced—reflects consumer equilibrium where goods are subject to the law of diminishing marginal utility: A lower price for a good increases its marginal utility or satisfaction per dollar, leading to an increase in the quantity of that good demanded.

I   REVIEW

A rational consumer will avoid purchases of one good if there are other goods that give greater _____ for the amount spent.

The additional satisfaction or marginal utility of a good _____ as more of it is consumed.

When a consumer acquires the bundle of goods that maximizes her utility or happiness, she is at a point of consumer _____ .

When people have spent their _____ on goods and services so that the marginal utility they receive per _____ spent is the same for every good, they have reached consumer equilibrium.

When the price of a good falls, consumers buy _____ of it because the marginal utility per dollar spent for the good _____ . As they buy more, the marginal utility per dollar spent _____ and a new equilibrium is reached.

The law of demand reflects consumer equilibrium where goods are subject to the law of _____ marginal utility.

II   TRUE/FALSE

_____1. By spending less on CDs and more on travel, Grete could make herself better off, but she doesn't because she is currently at consumer equilibrium.

_____2. Franco's mother buys three cans of ravioli and three cans of chili for his lunch every week. This week Franco does the shopping and buys four cans of chili and two cans of ravioli. Since each costs $2 per can, the marginal utility Franco gets from the fourth can of chili must be greater than he gets from the third can of ravioli.

_____3. Malcolm spends his income on two goods, books and soup. Books costs about $25 each while soup costs $1 a can. Malcolm is maximizing his utility because the marginal utility he received was the same for both the last book and last can of soup he purchased.

_____4. The law of diminishing marginal utility suggests that the demand curve would have a positive slope.

III   MULTIPLE CHOICE

1. When consumers have spent their income on goods and services in a way that maximizes their utility, they have reached
    A) monetary equilibrium.
    B) market equilibrium.
    C) consumer equilibrium.
    D) the end of the month.

2. Hamburgers cost $2 and hot dogs cost $1 and Juanita is in consumer equilibrium. What must be true about the marginal utility of the hamburger Juanita consumes?
    A) The marginal utility of the last hamburger is less than that of the last hot dog.
    B) The marginal utility of the last hamburger is equal to that of the last hot dog.
    C) The marginal utility of the last hamburger is greater than that of the last hot dog.
    D) The marginal utility of the last hamburger is equal to zero.

3. Werner has spent a week at the state fair and blown all of his money on carnival rides and hot dogs. Both hot dogs and rides cost $1 each. Werner realizes the last hot dog he ate increased his utility by 40 utils while the marginal utility of his last ride was only 20 utils. He was not in consumer equilibrium. What should Werner have done differently to make himself happier?
    A) He should have reduced the number of hot dogs he ate and increased the number of rides.
    B) He should have increased the number of hot dogs he ate and reduced the number of rides.
    C) He should have decreased the amount of hot dogs and rides he consumed.
    D) He should have increased the number of hot dogs and rides he consumed.

IV   APPLICATION AND DISCUSSION

The Consumer Price Index (CPI) measures changes in the cost of living by comparing the cost of buying a certain bundle of goods and services over time. The quantities of each commodity remain the same from year to year but their prices change, so changes in the index reflect weighted average of changes in the prices of goods and services.

Explain how the behavior assumed in the CPI conflicts with the way consumers actually respond to price changes. Do you think the CPI overestimates or underestimates the effect of price changes on consumers?

Chapter 7: Market Efficiency and Welfare

Questions

1. What do you think would happen to "all you can eat" buffets if the law of diminishing marginal utility were repealed?

2. Do you think the law of diminishing marginal utility saved Mom's Chinese Buffet from losing money on Jim Lowell and his pal?

111

CHAPTER 10
PRODUCTION AND COSTS

SECTION 10.1
PROFITS: TOTAL REVENUE MINUS TOTAL COSTS

KEY POINTS

- Recall that costs exist because resources are scarce and have competing uses—to produce more of one good means forgoing the production of another good. The cost of producing a good is measured by the worth of the most valuable alternative that was given up to obtain the resource: the opportunity cost.

- **Explicit costs** are input costs that require a monetary payment. They are out-of-pocket expenses, such as wages, that are relatively easy to measure by the money spent on the resources used.

- **Implicit costs** do not represent an explicit outlay of money, but they are still real, representing the implicit opportunity costs of alternatives that must be forgone. The opportunity cost of using one's own land, labor, or capital are examples.

- Whenever we talk about costs—explicit or implicit—we are talking about opportunity cost.

Chapter 10: Production and Costs

- Economists generally assume that the ultimate goal of the firm is to maximize **profits**. In other words, firms try to maximize the difference between what they receive for their goods and services—their total revenue—and what they give up for their inputs—their total costs (explicit and implicit).

- Profits are the difference between the total revenues (*TR*) of a firm and its total costs (*TC*). **Accounting profits** equal actual revenues minus actual expenditures of cash (explicit costs), so they do not include implicit costs. **Economic profits** equal actual revenues minus all explicit and implicit costs.

- Economists consider a zero economic profit a normal profit because it means that the firm is covering both implicit and explicit costs: the total opportunity cost of its resources. This is different from earning zero accounting profits.

- **Sunk costs** are costs that have already been incurred and cannot be recovered. As a result, sunk costs are irrelevant for any future action.

I   REVIEW

When economists explain the behavior of firms they assume the firm's ultimate goal is to maximize _____, which is the difference between the _____ the firm earns and its _____.

There are two types of costs. _____ costs are measured by the money payments for resources. The opportunity costs of using the resources owned by the firm are _____ costs; these costs even though no _____ is spent.

_____ profits are the difference between total revenue and explicit costs.

_____ profits will be less than accounting profits because they include as a cost the opportunity cost of the firm's resources or its implicit costs.

A(n) _____ economic profit means that the firm's revenue is just sufficient to cover its total opportunity costs. Even with a zero economic profit, the firm's owners would be _____ for the time and money they put in to the business.

When costs have been incurred and cannot be recovered they are called _____ costs. These costs are _____ for any future decisions since they will not be changed by any decision.

II   TRUE/FALSE

_____1. Eddy Sun is a lawyer who has invented a better mousetrap. Eddy works fewer hours as a lawyer in order to build and distribute mousetraps for his company, Smashmouse Inc. Smashmouse does not pay Eddy a wage, so his time imposes no cost on the firm.

_____2. Carrie neglected to include her electric bill when she calculated her profits for the first month she operated her bookstore. When she includes the electric bill, her profits will be lower.

_____3. Economic profits will always be greater than accounting profits.

_____4. Hank O'Hara has run his company, Hank's Towing and Wrecking, for three years and made an accounting profit of $20,000 each year. As long as Hank continues to make accounting profits, staying in the towing business is a rational decision.

III   MULTIPLE CHOICE

1. Mammoth Drug Company spent $2.5 million to develop its new intelligence-increasing drug, Iqgra, or $0.25 per pill. Production costs are $0.75. Studies show the pill will only sell if priced at $0.80. Mammoth's economist says the pill should still be produced even though the price is less than the $1 per unit cost. Why would he make this recommendation?
    A) He is close to retirement and doesn't care that much.
    B) He is predicting the price will rise with inflation but not the cost.
    C) The development costs are sunk costs and irrelevant to production decisions.
    D) He knows that the company never intended to recover the development costs.

2. P. C. Brown sells three hundred jars of honey each month at a price of $3 per jar. He pays $200 each month for jars and other materials and $150 for labor. He uses his own land, which he could rent for $100 per month, and his time, which has an opportunity cost of $300 per month. What are his economic profits?
    A) $550
    B) $400
    C) $300
    D) $150

3. LaTisha is an entrepreneur who sets up a single checking account for her business. She deposits all of her receipts in her checking account and pays all of the firm's bills by writing checks on her account. The change in her account balance over the year is equal to
    A) her firm's yearly total revenue.
    B) her firm's yearly total costs.
    C) her firm's yearly accounting profits.
    D) her firm's yearly economic profits.

IV   APPLICATION AND DISCUSSION

The salmon fishery in Alaska's Bristol Bay has historically been one of the world's richest. Over the past few years, poor returns of salmon to the Bay and competition from farm-raised salmon have reduced the economic returns to the fishermen. One response to lower revenues has been for fishermen to use family members instead of hiring crew "in order to reduce their costs."

Evaluate this business strategy. Will employing relatives really keep profits from falling? Under what conditions is this a good strategy?

SECTION 10.2
PRODUCTION IN THE SHORT RUN

KEY POINTS

- Since it takes more time to vary some inputs than others, we must distinguish between the short run and the long run.

- The **short run** is defined as a period too brief for some inputs to be varied. In the short run, the inputs that do not change with output are called fixed inputs.

- The **long run** is a period of time in which the firm can adjust all inputs. In the long run, all inputs are variable and will change as output changes. The long run can vary considerably in length from industry to industry.

- **Total product (*TP*)** shows the total amount of output generated as the level of the variable input increases. Total product will start at a low level and increase—perhaps rapidly at first, and then more slowly—as the amount of the variable input increases. It will continue to increase until the quantity of the variable input becomes so large in relation to the quantity of others that further increases in output become more and more difficult or even impossible.

- The **marginal product (*MP*)** of any single input is defined as the change in total product resulting from a small change in the amount of that input used. Marginal product first rises as the result of more effective use of fixed inputs, and then falls.

- As the amount of a variable input is increased, the amount of other (fixed) inputs being held constant, a point ultimately will be reached beyond which marginal product will decline. This is called **diminishing marginal product,** which stems from the crowding of the fixed input with more and more of the variable input.

- A firm never knowingly allows itself to reach the point where the marginal product becomes negative, the situation in which the use of additional variable input units actually reduces total product. In such a situation, there are so many units of the variable inputs—inputs with positive opportunity costs—that efficient use of the fixed input units is impaired.

I   REVIEW

To produce a certain level of _____ a firm must use _____ in certain combinations.

The period of time that is too short for the firm to change the amount of some input is called the _____ run. Inputs that cannot be varied during this time period are called _____ inputs.

The long run is the period of time in which all inputs are _____ inputs. The actual time in this period _____ from industry to industry.

The maximum amount of product a firm can produce with a given combination of inputs is determined by the existing _____ and described by firm's _____ function.

The total amount of a firm's output is called its total _____. The _____ product is the amount total product changes when one input is increased by a small amount.

Diminishing _____ product states that in the _____ run, when some input is fixed, increasing the amount of the _____ input will add to total product but after some point marginal product will decline.

II   TRUE/FALSE

_____1. Jed and Ellie May Derrick would like to increase the oil produced from their oil fields. Since it takes over a year to drill new wells, they are increasing labor and other variable inputs to produce more oil from existing wells. They are making short-run production decisions.

_____2. Beth's delivery service currently has two trucks and it will take a few months to add another truck. The trucks, the drivers, and the gasoline used in the trucks are all fixed inputs.

_____3. When Henry Ford introduced the assembly line in auto production, he changed the number of cars that a given amount of labor and capital could produce. This was a change in the production function for automobiles.

Chapter 10: Production and Costs

III   MULTIPLE CHOICE

1. The U.S. Office of Production Standardization wants the short run to be of equal length for all firms for easier record keeping. The short run cannot be the same for all firms and industries because
    A) entrepreneurs have different tastes and preferences.
    B) the time it takes firms to change the amount of fixed inputs varies.
    C) the law of diminishing marginal product occurs at different points.
    D) firms don't listen to what government officials say even if it is a good idea.

2. Cal's Candy Company recently hired its twelfth employee. The company can hire all the labor it needs for $70 per day. Given its production function, the company has entered the range of diminishing marginal product. Why is this important to Cal's company?
    A) It limits the amount that can be produced in the long run.
    B) It means the quality of the available labor has diminished.
    C) It means the total product will begin to decline as Cal hires more workers.
    D) It means smaller increases in output for every additional $70 Cal spends on labor.

EXHIBIT 1 WILLIE'S WATER PARK SHORT-RUN PRODUCTION FUNCTION

Labor	Total Product	Marginal
(Workers)	(Visitors per hour)	Product
0	0	
1	10	10
2	22	12
3	31	9
4	39	8
5	43	4
6	41	-2

3. Referring to Exhibit 1 above, Willie's Water Park experiences diminishing marginal product beginning with the
    A) first worker.
    B) sixth worker.
    C) third worker.
    D) second worker.

4. Which of the following aphorism best describes the Law of Diminishing Marginal Product?
    A) Don't cry over spilled milk.
    B) Too many cooks spoil the soup.
    C) You can lead a horse to water but you can't make him drink.
    D) A penny saved is a penny earned.

IV   APPLICATION AND DISCUSSION

Harry Hat Company makes hats using the technology described below:

With 3 Machines:

Labor	Total Product (Hats)	Marginal Product (Hats)
1 day	8	_____
2 days	18	_____
3 days	30	_____
4 days	45	_____
5 days	57	_____
6 days	67	_____
7 days	72	_____

With 4 Machines:

Labor	Total Product (Hats)	Marginal Product (Hats)
1 day	9	_____
2 days	20	_____
3 days	35	_____
4 days	55	_____
5 days	76	_____
6 days	88	_____
7 days	95	_____

A) Fill in the Marginal Product columns of these tables.

B) At what point does diminishing marginal product set in with three machines? With four?

C) Why is the point of diminishing marginal product different in each case?

SECTION 10.3
COSTS IN THE SHORT RUN

KEY POINTS

- The short-run total costs of a business fall into two distinct categories: fixed costs and variable costs.

- **Fixed costs** are costs that do not vary with the level of output. Fixed costs have to be paid even if no output is produced. In the short run, fixed costs cannot be avoided without going out of business.

- The sum of the firm's fixed costs is called its **total fixed cost (*TFC*)**.

- Costs that are not fixed are called **variable costs**. Variable costs vary with the level of output, such as expenditures for wages and raw materials.

- The sum of the firm's variable costs is called its **total variable cost (*TVC*)**.

- The sum of the firm's total fixed costs and total variable costs is called its **total cost (*TC*).**

- Sometimes we find it convenient to discuss costs on a per-unit-of-output, or average, basis. **Average total cost (ATC)** equals total cost divided by the level of output produced. **Average fixed cost (*AFC*)** equals total fixed cost divided by the level of output produced. **Average variable cost (*AVC*)** equals total variable cost divided by the level of output produced.

- The most important single cost concept is marginal cost. **Marginal cost (*MC*)** shows the change in total costs associated with a change in output by one unit, or the costs of producing one more unit of output. Marginal costs are a useful way to view variable costs—costs that vary as output varies. Marginal costs are the additional, or incremental, costs associated with the "last" unit of output produced.

Chapter 10: Production and Costs

- The various cost concepts can be illustrated graphically. A total fixed cost (TFC) curve is always a horizontal line because, by definition, fixed costs are the same at all output levels. The total cost (*TC*) curve is the summation of the total variable cost (*TVC*) and total fixed cost (*TFC*) curves. Because the total fixed cost curve is horizontal, the total cost curve runs above and parallel to the variable cost curve.

- The average fixed cost (*AFC*) curve constantly declines, approaching but never reaching zero. The marginal cost (*MC*) curve crosses the average variable cost (*AVC*) and average total cost (*ATC*) curves at those curves' minimum points.

I   REVIEW

In the short run, a firm's _____ costs are those expenses that are not affected by the level of output.

Those costs that change as the level of output changes are called _____ costs.

_____ costs are the sum of the firm's fixed and variable costs.

Average total, fixed, and variable costs present the firm's costs on a per _____ of output basis.

The change in the firm's total costs that results from an increase in output by one unit is the _____ cost. This is another way to look at the firm's variable costs.

As a firm increases its output, its fixed costs become a _____ share of total costs and its average fixed costs _____.

Marginal costs equal average variable and average total costs at their _____ points. When marginal costs are above average variable and average total costs, these costs _____.

II   TRUE/FALSE

_____1. To operate her consulting business, Ming-Na pays $750 a month to rent an office for which she has signed a one-year lease. She also pays $7 per hour for secretarial services, of which she usually uses twenty hours a month. Ming-Na's monthly total variable costs are $890.

_____2. Tremaine knows that the fixed costs for the Spokane branch of his lumber business will be $12,000 this year. His average fixed costs will not be affected by the amount of lumber he sells.

_____3. A firm's marginal costs are not its per unit variable costs.

_____4. As a firm's output increases, its average variable costs will eventually be greater than its average total costs.

III   MULTIPLE CHOICE

1. Roger Weave promotes boxing matches. He makes $6,500 per fight. Which costs are most relevant to his decision to promote one more fight?
   A) total costs
   B) marginal costs
   C) average fixed costs
   D) average total costs

2. Omar knows that he is currently producing a level of output at which his marginal costs equal his average variable costs. What is true about Omar's average variable costs at this level of output?
    A) It is at a minimum.
    B) It is at a maximum.
    C) It is at neither its maximum nor its minimum.
    D) It is greater than the average total costs.

Answer questions 3 through 6 by referring to Exhibit 2, which describes a firm's costs.

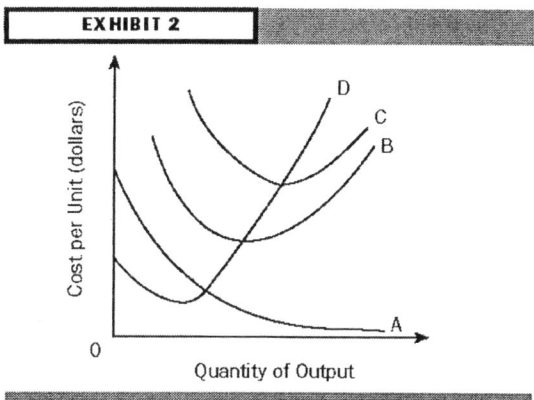

3. The average fixed cost curve is the curve labeled
    A) A.
    B) B.
    C) C.
    D) D.

4. What does the curve labeled D describe?
    A) The firm's average variable costs.
    B) The firm's average total costs.
    C) The firm's average fixed costs.
    D) The firm's marginal costs.

5. Which curve describes average variable costs?
    A) A
    B) B
    C) C
    D) D

6. Which curve describes the average total costs?
    A) A
    B) B
    C) C
    D) D

IV   APPLICATION AND DISCUSSION

Complete the following table describing the short-run daily costs of the Attractive Magnet Co. for 2002.

Total Product (Magnets)	Total Fixed Costs	Total Variable Costs	Total Costs	Average Fixed Costs	Average Variable Costs	Average Total Costs	Marginal Costs
1	$100	$30	$130	$100	$30	$130	$30
2	___	___	___	___	25	___	20
3	___	___	___	___	20	___	___
4	___	___	___	___	16	___	___
5	___	___	___	___	18	___	___
6	___	___	___	___	21	___	___
7	___	___	___	___	24	___	___
8	___	218	318	___	___	___	___

SECTION 10.4
THE SHAPE OF THE SHORT-RUN COST CURVES

KEY POINTS

- The relationship between the marginal and the average is simply a matter of arithmetic. When a number (the marginal cost) being added into a series is smaller than the previous average, the new average will be lower; when a number (the marginal cost) being added into a series is larger than the previous average, the new average will be higher.

- The behavior of marginal cost (MC) is related to marginal production (MP). When MP of an input is rising the MC of expanding output will be falling. When MP falls, MC rises.

- The average total cost (ATC) curve is usually U-shaped. The average cost per unit declines as output expands, but then starts increasing again as output expands still further beyond a certain point.

- The reason for high average total costs when the firm is producing a very small amount of output is the high average fixed costs. It is the declining AFC that is primarily responsible for the falling ATC.

- The average total cost curve rises at high levels of output because of diminishing marginal product. Diminishing marginal product sets in at the very bottom of the marginal cost curve. Diminishing marginal product causes MC to increase, eventually causing the AVC and ATC curves to rise.

- A relationship exists between average and marginal costs when AVC is falling, MC must be less than AVC; and when AVC is rising, MC must be more than AVC. MC is equal to AVC at the lowest point on the AVC curve. The same is true for the ATC curve□MC is equal to ATC at the lowest point on the ATC curve.

Chapter 10: Production and Costs

The average total cost curve is roughly "_____" shaped.

Average total costs initially fall with increased production in the short run because average _____ costs fall rapidly at small amounts of production.

As production increases marginal costs rise since _____ variable input has to be used to increase output by the same amount.

Diminishing _____ product is the reason average total costs rise in the short run.

When marginal product is rising, marginal costs are _____. When marginal product is falling, marginal costs are _____.

When marginal costs exceed average costs, average costs are _____. When marginal costs are below average costs, average costs are _____.

II   TRUE/FALSE

_____1. The shape of the average total and variable cost curves resembles most closely the letter "n."

_____2. If diminishing marginal product were not a factor, average total costs would never increase in the short run.

_____3. Sara's first three econ quiz scores were 10, 20, and 15 for an average score of 15. If her score on her fourth quiz is 18, her average score will rise.

_____4. As Sofia expands production in her bakery, her per unit fixed costs will fall but her average total costs will always rise.

III   MULTIPLE CHOICE

1. Silicon Valley Brick Works has opened a new brick factory in San Jose, California. Why do their average total costs fall as they expand brick production?
   A) They find cheaper and cheaper concrete to buy as they produce more.
   B) The marginal product of their labor input declines as they produce more.
   C) Their average variable costs rise less than the per unit costs of inputs.
   D) Their fixed costs are being spread over more units of output.

2. Ellis Finn realizes his firm, Ring Carpet Cleaning, is operating in the region of diminishing marginal product. As he cleans more carpets in the short run, what will happen to the marginal cost of carpet cleaning?
   A) Marginal costs will increase.
   B) Marginal costs will decrease.
   C) Marginal costs will stay the same.
   D) It is impossible to say anything about marginal costs.

3. When average total cost is increasing with increases in output,
   A) average fixed costs will also be increasing.
   B) average variable costs will be falling.
   C) marginal costs will be above average total costs.
   D) marginal costs will be below average total costs.

IV   APPLICATION AND DISCUSSION

1.   The Lighthouse Safety Vest Co. makes flotation vests for recreational boaters. They currently employ 50 people and produce 12,000 vests per month. Lighthouse managers know that when they hire one more person, monthly vest production will increase by 200 vests. They pay workers $1600 per month. What is the marginal product of labor? What is the marginal cost to produce one more vest? (*Hint:* Think of the marginal cost as the additional worker's pay divided by the changes in output.) If labor is the only variable factor of production, will the average variable cost of production rise or fall? Why?

2.   What happens to the marginal cost of a vest when the fifty-second worker is added and the marginal product drops to 160 vests per month?

SECTION 10.5
COST CURVES: SHORT RUN VERSUS LONG RUN

KEY POINTS

- Over long enough time periods, firms can vary all of their productive inputs. However, in the short run, a company cannot vary its plant size and equipment. In the short run the firm can only expand output by employing more variable inputs.

- The long run average total cost curve lies equal to or below the short run average cost curves. In the long run, costs are lower because firms have greater flexibility in changing inputs that are fixed in the short run.

- **Economies of scale** occur when per unit costs fall as output expands. When the per unit costs does not vary with output, the firm faces **constant returns to scale**. When the per unit costs rises as output expands, there are **diseconomies of scale**.

- The typical firm may experience economies of scale at low levels of output, constant returns to scale at higher levels of output, and diseconomies of scale at still higher levels of output. At the **minimum efficient scale**, a firm has exhausted its economies of scale and the long-run average total costs are minimized.

- Economies of scale may exist because a firm can use mass production techniques or capture gains from further labor specialization not possible at lower levels of output. Diseconomies of scale may occur as a firm finds it increasingly difficult to handle the complexities of large-scale management.

I   REVIEW

In the long run, firms can _____ capital for labor if that will reduce the cost of producing a given amount of output.

The effects of diminishing marginal product are reduced in the long run because the firm can _____ all of its inputs.

In the long run, average costs associated with expanding output are _____than in the short run because of the greater _____ firms have in choosing inputs.

In the long run, firms experience _____of scale when increased output results in declining per unit costs.

When per unit costs increase with output, firms experience _____ of scale.

In the long run, firms can often expand output and keep average costs the same. This is the range of _____ returns to scale.

When economies of scale are exhausted, firms are producing at the minimum _____ scale in the long run.

II   TRUE/FALSE

_____1. Edith Hear has to wait eight months for her restaurant to be remodeled. These changes will allow her to reduce the number of waiters and bus people she uses to serve her current customers. Her average costs will fall when the remodel is completed.

_____2. In the long run, a firm is operating in the range of diseconomies of scale when an increase in output results in no change in its per unit cost of production.

III   MULTIPLE CHOICE

1. If a firm doesn't expect either an increase in input prices or an increase in its sales, why would it build an additional factory?
    A) In the long run, the cost of building a factory will rise so building it now will save money.
    B) If the firm is in the range of diseconomies of scale, a factory will help reduce costs.
    C) In the long run, using more capital will reduce total costs as long as the firm is operating with economies of scale.
    D) In the long run, firms may reduce per unit costs of production by substituting capital for labor.

2. Max Prophet sells hot dogs from a street-side stand. The city imposes a new permit fee that Max must pay to sell hot dogs. Which of the following statements is true?
    A) This fee will not affect Max's cost curves.
    B) This fee will increase Max's short-run average fixed cost.
    C) This fee will increase Max's short-run average variable cost.
    D) This fee will have no effect on Max's long-run costs.

Chapter 10: Production and Costs

Answer Questions 3, 4, and 5 by referring to the cost curves in Exhibit 3.

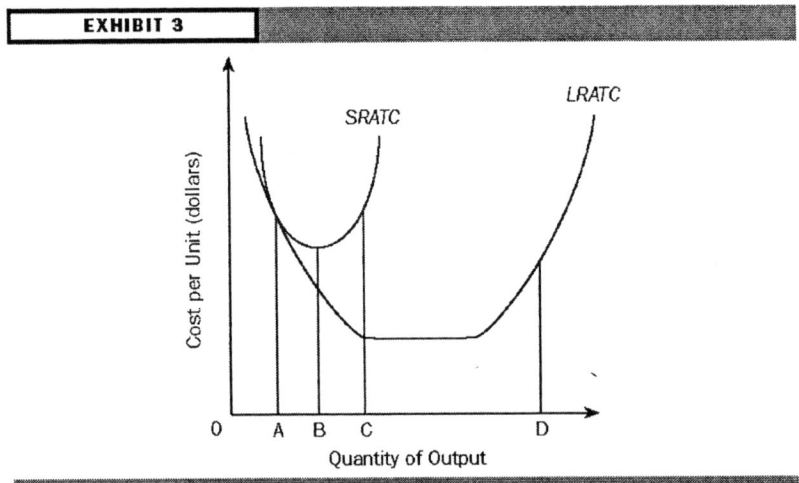

3. The lowest level of output at which the efficient scale of production is reached in the long run is
   A) A.
   B) B.
   C) C.
   D) D.

4. In the short run, described by *SRATC*, the efficient output level is
   A) A.
   B) B.
   C) C.
   D) D.

5. When the firm is producing at the level of output described by D, it will be experiencing
   A) economies of scale.
   B) diseconomies of scale.
   C) constant economies of scale.
   D) real returns to scale.

IV   APPLICATION AND DISCUSSION

Buffalo Bill has a potato chip company, Buffalo's Chips. He is currently losing money on every bag of chips he sells. Mrs. Bill, who has just completed an economics class, tells Bill he could make a profit if he adds more machines and produces more chips. How could this be possible? What is Mrs. Bill assuming about the output range in which Bill is currently producing?

Questions

1. In this example, what is the variable input that is causing the problem of diminishing marginal product?

2. What are the fixed inputs?

3. Who do you think has the highest marginal productivity, the first worker Mr. Lowell hired, or the last?

CHAPTER 11
PERFECT COMPETITION

SECTION 11.1 THE FOUR MARKET STRUCTURES

SECTION 11.2 AN INDIVIDUAL PRICE TAKER'S DEMAND CURVE

SECTION 11.3 PROFIT MAXIMIZATION

SECTION 11.4 SHORT-RUN PROFITS AND LOSSES

SECTION 11.5 LONG-RUN EQUILIBRIUM

SECTION 11.6 LONG-RUN SUPPLY

SECTION 11.1
THE FOUR MARKET STRUCTURES

KEY POINTS

- Economists have identified four different market structures in which firms operate: perfect competition, monopoly, monopolistic competition, and oligopoly. Each structure or environment has certain key characteristics that distinguish it from the other structures.

- **Perfect competition** is a market structure involving a large number of buyers and sellers, a homogeneous (standardized) product, and easy market entry and exit.

- In perfect competition, no single firm produces more than an extremely small proportion of output, so no firm can influence the market price or quantity. Firms are price takers and must accept the market price as determined by the forces of demand and supply.

- At the other end of the continuum of market environments is pure **monopoly**, where there is a single seller, and the seller sets the price that will maximize its profits.

- **Monopolistic competition** falls between perfect competition and monopoly, where firms have both an element of competition and an element of monopoly power. Because each firm's product is differentiated at least slightly from that of other competitors, each has some monopoly power. However, because there are so many competitors, it also has an element of competitive markets.

- **Oligopoly** also falls between perfect competition and monopoly, where a few firms produce similar or identical goods, as opposed to one firm or many. Unlike monopoly, oligopoly allows for some competition between firms; unlike competition, individual firms have a significant share of the total market for the good being produced.

Chapter 11: Perfect Competition

- An oligopolist is very conscious of the actions of competing firms, unlike other market structures. An oligopolist's behavior is closely related to that of its competitors. It does have some control over price and thus is a price searcher.

- Consumers believe that all firms in a perfectly competitive market sell identical (homogeneous) products, so that the products of all the firms are perfect substitutes.

- Product markets characterized by perfect competition have no significant barriers to entry or exit. This means that it is fairly easy for entrepreneurs to become suppliers of the product or, if they are already producers, to stop supplying the product.

- While the assumptions for perfect competition may seem a bit unrealistic, the model of perfect competition is useful because there are many markets that resemble perfect competition in that firms face very elastic demand curves and relatively easy entry and exit. It also gives us a standard of comparison.

I   REVIEW

Economists have identified four different market structures: _____ _____, _____,
_____, and _____.

Perfect competition is one market type that is characterized by (1) _____ buyers and sellers, (2) selling a _____ product, and (3) _____ market entry and exit.

Firms in this type of market produce homogenous products or products that are _____.

In a perfectly competitive market there are so many buyers and sellers that each feels they have little _____ over the prices. Firms in this type of market are price _____ and take the market price as given.

In a perfectly competitive industry it is fairly easy for entrepreneurs to become suppliers of a product because there are no significant _____ to entry or exit.

II   TRUE/FALSE

_____1. Many firms make nails. Since it is hard to distinguish the nails made by one firm from another, nail firms produce a homogeneous product.

_____2. The city of Coney Island, Nebraska, limits the number of hot dog vendors in its downtown to five. Cecilia paid $3,000 for one of these permits and opened a hot dog cart. Since all hot dogs are the same, Cecilia is in a perfectly competitive market.

_____3. The egg business is a perfectly competitive market. When the market price of eggs is $2.50 a dozen, Farmer Brown would be able to sell his eggs at $3 a dozen.

III   MULTIPLE CHOICE

1. Why can't firms in a perfectly competitive industry raise the price of their product above the market clearing price?
   A) The government has established laws against raising prices.
   B) The firms in a perfectly competitive industry face barriers to entry.
   C) These type of firms are price searchers.
   D) Many other sellers produce the same product and charge the market price.

2. Which of the following is not an example of a barrier to entry?
   A) There is limited information about the profits available raising nutria.
   B) The city government limits the number of taxis to 200.
   C) The cost of labor in the pickle business is $50 a day.
   D) A firm must invest billions of dollars before it could launch a moon rocket.

3. Which of the following is not a true statement about the different market structures found around the world?
   A) In perfect competitive sellers are price takers.
   B) In monopoly the seller sets the price that maximizes profits.
   C) Firms in a monopolistic competitive market produce similar but not identical products.
   D) Oligopoly is a market structure with no competition between firms.

IV   APPLICATION AND DISCUSSION

Using the following information, which of the industries described below are perfectly competitive? Check the perfectly competitive market characteristics each industry possesses and determine whether it is a perfectly competitive industry.

Industry	Many Firms and Buyers	Identical Products	Ease of Entry and Exit	Perfectly Competitive Market?
New York taxi business: City issues a limited number of permits.	☐	☐	☐	____
Commercial aircraft industry: The costs of starting such a business are significant.	☐	☐	☐	____
Window washing business: Low cost of entry and limited specialized training.	☐	☐	☐	____
Fast-food business: Restaurant chains produce meals that are distinct.	☐	☐	☐	____
Broccoli farming: There are many producers of broccoli, which requires no special growing conditions.	☐	☐	☐	____

SECTION 11.2
AN INDIVIDUAL PRICE TAKER'S DEMAND CURVE

KEY POINTS

- Perfectly competitive firms are price takers; that is, they must sell at the market-determined price. An individual seller cannot sell at any figure higher than the current market price, and he certainly would not knowingly charge a lower price because he could sell all he wants at the market price.

- In a perfectly competitive market, an individual seller can change his output and it will not alter the market price. Each producer provides such a small fraction of the total supply that a change in the amount she offers does not have a noticeable effect on market price. In a perfectly competitive market, then, an individual firm can sell as much as it wishes to place on the market at the prevailing price. In other words, the demand, as seen by the seller, is perfectly elastic at the market price.

- While perfectly competitive firms are price takers, the position or height of each firm's demand curve varies with every change in the market price. In effect, sellers are provided with current information about market demand and supply conditions as a result of price changes. The perfectly competitive model does not assume any knowledge on the part of individual buyers and sellers about market demand and supply—they only have to know the price of the good they sell.

I   REVIEW

Firms in a perfectly competitive industry sell at the market-determined price, so they are price _____.

If a perfectly competitive firm charged a higher then market price, buyers would purchase the product from _____ sellers.

A seller is such a _____ fraction of the market they can place as much of their product as they want on the market with no effect on the market price. They have no reason to _____ their price below the market price since they can sell all they want.

The demand facing the perfectly competitive seller is _____ elastic.

Changes in the market demand for a firm's product will change the _____ of the firm's demand curve.

Price changes provide sellers with current _____ about market demand and supply conditions. Sellers alter their _____ decisions in response to the price signals.

II   TRUE/FALSE

_____1. When a firm faces a perfectly elastic demand curve, the firm will not lose all of its customers when it raises its price.

_____2. Brooke has a rafting business on the Rolling River. She has one of many rafting firms selling the same product. New rafting companies are starting up all the time. Brooke would be smart to lower her price below the market price because customers would flock to her business.

_____3. In a perfectly competitive market, price changes summarize all the information entrepreneurs need to know when making production decisions.

III   MULTIPLE CHOICE

Use Exhibit 1 to answer questions 1 and 2.

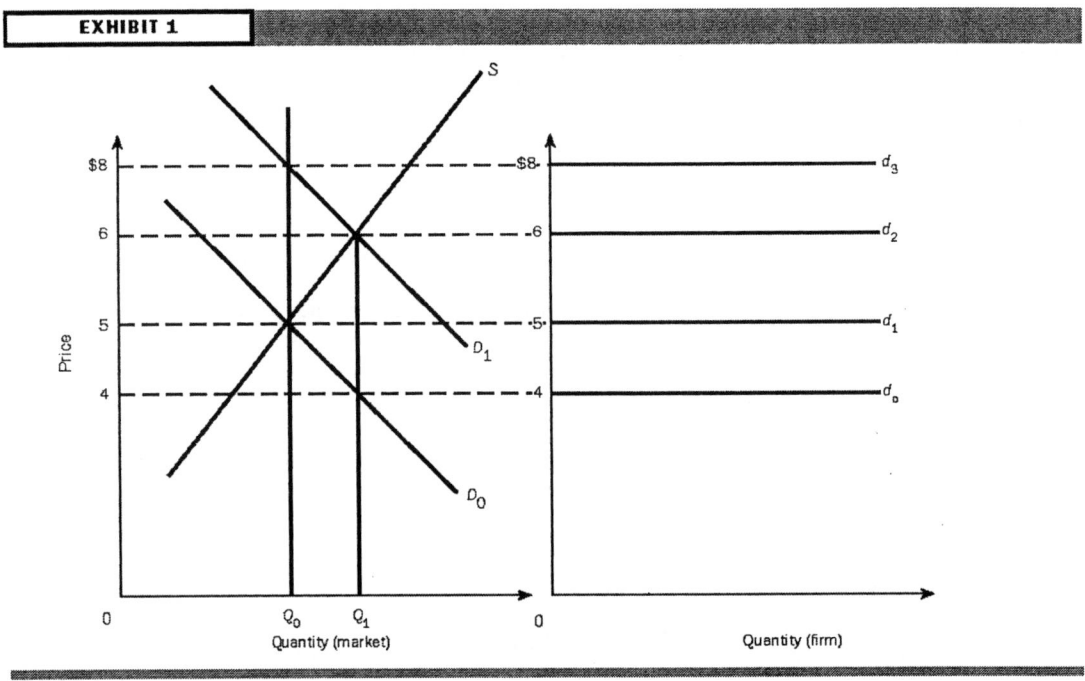

1. When market demand is D_0, the firm will face a perfectly elastic demand curve at a price of
   A) $8.
   B) $6.
   C) $5.
   D) $4.

2. When market demand increases to D_1, the demand facing the firm will be
   A) d_1.
   B) d_2.
   C) d_3.
   D) d_4.

3. Johnny Apple and his Granny Smith own an apple orchard. If American tastes change so that people like apples more, how will Johnny and Granny find this out?
   A) The newspaper headline will be "America's Apple Taste Change."
   B) The taste change will be the big piece of gossip at the apple growers' picnic.
   C) They will receive bulletins from the government taste watchers.
   D) Prices for apples will rise and they will face a new demand curve.

IV   APPLICATION AND DISCUSSION

Most farm products have industry councils that promote the consumption of particular types of farm products. These groups urge us to "Drink Milk" or "Eat Apples." Very little advertising is done by individual farmers. Using your understanding of the perfectly competitive market, explain this advertising strategy.

SECTION 11.3
PROFIT MAXIMIZATION

KEY POINTS

- The objective of the firm is to maximize profits. It wants to produce the amount that maximizes the difference between its total revenues and total costs.

- **Total revenue (*TR*)** is the revenue that the firm receives from the sale of its products. Total revenue for a perfectly competitive firm equals the market price of the good (*P*) times the quantity (*q*) of units sold ($TR = P \times q$).

- **Average revenue (*AR*)** equals total revenue divided by the number of units sold of the product (TR/q, or $P \times q/q$). So, in perfect competition, average revenue is equal to price of the good.

- **Marginal revenue (*MR*)** is the additional revenue derived from the sale of one more unit of the good. In a perfectly competitive market, because additional units of output can be sold without reducing the market price of the product, marginal revenue is constant and equal to the market price, which is also the average revenue.

- In perfect competition, we know that marginal revenue, average revenue, and price are all equal: $P = MR = AR$.

- In all types of market environments, firms will maximize profits at that output where one maximizes the difference between total revenue and total costs, which is the same output level where marginal revenue equals marginal costs.

- The importance of equating marginal revenue and marginal costs for maximizing profits is straightforward. As long as the marginal revenue derived from expanded output exceeds the marginal cost of that output, the expansion of output creates additional profits. However, expansion of output when the marginal cost of production exceeds marginal revenue will lead to losses on the additional output, decreasing profits.

- The **profit-maximizing output rule** says a firm should always produce where its $MR = MC$.

I   REVIEW

The objective of a firm is to maximize _____, the difference between total revenue and total costs.

The firm wants to produce the amount of output that _____ the difference between total revenue and total costs.

Total revenue equals the product price times the _____ of output sold.

Average revenue is total revenue _____ by quantity. It is equal to the _____ of the product in perfect competition.

Chapter 11: Perfect Competition

The additional revenue from producing and selling one more unit of output is _____ revenue. In a perfectly competitive firm, it also equals the price and average revenue.

As long as marginal revenue is greater than marginal costs, revenues increase by more than costs when output increases so profits _____.

The output level where marginal revenue _____ marginal costs is the output where the difference between total revenue and total costs is greatest or where profits are maximized.

II   TRUE/FALSE

_____1. For a perfectly competitive firm, marginal revenue equals total revenue divided by the quantity of output.

_____2. The Bob and Lou Review is a Cuban band that will earn $4,500 for each concert they perform in the United States in 2003. Additional travel and maintenance expenses will cause their per concert marginal cost to increase after the fifth concert. Since Bob and Lou's per concert marginal revenue is constant, they would never perform more than five concerts.

_____3. Francis is a blacksmith who charges $35 per hoof shoed. During 2001, she shoed 100 horses. Her total revenue was $14,000.

III   MULTIPLE CHOICE

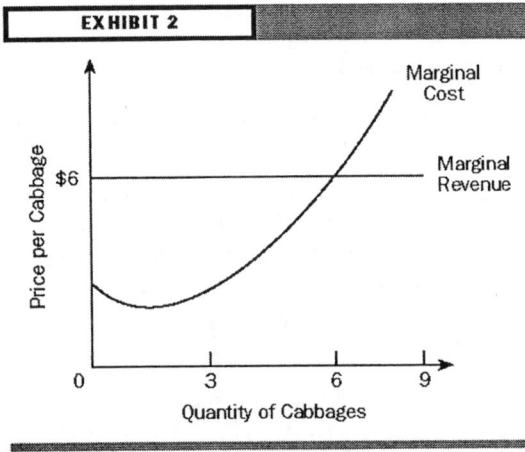

1. The graph in Exhibit 2 shows the marginal costs and marginal revenue of Mr. MacGregor's cabbage patch. What is the profit-maximizing number of cabbages?
    A) 0
    B) 3
    C) 6
    D) 9

2. Jim owns a firm in the perfectly competitive pencil industry. In one year he sells 10,000 pencils and charges $.25 a piece. Which of the following is a true statement about his average revenue?
   A) It is equal to the price of $.25.
   B) It is greater than $.25 since marginal revenue is rising.
   C) It is less than the firm's marginal revenue.
   D) It equals $2,500 since this was an average year.

3. In a perfectly competitive firm, marginal revenue always equals
   A) average total cost.
   B) the price of the product.
   C) average fixed cost.
   D) total revenue.

IV   APPLICATION AND DISCUSSION

1. Complete the following table and identify the profit-maximizing output.

Quantity	Price	Total Revenue	Marginal Revenue	Marginal Cost	Total Profit
10	$12	$120	$12	$ 8	$25
11	12	_____	_____	9	_____
12	12	_____	_____	11	_____
13	12	_____	_____	12	_____
14	12	_____	_____	14	_____

2. What is true about marginal revenue and marginal costs when profit is maximized?

3. What would be the profit-maximizing level of output if price fell to $9?

SECTION 11.4
SHORT-RUN PROFITS AND LOSSES

KEY POINTS

- Producing at the profit-maximizing output level does not mean that a firm is actually generating profits; it merely means that a firm is maximizing its profit opportunity at a given price level. At that point, a firm could be earning profits, generating losses, or breaking even.

- If total revenue is greater than total costs at the profit-maximizing output level, the firm is generating economic profits. If total revenue is less than total costs, the firm is generating economic losses. If total revenue equals total cost, so the firm is earning zero economic profits, the firm is covering both its implicit costs and explicit costs. Economists sometimes call this zero economic profit a **normal rate of return.**

- At price levels greater than or equal to average variable costs, a firm may continue to operate in the short run even if average total costs and variable and fixed costs are not completely covered. Because fixed costs continue whether the firm produces or not, it is better to earn enough to cover a portion of these costs rather than earn nothing at all.

Chapter 11: Perfect Competition

- When the price a firm is able to obtain for its product is below its average variable costs at all ranges of output, it is unable to cover even its variable costs in the short run. Since it is losing even more than the fixed costs it would lose if it shut down, it is most logical for the firm to cease operations.

- At all prices above minimum AVC, the firm produces in the short run, even if ATC is not completely covered, and at all prices below the minimum AVC the firm shuts down. Therefore the **short-run supply curve** of an individual competitive seller is identical with that portion of the MC curve that lies above the minimum of the AVC curve.

- The **short-run market supply curve** is the horizontal summation of the individual firms' supply curves, providing that input prices are not affected by increased production of existing firms. Because the short run is too brief for new firms to enter the market, the market supply curve is the horizontal summation of existing firms.

I   REVIEW

The firm can make economic profits, suffer economic losses, or make zero profits at the profit-_____ level of output.

The profit-maximizing output is where price equals marginal _____. At this output a firm will make an economic profit if total revenue is _____ than total cost.

At this output a firm will suffer an economic _____ if total revenue is less than total cost.

If total revenue equals total cost at this output, the firm earns _____ economic profit. Entrepreneurs are covering their _____ and explicit costs. They produce since they are doing as _____ as they could anywhere else.

In the short run the firm will continue to produce when it suffers an economic loss as long as price is _____ than average variable costs. It reduces its loss by producing since it can use the excess to cover some of its _____ costs.

A firm will shut down in the short run if price is _____ than average variable cost, since it will lose more than its fixed cost by producing.

The short-run supply curve of an individual competitive seller is that portion of the marginal cost curve that lies _____ the minimum of the average variable cost curve.

The short-run _____ supply curve for a competitive industry is the horizontal summation of the individual firms' supply curves.

II   TRUE/FALSE

_____1. The profit-maximizing output is where marginal revenue equals marginal costs. A perfectly competitive firm will always produce at this level of output.

_____2. Marge and Al own a laundry that specializes in shirts and blouses. They know that 750 shirts a month is the output at which marginal revenue and costs are equal. They charge $1 per shirt and their average variable cost is $.59. They have a total fixed cost of $350 a month. They are making an economic loss.

_____3. The fact that many large corporations continue to operate even though they suffer economic losses illustrates that these firms are completely irrational.

III   MULTIPLE CHOICE

1. The main reason an entrepreneur is not disappointed with zero economic profits is that
    A) at least the entrepreneur is covering her explicit costs so she pays her bills.
    B) the entrepreneur is only losing an amount equal to her implicit costs.
    C) economic profits may be zero but accounting profits are positive.
    D) with zero economic profit she is doing as well as she could in her next best alternative.

Answer questions 2 and 3 with reference to Exhibit 3, which shows a firm's short-run cost curves.

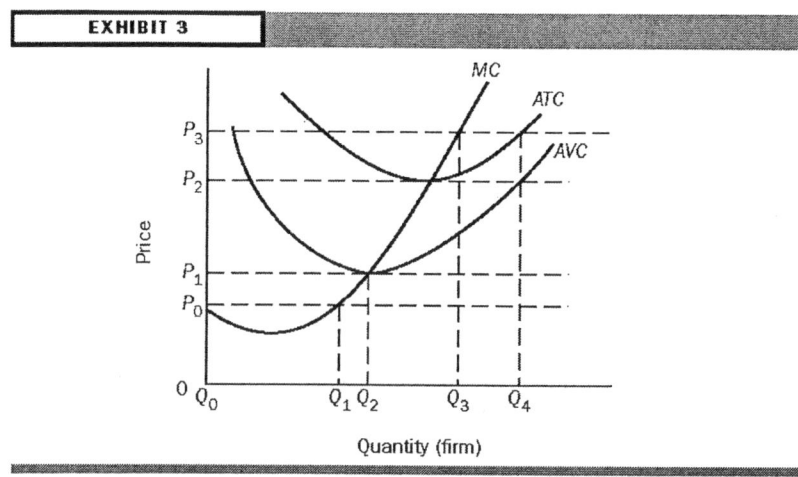

2. How much will the firm produce at a price equal to P_0?
    A) Q_0
    B) Q_1
    C) Q_2
    D) Q_3

3. What is the lowest price at which the firm will produce?
    A) P_0
    B) P_1
    C) P_2
    D) P_3

4. Loren fishes for abalone. When the price is $2.50 a pound, he continues to fish even though he does not earn enough to meet his boat payment, but he stops fishing when the price falls to $2. What do we know about Bob's average variable costs?
    A) It is greater than $2.50.
    B) It is less than $2.00.
    C) It is greater than $2.00 and less than $2.50.
    D) It is rises with increased production.

135

IV   APPLICATION AND DISCUSSION

At a price of $5 the profit-maximizing output for a perfectly competitive firm is 1,000 units per year. If the average total cost is $3 per unit, what will be the firm's profit? If the average total cost is $6 per unit, what will be the firm's profit? What is the relationship between profit, price, and average total cost?

SECTION 11.5
LONG-RUN EQUILIBRIUM

KEY POINTS

- If perfectly competitive producers are able to make economic profits, there will be a supply response: the market supply curve will shift to the right over time as more firms enter the industry and existing firms expand. The impact of increasing supply, other things equal, is to reduce the equilibrium price.

- As entry into the profitable industry pushes down the market price, producers will move from making a profit ($P > ATC$) to zero economic profits ($P = ATC$). In long-run equilibrium, perfectly competitive firms make zero economic profits, earning a normal return on the use of their capital.

- Zero economic profits is an equilibrium or stable situation because any positive economic (above-normal) profits signal resources into the industry, beating down prices and thus revenues to the firm; economic losses signal resources to leave the activity, leading to supply reductions that lead to increased prices and higher firm revenues to the remaining firms. Only at zero economic profits is there no tendency for firms to either enter or leave the business.

- The long-run equilibrium output in perfect competition occurs at the lowest point on the average total cost curve, so the equilibrium condition in the long run in perfect competition is for firms to produce at that output that minimizes per-unit total costs.

I   REVIEW

Positive economic profits in a perfectly competitive industry are signals that _____ additional resources to the industry in the long run.

As more firms enter the industry, the market supply will _____ and the market supply curve will shift to the _____. The impact of this shift is a _____ in the equilibrium price of the product.

As the product price falls, the economic profit earned by firms in the industry will _____. New firms will stop entering the industry only when firms in the industry are earning _____ economic profits.

When firms in an industry suffer economic _____, resources will leave the industry causing market supply to decline and prices to _____. Firms will stop leaving the industry when no firm earns an economic _____.

Zero economic profit is a(n) _____ situation in the long run because there is neither a signal for firms to leave nor enter the industry.

Chapter 11: Perfect Competition

Long-run equilibrium results in each firm producing at its _____ average total costs, the point where price equals marginal costs and average total costs.

II   TRUE/FALSE

_____1. Entrepreneurs enter an industry when there are economic profits in order to make themselves better off, and their entry makes consumers better off.

_____2. Daisy can earn an economic profit by increasing the resources she devotes to poinsettia production when the price of her poinsettias is $4 a plant. The price will remain at $4 for the long run.

_____3. Competition has driven the economic profits in the video rental business to zero. Johnny Rocco would be better off leaving this industry for another alternative.

III   MULTIPLE CHOICE

1. Economic losses caused firms to leave the car wash business in Toledo. Though prices have risen, firms are still leaving. What does this tell us about economic profits in the Toledo car wash business?
   A) Economic profits exist but they are not as high as in other industries.
   B) Economic profits are zero and firms won't stay in the industry with no profit.
   C) Economic profits are still negative or firms are earning an economic loss.
   D) Economic profits have decreased because of the exit of existing firms.

2. If costs remain the same for firms in the industry, what would you expect to be the long-run effect of an increase in demand on an industry currently in long-run equilibrium?
   A) There will be more firms but the price will remain the same.
   B) There will be fewer firms but the price will remain the same.
   C) There will be more firms and the price will be higher.
   D) There will be fewer firms and the price will be lower.

3. Larry owns a firm that makes golf clubs. At the current price of clubs, Larry is suffering an economic loss. Which of the following is a true statement about the value of Larry's time and his other resources?
   A) Larry has always been in the golf club business so his resources have no value in other industries.
   B) Larry is not covering his implicit cost, which means his resources are more valuable in some other use.
   C) Larry should retire since his resources have no value in any use.
   D) Larry should stay in the golf business as long as he covers his explicit cost.

IV   APPLICATION AND DISCUSSION

In *The Wealth of Nations,* Adam Smith wrote,

Every individual endeavors to employ his capital so that its produce may be of greatest value. He generally neither intends to promote the public interest, nor knows how much he is promoting it. He intends only his own security, only his own gain. And he is led by an invisible hand to promote an end which was no part of his intention. By pursuing his own interest he frequently promotes that of society more effectively than when he really intends to promote it.

How does the story of long-run equilibrium in a perfectly competitive industry illustrate Adam Smith's invisible hand?

SECTION 11.6
LONG-RUN SUPPLY

KEY POINTS

- When the output of an entire industry changes, the shape of the long-run supply curve depends on the extent to which input costs change when there is entry or exit of firms in the industry.

- In a **constant-cost industry**, the prices of inputs do not change as output is expanded. The industry does not use inputs in sufficient quantities to affect input prices.

- If it is a constant costs industry, industry expansion does not alter firms' cost curves, and the industry long-run supply curve is horizontal. That is, once the short-run higher profits from an increase in demand has attracted entry until long run-equilibrium is again reached, the long-run equilibrium price is at the same level that prevailed before demand increased; the only long-run effect of the increase in demand is an increase in industry output.

- In an **increasing-cost industry**, the cost curves of the individual firms rise as the total output of the industry increases. When an industry utilizes a large portion of an input, input prices will rise when the industry uses more of that input as it expands output, which will shift firms' cost curves upward. The new long-run equilibrium is at a higher price. The long-run industry supply curve in this case has a positive slope.

- The long-run supply is usually more elastic than the short-run supply because in the long run, firms can enter and exit the industry.

- The output that results from equilibrium conditions of market demand and market supply in perfectly competitive markets is economically efficient. Only at this outcome can maximum output be obtained from our scarce resources.

I   REVIEW

When the output of an entire industry changes there is a likelihood that _____ will be affected.

As the industry output increases, the industry's _____ for the inputs it uses will also increase.

If the industry uses a significant share of any particular input, this increased demand will cause input prices to _____ or the quality of the input to _____.

In a(n) _____-cost industry, the cost curves of the individual firms shift up as the industry output increases because input prices _____ or input quality _____.

When an industry's use of inputs is a relatively _____ share of the total available, the increased demand that results from expanding output will have little effect on input prices.

In a(n) _____-cost industry, the cost curves of the individual firms will not change as the industry output increases since input prices will not be effected by the change.

In a constant cost industry, increased demand will result in a new equilibrium at the _____ equilibrium price. The long-run supply curve will be _____ elastic at a price equal to the minimum average total cost of production.

In an increasing cost industry, increased demand will result in a new equilibrium at a _____ price than the original equilibrium. The long-run supply curve will have a _____ slope, since increasing output results in higher costs.

The long-run supply curve will be _____ elastic than the short-run supply curve in a competitive industry because firms can enter and exit.

At the competitive industry equilibrium resources are used _____.
•

II   TRUE/FALSE

_____1. It takes time to train a pilot who can fly commercial passenger aircraft. The U.S. commercial airline industry uses the vast majority of these pilots. The airline industry is most likely to be an increasing cost industry.

_____2. Marita runs the Roulette Wedding Chapel in Las Vegas. The wedding business does not use a significant share of any of the inputs to produce weddings. Because of a recent increase in the demand for weddings, Marita will be able to raise her long-run price.

III   MULTIPLE CHOICE

1. If the windshield wiper industry is a constant-cost industry, which of the following would *not* be a true statement about their inputs?
   A) It uses no input specialized to windshield production.
   B) It uses a relatively small share of the inputs it uses in production.
   C) The inputs it uses do not vary much in quality.
   D) It uses an input that is available in fixed supply.

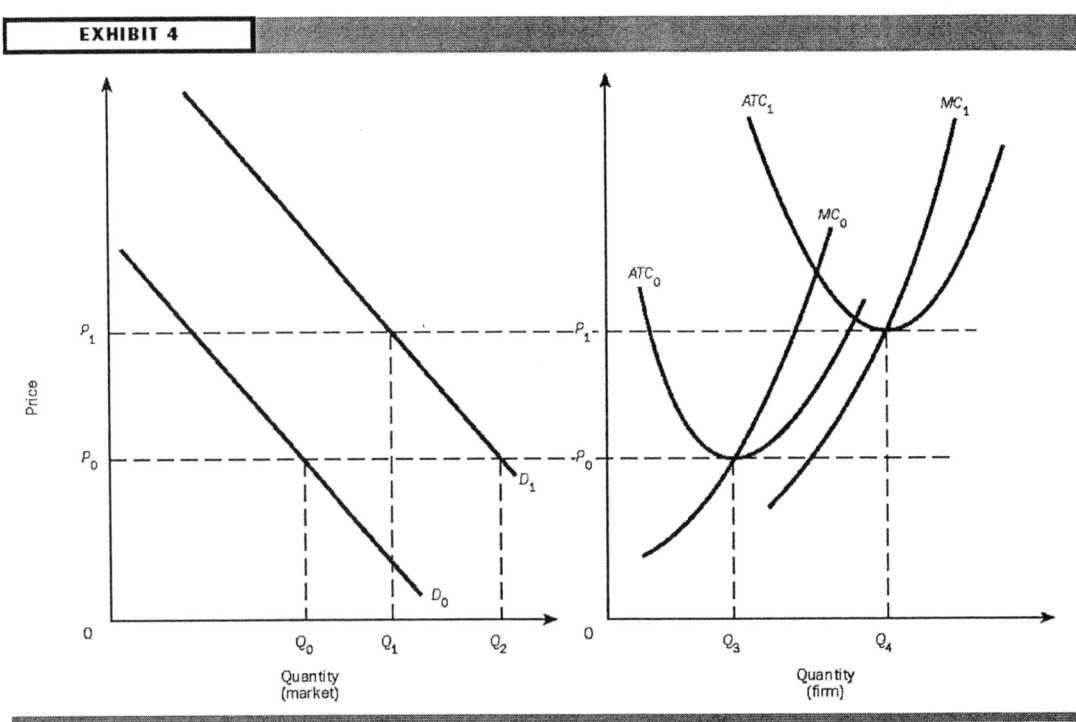

EXHIBIT 4

2. The microbrew industry uses a significant share of the beer bottles made in the United States. Any increase in demand for beer is likely to result in an increase in bottle prices. In Exhibit 4, as demand for beer increases from D_0 to D_1, costs rise for the typical microbrewery from ATC_0 to ATC_1. Which of the following is a point on the long-run industry supply curve?

    A) P_1, Q_1
    B) P_0, Q_2
    C) P_0, Q_3
    D) P_1, Q_4

IV   APPLICATION AND DISCUSSION

Given the industry description, identify each of the following as an increasing- or constant-cost industry.

Industry	Input Market	Increasing or Constant Costs?
Major League Baseball	Uses the majority of pitchers. As the number of pitchers used increases, the quality declines.	_____
Fast-Food Restaurants	Uses a relatively small share of land and unskilled labor in most cities.	_____
Trucking Industry	Uses a large portion of the trained and experienced drivers, especially long-distance drivers.	_____

Questions

1. Is the wheat market an example of perfect competition? Why?

2. What is the flaw in Uncle Ed's scheme?

CHAPTER 12
MONOPOLY

SECTION 12.1
MONOPOLY: THE PRICE MAKER

KEY POINTS

- A true or pure **monopoly** exists where there is only one seller of a product for which no close substitute is available. The firm and "the industry" are one and the same.

- Because a monopoly firm faces the industry demand curve, it can pick the most profitable point on that demand curve. Monopolists are price makers (rather than takers) who try to pick the price that will maximize their profits.

- Pure monopolies are a rarity because few goods and services truly have only one producer. Near-monopoly conditions may exist, such as with many public utilities, but absolute total monopoly is rather unusual. However, the number of situations where monopoly conditions are closely approximated are numerous enough to make the study of monopoly useful.

- For a monopoly to persist as a market structure, it must be virtually impossible for other firms to overcome **barriers to entry.** Barriers to entry can include legal barriers, economies of scale, and control of important inputs.

Chapter 12: Monopoly

- Legal barriers to entry include franchising, licensing, and patents.

- The situation in which one large firm can provide the output of the market at a lower cost than two or more smaller firms is called a **natural monopoly.** With natural monopoly it is more efficient to have one firm produce the good. The reason for the cost advantage is economies of scale.

- Another barrier to entry is control over an important input, such as Alcoa's control over bauxite in the 1940s and DeBeers control over much of the world's output of diamonds.

I   REVIEW

A pure monopoly exists when there is only _____ seller of a product, which has no available close _____.

Examples of pure monopoly are _____ to find because most goods have some available _____.

_____ to entry are necessary for a monopoly to persist.

Government's award of franchise, occupational licenses, and patents for new inventions are examples of _____ barriers to entry.

A _____ monopoly exists when economies of scale give one firm a cost advantage over production by a number of firms. Government may grant these firms _____ rights and erect another barrier to entry.

One firm's control of the _____ of an important input to production, such as DeBeers control over diamonds, provides another a barrier to entry.

II   TRUE/FALSE

_____ 1. Many stores in town sell regular-sized bagels, but Betty's Big Bagels is the only store in town that sells bagels with a circumference of one foot. Since Betty's is the only one, she has a pure monopoly.

_____ 2. Watertown, Massachusetts, recently allowed competition in the water business. Its public utility, Watertown Waterworks, had to compete with two new companies. If providing water was a natural monopoly, we would expect to see the average cost of water production increase.

III   MULTIPLE CHOICE

1. Government postal services in most countries have historically been pure monopolies protected by legislation. Which of the following is *not* a reason postal services are no longer pure monopolies?
   A) the widespread use of e-mail and fax machines
   B) the invention and far-reaching use of the telephone
   C) the increase in postal rates over time
   D) the creation of the overnight delivery service by firms like FedEx and UPS

2. Your rich Aunt Eunice left you a large inheritance. You want to use the money to pursue your dream of becoming a pure monopolist. Which of the following is the best investment for your dream?
    A) buy a soybean farm in Iowa
    B) buy the first and only fast-food restaurant in your hometown
    C) buy the town's only newspaper
    D) buy the water utility, by law the town's only producer and distributor of water

IV APPLICATION AND DISCUSSION

Barriers to entry are important in the creation of monopolies because they keep competitors out of the industry. Although many types of barriers exist, historically, ownership of an essential resource, government patents and licenses, and large entry costs have served as the primary barriers to entry. For each of the following cases check the box that identifies the general type of barrier that created the monopoly.

Monopoly case:	Government patents or license	Ownership of essential resource	Large entry costs
In the 1940s, Aluminum Company of America owns all of the world's known bauxite deposits.	☐	☐	☐
Local cable TV company has the only government issued license to supply services in the area.	☐	☐	☐
The pharmaceutical company, MAXCO, invented and patented a new baldness drug.	☐	☐	☐
In the 1950s, AT&T provided long-distance telephone service by stringing millions of miles of copper wiring across the United States.	☐	☐	☐

SECTION 12.2
DEMAND AND MARGINAL REVENUE IN MONOPOLY

KEY POINTS

- In monopoly, the market demand curve may be regarded as the demand curve for the firm's product because the monopoly firm is the market for that particular product.

- Unlike in perfect competition, in monopoly the demand curve for the firm's product is downward sloping because the market demand curve is downward sloping. If the monopolist reduces output, the price will rise; and if the monopolist expands output, the price will fall.

- The marginal revenue curve for a monopolist lies below the demand curve. In order to get revenue from marginal customers, the firm has to lower the price, so that marginal revenue is always less than price.

- In monopoly, if the seller wants to expand output, it will have to lower its price on all units. So when the monopolist cuts price to attract new customers, the old customers benefit. That means that the monopolist receives additional revenue from the new unit sold, but it will receive less revenue on all of the units it was previously selling.

- There is a relationship between the elasticity and marginal and total revenue. In the elastic portion of the curve, when the price falls, total revenue rises, so that marginal revenue is positive. In the inelastic portion of the curve, when the price falls, total revenue falls, so that marginal revenue is negative.

- A monopolist will never knowingly operate in the inelastic portion of its demand curve because increased output will lead to lower total revenue and higher total cost in that region.

I   REVIEW

The _____ demand curve is the demand curve of the monopoly firm.

The firm faces a _____-sloping demand curve. The monopolist can increase price by _____ output. _____ output will cause price to fall.

To sell more the monopolist must lower his price to _____ customers. The _____ revenue from selling one more unit is offset by the _____ revenue from the lower price; the monopolist's marginal revenue is _____ than price. The marginal revenue curve lies _____ the demand curve.

Monopolists will always produce where marginal revenue is _____ and this is on the _____ portion of the demand curve.

II   TRUE/FALSE

_____1. According to the charter for the town of Upper Poesy, New Hampshire, only the electric utility, Watts UP, can sell electricity in town. Watts UP, a pure monopoly, can sell as much electricity as they want at whatever price they set.

_____2. A pure monopoly will never produce at a level of output for which marginal revenue is negative.

_____3. At any given price a pure monopolist sells an amount that is less than the market quantity demanded of the product.

III   MULTIPLE CHOICE

1. Joan owns the town's natural gas monopoly. She currently sells 100 cubic feet of gas at $1.10 per cubic foot. To sell one more cubic foot she must lower her price to $1.09. Which of the following best describes Joan's marginal revenue?
   A) Her marginal revenue equals the price of $1.09.
   B) The marginal revenue equals the change in price of $.01.
   C) The marginal revenue is less than the price of $1.09.
   D) The marginal revenue is greater than $1.09 but less than $1.10.

2. Why can't a perfectly competitive firm be a price maker?
   A) They would not know what price to set because the market price is hard to find.
   B) If they raise the price above the market price, customers would buy from competitors.
   C) They face a negatively sloped demand curve and they can't set the price.
   D) If they were price makers, the elasticity of demand would be greater.

3. Billy and Bob Duke own the only drag strip for hundreds of miles. When they raise the price they charge spectators, the strip gets fewer customers, but their total revenue increases. Which of the following describes Billy and Bob's situation?
   A) They are perfect competitors who are price takers.
   B) They are monopolists operating on the inelastic part of their demand curve.
   C) They are competitors operating on the elastic part of their demand curve.
   D) They are monopolists operating on the elastic portion of their demand curve.

IV   APPLICATION AND DISCUSSION

1. The Mobile Phone Company has served Mobile, Alabama, since the 1930s as a government-authorized natural monopoly. Exhibit 1 describes a portion of the demand curve for long-distance service facing Mobile Phone. Complete the table.

EXHIBIT 1 MOBILE PHONE COMPANY DEMAND FOR PHONE HOURS

Quantity	Price	Total Revenue	Marginal Revenue	Elastic or Inelastic ?
30	$3.65			
31	3.58			
32	3.50			
33	3.43			
34	3.35			
35	3.27			
36	3.20			
37	3.12			
38	3.05			
39	2.97			
40	2.89			
41	2.82			
42	2.74			
43	2.67			
44	2.59			
45	2.51			
46	2.44			
47	2.36			
48	2.29			
49	2.21			
50	2.13			

A) How does the company's marginal revenue change as the price changes? What is the relationship between marginal revenue and price?

B) At what price does demand become inelastic?

C) What will happen to the elasticity of demand when a new company, Mobile Phones of Mobile, starts a competing wireless phone company?

SECTION 12.3

THE MONOPOLIST'S EQUILIBRIUM

KEY POINTS

- The monopolist, like the perfect competitor, will maximize profits at that output where $MC = MR$. Profits continue to grow until that output is reached. Therefore, the equilibrium output is where marginal costs and marginal revenues are equal.

- In perfect competition, profits in an economic sense will persist only in the short run because in the long run, new firms will enter the industry, increasing industry supply and thus driving down the price of the good. With this, profits are eliminated. In monopoly, however, profits are not eliminated because one of the conditions for monopoly is that barriers to entry exist. Other firms cannot enter, so economic profits can persist in the long run.

- Being a sole supplier does not guarantee that consumers will demand your product. A monopolist will incur a loss if there is insufficient demand to cover average total costs at any price and output combination along the demand curve.

- Patents and copyrights are given as examples of government created monopoly power designed to provide an incentive to develop new products.

I   REVIEW

The monopolist, like the perfect competitor, maximizes profits by producing the output where marginal
_____ equals marginal _____.

The monopolist's equilibrium output level determines the _____ it will charge. The monopolist will charge the maximum price consumers are _____ to pay for the equilibrium output.

The monopolist's total profit at the equilibrium output equals the difference between the _____ times output and average total _____ times output.

In perfectly competitive industries, economic profits will be eliminated in the _____ run by competition. Monopolists can earn profits in the _____ run because _____ to entry keep competitors out of the market.

Monopolies have gone out of business. Being a sole provider does not mean consumers will _____ your product. Monopolies can suffer loses when average revenue is _____ than average total costs at its equilibrium output.

Patents and copyrights are forms of _____ power granted by government. The patent holder has the _____ right to make a product for twenty years. Patents give producers the _____ to undertake the expensive research effort required to develop new products.

II   TRUE/FALSE

_____1. The monopolist's profit-maximizing rule is different than the rule that perfect competitors follow.

_____2. Dwayne's plumbing business has really become profitable since he received a patent on his computerized "Fast Drain." Since Dwayne doesn't have to worry about competitors, he will be able to earn economic profits for a long time.

_____3. Patrice has a pure monopoly because she has the only license to import watonga and watonga-tree products. Patrice will charge a price that equals her marginal cost at the equilibrium output.

III   MULTIPLE CHOICE

Answer the following questions by referring to Exhibit 2.

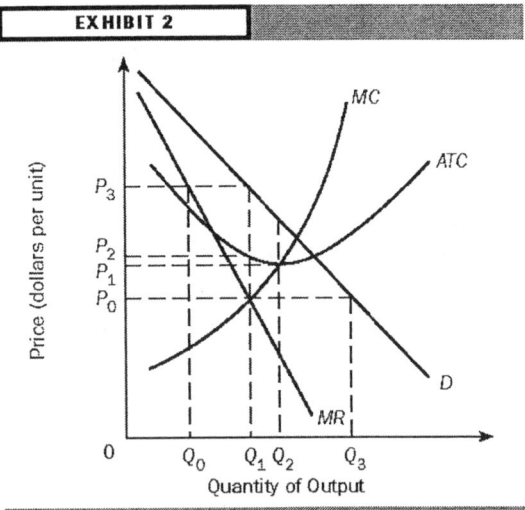

EXHIBIT 2

1. The monopolist's profit-maximizing level of output is
    A) Q_0.
    B) Q_1.
    C) Q_2.
    D) Q_3.

2. If this firm charged a price equal to P_0 and produced output Q_1, we would expect to find
    A) excess demand equal to $Q_3 - Q_1$, which would result in prices increasing to P_3.
    B) excess demand equal to $Q_3 - Q_1$, which would result in output increasing to Q_3.
    C) excess demand equal to $Q_2 - Q_1$, which would result in price and output increasing to P_1, Q_2.
    D) excess demand equal to $Q_1 - Q_0$, which would result in price increasing to P_3 and output falling to Q_0.

3. The monopolist's profit equals the equilibrium output times
    A) per-unit profit of P_3.
    B) per-unit profit of $P_3 - P_0$.
    C) per-unit profit of $P_3 - P_2$.
    D) per-unit profit of $P_3 - P_1$.

IV   APPLICATION AND DISCUSSION

1. Exhibit 3 shows the demand for water and cost conditions for the New South Springdale Water Utility, a pure monopoly. Complete the table.

EXHIBIT 3

QUANTITY (GALLONS)	PRICE (PER GALLON)	TOTAL REVENUE	MARGINAL REVENUE	MARGINAL COSTS	AVERAGE COSTS	TOTAL PROFIT
100	$1.28	_____	_____	$0.15	$1.252	_____
101	$1.27	_____	_____	$0.18	$1.241	_____
102	$1.26	_____	_____	$0.21	$1.231	_____
103	$1.25	_____	_____	$0.23	$1.221	_____
104	$1.24	_____	_____	$0.26	$1.212	_____

2. What is true about the relationship between marginal revenue and marginal costs when profit is the greatest?

3. Suppose the government imposed a tax on the firm of $103, which the firm had to pay even if it went out of business. What would be the profit-maximizing level of output? What would happen to profits? Would the firm stay in business?

SECTION 12.4
MONOPOLY AND WELFARE LOSS

KEY POINTS

- The most serious objection to monopoly is that monopolies result in market inefficiencies. Monopoly leads to lower output and to higher prices than would exist under perfect competition.

- The monopolist produces an output where the price is greater than its cost, so that the value to society from the last unit produced is greater than its cost. The monopoly is not producing enough of the good from society's perspective, creating a welfare loss.

- Another argument against monopoly is that a lack of competition tends to retard technological advance. Monopolists become comfortable reaping monopolistic profits, so they do not work hard at product improvement, technical advances designed to promote efficiency, and so forth.

- However, the notion that monopoly retards all innovation can be disputed. Innovation helps firms initially obtain a degree of monopoly status. Even monopolists want more profits, and any innovation that lowers costs or expands revenues creates profits for a monopolist. Therefore, the incentive to innovate may well exist in monopolistic market structures.

I   REVIEW

A monopoly will result in a _____ output and a _____ price than would exist if the industry were organized under perfect competition. This is the main objection economists have to monopoly.

Monopolists produce where _____ is greater than marginal cost. This means monopolists do not produce _____ of the product. A welfare loss results because the monopolist stops producing even though the value to society of the last unit produced is _____ than its cost.

Chapter 12: Monopoly

Critics argue that monopoly is bad because it results in market _____ and that monopolists have no incentive to _____.

Some dispute the notion that monopoly retards innovation. Many important _____, like AT&T and IBM, have been near-monopolists. To expand profits, monopolists may innovate to _____ costs, expand revenues, or _____ their monopoly power.

II   TRUE/FALSE

_____1. The welfare loss from monopoly is not really a loss to society as a whole since it is just a transfer from consumers to producers.

_____2. Rita Bega has pulled a real coup and taken over the entire beet industry. This changes the industry from a perfectly competitive one to a monopoly. Even though the technology and input prices remain the same, consumers should expect real changes in the beet business.

_____3. Economists are in agreement that monopolies retard innovation.

III   MULTIPLE CHOICE

1. Which of the following supports the argument that monopolies retard innovation?
    A) the research work at AT&T's Bell Labs
    B) American railroad industry spending on research and development in the first part of the twentieth century
    C) early innovations in computers by IBM
    D) the Xerox Company's innovation and invention

2. The surplus lost because a monopolist reduces the amount produced represents a welfare loss because
    A) the loss shows up as increased producer profits.
    B) the society is not using its scarce resources in the best way.
    C) the price is higher than consumers would pay for the monopolist's equilibrium output.
    D) less output means reduced taxes so fewer people can be supported on welfare.

3. From society's point of view, why is the monopoly result inefficient?
    A) Monopolies earn a profit and produce more of the good than we want or need.
    B) Monopolies retard innovation but give us too many of the newer goods that we don't need.
    C) Monopolies raise the cost of production, so it costs more to get the same amount as in a competitive industry.
    D) Monopolies stop production when the value of additional production is greater than the cost.

IV   APPLICATION AND DISCUSSION

1. A patent gives a firm a monopoly in production of the patented good. While the monopoly profits provide an incentive for firms to innovate, the monopoly power imposes a cost on consumers. Why do consumers suffer a cost? Is it greater than the profits earned by the monopolist?

2. Why would a program that bought companies' patent rights and created competition in place of monopolies make consumers better off even though consumers' tax money was used to pay off the monopolists?

SECTION 12.5
MONOPOLY POLICY

KEY POINTS

- Two major approaches to dealing with the monopoly problem are commonly used: antitrust policies and regulation.

- Antitrust policies make monopoly practices illegal. Government uses civil lawsuits and criminal action to limit monopoly behavior.

- The success of antitrust policies can be debated. It is very likely that at least some anticompetitive practices have been prevented simply by the very existence of laws prohibiting monopoly-like practices. While the laws have probably been enforced in an imperfect fashion, on balance, they have probably successfully impeded monopoly influences to some degree.

- Government regulation is an alternative approach to dealing with monopolies. The goal is to achieve the efficiency of large-scale production without permitting the high monopoly prices and low output that can promote allocative inefficiency.

- Regulators often face a basic policy dilemma. Without regulation, the profit-maximizing monopolist will produce where marginal cost equals marginal revenue. At that output, the price exceeds average total cost, so economic profits exist. However, the monopolist is producing relatively little output, is charging a relatively high price, and is producing at a point where price is above marginal cost.

- From society's point of view, **allocative efficiency** occurs where the price of the good is equal to marginal cost. But with natural monopoly, this optimal output produces losses for the producer. It would be impossible to attract new capital to the industry.

- A compromise between unregulated monopoly and marginal cost pricing is **average cost pricing**, where price equals average total cost. The monopolist is permitted to price the product where economic profits are zero, meaning that a normal return is being permitted, like firms experience in perfect competition in the long run.

- The actual implementation of a rate (price) that permits a "fair and reasonable" return is difficult. The calculations of costs and values is very difficult, often forcing regulatory agencies to use profits as a guide instead. Another problem is that average cost pricing gives the monopolist no incentive to reduce costs.

- Decisions about rates are influenced by the arguments of special interests. Consumer groups are constantly battling for lower rates, while the utilities themselves are lobbying for higher rates so that they can achieve some monopoly profits. The temptation is great for the commissioners to be generous to the utilities. On the other hand, there may be a tendency for regulators to bow to pressure from consumer groups.

I   REVIEW

Two approaches government has taken to dealing with monopoly are _____ policies and
_____.

_____ policies make monopolies illegal and impose costs on monopolists. These policies attack
restrictions placed on price _____ such as limits to advertising in industries or firms collectively
setting prices.

Chapter 12: Monopoly

To achieve the _____ of large scale, privately owned natural monopolies, government regulates _____ and other monopoly practices of these firms.

Allocative _____ occurs when firms produce the amount of the good for which the _____ consumers receive from the last unit just equals the opportunity _____ of producing it. This occurs where _____ equals marginal cost.

Without regulation a natural monopoly will _____ where marginal revenue equals marginal costs and earn an economic profit. This is not a point of _____ efficiency.

When a firm produces an output where average costs are falling, marginal cost is _____ average total costs. At the equilibrium output if regulators set price equal to marginal cost, the monopolist would suffer _____ since price will be less than average total cost.

A regulatory compromise is _____ cost pricing. Prices are set so that average revenue will just equal average costs or where the demand curve crosses the average total cost curve.

Average cost pricing sets price so that economic profits are _____ but allows firms to earn a _____ rate of return.

One problem with implementing average cost pricing is the difficulty of calculating the _____ rate of return.

Another problem is average cost pricing gives monopolist no _____ to reduce costs. The price will be set so that a firm earns a normal rate of return _____ of costs.

A final problem with average cost pricing is that rates are set in a _____ arena so the outcome reflects the power of _____ interest groups.

II   TRUE/FALSE

_____1. A firm that is a natural monopoly will choose to produce at the point of allocative efficiency.

_____2. Firms operating as regulated natural monopolies trade off some control over their production and pricing decisions for the exclusive right to produce their product.

_____3. Regulation and anti-trust policy have the same objective, the elimination of monopolies in the United States.

III   MULTIPLE CHOICE

Answer questions 1 through 3 by referring to Exhibit 4, which shows the costs curves and demand facing a natural monopolist.

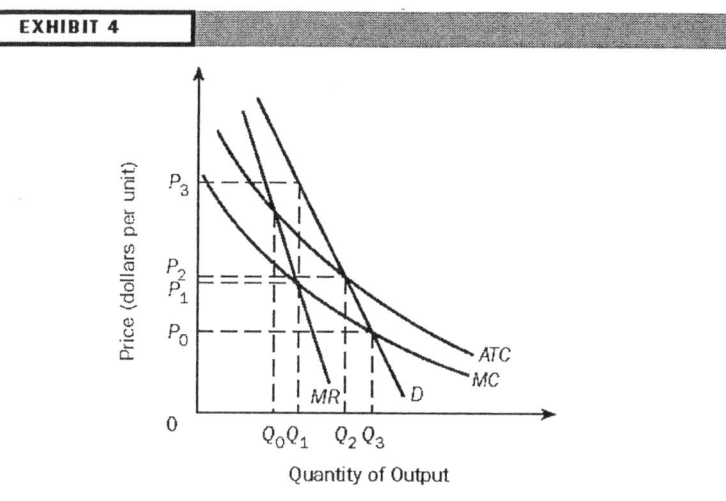

EXHIBIT 4

1. If the monopolist produced at the point of allocative efficiency, she would produce an output____ and charge a price _____.
   A) $Q_1; P_3$
   B) $Q_1; P_1$
   C) $Q_2; P_2$
   D) $Q_3; P_0$

2. A firm that is operating as a natural monopoly would choose to produce which quantity?
   A) Q_0
   B) Q_1
   C) Q_2
   D) Q_3

3. Government regulation of a natural monopoly would set the price equal to
   A) P_0.
   B) P_1.
   C) P_2.
   D) P_3.

4. The local chapter of the Piano Teachers of America has voted to refrain from advertising the prices charged by their member teachers. This move helps their members more than consumers because it
   A) reminds the instructors that piano teaching is an art, not a business.
   B) is a way to restrict price competition among teachers.
   C) reminds the instructors, who are mostly people's aunties, to trust one another.
   D) allows the instructors to focus on output and not price.

5. Which of the following is *not* a limitation regulators face when they implement average cost pricing?
   A) Average cost pricing provides no incentive for firms to keep costs down.
   B) The accurate calculations of costs and values is difficult.
   C) Decisions are political and often influenced by special interests.
   D) Marginal costs are usually less than average costs.

IV   APPLICATION AND DISCUSSION

Governments around the world are allowing competition in the production of goods and services that have historically been considered natural monopolies. Competition has been introduced in industries such as the local telephone service and electricity provision. Why might the introduction of competition increase the efficiency of these industries?

SECTION 12.6
PRICE DISCRIMINATION AND PEAK LOAD PRICING

KEY POINTS

- **Price discrimination** is when sellers charge different customers different prices for the same good or service even though the cost does not differ.

- To practice price discrimination three conditions must hold: 1) Firms must have monopoly power, 2) Demand curves for different groups must be different, 3) Resale between groups must be prevented.

- A profit-maximizing seller will price where marginal cost equals marginal revenue for each different group of demanders, resulting in a higher price for more inelastic demanders (such as adult movie-goers) and a lower price for more elastic demanders (such as children).

- Quantity discounts, coupons, airline tickets, and college tuition are forms of price discrimination.

- A firm is able to perfectly price discriminate when each unit is sold at the maximum price the customer would be willing to pay.

- When a firm practices perfect price discrimination it produces where price equals marginal cost. This is an efficient level of output. All of the surplus goes to the producer.

- Sometimes producers charge different prices in different periods because demand and cost vary. Peak load pricing charges customer's higher prices to reflect higher marginal cost of production in peak times.

- The most economically efficient solution is to charge a lower price during the non peak period and a higher price during the peak period. Customers have an incentive to shift their use from peak to non peak periods.

I   REVIEW

Price _____ occurs when producers charge different customers different prices for the same good or service.

Producers' motive for price discrimination is _____ maximization.

Even though the marginal cost is the same, producers charge different prices to groups of consumers who differ in the _____ for the product.

Price discrimination is possible only with _____ or where members of a small group of firms follow identical pricing policies. Competitors would _____ the high prices charged to certain groups.

Price discriminating monopolists must also prevent _____ of the product by the group that is charged the lower price.

A firm that perfectly price discriminates sets the price for each unit at the _____ amount customers will pay.

Chapter 12: Monopoly

Perfect price discrimination results in a monopoly producing a(n) _____ level of output.

Higher peak load prices lead to greater efficiency because they reflect higher _____ _____ of production.

II   TRUE/FALSE

_____1. Producers should never price discriminate since charging one group a lower price will reduce their profits.

_____2. Airlines require a picture identification card to use an airline ticket. While this requirement was originally introduced for security, it also helps airlines price discriminate.

_____3. Farmer Geraldo raises tomatoes. He knows that men's demand for tomatoes differs from women's demand. Geraldo could successfully price discriminate.

_____4. Because perfect price discrimination is efficient, consumers are happy with monopolist who do this.

III   MULTIPLE CHOICE

1. Which of the following is *not* a characteristic of a successful price discriminator?
   A) monopoly power
   B) can prevent resale of the product
   C) marginal costs differ between customers
   D) demand differs across customers

2. Why does a firm charge different customers different prices?
   A) The firm wants to drive certain types of people away.
   B) Entrepreneurs don't understand business.
   C) Consumers are ignorant.
   D) They can increase their profits by doing this.

3. If your hometown electric utility were to start peak load pricing, how would it affect consumer behavior?
   A) People would consume the same amount of electricity and pay higher prices.
   B) People would consume more electricity during the peak period since more electricity is produced then.
   C) People would shift some of their electricity consumption to off peak hours to take advantage of lower rates.
   D) People would completely stop using electricity and switch to natural gas.

IV   APPLICATION AND DISCUSSION

The Mississippi Bridge Authority operates a toll bridge that crosses the river near St. Louis. Traffic over the bridge includes tourist traffic and commercial traffic. It also includes commuters who work in St. Louis but live on the Illinois side of the river.

1. Would you expect demand for bridge use to differ at different times during the day? Why?

2. How might costs differ in these time periods?

3. What would be the effects of charging a higher toll to cross the bridge during busy times?

Questions

1. Could the closing of Cinema City and higher prices at the Megaplex be related? How?

2. Do you think higher prices at the Megaplex are permanent? What types of changes could cause the Megaplex to lower their prices?

CHAPTER 13
MONOPOLISTIC COMPETITION AND OLIGOPOLY

SECTION 13.1
MONOPOLISTIC COMPETITION

KEY POINTS

- Many goods and services are traded in circumstances that contain elements of both monopoly and competition. Theories of monopolistic competition and oligopoly deal with markets that lie between the extreme cases of perfect competition and monopoly.

- **Monopolistic competition** is a market structure where many producers of somewhat different products compete with one another.

Chapter 13: Monopolistic Competition and Oligopoly

- Monopolistic competition has features in common with both monopoly and perfect competition. Like monopoly, individual sellers believe that they have some market power; but unlike monopoly, there are many close substitutes coming from other monopolistically competitive firms.

- Firms in monopolistically competitive markets recognize the existence of competitors, imposing a limit on the prices they can charge and still sell a particular level of output, but they do not consider competitors as rivals who are watching them closely.

- Because of the relatively free entry of new firms, the long-run price and output behavior and zero long-run economic profits of monopolistic competition are similar to that of perfect competition. However, the monopolistic competitive firm produces a product that is differentiated from others, which leads to some degree of monopoly power.

- The theory of monopolistic competition is based on three characteristics: product differentiation, many sellers, and free entry

- **Product differentiation** is the accentuation of unique product qualities, real or perceived, to develop a specific product identity. The significant feature of differentiation is the buyers' beliefs that the products of the various sellers are not the same, whether the products are actually physically different or not.

- When many firms compete for the same customers, any particular firm has little control over or interest in what other firms do.

- Entry in monopolistic competition is relatively unrestricted in the sense that new firms may easily start the production of close substitutes for existing products. Because of relatively free entry, economic profits tend to be eliminated in the long run, as is the case in perfect competition.

I   REVIEW

Monopolistic competition is similar to both _____ and perfect competition. As in monopoly, firms have some control over market _____, but as in perfect competition, they face _____ from many other sellers.

Due to the free entry of new firms, long-run economic profits in monopolistic competition are _____.

Firms in monopolistic competition produce products that are _____ from those produced by other firms in the industry.

In monopolistic competition, firms use _____ names to gain some degree of control over price.

The theory of monopolistic competition is based on three characteristics: (1) product _____, (2) many _____, and (3) free _____.

Product differentiation is the accentuation of _____ product qualities to develop a product identity.

II   TRUE/FALSE

_____ 1. Monopolistic competition is a mixture of monopoly and perfect competition.

_____ 2. Like pure monopolists, firms in monopolistically competitive industries can earn economic profits in the long run.

_____ 3. By differentiating their products and promoting brand-name loyalty, firms in monopolistic competition can raise prices without losing all their customers.

_____4. In monopolistic competition, as in perfect competition, all firms in an industry charge the same price.

III   MULTIPLE CHOICE

1. Which of the following is *not* a source of product differentiation?
    A) physical differences in products
    B) differences in quantities that firms offer for sale
    C) differences in service provided by firms
    D) differences in location of sales outlets

2. Which of the following characteristics do monopolistic competition and perfect competition have in common?
    A) Individual firms believe that they can influence market price.
    B) Firms sell brand-name products.
    C) Firms are able to earn long-run economic profits.
    D) Competing firms can enter the industry easily.

3. Firms in monopolistically competitive industries cannot earn economic profits in the long run because
    A) government regulators, whose first interest is the public good, will impose regulations that limit economic profits.
    B) the additional costs of product differentiation will eliminate long-run economic profits.
    C) economic profits will attract competitors whose presence will eliminate profits in the long run.
    D) whenever one firm in the industry begins making economic profits, others will lower their prices thus eliminating long-run economic profits.

IV   APPLICATION AND DISCUSSION

Product differentiation is a hallmark of monopolistic competition and the text lists four sources of such differentiations: physical differences, prestige, location, and service. How do firms in the industries listed below differentiate their products? How important are each of the four sources of differentiation in each case? List the most important source of differentiation in each case.

1. Fast-food restaurants

2. Espresso shops/carts

3. Hair stylists

4. Soft drinks

5. Wine

SECTION 13.2

PRICE AND OUTPUT DETERMINATION IN MONOPOLISTIC COMPETITION

KEY POINTS

- Monopolistic competitive sellers are price searchers rather than price takers. Because each firm sells a slightly different product, each firm's demand curve is downward sloping, but quite flat (elastic) because of many close substitutes.

- The intersection of marginal revenue and marginal cost curves indicates the short-run equilibrium output under monopolistic competition. By observing the price on the demand curve at which that output can be sold, we then find the short-run equilibrium price.

- The short-run equilibrium situation, whether involving profits or losses, will probably not last long because there is entry and exit in the long run. If market entry and exit are sufficiently free, new firms will enter when there are economic profits, and some firms will exit when there are economic losses.

- As new firms enter to take advantage of the economic profits being earned by existing firms, the demand curves for each of the existing firms to fall and become more elastic due to each firm's products having more substitutes.

- When monopolistically competitive firms are making economic losses, some firms will exit the industry. As some firms exit, it increases the demand curves for the remaining firms to the right and makes them more inelastic due to each firm's products having fewer substitutes.

- Long-run equilibrium occurs when each firms' demand curve is just tangent to its *ATC* curve. The point of tangency will occur at the output level where marginal cost is equal to marginal revenue. At this equilibrium point, there are zero economic profits and there are no incentives for firms to either enter or exit the industry.

I   REVIEW

Monopolistic competitive sellers are price _____ like monopolists, and they do not regard price as given by the market. Because products in the industry are slightly different, each firm faces a(n) _____- sloping demand curve.

In the short run, equilibrium output is determined where marginal revenue equals marginal _____. The price is set equal to the _____ the consumer will pay for this amount.

When price is greater than average total costs, the monopolistic competitive firm will make an economic _____.

Barriers to entry do not protect monopolistic competitive firms in the _____ run. Economic profits will _____ new firms to the industry. Similarly, firms will leave when there are economic _____.

As new firms enter an industry, the demand curve of existing firms will shift to the _____. Entry will continue until there are _____ economic profits or _____ just equals average total cost. This is the point where the demand curve for the typical firm is _____ to the long run average total cost curve.

When there are economic losses, firms will leave the industry and the demand curve of remaining firms will shift to the _____. Firms will exit the industry until the economic loss is _____.

Chapter 13: Monopolistic Competition and Oligopoly

Long-run equilibrium in a monopolistic competitive industry occurs when there are _____ economic profits or losses, so there is no incentive for firms to _____ or _____ the industry.

II   True/False

_____1. Frank's location and his secret sauce make "Frank's Hot Dog Shop" a monopolistic competitor in the restaurant industry. The competitive character of the industry means Frank maximizes profits by producing where price equals marginal cost.

_____2. Monopolies, Competitive Firms, and Monopolistic Competitive firms all follow the same general rule when deciding how much to produce.

III   MULTIPLE CHOICE

1. Maria's West Side Bakery is the only bakery on the West Side of the city. She is a monopolistic competitor and she is open for business. Which of the following *cannot* be true about Maria's profits?
   A) She is making an economic profit.
   B) She is making neither an economic profit nor loss.
   C) She is making an economic loss that is less than her fixed cost.
   D) She is making an economic loss that is greater than her fixed cost.

2. Claire is considering buying the only Hungarian restaurant in Boise, Idaho. The restaurant's unique food means it faces a negatively sloped demand curve and it is currently earning an economic profit. Why shouldn't Claire assume the current profits will continue when she makes her decision?
   A) Claire will not earn those profits right away because she doesn't know much about cooking.
   B) The firm is a monopolist and this will attract government regulation.
   C) Current economic profits will be eliminated by the entry of competitors.
   D) While economic profits are positive, accounting profits may be negative.

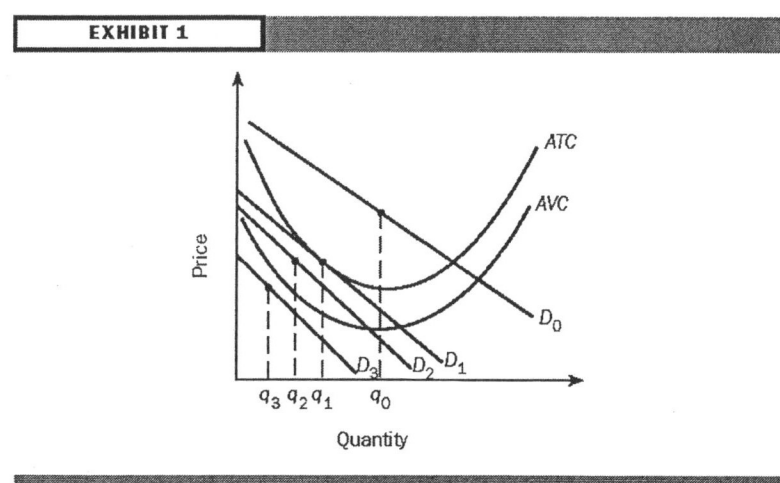

EXHIBIT 1

Answer questions 3 and 4 with reference to Exhibit 1, which shows a monopolistic competitor's cost curves and four demand curves, each with its profit-maximizing output.

3. Which of the demand curves in Exhibit 1 represents a long-run equilibrium for the firm?
   A) *D0*
   B) *D1*
   C) *D2*
   D) *D3*

4. Which of the demand curves in Exhibit 1 will result in the firm shutting down in the short run?
   A) *D0*
   B) *D1*
   C) *D2*
   D) *D3*

IV   APPLICATION AND DISCUSSION

How are monopolistically competitive firms and perfectly competitive firms similar? Why don't monopolistically competitive firms produce the same output in the long run as perfectly competitive firms, which face similar costs?

SECTION 13.3

MONOPOLISTIC COMPETITION VERSUS PERFECT COMPETITION

KEY POINTS

- Product differentiation allows a monopolistic competitor to have some influence over price. Consequently, a monopolistically competitive firm has a downward-sloping demand curve that, because of the large number of good substitutes is more elastic than the demand curve for a monopolist.

- The downward slope of the demand curve means the long run equilibrium output will not be at the lowest average cost. Therefore, even when long-run adjustments are complete, firms will not be operating at a level that permits the lowest average cost of production—the efficient scale for the firm. The existing plant, even though optimal for the equilibrium volume of output, will not be used to capacity. That is, **excess capacity** will exist at that level of output.

- Unlike a perfectly competitive firm, a monopolistically competitive firm could increase output and lower its average total costs. However, any attempt to increase output to attain lower average costs would be unprofitable because the price reduction necessary to sell the greater output would cause *MR* to fall below *MC* at the increased output. In monopolistic competition, there is a tendency toward too many firms in the industry, each producing a volume of output less than that which would allow lowest cost.

- Productive inefficiency is not the only problem with monopolistic competition. Firms are also not operating where price is equal to marginal cost. This means that society is willing to pay more for the product (the price) than it costs society to produce it. In this case, the firm is failing to reach allocative efficiency.

- In monopolistic competition, the higher average costs and the slightly higher price and lower output may just be the price we pay for differentiated products and variety.

- Perfect competition meets the test of allocative and productive efficiency and monopolistic competition does not.

- The significance of the difference between the relationship of long-run marginal cost to price in monopolistic competition and in perfect competition can easily be exaggerated. As long as preferences for various brands are not extremely strong, the demand for the products of firms will be highly elastic. Accordingly, the points of tangency with the *ATC* curves are not likely to be far above the point of lowest cost, and excess capacity will be small. Only if differentiation is very strong will the difference between the long-run price level and that which would prevail under perfectly competitive conditions be significant.

I   REVIEW

Because it faces competition, a monopolistically competitive firm has a _____-sloping demand curve that tends to be more _____ than the demand curve for a monopolist.

Even in the long run, monopolistically competitive firms do not operate at levels that permit the full realization of _____ of scale.

Unlike a perfectly competitive firm in long-run equilibrium, a monopolistically competitive firm will produce with _____ capacity. The firm could lower average costs by increasing output but this would reduce _____.

In monopolistic competition there is a tendency toward too _____ firms in the industry. Monopolistically competitive industries will not reach _____efficiency since firms in the industry do not produce at the _____ per unit cost.

In monopolistic competition, firms operate where price is _____ than marginal cost which means that consumers are willing to pay _____ for the product than it costs society to produce it. In this case, the firm fails to reach _____ efficiency.

Although average costs and prices are higher under monopolistic competition than they are under perfect competition, society gets a benefit from monopolistic competition in the form of _____ products.

II   TRUE/FALSE

_____1. A monopolistic competitor's demand curve is relatively more inelastic than a monopolist's demand curve.

_____2. Unlike purely competitive firms, firms in monopolistic competition will operate with excess capacity, even in the long run.

_____3. Although there are certain inefficiencies associated with monopolistic competition, society receives a benefit from monopolistic competition in the form of differentiated goods and services.

III   MULTIPLE CHOICE

1. In the long run, firms in monopolistic competition do not attain productive efficiency because they produce
   A) at a point where economic profits are positive.
   B) at a point where marginal revenue is less than marginal cost.
   C) at a point to the left of the low point of their long-run average total cost curve.
   D) where marginal cost is equal to long-run average total cost.

2. In the long run, firms in monopolistic competition do not attain allocative efficiency because they
   A) operate where price equals marginal cost.
   B) do not operate where price equals marginal cost.
   C) produce more output than society wants.
   D) charge prices that are less than production costs.

3. Compared to perfect competition, firms in monopolist competition in the long run produce
   A) less output at a lower cost.
   B) less output at a higher cost.
   C) more output at a lower cost.
   D) more output at a higher cost.

IV DISCUSSION AND APPLICATION

As you know, there are important differences between perfect competition and monopolistic competition. Show your understanding of these differences by listing the following terms under either "perfect competition" or "monopolistic competition."

Terms		Perfect Competition	Monopolistic Competition
standardized product	productive efficiency	_____	_____
differentiated product	horizontal demand curve	_____	_____
allocative efficiency	downward-sloping demand curve	_____	_____
excess capacity	no control over price	_____	_____

SECTION 13.4
ADVERTISING

KEY POINTS

- Advertising is an important non-price method of competition that is commonly used in monopolistic competition.

- A successful advertising campaign can increase demand and decrease elasticity by convincing buyers that a firm's product is truly different. The result would be greater profits.

- Critics have argued that advertising manipulates consumer tastes, wastes billions of dollars annually, and creates "needs" for trivial products. They also suggest that it is sometimes based on misleading claims, so people find themselves buying products that do not provide the satisfaction or results promised in the ads. Finally, advertising itself requires resources, which raises average costs.

- Advertising can raise average total costs. When there are significant economies of scale, the increase demand from advertising may reduce average total cost. However, firms in monopolistic competition are not likely to experience substantial cost reductions as output increases. Therefore, they probably will not be able to offset advertising costs with lower production costs.

- Advertising may add to total cost but it also conveys information. Through advertising, customers become aware of options that they have in terms of product choice. Advertising helps the customer arrive at a choice of price and product that best meets their needs, and it also informs price-conscious customers about the cost of the product.

- Advertising reduces information costs, so customers know about more products that may be substitutes for the products they currently buy. Consequently, this leads to increasingly competitive markets. Studies in the eyeglass, toy, and drug industries have shown that advertising has increased competition and led to lower prices in these markets.

I   REVIEW

Advertising is an important type of _____ competition that firms use to _____ the demand for their products.

Advertising may not only increase the demand facing a firm, it may also make the demand facing the firm more _____ if it convinces buyers the product is truly different. A more inelastic demand curve means price changes will have relatively _____ effects on the quantity demanded of the product.

Critics of advertising assert that it _____ average total costs while manipulating consumer's tastes. However, if people are _____, this argument loses some of its force.

When advertising is used in industries with significant economies of _____, per-unit costs may decline by more than per-unit advertising costs.

An important function of advertising is to lower the cost of acquiring _____ about the availability of substitutes and the _____ of products.

By making information about substitutes and prices less costly to acquire, advertising will increase the _____ in industries, which is good for consumers.

II   TRUE/FALSE

_____1. While advertising will add to the cost of production, when there are significant economies of scale, advertising may lower the per-unit total cost.

_____2. Misleading claims and preposterous bragging about products is a type of advertising that will result in increased demand for a firm's products.

III   MULTIPLE CHOICE

1. If Rolf wants to use advertising to reduce the elasticity of demand for his chiropractic services, he must make sure the advertising
   A) clearly states the prices he charges.
   B) shows that he is producing a product like the other chiropractors in town.
   C) shows why his services are truly different from the other chiropractors in town.
   D) explains the hours and days that he is open for business.

2. Advertising about prices by firms in an industry will make an industry more competitive because it
   A) reduces the cost of finding a substitute when one producer raises his price.
   B) assures the consumers that prices are the same every where.
   C) increases the cost for all firms because of the existence of scale economies.
   D) reduces the number of firms because of the existence of scale economies.

IV   APPLICATION AND DISCUSSION

In what way is the use of advertising another example of Adam Smith's "Invisible Hand" in which entrepreneurs pursuing their own best interest make consumers better off?

Questions

1. Lowell Construction and Acme Roofing provide similar services. In this case, what differentiates the two companies?

2. Why do you think Mr. Lowell is able to charge a higher price than Acme?

SECTION 13.5
OLIGOPOLY

KEY POINTS

- **Oligopolies** exist where relatively few firms control all or most of the production and sale of a product. The products may be homogeneous or differentiated, but the barriers to entry are often very high, which makes it difficult for firms to enter into the industry. Consequently, long-run economic profits may be earned by firms in the industry.

- Oligopoly is characterized by **mutual interdependence** among firms; that is, each firm shapes its policy with an eye to the policies of competing firms. Oligopoly occurs when the number of firms in an industry is so small that any change in output or price by one firm appreciably impacts the sales of competing firms, so competitors respond directly to these actions in determining their own policy.

- Oligopoly is a result of the relationship between technological conditions of production and potential sales volumes. For many products, a reasonably low cost of production cannot be obtained unless a firm is producing a large fraction of the market output. In other words, substantial economies of scale are present.

- Economies of large-scale production make operation on a small scale during a new firm's early years extremely unprofitable. A firm cannot build up a large market overnight; in the interim, average total cost is so high that losses are heavy. Recognition of this fact discourages new firms from entering the market.

Chapter 13: Monopolistic Competition and Oligopoly

- With mutual interdependence, an oligopolist generally faces considerable uncertainty as to the shape of its demand and marginal revenue curves. In order to know anything about its demand curve, a firm must know how other firms will react to its prices and other policies. Thus, in the absence of additional assumptions, equating marginal revenue and marginal cost is relegated to guesswork. Thus oligopolists have difficulty determining the most profitable price and output.

I   REVIEW

Oligopolies exist when only a _____ firms control all or most of the production and sale of a product.

In oligopoly, products may be either homogeneous or _____.

In oligopoly, _____ to entry are often very high, preventing competing firms from entering the market.

In oligopoly, firms can earn long-run _____ profits.

Oligopoly is characterized by mutual _____ among firms. Oligopolists must _____ because the number of firms in the industry is so small that changes in one firm's price of output will affect the sales of competing firms.

In oligopoly, barriers to entry in the form of large start-up costs, economies of scale, or _____ are usually present.

The economy of large-scale production _____ new firms from entering a market because high initial average total costs impose heavy losses on new entrants.

Mutual interdependence means that no firm knows with _____ what its demand curve looks like. The demand curve and the profit-maximizing price and output will depend on how others _____ to the firm's policies.

II   TRUE/FALSE

_____1. Under oligopoly, individual firms produce only an infinitesimal share of total output.

_____2. The auto industry is an example of oligopoly.

_____3. Under oligopoly, as in perfect competition and monopolistic competition, firms cannot earn economic profits in the long run.

III   MULTIPLE CHOICE

1. Which of the following is *not* a characteristic of oligopoly?
    A) A few firms control most of the production and sale of a product.
    B) Firms in the industry make price and output decisions with an eye to the decisions and policies of other firms in the industry.
    C) Competing firms can enter the industry easily.
    D) Substantial economies of scale are present in production.

2. Under oligopoly, a few large firms control most of the production and sale of a product because
    A) economies of scale make it difficult for small firms to compete.
    B) diseconomies of scale make it difficult for small firms to compete.
    C) average total costs rise as production expands.
    D) marginal costs rise as production expands.

3. In an oligopoly like the U.S. domestic airline industry, a firm like United Airlines would
    A) carefully anticipate Delta, American, and Southwest's likely responses before it raised or lowered fares.
    B) pretty much disregard Delta, American, and Southwest's likely responses when raising or lowering fares.
    C) charge the lowest fare possible in order to maximize market share.
    D) schedule as many flights to as many cities as possible without regard to what competitors do.

IV   APPLICATION AND DISCUSSION

Important differences exist between perfect competition and oligopoly. Show your understanding of these differences by listing the following terms under either "perfect competition" or "oligopoly."

Terms		Perfect Competition	Oligopoly
allocative efficiency	large economies of scale	_____	_____
many small firms	productive efficiency	_____	_____
high barriers to entry	horizontal demand curve	_____	_____
few large firms	mutual interdependence	_____	_____
downward-sloping demand curve	no control over price	_____	_____

SECTION 13.6
COLLUSION AND CARTELS

KEY POINTS

- The uncertainties of pricing decisions are substantial in oligopoly. Because of this uncertainty, some believe that oligopolists change their prices less frequently than perfect competitors do. The empirical evidence, however, does not clearly indicate that prices are in fact always slow to change in oligopoly situations.

- Because the actions and profits of oligopolists are so dominated by mutual interdependence, the temptation is great for firms to **collude**□to get together and agree to act jointly in pricing and other matters. If firms believe they can increase their profits by coordinating their actions, they will be tempted to collude. Collusion reduces uncertainty and increases the potential for monopoly profits.

- Unfortunately, from society's point of view, collusion has the same disadvantages monopoly does; namely, it creates a situation in which goods become overpriced and underproduced, with consumers losing out from a misallocation of resources.

- A collusive oligopoly that involves all firms in an industry could act as the equivalent of one firm with several "plants" from the standpoint of pricing and output decisions. Acting in this matter, the economic effect of the collusive oligopolist is exactly the same as a monopolist. Once the profit-maximizing price is determined, they can agree on how much output each firm in the group will offer for sale.

- A **Cartel** is a collection of firms making an agreement on sale, pricing, and other decisions.

- Cartels may lead to **joint profit maximization**, which requires the determination of price on the basis of the marginal revenue function derived from the total (or market) demand schedule for the product and the marginal cost schedules of the various firms.

- Collusion facilitates joint profit maximization for an oligopoly. Like monopoly, if the oligopoly is maintained in the long run, it charges a higher price, produces less output, and fails to maximize social welfare relative to perfect competition.

- Most strong collusive oligopolies are rather short lived for two reasons. First, in the United States and in some other nations, collusive oligopolies are strictly illegal under antitrust laws. Second, for collusion to work, firms must agree to restrict output to a level that will support the profit-maximizing price. At that price, firms can earn positive economic profits. Yet there is a great temptation for firms to cheat on the agreement of the collusive oligopoly, and because collusive agreements are illegal, the other parties have no way to punish the offender.

- Oligopolists have a strong incentive to cheat on a cartel because any individual firm could lower its price slightly and increase sales and profits, as long as it is undetected. Undetected price cuts could bring in new customers, including rivals' customers. In addition, there are non-price forms of defection.

I   REVIEW

Because they are mutually interdependent, oligopolists are tempted to get together and agree to act jointly or to _____ in order to reduce uncertainty and raise profits.

Collusion has the same effects that monopoly does; goods that are priced too _____ and outputs that are too _____.

International agreements between firms regarding sales, pricing, and other decisions are called _____ agreements.

Although collusive oligopolies may be profitable for participants they are often short-lived because firms have a great temptation to _____ on their fellow colluders.

II   TRUE/FALSE

_____1. When firms in an oligopolistic industry collude, the effects are the same as under monopoly.

_____2. When firms collude to set prices, their individual demand curves become relatively more elastic.

_____3. Although they are difficult to establish, most collusive oligopolies last indefinitely.

III   MULTIPLE CHOICE

1. One of the reasons that collusive oligopolies are usually short-lived is that
    A) they are unable to earn economic profits in the long run.
    B) they do not set prices where marginal cost equals marginal revenue.
    C) they set prices below long-run average total costs.
    D) parties to the collusion often cheat on one another.

2. In a collusive oligopoly, joint profits are maximized when a price is set based on
    A) its own demand and cost schedules.
    B) the market demand for the product and the summation of marginal costs of the various firms.
    C) the price followers' demand schedules and the price leader's marginal costs.
    D) the price leader's demand schedule and the price followers' marginal costs.

IV   APPLICATION AND DISCUSSION

One of the world's most successful cartels has been the Central Selling Organization (CSO) which controls about three quarters of the world's diamonds. This collusive oligopoly kept diamond prices high by restricting supply, like a monopolist. The CSO also promoted diamonds through advertising and marketing, promoting the general consumption of diamonds. New supplies of diamonds have been found in Canada and Russia. These new mines, which are outside the direct control of the CSO, want to sell their diamonds on the open market.

1.   What would you predict will happen in the market for diamonds if these new mines do not cooperate with the cartel?

2.   What do you think will happen to CSO diamond advertising?

SECTION 13.7
OTHER OLIGOPOLY MODELS

KEY POINTS

- Prices in some oligopolistic industries tend to be quite stable, or rigid. If demand or cost were to increase, firms might be tempted to increase their prices, but may not do so because of the fear that rivals will not raise prices and they will lose customer sales. They may also be reluctant to lower their prices because it might set off a price war.

- The idea that there is price rigidity in oligopoly is the basis of the **kinked demand curve** model. In it, each firm faces a demand curve that is kinked at the market price because of the greater tendency of competitors to follow price reductions than price increases. A price reduction takes business away from other firms and forces them to cut prices to protect their sales, while an increase does not necessitate a readjustment, since other firms gain customers if a competitor increases its price.

- One important consequence of the kink in the demand curve is that the firm may be slow to adjust price in response to cost changes. Because of the kink in the demand curve, the marginal revenue curve is discontinuous. Therefore, the *MC* curve can move up or down over a substantial range without affecting the optimal level of price.

- In the real world, when a firm raises its price, but other firms do not, the price-raising firm will face the prospect of a major sales decline and so will usually retreat from the price increase. The explanation for the price rigidity comes from the idea that firms do not want to engage in destructive price competition.

- Not all oligopolies experience price rigidity. It is more likely when there is excess capacity, like during a recession, because firms are likely to match a price cut but not a price hike.

- A form of tacit collusion is price leadership. In some oligopolistic industries a dominant firm signals increases in prices. Competitors that go along with the pricing decision are price followers.

- Mutual interdependence is no guarantee of economic profits, even if the firms in the industry succeed in maximizing joint profits. The extent to which economic profits disappear depends on the ease with which new firms can enter the industry.

- When entry is easy, excess profits attract newcomers. New firms may break down existing price agreements by cutting prices in an attempt to establish themselves in the industry. Older firms may reduce prices to avoid excessive sales losses. As a result, the general level of prices will begin to approach average total cost.

- Oligopolists often initiate pricing policies that reduce the entry incentive for new firms, holding prices below the maximum-profit point. This lower-than-profit-maximizing price may discourage newcomers from entering. Because new firms would likely have higher costs than existing firms, the lower price may not be high enough to cover their costs. However, once the threat of entry subsides, the market price may return to the profit-maximizing price.

- If the price is deliberately kept low (below average variable cost) to drive a competitor out of the market, it is called **predatory pricing**. However, it is difficult to distinguish predatory pricing from vigorous competition.

I   REVIEW

Prices in some oligopolistic industries tend to be stable or _____. One explanation of this is the _____ demand model.

This model recognizes a firm's demand curve is _____ on the actions and reactions of competing firms. The kinked demand curve is a result of the greater tendency of competitors to follow a firm's price _____ than price increases. Demand is very _____ above an established price but relatively _____ below this price. One consequence of this is that firms are _____ to adjust price in response to cost changes.

In oligopoly, an understanding may develop under which one large firm will play the role of price _____, sending signals to competitors that they have changed their prices.

Competitors that go along with the pricing decisions of a price leader are called price _____.

Collusive behavior is no guarantee of economic profits in the _____ run.

Without _____ to entry, new firms will be attracted by the economic profits earned when firms act to maximize joint profits.

New firms will lower _____ and break down existing pricing agreements. Price competition will result in prices approaching the level of average total _____.

Oligopolists may charge a price lower than the profit-maximizing price to _____ new firms from entering the market. This strategy will be effective when new firms face _____ costs than existing firms in the industry do.

Chapter 13: Monopolistic Competition and Oligopoly

II   TRUE/FALSE

_____ 1. The new diamond industry in northern Canada will not threaten the economic profits earned by members of the international diamond cartel.

_____ 2. By the year 2050 the moon travel business consists of three international firms that create the International Moon Cartel, which restricts output and raises prices. Because this industry is an oligopoly, the existing firms' economic profits will be guaranteed for the long run.

III   MULTIPLE CHOICE

1. If existing firms in an oligopoly charge a price that is lower than the profit-maximizing price, this is an example of a
    A) price following strategy.
    B) kinked demand curve.
    C) barrier to entry.
    D) cartel.

2. Why does the kinked demand model suggests that demand will be more elastic when a firm raises its price above some established price than when it lowers its price?
    A) Demand is always more elastic above the midpoint of a straight-line demand curve than below.
    B) Demand will be more elastic since all firms sell less of the good as the price increases and all firms will sell more as the price falls.
    C) Demand will be more elastic because competitors will not follow price increases but will match price decreases.
    D) Demand will be more elastic because price increases will result in a decrease in quantity demanded while price reduction will result in an increase.

3. During the 1950s many profitable manufacturing industries in the United States, like steel, tires, and autos, were considered oligopolies. Why do you think such firms work hard to keep imports from other countries out of the U.S. market?
    A) Without import barriers, excess profits in the United States would attract foreign firms, break down existing price agreements and reduce profits of U.S. firms.
    B) Without import barriers, foreign firms would be attracted to the United States and cause the cost in the industry to rise.
    C) Without import barriers, foreign firms would buy U.S. goods and resell them in the United States causing profits to fall.
    D) Without import barriers, prices of goods would rise, so consumers would buy less of the products of these firms.

4. Over the past 20 years, Dominator, Inc., a large firm in an oligopolistic industry, has changed prices a number of times. Each time it does so, the other firms in the industry follow suit. Dominator, Inc. is a
    A) monopoly.
    B) perfect competitor.
    C) price leader.
    D) price follower.

IV   APPLICATION AND DISCUSSION

The U.S. Justice Department has worried that the nation's four largest air carriers, Delta, Northwest, American, and United, use low prices to limit competition at the busiest airports. Predatory pricing exists when the dominant carrier at an airport matches the low prices of any new low-fare competitors and sells more low fare seats. The major carrier holds these low prices until the new competition folds. The dominant carrier recovers any short-term losses with increased fares once the competition is eliminated.

The government thinks that this pricing response is an anti-competitive strategy. The dominant carriers have claimed that this response is simply a part of competition. Which is it? How would each of the following pieces of information affect your decision as to whether it is an anti-competitive strategy or a competitive response? Check the appropriate box.

Information	Anti-Competitive Strategy	Competitive Response
1. Large unrecoverable start up costs for new airlines.	☐	☐
2. Many airlines serve the airport.	☐	☐
3. Dominant airline drops price below average variable cost.	☐	☐
4. There is excess capacity on the dominant airline flights before the new airline enters the market.	☐	☐

SECTION 13.8
GAME THEORY AND STRATEGIC BEHAVIOR

KEY POINTS

- In oligopolistic industries, firms take certain actions not because they are necessarily advantageous in themselves but because they improve the position of the oligopolist relative to its competitors and may ultimately improve its financial position.

- Some economists analyze oligopoly behavior in terms of a strategic game. **Game theory** stresses the tendency of various parties in such circumstances to act in such a way that minimizes damage from opponents.

- With the game theory approach, there is a set of alternative actions, and the action that would be taken in a particular case depends on the specific policies followed by each firm. The firm may try to figure out its competitors' most likely countermoves to its own policies and then formulate alternative defense measures.

- Interactions between oligopolists can either be cooperative or noncooperative. Collusion is a **cooperative game**. However, enforcement costs are usually too high to keep all firms from cheating on collusive agreements. Consequently, most games are **noncooperative games** in which each firm sets its own price without consulting other firms.

- The primary difference between cooperative and noncooperative games is the contract. Players in a cooperative game can talk and set binding contracts, while those in noncooperative games are assumed to act independently with no communication and no binding contracts. Because antitrust laws forbid firms to collude, we will assume that most strategic behavior in the marketplace is noncooperative.

- A firm's decision makers must map out a pricing strategy based on a wide range of information. They also must decide whether their strategy will be effective and affected by their competitors' actions. A strategy that will be optimal regardless of the opponents' actions is called a **dominant strategy.**

- The **Prisoners' Dilemma** is a famous game that has a dominant strategy and demonstrates the basic problem confronting noncolluding oligopolists. Two suspects to a bank robbery are caught. The suspects are placed in separate cells in the county jail and are not allowed to talk with each other. There are four possible results in this situation: both prisoners confess, neither confesses, Prisoner A confesses but Prisoner B doesn't, or Prisoner B confesses but Prisoner A doesn't. The outcome of a Prisoner's decision to confess or not depends on the decision of the other prisoners.

- Looking at the Prisoners' Dilemma payoff matrix, if one prisoner confesses, it is in the best interest of the other prisoner to confess. Since both know the temptation of the other to confess, the dominant strategy is to confess. That is, the prisoners know that confessing is the way to make the best of a bad situation.

- Firms in oligopoly often behave like the prisoners in the Prisoners' Dilemma, carefully anticipating the moves of their rivals in an uncertain environment.

- At a **Nash equilibrium,** each firm is doing as well as it can, given the actions of its competitor. Each will make the choice that minimizes the risk of the worst scenario. The Nash equilibrium takes on particular importance because it is a self-enforcing equilibrium. That is, once this equilibrium is established, there is no incentive for either firm to move.

- If two firms were to collude, it would be in their best interest. However, each firm has a strong incentive to lower its price if this pricing strategy goes undetected by its competitor. However, if both firms defect by lowering their prices from the joint-profit-maximization level, both will be worse off than if they had colluded, but at least each will have minimized its potential loss if it cannot trust its competitor. This is the oligopolist's dilemma, which can also be played out over other strategic variables, such as advertising.

I   REVIEW

An approach to oligopoly that focuses on the tendency of firms to act in ways that minimize damage from opponents is called _____ theory.

Games can either be cooperative or _____ and the primary difference between them is the existence of _____.

In game theory, a strategy that will be optimal no matter what your opponent does is called a _____ strategy.

The _____ Dilemma is a famous game that has a dominant strategy and demonstrates the basic problem confronting noncolluding monopolists.

Firms in oligopoly often behave like the prisoners in the Prisoners' Dilemma because they carefully anticipate the moves of their rivals in a(n) _____ environment.

At a(n) _____ equilibrium, each player in a game is said to be doing as well as he can given the actions of his _____.

II   TRUE/FALSE

_____1. An oligopoly always has a dominant pricing strategy.

_____2. The Prisoners' Dilemma is an example of a cooperative game.

III   MULTIPLE CHOICE

1. The main difference between cooperative and noncooperative games is that
   A) in cooperative games players help each other and in noncooperative games they don't.
   B) in cooperative games both players can win while in noncooperative games there is a winner and a loser.
   C) in cooperative games players can communicate and set contracts while in noncooperative games they can't.
   D) cooperative games are legal in the eyes of the law while noncooperative games aren't.

2. Economists believe that oligopolists like American Airlines and the Kellogg Company
   A) make price and output decisions without regard to what their competitors might do.
   B) have no control over market price but produce output to the point where marginal costs equal total costs.
   C) have no control over price but produce to the point where demand is equal to marginal revenue.
   D) carefully watch and anticipate the moves of their competitors.

3. Noncollusive oligopolists behave like
   A) a family watching TV.
   B) a dog with a bone.
   C) players in a poker game.
   D) children at a picnic.

IV   APPLICATION AND DISCUSSION

Duke and Carmella each run one of the two airlines serving a small community. Both are considering implementing frequent-flyer programs that would provide upgrades and free tickets to customers who fly a lot. The payoff matrix below shows the expected monthly profits for each airline.

	Carmella has a frequent flyer program.		Carmella doesn't have a frequent flyer program.	
Duke has a frequent flyer program.	Carmella's	$20,000	Carmella's	$10,000
	Duke's	$50,000	Duke's	$25,000
Duke doesn't have a frequent flyer program.	Carmella's	$30,000	Carmella's	$15,000
	Duke's	$40,000	Duke's	$45,000

A) Does Carmella have a dominant strategy? If yes, what is it?

B) Does Duke have a dominant strategy? If yes, what is it?

C) If you were Carmella's economic advisor, what would you advise her to do?

D) If you were Duke's economic advisor, what would you advise him to do?

Questions

1. What oligopolistic practice is Mr. Lowell referring to when he says it looks like "follow the leader"?

2. What incentives does Jerry's Jiffy Gas and Kim's Family Service have to follow Blue Ribbon's price leadership?

3. What do you think would happen if Kim's didn't raise their prices?

CHAPTER 14
SUPPLY AND DEMAND IN INPUT MARKETS

SECTION 14.1
INPUT MARKETS

KEY POINTS

- Approximately 75 percent of national income goes to wages and salaries for labor services. The rest goes to owners of land and capital and the entrepreneurs who employ those resources to produce valued goods and services.

- The price and quantity of each of these inputs is determined by their supply and demand.

- In input or factor markets, the demand for an input is a **derived demand**—derived from consumers' demand for the good or service. The "price" of a productive factor is directly related to consumer demand for the final good or service.

Chapter 14: Supply and Demand in Input Markets

I REVIEW

The three major categories of productive resources are land, labor, and _____. _____ employ these resources for production.

The prices and quantities of productive resources are determined by the forces of supply and _____.

In the market for productive resources, the buyer's cost is the seller's _____.

An important thing to remember is that the demand for productive resources is _____ from the demand for the goods and services that those resources produce.

II TRUE/FALSE

_____1. The salaries of college professor are determined by the forces of supply and demand.

_____2. The demand for auto workers has no relationship to the demand for automobiles.

III MULTIPLE CHOICE

1. Another term for "productive resource" is
    A) financial resource.
    B) innovation.
    C) production possibilities curve.
    D) factor of production.

2. Why would an abnormally hot summer in California increase the demand for natural gas?
    A) The number of people in California would increase, which would increase the demand for all goods people consume, including natural gas.
    B) The price of petroleum would go up so Californians would substitute natural gas for gasoline in their cars.
    C) The demand for electricity for air conditioning would increase and natural gas is used to produce electricity.
    D) The supply of natural gas would increase as the price people are willing to pay increased and more natural gas would be consumed.

IV APPLICATION AND DISCUSSION

During the nineteenth century, American business generally supported liberal immigration laws while labor unions, who represented American workers, opposed it. From what you know about how prices of factors of production are determined, how can you explain these different attitudes toward immigration?

SECTION 14.2

SUPPLY AND DEMAND IN THE LABOR MARKET

KEY POINTS

- Firms are trying to maximize their profits so they try to make the difference between total revenue and total cost as large as possible. The attractiveness of a resource varies with what the resource adds to the revenues received by the firm relative to what it adds to costs.

- The demand for labor is determined by its **marginal revenue product (*MRP*)**, which is the additional revenue that a firm obtains from one more unit of input.

- The **marginal resource cost (*MRC*)** is the amount that an extra input adds to the firm's total costs. In a competitive labor market, its *MRC* is the market wage.

- A firm would find its profits growing by adding one more worker when the marginal revenue product associated with the worker exceeds the marginal resource cost of the worker. However, additional hiring would be unprofitable when the marginal resource cost exceeds the marginal revenue product.

- The demand curve for labor is downward sloping. Higher wages will decrease the quantity of labor demanded, while lower wages will increase the quantity of labor demanded.

- The major reason for the downward-sloping demand curve for labor is the law of diminishing marginal product: As increasing quantities of a variable input (say labor) are added to fixed quantities of another input, output will rise, but at some point it will increase by diminishing amounts. This occurs because the added output associated with one more worker—**marginal product**—declines as more workers are added and each has fewer fixed resources with which to work.

- The marginal revenue product (MRP) is the change in total revenue associated with an additional unit of input. The marginal revenue product is equal to the marginal product (the units of output added by a worker) multiplied by the marginal revenue (in the competitive output market case, this is price of the output). The marginal revenue product of labor declines because of the diminishing marginal product of labor.

- Profits are maximized if a firm hires only to the point where the wage equals the expected marginal revenue product. Therefore, value of the marginal revenue product (*MRP*) is the same as the demand curve for labor for a competitive firm. It is why raising wages, *ceteris paribus*, lowers employment.

- In a competitive labor market, many firms are competing for workers and no single firm is big enough by itself to have any significant effect on the level of wages. The ability to hire all one wishes at the prevailing wage is analogous to perfect competition in output markets, where a firm could sell all it wanted at the going price.

- Just as was the case in earlier discussions of the law of supply, there is a positive relationship between wage level and the quantity of labor supplied. As the wage rate rises, the quantity of labor supplied increases, *ceteris paribus;* as the wage falls, the quantity of labor supplied falls, *ceteris paribus*.

- Wage increases have two conflicting effects on the quantity of labor supplied by an individual: the substitution effect and the income effect. The **substitution effect:** a higher wage increases the opportunity cost of forgoing labor time to gain greater leisure time, leading to a substitution of labor for leisure. The **income effect:** at a higher wage a worker's income is higher, and since leisure is a normal good, a worker demands more leisure, reducing the quantity of labor supplied.

- There is the possibility of a **backward-bending individual labor supply curve.** Where the substitution effect dominates the income effect, the individual labor supply curve is upward sloping, but where the income effect dominates the substitution effect, the individual labor supply curve is backward bending.

Chapter 14: Supply and Demand in Input Markets

I REVIEW

In making hiring decisions, firms are guided by their desire to maximize _____.

The additional revenue a firm obtains from hiring one more unit of input is called the _____ revenue product.

The marginal _____ cost is the amount the extra unit of an input increases the firm's total costs.

A firm will hire one more unit of labor as long as that labor's marginal revenue product _____ the marginal resource cost. If the marginal resource cost of the labor is _____ than the marginal revenue product, hiring the labor will be unprofitable.

The _____ curve for labor is the same as the marginal revenue product.

The marginal revenue product for a firm in a competitive industry is equal to the _____ product multiplied by the price of the output.

There is a _____ relation between the wage and the quantity of labor demanded.

The demand curve for labor is downward sloping because of the law of _____ marginal product. This law states that as more labor is added to some fixed amount of another input, output _____ but by diminishing amounts.

The marginal revenue product declines as more labor is added to a fixed input because the marginal _____ of labor declines.

Profits are maximized if the firm hires only to the point where the marginal _____ cost equals the marginal _____ product.

The intersection of market demand and market supply determines the _____ wage rate.

The _____ supply of labor shows how much work effort people collectively are willing and able to supply to the market. There is a _____ relationship between wage level and the quantity of labor supplied.

For an individual, wage increases have two conflicting effects. The _____ effect of a wage increase increases the cost of leisure, so people consume _____ leisure and work more. The _____ effect of a wage increase increases a person's income, so people buy more leisure and work _____.

II TRUE/FALSE

_____1. Al owns a restaurant. He pays $25 per day in wages when he hires a waiter and $2.75 to the state's worker compensation fund. His marginal resource cost is equal to $25.

_____2. Margie's profits will rise if she hires Gail since Gail's contribution to revenue is $700 and Margie will only pay $500 in wages and other costs if she hires Gail.

_____3. The demand curve for labor is downward sloping because the quality of labor declines the more labor a firm hires.

_____4. The individual's supply curve of labor will always have a positive slope.

Chapter 14: Supply and Demand in Input Markets

III MULTIPLE CHOICE

1. Ernie's Auto Supply is a competitor in the labor market. Ernie decides to pay his workers less than the market wage to increase his profits. What is the most likely result of Ernie's decision?
   A) Ernie's profits will increase even if he doesn't change his output.
   B) Ernie's employees will find work with other employers who pay the market wage.
   C) Ernie will be able to increase the number of workers he hires because he is paying them less.
   D) Ernie will produce more even if he doesn't hire any more workers because his profits are higher.

2. When the wage is the only cost of hiring labor, a firm will hire labor up to the quantity where marginal revenue product equals the wage rate, so the marginal revenue product shows the
   A) cost of hiring labor.
   B) supply of labor.
   C) demand for labor.
   D) profits from hiring labor.

3. Marginal revenue product falls as more labor is hired because the
   A) price of the product must fall for a perfectly competitive firm to sell more.
   B) marginal resource cost of labor increases the more labor hired.
   C) marginal product of labor is negative as additional labor is hired.
   D) marginal product of labor falls as a result of the law of diminishing marginal product.

IV APPLICATION AND DISCUSSION

1. The following table compares the average salaries earned in major league sports with the salaries earned in 2001 in other occupations.

Occupation	2001 Average Earnings
Baseball Players	$2,264,403
Football Players	$1,169,470 (2000)
Engineers	$61,000
Nurses	$48,240
Carpenters	$36,110
Teachers	$45,370

Source: Sports salaries from www.USATODAY.com/sports/NFL/salaries; http://slam.canoe.ca/BaseballMoneyMatters/salaries. Other salaries from www.bls.gov/oes/2001.

Surely engineers, nurses, and carpenters provide services for society that are more important than the entertainment athletes provide. How can you explain the relative difference between salaries for professional athletes and others?

2. For each of the following changes, specify its effect on the marginal revenue product, marginal factor cost, and earnings of the occupational groups identified by specifying whether there would be an increase (+), decrease (−), or no change (0).

Event	Change in Marginal Revenue Product	Change in Marginal Factor Cost	Change in Earnings
A. Baseball Players: Television networks begin to broadcast major league baseball games.	_____	_____	_____
B. Football Players: New technology allows new football stadiums to be built twice as big as they currently are.	_____	_____	_____
C. Hockey Players: Teams begin to recruit European hockey stars to play in the NHL.	_____	_____	_____
D. Nurses: The time to earn a standard degree in nursing is increased by one and one-half years.	_____	_____	_____

SECTION 14.3
LABOR MARKET EQUILIBRIUM

KEY POINTS

- The equilibrium wage and quantity in competitive labor markets is determined by the intersection of labor demand and labor supply.

- At any wage higher than the equilibrium wage, the quantity of labor supplied exceeds the quantity of labor demanded, resulting in a surplus of labor. In this situation, unemployed workers will be willing to undercut the established wage in order to get jobs, pushing the wage down and returning the market to equilibrium.

- At a wage below the equilibrium level, quantity demanded would exceed quantity supplied, resulting in a labor shortage. In this situation, employers would be forced to offer higher wages in order to hire as many workers as they would like.

- Two important factors can shift the demand curve for labor: Increases in labor productivity or increases in the price of the good such as due to increases in the demand for a firm's product.

- Workers can increase productivity if they have more capital or land with which to work, if technological improvements occur, or if they acquire additional skills or experience. This increase in productivity will increase the marginal product of labor and shift the demand curve for labor to the right. However, if labor productivity falls, then marginal product will fall and the demand curve for labor will shift to the left.

- The greater the demand for the firm's product, the greater the firm's demand for labor or any other variable input. The higher demand for the firm's product increases the firm's marginal revenue, which increases marginal revenue product. If demand for the firm's product falls, the labor demand curve will shift to the left, as marginal revenue product falls.

- Several factors can cause the labor supply curve to shift, including immigration and population growth, the number of hours workers are willing to work at a given wage (worker tastes or preferences), nonwage income, and amenities.

- If new workers enter the labor force, it will shift the labor supply curve to the right. If there are fewer workers in the labor force, it will cause the labor supply curve to shift to the left.

Chapter 14: Supply and Demand in Input Markets

- If people become willing to work more hours at a given wage (due to changes in worker tastes or preferences), the labor supply curve will shift to the right. If they become willing to work fewer hours at a given wage, the labor supply curve will shift to the left.

- Increases in income from sources other than employment can cause the labor supply curve to shift to the left. A decrease in nonwage income might push a person back into the labor force, thus shifting the labor supply curve to the right.

- If there are amenities associated with a job, it will make for a more desirable work atmosphere, *ceteris paribus*. These amenities would cause an increase, or rightward shift, in the supply of labor. If job conditions deteriorate, it would lead to a reduction, or leftward shift, in the labor supply curve.

I   REVIEW

The wage in the labor market is established where the quantity of labor demanded is equal to the quantity of labor _____.

If, at the prevailing wage, the quantity of labor supplied exceeds the quantity of labor demanded, wages will tend to _____.

If the quantity of labor supplied is less than the quantity of labor demanded, wages will tend to _____.

An increase in labor productivity will _____ the marginal product of labor and shift the demand curve for labor to the _____. If labor productivity falls, the demand curve for labor will shift to the _____.

The greater the demand for a firm's product, the _____ the firms demand for labor will be.

An increase in labor demand will shift the demand curve for labor to the _____, while a decrease in labor demand will shift the demand curve for labor to the _____.

If new workers enter the labor force, the labor supply curve will shift to the _____.

If people become willing to work fewer hours at a given wage, the labor supply curve will shift _____.

Increases in income from sources other than employment can cause the labor supply curve to move _____.

If the amenities associated with work improve, the supply of labor is likely to _____.

An increase in labor supply shifts the supply curve to the _____, while a decrease in labor supply shifts the curve to the _____.

II   TRUE/FALSE

_____1. Wages in the labor market are determined in the same way as prices are determined in markets for goods and services.

_____2. A shortage of nurses will put downward pressure on nurses' wages.

_____3. Mindy unexpectedly inherited $1 million from a favorite aunt. This will probably not change Mindy's labor supply.

III   MULTIPLE CHOICE

1. Which of the following would cause the demand for carpenters to increase?
    A) a decrease in immigration
    B) an increase in the demand for housing
    C) an increase in the price of lumber
    D) a decrease in the productivity of carpenters

To answer questions 2, 3, and 4 refer to Exhibit 1.

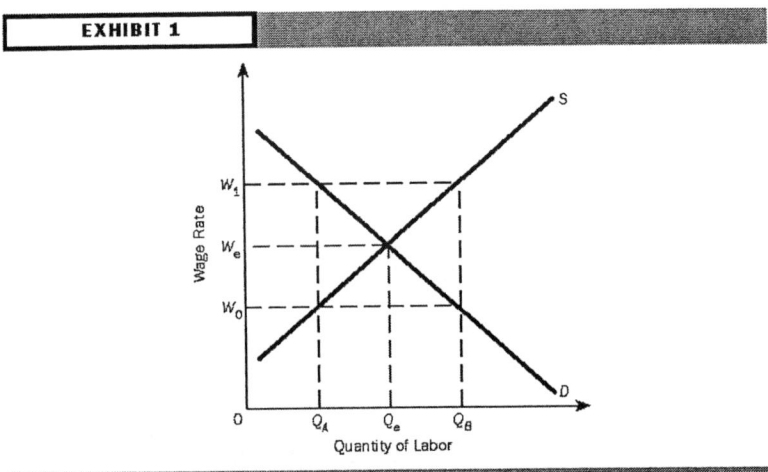

2. At wage rate W_e,
    A) the labor market will be in equilibrium.
    B) there will be a surplus of labor.
    C) there will be a shortage of labor.
    D) the quantity of labor supplied will be Q_A, while the quantity demanded will be Q_B.

3. At wage rate W_0,
    A) the labor market will be in equilibrium.
    B) there will be a surplus of labor.
    C) there will be a shortage of labor.
    D) the quantity of labor supplied will be Q_B, while the quantity demanded will be Q_A.

4. At wage W_1,
    A) the labor market will be in equilibrium.
    B) there will be a surplus of labor.
    C) there will be a shortage of labor.
    D) the quantity of labor supplied will be Q_A, while the quantity demanded will be Q_B.

IV   APPLICATION AND DISCUSSION

Using supply and demand curves, show how each of the following would affect the demand or supply of factory workers in the United States. In each case label the new equilibrium wage and quantity.

1.   Immigration increases dramatically.

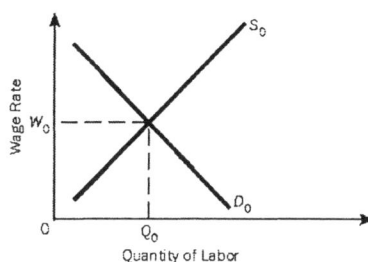

2.   Demand for U.S. manufactured goods declines.

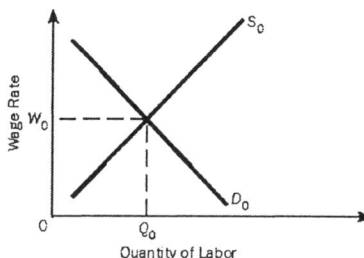

3.   New computerized technology increases productivity of U.S. factory workers.

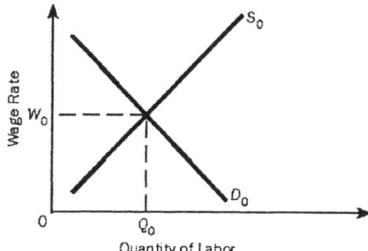

4. U.S. factory owners increase job amenities for workers.

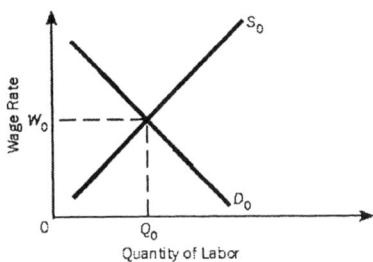

5. U.S. workers want more time off work to spend with their families.

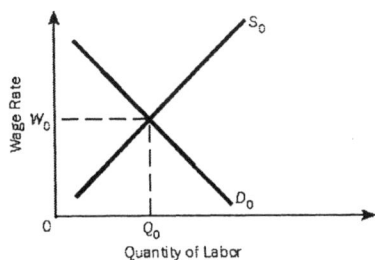

SECTION 14.4

LABOR PRODUCTIVITY AND STANDARD OF LIVING

KEY POINTS

- From the 1940s to the mid-1970s, the real wages of American workers rose an average of almost 3 percent a year, bringing about profound changes in the standard of living. The demand for labor increased faster than the supply.

- Since 1950, the supply of most forms of labor has increased, reflecting both a growing population and an increasing number of women participating in the labor force. At the same time, additions to capital per worker, technological advances, and higher skill levels in the labor force caused increases in marginal revenue product, leading to a rightward shift in the labor demand curve. When the demand effect exceeds the supply effect, as they did from 1950 to 1970, real wages and the equilibrium quantity of workers increase.

- However, real wages only increased 1.4 percent a year from the mid-70's to the mid-90's.

- Several culprits may help explain the productivity slowdown: a slowdown in capital formation; an increase in the number of unskilled and inexperienced workers; and an increase in the relative size of the service sector, where measured productivity tends to be lower (and less accurately measured).

- Real wages and productivity are related. When output per worker (labor productivity) rises, workers are paid more; when output per worker falls, workers are paid less.

Chapter 14: Supply and Demand in Input Markets

I   REVIEW

From the 1940s to the mid-1970s real wages in the United States _____ an average of about three percent per year.

Since 1950, the supply of most forms of labor in the United States has _____, causing the supply curve for labor to shift to the _____.

During the same time, the demand for most forms of labor has _____ even more than supply, causing real wage to _____.

Compared to the 1950–1970 period, the growth of labor productivity from 1970 to present has been _____.

Reasons for the reduction in the rate of worker productivity since the 1970s include a(n) _____ in capital formation, a(n) _____ in labor supply, and a(n) _____ in the proportion of workers in the service sector.

II   TRUE/FALSE

_____1. If the demand for school teachers increases faster than the supply, teachers' wages will rise.

_____2. A decrease in the supply of computer programmers will cause the wage of computer programmers to fall.

_____3. An increase in the supply of labor will always result in a decline in an economy's real wage.

III   MULTIPLE CHOICE

1. Between the 1940s and the mid-1970s, real wages of American workers increased at an average rate of 3 percent per year because
   A) the supply of labor increased faster than the demand.
   B) the demand for labor increased faster than the supply.
   C) the skills of American workers declined.
   D) increases in the wages of government workers offset declining wages of workers in the private sector.

2. Which of the following does *not* contribute to increased worker productivity?
   A) technological advance
   B) increased capital formation
   C) improvements in workers' skills
   D) increased labor supply

IV APPLICATION AND DISCUSSION

The "New Economy" has brought many changes to the labor market. Listed below are a number of changes described as being part of the "New Economy." If other important factors did not change (in other words, *ceteris paribus*), how would each of the following changes affect the U.S. demand for labor, supply of labor, and the real wage? (Indicate the effect of the change as +, 0, or −.)

Change in the Economic Environment	Change in the Demand for Labor	Change in the Supply of Labor	Change in the Real Wage
1. Increased corporate investment in efficiency enhancing equipment and computer software	_____	_____	_____
2. Increased immigration of working-age population	_____	_____	_____
3. Introduction of biotechnology innovations to agriculture	_____	_____	_____
4. Increases in the rate of college graduate in the workforce	_____	_____	_____
5. Laws that require companies to provide workers with ten weeks of vacation a year	_____	_____	_____

SECTION 14.5
LABOR UNIONS

KEY POINTS

- Labor unions are formed to increase their members' wages and to improve working conditions. Workers realize that acting together, as a union of workers, gives them more **collective bargaining power** than acting individually.

- Union membership has fallen from its peak of 25.5 percent in 1953 to about 16 percent today (and less than 10 percent of private-sector employment), reflecting structural shifts in the occupations of American workers.

- Blue-collar manufacturing positions in the North and East have been successfully unionized to a considerable extent. Unionization efforts have been particularly successful in the public sector. However, unions have traditionally found it difficult to organize workers in white-collar jobs, in the service industries, and in the South and West, where most recent job growth has been.

- Labor unions influence the quantity and the wages of union labor hired primarily through the ability to alter the supply of labor services to employers from what would exist if workers acted independently. By raising barriers to entry into a given occupation by restricting membership, unions can reduce the quantity of labor supplied to industry employers, and as a result, increase wages in that occupation.

- If unions are successful in obtaining higher wages, that will also cause employment to fall in the union sector. With a downward-sloping demand curve for labor, higher wages mean that less labor is demanded in the union sector. Those workers that are equally skilled but are unable to find union work will seek nonunion work, thus increasing supply in that sector and, in turn, lowering wages in the nonunion sector. Thus, comparably skilled workers will experience higher wages in the union sector than in the nonunion sector.

- Some argue that unions might actually increase worker productivity by increasing marginal productivity because unions provide a collective voice that workers can use to communicate their discontents more effectively. This might lower the number of union workers that quit their jobs, which is costly for firms. In addition, by handling workers' grievances, unions may increase workers' motivation and morale. Fewer resignations and improved morale could boost productivity. However, it appears that unions tend to lower the profitability of firms, not raise it.

I   REVIEW

When workers act collectively as a _____, they have more _____ power with the employer than they would individually.

The two primary objectives of labor unions are to increase members' _____ and _____ working conditions.

As a proportion of the workforce, union membership has _____ since 1947. However, union efforts have been successful in the _____ sector.

When unions successfully raise wage rates in the unionized sector, the downward-sloping demand curve for labor means that _____ labor will be hired in this sector. Workers released from the unionized firms will _____ the supply of labor to the nonunionized sector causing wages to _____.

Freeman and Medoff argue that unions increase worker productivity by reducing the number of _____ and _____ worker morale. However, the evidence, which suggests that unions tend to _____ the profitability of firms, weakens this argument.

II   TRUE/FALSE

_____1. According to Medoff and Freeman, happy workers are more productive workers, so unions can increase worker productivity by improving morale.

_____2. The primary objective of unions is to increase the number of job opportunities available in an industry.

_____3. While unions represent only a fraction of the unskilled workers in the U.S. labor market, any wage increase won by unionized workers is most likely shared with nonunion, unskilled workers.

_____4. Bargaining individually, stand-up comedians just "didn't get no respect" from employers. By forming the union, United Stand-Up Comedians, and bargaining collectively, they increased bargaining power.

III   MULTIPLE CHOICE

1. Which of the following is *not* a reason that it is harder to unionize in the fast growing service industry?
   A) Service sector jobs are in small firms.
   B) Jobs are more varied, making it harder to negotiate as a group.
   C) Employees work more closely with management.
   D) The service industry is growing most rapidly in the North and East.

2. A large portion of the painting jobs in the county are done by firms with union contracts. If the painters' union wins a 12 percent wage increase, what is most likely to happen in the nonunionized part of the painters' labor market?
   A) Nonunion painters will also get 12 percent wage increases.
   B) There will be no change because these sectors are not connected.
   C) Wage rates in the nonunion sector are likely to fall.
   D) Nonunion painters will find work for a firm with a union contract.

3. If unions increased worker productivity, we would *not* expect to find that _____ were(was) _____ in the union sector of an industry.
   A) profits; lower
   B) costs; higher
   C) quits; higher
   D) morale; lower

IV   APPLICATION AND DISCUSSION

1. To gain new members, unions have begun to focus on lower paying sectors of the economy. The low-wage sectors include workers in nursing homes, hospitals, hotels, and agriculture. Unions have also attempted to organize workers just off of welfare. Assume for now that all of these workers are subject to minimum-wage laws and are paid the legal minimum. What will happen in the low-wage sector of the labor market if unions are successful in organizing a portion of the industry and raising wages?

SECTION 14.6
THE MARKETS FOR LAND AND CAPITAL

KEY POINTS

- **Economic rent** is the price paid for land or any other factor that has a fixed supply—a perfectly inelastic supply curve. The supply of land is perfectly inelastic and not at all responsive to prices. There will be as much land available at a zero price as at a very high price.

- The price of using land—its rental price—is determined by demand and supply considerations. Changes in the demand for land will change the rental value. Because the supply curve is completely inelastic, the demand curve determines the price of the land. Only changes in the demand for land will change the price of land.

- The demand for land is derived from the demand for the products being produced.

- The concept of economic rent does not only apply to land. It is a very powerful tool to understanding labor. Differences in quality between productive resources give rise to variations in productivity and to variations in compensation.

- Labor resources that are in highly limited supply and in great demand will command a large amount in compensation. Those who receive their income because of a distinct, unique skill are collecting economic rent—compensation for a resource whose supply is perfectly inelastic over the relevant range of prices. Examples include star athletes, famous surgeons, and music stars.

- Resources like capital can be "leased" or "rented" for some stipulated period of time. Following the law of demand, the lower the rental price of a machine, the lower the cost of production when using it, and the greater the quantity of machines demanded.

- Following the law of supply, the greater the rental price of machines, the more willing owners of those machines are to supply them to entrepreneurs.

Chapter 14: Supply and Demand in Input Markets

- The price of borrowed funds is called the **interest rate.** At lower interest rates, the cost of financing the purchase of a machine is lower. At lower interest rates, capital costs are lower, and the quantity of funds demanded is greater.

- The lenders of funds will derive greater income the greater the interest rate, so the benefits to them of making a loan increase as interest rates (the price of funds) rise. Thus, the quantity of funds supplied is positively related to interest rates.

- The intersection of the upward-sloping supply curve for capital and the downward-sloping demand curve for capital determines the price of capital.

- We have treated the labor, capital and land markets independently. In reality, these markets are interdependent. For example, if wages rise and/or the rental price of capital falls, machines might be substituted for some workers.

I   REVIEW

The three productive _____ are labor, land, and capital.

The price of using land is determined by the _____ and demand for land.

The _____ for land is the marginal revenue product of land.

The supply of land can be thought of as fixed or perfectly _____. In this case, the price of land will be determined by changes in the _____ for land. Economic _____ is the price paid to any factor that has a fixed supply.

In the market for land, an increase in the prices of the commodities that are produced with land will _____ the demand for land and the _____ price of land.

Differences between the types of land and other resources result in variations in resource productivity. This results in variations in _____.

People who receive their income because of a distinct, unique skill, or talent are collecting economic _____ since they represent a resource whose supply is perfectly inelastic. _____ in various fields earn high salaries because there is a great demand for their services and their unique talents are in limited supply.

Economic rent represents a payment that the resource owner receives above its _____ cost.

Capital can be _____or borrowed for a stipulated period of time. The cost of borrowing these factors is the _____ price.

When entrepreneurs buy capital, they often borrow funds. The price of these borrowed funds is the _____ rate. The yearly interest cost of borrowing an amount of money equals the interest rate _____ the loan amount. The cost of buying capital will _____ when the interest rate rises and decline when the interest rate _____.

The interest rate is determined by the _____ of the supply and demand for capital. The demand curve for capital is downward sloping, reflecting the decline in the marginal revenue _____ of capital as more is used.

Resource markets are _____. Changes in the price of one resource may result in the increased demand for others if they are _____.

II   TRUE/FALSE

_____1. Since the supply of land is perfectly inelastic, the interaction of supply and demand has no role in land markets.

_____2. When Asian economies suffer a recession, their demand for American oranges declines and the rental price of farmland that can grow oranges in the United States will fall.

_____3. An increase in the wage rate has no effect on the market for capital.

III   MULTIPLE CHOICE

1. Frank Smith, the star first baseman for the Philadelphia Phillies baseball team, earns $5 million a year. He described his love of the game this way, "I love playing so much I'd play even if they only paid me $300,000 a year." What is the difference between his salary and the $300,000 called?
   A) economic rent
   B) opportunity cost
   C) excess earnings
   D) marginal revenue product

2. Harrison Ford earns approximately $25 million for each film he makes. If he was not an actor, Ford would pursue his career as a carpenter. Which of the following is a true statement about his earnings?
   A) This is purely economic rent.
   B) This represents his marginal revenue product.
   C) This is his opportunity cost.
   D) This is less than he could make as a carpenter, his next best alternative.

3. Guy and his sister, Dolly, decide not to open "Guy's and Dolly's Espresso Emporium" because only the local loan shark, Nathan Toledo, will loan them the $10,000 needed to buy the coffee machine. Nathan would charge 50 percent interest. What can we say about Guy and Dolly's expectation about the coffee business?
   A) They expect the machine's yearly marginal revenue product will be more than $5,000.
   B) They expect the machine's yearly marginal revenue product will be less than $5,000.
   C) They expect the machine's yearly marginal resource cost will be $10,000.
   D) They expect to get burnt working with Nathan Toledo.

4. What best explains the negative slope of the demand for capital curve?
   A) the law of less productive assets
   B) the law of supply and demand
   C) the law of diminishing marginal product
   D) the law of the minimum returns

IV   APPLICATION AND DISCUSSION

Nineteenth-century economist, Henry George, proposed a tax on economic rent as a "Single Tax" that could fund government. While George's idea was to tax land, there are many sources of economic rent that could be taxed today. If the United States established an economic rent tax on land and the incomes of stars, how would it change the behavior of landowners, movie stars, athletes, and other rent earners?

Questions

1. Would an economist agree with Mr. Lowell that "No hockey player is worth $3 million?"

2. How do you think Larry "The Shark" contributed to the Wolves' revenues when he played for them?

CHAPTER 15
INCOME DISTRIBUTION, POVERTY, AND HEALTH CARE

SECTION 15.1
INCOME DISTRIBUTION

KEY POINTS

- The ultimate purpose of producing goods and services is to satisfy the material wants of people.

- On balance, the evidence suggests that inequality of money income in the United States declined from 1935 to 1950, then remained rather stable until 1980. Since then, the distribution of income has become less equal. However, if we consider age distribution, institutional factors, and in-kind transfer programs, it is safe to say that the income distribution is considerably more equal than it appears.

- Failing to take into consideration differences in age, certain demographic factors, institutional factors, and government redistributive activities have all been identified as elements that influence the income distribution data and suggest that we might be overstating inequality.

- At any moment in time, middle-age persons tend to have higher incomes than younger and older persons because they are at an age when their productivity is at a peak and they are participating in the labor force to a greater extent. The increased proportion of Americans that are either very young or very old has tended to increase the observed inequality in the distribution of income.

Chapter 15: Income, Poverty, and Healthcare

- Demographic trends, like the increased number of divorced couples and the rise of two-income families (and DINKS—Double Income, No Kids), have also caused the measured distribution of income (measured in terms of household or family income) to appear more unequal.

- The impact of increased government activity should be considered in evaluating the measured income distribution. Government-imposed taxes and government programs affect different income groups differently. When taxes and in-kind income are included, many economists conclude that they have served to reduce levels of inequality significantly from the levels suggested by aggregate income statistics.

- While the distribution of current income is an important piece of information, it is also critical to know how much movement goes on between different income levels. The people that make up a given income group are not always the same people because there is substantial movement between income groups.

- Reasons some people make more income than others include differences in age, skill, education, training, and preferences toward risk and leisure.

- Income inequality is greater in the United States and United Kingdom than in Sweden and Japan. However, many developed countries have more equal distributions of income than developing countries.

- While income inequality within nations is often substantial, it is far less than income inequality among nations. A majority of income inequality reflects differences in living standards among countries rather than disparities within nations.

I   REVIEW

The proportion of income received by the top 5 percent of Americans _____ after 1935, but has gone _____ since the 1980s.

Since the 1980s, the share of measured income received by the lowest fifth of families has _____.

At any moment in time, middle-aged persons tend to have _____ incomes than younger or older persons.

Demographic trends like an _____ in the number of divorced couples and an _____ in the number of two-income families have caused the measured distribution of income to appear more unequal.

It has been argued that state-subsidized higher education has benefited the _____ and middle-income groups more than the _____.

On the other hand, government programs like food stamps and school lunch programs benefit the _____ rather than the _____.

If we consider age distribution, institutional factors, and in-kind transfers, the actual distribution of income in America is more _____ than it appears.

Generational studies suggest there is considerable income _____ between generations. In addition, most Americans experience significant year to year _____ in their economic well being.

Productivity and income are _____ related.

Income inequality is _____ in the United States and Great Britain than in Sweden and Japan.

The greatest disparities in income are found in _____-income countries like Mexico and India.

Income inequality within nations is far _____ than income inequality among nations.

II   TRUE/FALSE

_____1. Yin, a workaholic, is likely to have a higher income than his twin brother Yang, who prefers to read the tabloids and watch TV.

_____2. Tina, who washes windows at one-story strip malls, is likely to have a higher income than her twin Tanya, who washes windows on skyscrapers.

_____3. Paul, a worker whose income currently places him among the poorest 20 percent of Americans, is destined to remain in that lowest quintile for the next decade.

III   MULTIPLE CHOICE

1. On average, middle-aged people tend to have higher incomes than younger or older people because they
    A) receive more money from the government than younger or older people.
    B) are at an age where their productivity is at its peak.
    C) participate in the labor force to a lesser extant than the young or the old.
    D) are subject to lower rates of taxation than younger or older workers.

2. Demographic trends that cause the measured distribution of income to become more unequal include all of the following *except*
    A) the increased number of divorced couples.
    B) an increase in the proportion of the population that is either very young or very old.
    C) an increase in the number of two-income families.
    D) a decrease in the proportion of women in the labor force.

3. Which of the following government programs are actually likely to aid the rich rather than the poor?
    A) food stamps
    B) school lunch programs
    C) subsidies to airports
    D) housing subsidies

IV   APPLICATION AND DISCUSSION

Use the three factors that the book identifies as accounting for some income differences—*Skills and Human Capital*, *Worker Preferences*, and *Job Preferences*—to try and explain the following earnings differences between men. For example, which one or more of these factors explains why engineers make more than farm workers?

	2001 Median Hourly Earnings	Explanation
Engineers	$29.33	
Farm Workers	$8.56	
Police Officers and Detectives	$20.17	
Cooks	$9.24	
Engineers	$29.33	
Police Officers	$20.17	

Surgeons	$65.89
Medical and Clinical Lab Technicians	$14.52
Computer Programmers	$30.23
Sales Workers, Retail and Personal Services	$10.06
Bus Drivers	$14.15
Waiters and Waitresses	$7.36

Source: U.S. Bureau of Labor Statistics, "National Occupational Employment and Wage Estimates," *Occupational Employment Statistics*, www.bls.gov/oes/2001.

SECTION 15.2

THE PROS AND CONS OF INCOME EQUALITY

KEY POINTS

- Because of the difficulty of comparing the welfare of one person with another, it is impossible to "prove" that a given income distribution is better than another.

- Political and social changes in the past century or two have generally worked to reduce income inequality.

- The economic theory that is supportive of policies of income redistribution is derived from the principle of diminishing marginal utility, where increases in income generate less additional happiness (utility) at higher levels of income. Taking from the rich and giving to the poor could increase society's total utility if the rich family loses less utility than the poor family gains from the redistribution. The theoretical argument favoring income redistribution is based on the assumption that people are alike in how they experience diminishing marginal utility from increasing income, a proposition impossible to prove.

- Arguments against a radical redistribution of income to eliminate virtually all inequality include the equity argument. That is, some would argue that it is not "fair" to take most of the income of hard-working, talented persons who earn high incomes, particularly when some of it is given to persons who perhaps are shiftless and lazy.

I   REVIEW

Political and social changes in the last century have worked to _____ income inequality.

However, it is impossible to prove that one income distribution is _____ than another, because it is impossible to _____ the welfare of one person with another.

The principle of _____ marginal utility can be used to support policies that redistribute income. This principle suggests that increases in income will generate _____ additional happiness the higher the level of income.

If people have similar _____ for income, the _____ in utility that results from taking a given amount of income from high-income groups will be less than the _____ utility which results from giving this income to low-income groups.

The _____ that individuals have similar preferences is critical for this argument, since we cannot make utility _____ among individuals.

Chapter 15: Income, Poverty, and Healthcare

One argument against policies to redistribute income is that it is not _____ to take income from one group and give it to another.

II   TRUE/FALSE

_____1. All of the citizens of Stepford have the exact same preferences for income. If the Stepfordian government taxes the rich and gives this money to the poor, total happiness will be increased.

_____2. Government policies that redistribute income from the rich to the poor will always improve the nations welfare.

_____3. Robin Hood stole from the rich and gave to the poor. This type of redistribution effort will always improve the long-term welfare of the poor.

III   MULTIPLE CHOICE

1. The principle of diminishing marginal utility is not enough to guarantee that transferring income from the rich to the poor will increase society's utility because
    A) diminishing marginal utility does not hold for everyone.
    B) the rich get richer and the poor get poorer.
    C) the total utility of the rich would still be greater.
    D) it is difficult to make utility comparisons among individuals.

2. Steven is running for president promising to redistribute income and encourage economic growth. Why might these goals conflict?
    A) Taxing the incomes of the rich to transfer to the poor will result in the poor saving less.
    B) Taxing the incomes of the rich to transfer to the poor will result in the rich saving more.
    C) Taxing the incomes of the rich to transfer to the poor will provide disincentives for work and capital accumulation.
    D) Taxing the incomes of the rich to transfer to the poor will provide incentives for buying more from other countries.

IV   APPLICATION AND DISCUSSION

1. Surf City has just elected a new mayor, "The Dude." The Mayor has proposed a tax on the one business in town, "Surf City Donut Shop" to raise revenues to provide lunch money for the town's surfing population. "The Dude" says this policy is fair because the town's income is unfairly distributed since Donut Bob, the shop's owner, is the only person in town earning any income. Is the policy fair? Evaluate the mayor's argument.

SECTION 15.3
THE ECONOMICS OF DISCRIMINATION

KEY POINTS

- **Job-entry discrimination** is where a worker is denied employment on the basis of some factor without regard to the productivity of the worker. **Wage discrimination** is where workers are given employment at wages lower than that of other workers on some basis other than productivity differences.

- In a world where sex and race have absolutely no bearing whatsoever on the employment circumstances of persons (e.g., talent, education, willingness to work, move, . . .), every occupation would, apart from random variations, have a work force with the same sex and race proportions as the population at large.

- A strong statistical correlation exists between lifetime earnings and years of schooling.

- Merely demonstrating that wages are lower for blacks and females does not in itself prove wage discrimination, although it is consistent with the notion that discrimination occurs. However, if occupational and wage differentials are not caused by discrimination, what are the causes? Several scholars have developed statistical models that argue that a great deal of the earnings differentials across the sexes and races can be explained by differences in productivity. In other words, employers hire and pay workers roughly an amount equal to their perceived contributions (marginal revenue product).

- An environmental explanation of productivity differences does not rule out discrimination, but rather argues that past discrimination's perverse influences on the environment of women and nonwhites has caused them to have an inferior endowment of human capital now, even if present-day employers were color- and sex-blind in terms of paying workers.

- It might appear that discrimination is totally inconsistent with rational utility maximization. To maximize profits, a firm should minimize costs by hiring the best persons available per dollar of wage expenditure, regardless of the age, sex, race, or other attribute of the worker.

- Discrimination may reflect information costs. Based on past experience, race or sex may be used as a screening device to narrow the list of job candidates, because it costs money and time to evaluate the prospects of every applicant.

- In competitive industries, firms that discriminate may lose out ultimately to those firms that do not. The nondiscriminating firm can hire the unfavored but equally competent workers and have a cost advantage, allowing it to undercut discriminating competitors' prices and either force them out of business or make them change their hiring practices. In the long run, competition has the potential to reduce discrimination.

- The primary means used to address economic discrimination in our country is affirmative action programs, in which employers are strongly encouraged to hire more minority group workers in occupations where those groups are now relatively under-represented and to correct wage and salary inequities. There is some evidence that these various efforts have met with some success. Still, the economic differences between different races and sexes are large.

- Affirmative action job hiring programs are controversial. Affirmative action increases the probability that some persons will be hired on some basis other than productivity. While this may be desirable from the standpoint of equalizing opportunities between demographic groups, it also can serve to lower the output of society as a whole and profits to firms.

I   REVIEW

When someone is denied employment on the basis of some noneconomic factor like race, religion, or gender, it is called job-entry _____.

Chapter 15: Income, Poverty, and Healthcare

When some workers are paid lower wages than others because of something other than productivity differences, it is called _____ discrimination.

Women earn _____ than men in most job categories and white men earn _____ than black men.

White males in general have acquired _____ years of schooling than black males.

Merely demonstrating that wages are lower for blacks and females does not in itself prove wage _____.

Several scholars have developed statistical models that argue that a great deal of the earnings differentials across the sexes and races can be explained by differences in _____.

The primary means used to address economic discrimination in the United States is _____ action programs, in which employers are encouraged to hire more _____ group workers in occupations where those groups are under-represented.

II   TRUE/FALSE

_____1. The fact that there are fewer male nurses than females is proof that discrimination exists in this occupation.

_____2. If Marla's wages are 10 percent higher than Antonio's, economists would call it "wage discrimination," even if she were 10 percent more productive than he.

_____3. There is a strong, positive correlation between educational attainment and lifetime earnings.

III   MULTIPLE CHOICE

1. When a construction firm doesn't hire Jane the carpenter simply because she is female, it is called
    A) wage discrimination.
    B) job-entry discrimination.
    C) affirmative action.
    D) fascism.

2. Which of the following statements is *not* consistent with the "environmental explanation" of wages and productivity?
    A) "Women are more likely than men to leave the labor force to care for children and, hence, have less work experience than men."
    B) "Blacks and other minorities don't get the same quality education as whites."
    C) "Boys are more likely than girls to receive moral and financial support from their families to attend college."
    D) "Employers discriminate systematically against blacks and women."

3. Captain Ahab thinks that hiring women to work on fishing boats is bad luck, while Captain Bob has no such prejudice. Why might this give Captain Bob a profit advantage?
    A) Bob can apply to the government for assistance since he hires women.
    B) Bob will be able to increase his utility because of his "taste for discrimination."
    C) Bob will be able to hire women sailors for less since discrimination limits the opportunities open to them.
    D) Bob will save money by not screening potential employees by using gender as a proxy for quality worker.

IV APPLICATION AND DISCUSSION

After all of the legal and social effort to end wage discrimination, the median weekly earnings for full-time female workers remains approximately seventy-five percent of the earnings of a similar male worker. One fact, which is often lost in the discussion of this "wage gap," is that the gap has been closing over time. In 1963 when the Equal Pay Act, which outlawed wage discrimination between men and women, was passed women earned less than 60 percent of the equivalent male.

Use the three factors that are identified in Section 15.1, *Skills and Human Capital, Worker Preferences*, and *Job Preferences*, to explain the change in women's earnings as a percent of men's over this period. What has happened since 1963 to the amount of education and training that women have gotten? To their attitudes about their work? To the kinds of occupations they enter? Use the table below to organize your answer.

Explaining the Change in Women's Relative Earnings

A) Skills and Human Capital:

B) Worker Preferences:

C) Job Preferences:

SECTION 15.4
POVERTY

KEY POINTS

- The federal government measures poverty by using a set of money income thresholds that vary by family size. If the family's total income is less than the established threshold—the **poverty line**—it is considered poor. The **poverty rate** is the proportion of persons who fall below that absolute standard.

- The poverty rate for the United States is currently set at three times the cost of providing a nutritionally adequate diet—slightly less than $20,000 for a family of four. The poverty rate may overstate the level of poverty because it does not include noncash benefits, such as public housing, Medicaid, and food stamps.

- One cure for poverty, as defined by some absolute income or standard of living criterion, is economic growth. The greater the rate of economic growth, the more rapidly poverty will be eradicated.

- Many "poor" individuals in the United States, using the official definition, would be considered well off, even "rich" in many less-developed countries.

- Rather than being classified by an ability to buy some specific basket of goods and services, poverty is often thought of as a relative income concept. (A person is "poor" if his or her income is low relative to the incomes of most other persons in the same geographical area.)

- Using definitions of poverty based on relative income measures, as economic growth proceeds, the income necessary to avoid being considered poor by this measure increases. Using this definition, then, poverty cannot be eradicated by economic growth, but only by income redistribution.

- In the U.S. the progressive income tax system redistributes income and reduces disparities among individuals.

Chapter 15: Income, Poverty, and Healthcare

- Transfer payments also redistribute income. These are payments to individuals in which no goods and services are exchanged. Examples include social security, Medicare, Unemployment Compensation, and Welfare programs.

- Government revenues are also used to subsidize services for the less affluent.

I   REVIEW

The poverty rate in the United States is defined as the _____ of the population who fail to earn a minimum _____ income standard.

The income standard varies with family _____.

Poverty rates in the United States have generally _____ since the 1960s. However, during recessions as unemployment _____, the poverty rate also tends to _____.

Unless lower income groups do not share at all in the rising income, one cure for poverty as defined by the absolute income criterion is economic _____.

An alternative definition of poverty compares incomes between people and considers a person poor if their income is low _____ to others is the same geographical area.

Poverty defined using relative income cannot be eliminated by economic _____, only by income _____.

Government uses taxes, transfer payments and subsidies to _____ income.

II   TRUE/FALSE

_____ 1. In 1964, the U.S. Department of Agriculture established the poverty threshold as the cost of a family economy food plan multiplied by three. This index provides a measure of relative poverty.

_____ 2. In Transferia, any family with an income of less than the country's average income is considered poor. Rose, the new President of Transferia, has little chance of fulfilling her pledge to eliminate poverty in the next decade by promoting economic growth.

_____ 3. All transfer payments redistribute money from the rich to the poor.

III   MULTIPLE CHOICE

1. In the United States, there are a number of programs that provide goods and services, like food, medical care, and housing to the poor. How should these programs affect the income standard for defining absolute poverty?
   A) The income standard should increase since it costs money to provide these goods.
   B) The income standard should decrease since it takes less income meet a minimum standard of living.
   C) The income standard shouldn't change because these programs provide goods and services, not money.
   D) The income standard should change because these programs will affect the relative measure of poverty.

2. Which of the following government programs is most likely to eliminate relative poverty?
   A) promoting economic growth
   B) providing college scholarships to the country's smartest students
   C) providing incentives to increase the level of capital formation
   D) transferring income from the richest to the poorest citizens

IV   APPLICATION AND DISCUSSION

1. How will each of the following changes affect the level of absolute and relative poverty? Place a (+) in the appropriate box for an increase; a (–) in the appropriate box for a decrease; and a (0) if the effect is indeterminate.

Change in Economic Environment	Change in Relative Poverty	Change in Absolute Poverty
With no changes in income, the cost of food and housing increases by 25 percent.	_____	_____
The stock market booms and the 45 percent of Americans who have invested in the market experience significant income gains.	_____	_____
Government transfer and tax programs reduce the difference between the highest and lowest incomes in the United States.	_____	_____
The economy grows by 6 percent during the year.	_____	_____

SECTION 15.1
HEALTHCARE

KEY POINTS

- Like the production of any other good or service, healthcare involves the utilization of scarce resources. Not only must the healthcare sector compete with other sectors for resources, but those resources must be allocated across patients facing vastly different circumstances.

- The United States spends more money on healthcare per person and as a percentage of national income than any other industrialized nation.

- The utilization of medical care involves trade-offs. Scarce resources allocated toward the production of health services cannot be used in the production of other goods and services.

- Investment in healthcare bears similarities to investment in human or physical capital. By promoting health and removing disabilities, medical care may (1) improve the productivity of workers on the job and reduce missed workdays; and (2) extend the average number of years of participation by people in the labor force.

- Both the demand for and supply of healthcare have increased over the last several decades. The increase in demand for medical care has been particularly significant due to changes in income, insurance coverage, and population demographics. Consequently, the price of medical care has risen at the same time the utilization of services has increased.

- Rising U.S. real income has contributed to the increase in demand for medical services. Most healthcare services are normal goods.

- The quantity of medical care demanded appears to be quite insensitive to changes in price. Healthcare is considered a necessity with few good substitutes, particularly when it comes to serious illness

- The health services market differs from many others in that, due to insurance, the consumer often pays only a fraction of the direct cost of care. Third-party payers, such as insurance companies or health maintenance organizations, play significant roles in this industry, which alter the behavior of both patients and providers.

- In addition to increasing the quantity of healthcare demanded by reducing price, insurance alters the incentive of patients in other ways. Insurance reduces the cost to the insured of undertaking risky activities. This creates what economists call a "moral hazard" problem.

- Insurance may pose additional problems for the healthcare industry. A situation of asymmetric information exists whenever patients know more about their own health status than prospective insurers. This is known as "adverse selection" because the chronically ill are more likely to demand health insurance than those who are in good health.

- The aging of the U.S. population is an additional factor that explains the increase in demand for healthcare. The elderly consume a disproportionate share of healthcare services (three to four times as much as the rest of the population).

- The supply of healthcare has increased slowly since 1960. The number of providers has increased but has not kept up with the demand for medical services. There has been an increase in the cost of medical education and training as well as a greater use of high-cost technological equipment in the healthcare industry.

- Medical research and technological progress has vastly improved the quality of medical care. Innovative therapies help reduce disability, improve health, and prolong life. Some innovations undoubtedly reduce the overall cost of healthcare. Insured patients who bear a small fraction of healthcare costs naturally desire the best possible care, contributing to a rise in healthcare costs that far exceeds the average level of inflation.

- Healthcare markets are imperfectly competitive for several reasons, including the presence of legal or administrative barriers to entry, economies of scale, collusion, and restrictions on advertising.

- In Canada, where a national healthcare program controls prices and strictly rations care, conditions of excess demand for surgery prevail.

I   REVIEW

Healthcare involves the utilization of _____ resources; resources used for healthcare can't be used to produce other goods and services. Decisions about the allocation of scarce resources to healthcare uses are _____ because of the ethical and equity considerations.

The United States spends _____ money per capita on healthcare than other industrialized nations. The United States also spends a larger share of its _____ and this share has been increasing since 1960.

Healthcare can be thought of as a type of _____ capital investment increasing the quality and quantity of labor.

The demand for medical services in the United States has increased because our real income has increased and healthcare services are _____ goods. The demand has also increased as a result of the _____ of the U.S. population, since the elderly consume a _____ share of healthcare services.

Most consumers in the United States do not pay the _____ cost of healthcare because of third-party payers, such as insurance companies. _____ provide the majority of this insurance coverage. Insurance lowers the cost consumers pay for using healthcare services and _____ the expenditure on healthcare services. Insurance creates a _____ hazard by lowering the cost of risky behavior; it may increase this behavior that requires more healthcare services.

Chapter 15: Income, Poverty, and Healthcare

Health maintenance organizations combine the provision and the _____ of healthcare. HMOs attempt to control the _____ of healthcare by attempting to control a patient's choice of treatment options.

Innovations in the healthcare industry may _____ as well as lower costs by introducing treatment options where none had been available.

Healthcare markets are _____ competitive because of the existence of barriers to entry that may be justified as ways to protect the patient from inferior quality. Economies of _____ in healthcare provision may also create "natural monopolies" in some areas. Costs will be _____ because of the lack of competition.

In situations where prices are controlled, such as in the Canadian healthcare sector, there will be _____.

II   TRUE/FALSE

_____1. Healthcare is an essential service, so while insurance may reduce the cost of medical services to consumers, it will not change the way they behave.

_____2. When doctors operate on a fee-for-service basis, they have an incentive to make recommendations that increase the demand for healthcare.

_____3. Costs associated with organ transplants are kept low by preventing the trade in body parts.

III   MULTIPLE CHOICE

1. Asymmetric information about the health status of individuals poses a problem for insurance companies. Which of the following is an example of the problem of adverse selection?
   A) Insurance reduces the cost of risky behavior, so people do risky things that increase their use of medical services.
   B) Doctors, paid on a fee-for-service basis, prescribe adverse treatment that people will follow because the doctor knows more than the patient.
   C) Insurance companies choose the inexpensive but adverse types of medical innovations to save money.
   D) The chronically ill are more likely to buy health insurance than the healthy, which will increase the cost of insurance.

2. All but which one of the following changes would be responsible for increasing the U.S. expenditure on healthcare?
   A) the introduction of cholesterol reducing drugs
   B) rising per capita incomes
   C) the aging of the baby boom population
   D) employer provided health insurance

3. Strict licensing requirements for doctors, nurses, and dentists have what effect on the medical services market?
   A) decrease the supply and increase the price of services
   B) increase the supply and increase the price of services
   C) decrease the demand and increase the price of services
   D) increase the demand and increase the price of services

IV   APPLICATION AND DISCUSSION

Governments often make the mistake and assume that healthcare industry problems are the result of market imperfections that call for some type of market intervention. But these problems may simply result from poor incentives. How does each of the following changes affect incentives in the healthcare industry? Do you think each change would reduce or increase healthcare costs?

A) Employers introduce "Wellness Programs" that compensate employees for adopting healthy lifestyles.

B) Insurance companies change the way they reimburse dentists, paying them by the cavity filled instead of by the visit.

C) Instead of paying a portion of the fee for medical service, insurance companies pay a set amount for each type of illness or procedure, which is independent of the actual amount the consumer pays.

D) State's abandon laws that mandate the treatments that any employers' health insurance must include.

E) Congress eliminates patent protection on new medicines so that companies do not have a monopoly on the drugs they develop.

Questions

1. Why is Julie's wage rate higher than Carmen's even though they both work behind the counter at fast food restaurants?

2. Who do you think is happier with her job, Julie or Carmen?

CHAPTER 16
THE ENVIRONMENT

SECTION 16.1 NEGATIVE EXTERNALITIES AND POLLUTION

SECTION 16.2 PUBLIC POLICY AND THE ENVIRONMENT

SECTION 16.3 PROPERTY RIGHTS

SECTION 16.1
NEGATIVE EXTERNALITIES AND POLLUTION

KEY POINTS

- Whenever an economic activity has benefits or costs that are shared by persons other than the demanders or suppliers of a good or service, an externality is involved. **Negative externalities** exist anytime the **social costs** of producing a good or service exceed the private costs.

- When a negative externality is involved, the marginal social costs of production are higher than the firm's private costs by the costs that spillover to other members of society from the pollution produced. The firm does not pay all of the social costs, and therefore creates too much output and too much pollution.

- The optimal output occurs where the marginal social costs are equal to the marginal social benefits.

- When negative externalities are **internalized**—persons who incur the costs of pollution are compensated—firms produce less output and charge higher prices.

- It is generally accepted that in the absence of intervention, the market mechanism will underproduce goods and services with positive externalities and overproduce those with negative externalities. But the exact extent of these market misallocations is quite difficult to establish in the real world because the divergence between social and private costs and benefits is often difficult to measure. No one really knows because no market fully measures those costs. Indeed, the costs are partly **non-pecuniary,** meaning that no outlay of money occurs.

Chapter 16: The Environment

I   REVIEW

When people other than those making the demand and supply decisions share the benefits or costs of an activity, an _____ occurs.

A _____ externality occurs when a decision imposes costs on people other than those making the decisions about production or consumption.

The costs that accrue to the total population are called _____ costs. Those costs that are incurred by the producer or consumer who makes the decision are called _____ costs.

When a negative externality exists, social costs are _____ than private costs.

The amount of a good or service producers choose to produce reflects _____ and demand. When there are only negative externalities, the demand curve represents the marginal social _____ of the good while the supply curve represents the marginal _____ costs.

For society, the optimal level of output occurs where the marginal social cost _____ the marginal social benefits for the last unit produced.

When there are negative externalities in the production of a good, output will be _____ than and price will be _____ than the optimal level.

One reason the extent of any negative externality is difficult to measure is that certain external costs may be _____ and not involve money.

II   TRUE/FALSE

_____1. Mac produces pork. His hogs smell. Because he is a perfect competitor who produces the output where price equals marginal costs, Mac always produces the optimal amount of pork.

_____2. Paul and Polly both own homes in the neighborhood that borders the city's International Airport. Paul moved into his house before the airport was built. Polly moved into her home after the airport was built. Even though they both suffer from the airport noise, only Paul has not been compensated for suffering the cost of the airport noise.

_____3. Che's School of Latin Dance is located in a room above Edna's English Tea Room. Che is missing an opportunity for profits by not compensating Edna for the costs his dance classes impose on her business.

III   MULTIPLE CHOICE

1.   If the government is able to force a firm to internalize the external cost of its production, we would expect to see
   A) the firm produce more to make up for the higher private cost.
   B) the firm reduce the price it charges to compensate for the higher private cost.
   C) the firm produce less and charge more because marginal private cost have increased.
   D) the firm would produce more and charge a higher price because marginal social cost has increased.

2.   We know that when Adam's House of Ribs serves one more dinner, Adam pays $5 in extra labor costs and $1.33 in extra utility costs. The extra smoke from the cook pit also increases the cleaning bills in the neighborhood by $.45. How much is the social cost of a rib dinner?
     A) $.45
     B) $6.33
     C) $1.78
     D) $6.78

3.   Which of the following is the best example of a nonpecuniary external cost?
     A) wages paid to workers in a steel mill
     B) the medical costs associated with increased asthma caused by steel mill pollution
     C) the cost of repainting cars because of steel mill pollution damage
     D) the cost to steel mill neighbors of suffering from the obnoxious odors from the pollution.

IV   APPLICATION AND DISCUSSION

The source of negative externalities is not always a bad thing. Often negative externalities result from activities that seem good or even noble. In the following table, identify the external cost of the following actions and explain why each will impose negative externalities on the identified group.

Action	Affected Group	External Cost
A mother reads a Dr. Seuss book to her children in a doctor's waiting room	The other patients in the waiting room	_____
An entrepreneur opens a flavored popcorn stand next to an espresso cart. (Hint: The popcorn smells of the various flavors.)	Owners of the espresso cart	_____
A church decides to celebrate the holiday by playing Christmas music on its external speakers twenty-four hours a day.	The neighbors of the church	_____
Your neighbor plants fifteen large deciduous trees right on the border between your house and hers. (Hint: Think fall.)	You	_____

SECTION 16.2
PUBLIC POLICY AND THE ENVIRONMENT

KEY POINTS

- While measuring externalities, both negative and positive, is often nearly impossible, that does not necessarily mean that it is better to ignore the externality and allow the market solution to operate. The market solution will almost certainly result in excessive output by polluters unless some intervention occurs.

- One approach to dealing with externalities is to require private enterprise to produce their output in a manner that would reduce the negative externality below the amount that would persist in the absence of regulation. Using the compliance standards approach, a regulatory agency such as the EPA identifies and then enforces a standard equal to the maximum amount of pollution that firms can produce per unit of output per year. The standards, then, force companies to find less pollution-intensive ways of producing goods and services.

- It would appear that the compliance standards approach to limiting key pollutants has led to some reduction in pollution levels from what would otherwise be the case.

- In many respects, a clean environment is no different from any other desirable good. In a world of scarcity, we can increase our consumption of a clean environment only by giving up something else. Only by considering the additional cost as well as the additional benefit of increased consumption of all goods, including clean air and water, can decisions on the desirable combination of goods to consume be properly made.

- Pollution elimination, like nearly everything else, is subject to diminishing returns. A large amount of pollution can be eliminated fairly inexpensively initially, but getting rid of still more pollution may prove more costly. Likewise, it is also possible that the benefits from eliminating "crud" from the air might decline as more and more pollution is eliminated. Some pollution elimination initially might have a profound impact, but as pollution levels fall, further elimination of pollutants brings fewer marginal benefits.

- Optimum pollution control occurs when the marginal benefits from the reduction of pollution equal the marginal costs, both pecuniary and nonpecuniary, of the pollution control. Because of measurement problems, however, it is difficult to state whether we are not generally below, at, or above the optimal pollution level.

- It is practically impossible to get widespread agreement on what the appropriate level of pollution should be. People with different preferences and situations are simply going to have different ideas about the costs and benefits of pollution abatement. Conflicts are inevitable because different people have different preferences and face different costs. Those most eager to clean up the environment are often those who will reap many of the benefits and pay few of the costs.

- If everyone could pay for and consume a preferred level of environmental quality, independent of the level paid for and consumed by others, controversy over environmental protection would largely disappear.

- One means of solving the misallocation problem posed by the existence of externalities is for the government to create incentives for firms to internalize the external costs or benefits resulting from their activities. If the government were to then levy a pollution tax equal to the external costs imposed, the firm's costs would then be equal to the true marginal social cost. A major objection is that it is very difficult or even impossible to measure externalities with any precision. Choosing a tax rate involves some guesswork, and poor guessing might lead to a solution that is far from optimal.

- Economists see an opportunity to control pollution through a government-enforced system of property rights. In this system, the government issues **transferable pollution rights** that give the holder the right to discharge a specified amount of pollution into the air. Firms have an incentive to lower their levels of pollution because they can sell their permits if they go unused.

- Faced with a positive price for pollution rights, each polluter has every motivation to discover the cheapest way to reduce pollution and to utilize it. Each polluter is motivated to reduce pollution as long as the cost of reducing one more unit is less than the price of pollution rights. The information and incentives generated by private ownership and market exchange of these pollution rights automatically leads to the desirable pattern of pollution abatement.

- The pollution-rights approach also creates an incentive for polluters to develop improved pollution-abatement technologies.

- The objectives of an ideal pollution control policy are (1) reducing pollution to the efficient level, (2) achieving pollution reduction as cheaply as possible, and (3) motivating advances in abatement technology. Without market information, there is no way of determining the efficient level of air or water pollution. In the absence of market exchange, we have to rely on the political process to determine the efficient level of pollution.

I   REVIEW

To be effective, compliance standards, such as those established by the Environmental Protection Agency (EPA), must result in _____ pollution than would exist in the absence of those standards.

Compliance standards have led to a _____ in some types of pollution, such as auto emissions.

Chapter 16: The Environment

In a world of scarcity, society must incur _____ in order to have the benefits of a cleaner environment.

People with different preferences and situations are likely to have _____ ideas about the costs and _____ of pollution abatement.

Because of the principles of diminishing marginal utility and increasing marginal cost, the benefits of further expenditures on pollution control will, sooner or later, fall _____ the added costs to society imposed by stricter controls.

One means of solving problems posed by the existence of negative externalities is for government to create incentives for firms to _____ the costs resulting from their activities.

When pollution taxes are imposed on activities that cause pollution, the amount of pollution caused by those activities goes _____.

Rights that allow the holder to discharge a specific amount of pollution are called transferable _____ rights.

Transferable pollution rights give firms an incentive to lower their levels of pollution because they can _____ their permits if they don't use them. The market will allocate these rights among firms so that those firms with the _____ clean up costs are doing most of the cleaning up. Placing market prices on the right to pollute also gives firms an incentive to invest in new _____.

The ideal pollution control policy would do three things: 1) achieve the _____ level of pollution; 2) achieve pollution reduction at the _____ cost; and 3) motivate advances in pollution clean up _____.

II   TRUE/FALSE

_____1. The main disadvantage of compliance standards as a pollution-control policy is that they can create situations where the marginal costs of eliminating pollution exceed the marginal benefits.

_____2. Under a system of transferable pollution rights, firms with relatively high abatement costs will sell rights to pollute to firms with relatively low abatement costs.

III   MULTIPLE CHOICE

1.   The main duty of the Environmental Protection Agency (EPA) is to
A) prevent crime.
B) enforce environmental standards.
C) regulate air transport.
D) assure safe work places.

2.   For society as a whole, the optimal amount of pollution control exists when
A) no pollution is permitted at all.
B) firms can produce as much pollution as necessary to make the goods people want.
C) the marginal costs of pollution control are equal to the marginal benefits.
D) the marginal costs of pollution control exceed the benefits.

3. Taxes on activities that cause pollution tend to reduce pollution because they
    A) increase the quantity of output the firm must produce to make a profit.
    B) require firms to lower prices, resulting in an increase in the quantity of output purchased.
    C) lower production costs and lead to increased output and lower prices.
    D) raise production costs and lead to reduced output and higher prices.

4. Which of the following is *not* an advantage of transferable pollution rights?
    A) They create incentives for polluters to develop cheaper ways to reduce pollution.
    B) They allow the greatest value of output to be produced with a given amount of pollution.
    C) They require polluters to eliminate pollution no matter what the cost.
    D) The rights are private property and may be bought or sold freely.

IV   APPLICATION AND DISCUSSION

As the text points out various policies are used by government to limit the creation of negative externalities, including *compliance standards, pollution taxes,* and *transferable pollution rights*. Consider the list of government initiatives below, identify the negative externality they are designed to limit, and classify the initiative according to policy type (i.e., whether it is a compliance standard, pollution tax, or an example of transferable pollution rights).

Initiative	Negative Externality Involved	Policy Type
1. Alaska levies a $1 per pack state tax on cigarettes.		
2. The Federal Government makes it illegal to smoke inside a federal building.		
3. The 1990 Clean Air Act allocates transferable rights to emit sulphur dioxide to U.S. electrical utilities.		
4. Residents of Singapore face stiff fines if they spit on the sidewalk.		
5. The Environmental Protection Agency requires new automobiles to pass tests that show that their emissions do not exceed specified limits.		
6. Germany taxes industrial plants according to how much air and water pollution they cause. The more pollution, the higher the tax.		

SECTION 16.3
PROPERTY RIGHTS

KEY POINTS

- The existence of externalities and the efforts to deal with them in a manner that will enhance the social good can be looked at as largely being a question as to the nature of property rights. Dealing with externalities evolves into a question of how property rights should be altered. Externalities is one area where law and economics merge.

- Professor Ronald Coase observed that if the benefits are greater than the cost of an action like environmental cleanup, there must be potential transactions that make some people better off without making anyone worse off. Where property rights are clearly defined and transactions costs are low, voluntary exchange will eliminate externalities.

- Voluntary exchange will not eliminate externalities when transactions cost are not low. Private negotiations are limited because of ambiguity regarding the property rights involved, high transactions costs when large numbers of people are affected, and the fact that people cannot be excluded from the benefits from environmental cleanup if they don't contribute to the costs involved. Hence, in practice, private agreements are unlikely to solve many problems of market failure.

- Goods that are owned by everyone and so owned by no one are called common property. There is little incentive to conserve or use these goods efficiently.

I   REVIEW

The problem of externalities can be examined as a question of _____ rights. Solutions to externality problems involve questions of how to _____ existing property rights.

Because solutions to externality problems involve the evaluation of the legal arrangements of property rights, this is one area where _____ and economics merge.

The _____ Theorem states that if the benefits of some action exceed the costs there is some potential transaction that would make someone better off and no one worse off. As long as ownership or property rights are well defined, there would be _____ externality problem.

If the polluter owns the right to pollute and the benefits of cleaning up the pollution are _____ than the costs, those who suffer from the pollution could pay the polluter's clean-up costs and all would be better off.

If those who suffer from the pollution owned the right to pollute and the benefits from pollution exceed the costs, they could make the polluter _____ them for their suffering and all would be better off.

_____ costs are the cost of negotiating and executing an exchange. They do not include the cost of the good or service purchased.

The ability of voluntary exchange to limit externality problems depends on the existence of _____ transaction costs. Transaction costs _____ as the number of participants in the exchange increases.

There are three reasons voluntary exchange and private negotiations have not been used to address pollution problems. First, _____ rights in environmental resources are ambiguous. Second, transaction costs are usually _____ because of the number of people and firms involved. Finally, the market is likely to _____, because people cannot be excluded from enjoying the benefits of improved air and water quality.

Chapter 16: The Environment

II TRUE/FALSE

_____1. Zoning laws often limit the types of land use on particular parcels of land because those uses would negatively affect the welfare of their neighbors. Zoning laws are examples of changes in property rights in order to limit an externality problem.

_____2. The Coase Theorem suggests that well-defined property rights will internalize the externality only when transaction costs are high.

_____3. One reason private agreements are unlikely to solve air pollution problems is that clean air is a good that allows free riding since it is impossible to insure that only the people who pay for cleaner air enjoy the benefits of it.

III MULTIPLE CHOICE

1. While the planes don't actually drop any bombs, the noise from the low-altitude combat training the Air Force conducts over the Yippy I-O Ranch causes the ranch cattle to lose weight. Which of the following actions is *not* consistent with recognition that the Yippy I-O has a property right to its skies?
   A) The Air Force equips its planes with mufflers.
   B) The Air Force compensates the Yippy I-O for the value of the lost weight.
   C) The ranch compensates the Air Force for the cost of moving the exercises to another location.
   D) The Air Force pays for cow ear plugs for the ranch herd.

2. The manufacture of goods and services often imposes external costs on other activities. For which of the following examples would the externalities most likely be internalized through private negotiation and voluntary exchange?
   A) Farmer Brown's harvesting machine makes a noise that disturbs his neighbor Mr. Rogers.
   B) The Alabama Steel Co. mill pollutes the air, which affects the health of all asthma sufferers in Birmingham.
   C) Gold mining along the Porcupine River puts arsenic and mercury into the river, which kills fish.
   D) Auto emissions cause health problems for the citizens of Mexico City.

3. Which of the following is *not* an example of a common good?
   A) Tuna in the Pacific Ocean.
   B) The air in Los Angeles.
   C) Light bulbs like everyone has.
   D) Deer in a state park.

IV   APPLICATION AND DISCUSSION

The Rock Island Railroad track is close to Dr. Dan's dentist office. When a train rolls past it shakes the office with significant consequences for dental patients. Dr. Dan must stop work when a train passes by, which results in a loss of business and income. The Rock Island has an alternative route but it would add an additional cost of $50 per train. The table below shows Dan's marginal income loss from additional train traffic.

Trains Per Week	Marginal Income Loss
0	$0
1	15
2	32
3	50
4	70
5	95
6	125
7	160
8	200

A) If Dan owned the property rights to the peace and quiet of his office, what would be the result?

B) If the Rock Island owned the rights, what would be the result?

Questions

1. What are the positive externalities that Julie and Carmen encounter at the beach?

2. Why does Tony generate a negative externality?

CHAPTER 17
INTERNATIONAL TRADE

SECTION 17.1 THE GROWTH IN WORLD TRADE

SECTION 17.2 COMPARATIVE ADVANTAGE AND GAINS FROM TRADE

SECTION 17.3 SUPPLY AND DEMAND IN INTERNATIONAL TRADE

SECTION 17.4 TARIFFS, IMPORT QUOTAS, AND SUBSIDIES

SECTION 17.1
THE GROWTH IN WORLD TRADE

KEY POINTS

- In a typical year, about 15 percent of the world's output is traded in international markets.
- While the importance of the international sector varies enormously from place to place, the volume of international trade has increased substantially.

I   REVIEW

Although it varies from country to country, in a typical year about _____ percent of the world's output is traded in international markets. In 1998, about _____ percent of U.S. output was _____, and imports amounted to over _____ percent of GDP.

The United States has important trading relations with many countries, but our three most important partners are _____, _____, and Japan.

II   TRUE/FALSE

_____1. In 1998, U.S. imports of goods from Canada were over twice as large as our imports of goods from China.

_____2. Over time, trade with other countries has remained insignificant to the United States.

III   MULTIPLE CHOICE

1. The Canadian politician Terry F. Razer wants to limit trade in goods with the United States to preserve Canadian culture. Why would this action be more important to the U.S. economy than the same type of policy in Italy?
    A) Canadians speak English so U.S. citizens are more interested in what they do.
    B) Canada ranks behind only the United Kingdom as our second most important trade partner.
    C) Canada accounts for approximately one-fifth of all U.S. exports and imports of goods.
    D) Canada exports most of the hockey players who play for the National Hockey League.

2. Dr. Mary K. Furst uses her 1940 dissertation research to justify her isolationist view that the U.S. economy would be affected only slightly if it were isolated from the rest of the world. Why might her conclusion be more correct in 1940 than it is today?
    A) The last 50 years have seen a dramatic increase in the importance of international trade to the U.S. economy.
    B) Technological changes over the last 50 years have reduced the importance of international trade throughout the world.
    C) The last 50 years have seen a dramatic reduction in the importance of international trade to the U.S. economy.
    D) Over the last 50 years, international trade has increased in importance in the world but not for the United States.

IV   APPLICATION AND DISCUSSION

In 1999, the countries of the world *exported* a total of $6.7 trillion dollars worth of goods and service. From this information, can you tell how many total dollars worth of goods and services they *imported* in 1999?

SECTION 17.2
COMPARATIVE ADVANTAGE AND GAINS FROM TRADE

KEY POINTS

- The very existence of trade suggests that trade is economically beneficial. Because almost all trade is voluntary, it would seem that trade occurs because the participants feel that they are better off because of the trade. Both participants of an exchange of goods and services anticipate an improvement in their economic welfare.

- The classical economist David Ricardo's theory that explains how trade can be beneficial to both parties centers on the concept of comparative advantage. A person, a region, or a country can gain from trade if it produces a good or service at a lower opportunity cost than others. That is, an area should specialize in producing and selling those items where it has a **comparative advantage.**

- What is important for mutually beneficial specialization and trade is comparative advantage, not **absolute advantage**.

- The gains from comparative advantage—specialization where one has a lower opportunity cost—can be illustrated with a production possibility curve. The differences in opportunity costs provide an incentive to gain from specialization and trade.

I   REVIEW

We know trade is economically _____ because it exists. Since trade is _____ and people _____ utility, participants must expect trade to make them better off.

David Ricardo developed the explanation of the mutual _____ of trade. His theory is the Principle of _____ Advantage.

The Principle of Comparative Advantage states that a nation can gain from trade by _____ in the production of those goods it can produce at a _____ opportunity cost than other countries. This principle also applies to regions and individuals.

A country has a(n) _____ advantage in producing a good when it uses fewer resources to produce a given level of output. A country may have a comparative advantage in a good without having an absolute advantage when the production of the good has _____ opportunity costs than its trading partner.

By specializing in the production of goods and services for which they have the lowest opportunity cost, trading partners can produce _____ of all of the goods they trade. _____ in opportunity costs between trading partners provide the _____ to gain from specialization and trade.

II   TRUE/FALSE

_____1. People and nations trade because trade makes them better off.

_____2. History has shown that specialization and trade are often in conflict with economic growth.

_____3. In the United States, one person working for 8 hours can produce 20 shirts, while in Malawi it would take one person 16 hours to produce 20 shirts. In trade with Malawi, the United States will always have a comparative advantage in the production of shirts.

Chapter 17: International Trade

III   MULTIPLE CHOICE

1. In France it takes one worker one year to produce either 500 bottles of wine or 1,000 bottles of sparkling water. If resources in France are fully employed, what is the opportunity cost of a bottle of French wine?
   A) 1,000 bottles of water
   B) one-half a bottle of water
   C) $3.25
   D) two bottles of water

2. In Bangladesh, one person can produce 330 pounds of rice or 110 shirts in one year. In Singapore, one person can produce 400 pounds of rice or 200 shirts in one year. Which of the following statements is true?
   A) Bangladesh has an absolute advantage in the production of rice.
   B) Bangladesh has a comparative advantage in the production of rice.
   C) Singapore has both an absolute and comparative advantage in the production of rice.
   D) Singapore has a comparative advantage in the production of rice.

IV   APPLICATION AND DISCUSSION

1. Bud and Larry have been shipwrecked on a deserted island. Their economic activity consists of either gathering berries or fishing. We know that Bud can catch four fish in one hour or harvest two buckets of berries. In the same time Larry can catch two fish or harvest two buckets of berries.

   A) Fill in the following table assuming that they *each* spend four hours a day fishing and four hours a day harvesting berries.

	Fish per day	Buckets of Berries per day
Bud	_____	_____
Larry	_____	_____
Total	_____	_____

   B) If Bud and Larry don't trade with each other, who is better off? Why?

   C) Assume that Larry and Bud operate on straight-line production possibility curves.

       Fill in the following table.

	Opportunity Cost of a Bucket of Berries	Opportunity Cost of a Fish
Bud	_____	_____
Larry	_____	_____

   D) If they traded, who has the comparative advantage in fish? In berries?

   E) If Larry and Bud specialize in and trade the good in which they have a comparative advantage, how much of each good will be produced in an eight hour day? What are the gains from trade?

SECTION 17.3
SUPPLY AND DEMAND IN INTERNATIONAL TRADE

KEY POINTS

- The difference between the most a consumer would be willing and able to pay for a quantity of a good and what a consumer actually has to pay is called **consumer surplus.** The difference between the least amount for which a supplier is willing and able to supply a quantity of a good or service and the revenues a supplier actually received for selling it is called **producer surplus.** With the tools of consumer and producer surplus, we can better analyze the impact of trade.

- The demand curve represents a collection of maximum prices that consumers are willing and able to pay for different quantities of a good or service while the supply curve represents a collection of minimum prices that suppliers require to be willing to supply different quantities of that good or service. Trading at the market equilibrium price generates both consumer surplus and producer surplus.

- Once the equilibrium output is reached at the equilibrium price, all of the mutually beneficial opportunities from trade between suppliers and demanders will have taken place; the sum of consumer surplus and producer surplus is maximized.

- The total gains to the economy from trade is the sum of consumer and producer surplus. That is, consumers benefit from additional amounts of consumer surplus and producers benefit from additional amounts of producer surplus.

- When the domestic economy has a comparative advantage in a good because it can produce it at a lower relative price than the rest of the world, international trade raises the domestic market price to the world price, benefitting domestic producers but harming domestic consumers. However, while this redistributes income from consumers to producers, there are net benefits from allowing free trade because producer surplus increases more than consumer surplus decreases. While domestic consumers lose from the free trade, those negative effects are more than offset by the positive gains captured by producers. In net, export trade increases domestic wealth.

- When a country does not produce a good relatively as well as other countries, international trade will lower the domestic price to the world price, with the difference between what is domestically supplied and what is domestically demanded supplied by imports. Domestic consumers benefit from paying a lower price for the good, increasing their consumer surplus. But domestic producers lose because they are now selling at the lower world price. However, while this redistributes income from producers to consumers, there is a net increase in domestic wealth from free trade and imports because the consumer surplus increases more than producer surplus decreases.

I   REVIEW

The difference between what a consumer is willing to pay for a given amount of a good and what they have to pay is called consumer _____. Consumers benefit from paying less than they would be willing to pay.

Producer _____ is the difference between the revenue the producer receives for selling a given amount of the good and the amount the producer is willing to accept. Producers benefit from receiving more than they would be willing to accept.

The demand curve represents the _____ prices consumers are willing and able to pay for different quantities of a good or service. The supply curve represents the _____ prices at which suppliers are willing to offer different quantities of the good or service.

As long as the maximum price the consumer is willing to pay _____ the minimum price the supplier requires for one more unit of a good or service, there are mutually _____ opportunities for trade.

Chapter 17: International Trade

When markets reach the _____ price, all the opportunities for mutually beneficial trade have taken place and the sum of consumer and producer surplus is _____.

When a country trades with the rest of the world, the price of the exported good is _____ after trade than before. Domestic consumers _____ from free trade because their consumer surplus is _____. However, these losses are offset by the positive gains captured by domestic _____. On net, export trade _____ domestic wealth.

When an economy trades with the rest of the world, the price of the imported good is _____ after trade than before. Domestic consumers _____ from free trade because their consumer surplus is _____. However, domestic producers lose because their producer surplus is _____. On net, import trade _____ domestic wealth since the gain to consumers _____ the loss to producers.

II   TRUE/FALSE

_____1. Trade between producers and consumers will occur as long as consumers benefit.

_____2. If the farming industry vigorously supports free trade while the cement industry opposes free trade, we could assume our country's comparative advantage is in farm products and not cement.

_____3. The price of bananas in Greece is higher than the world price. Ms. Margaret Stake is correct to assert that Greece has a comparative advantage in banana production.

III   MULTIPLE CHOICE

1. The difference between the price the seller receives for a good or service and the minimum price he would be willing to accept is called
    A) the market price.
    B) the producer surplus.
    C) the consumer surplus.
    D) the equilibrium difference.

Answer questions 2 through 4 by referring to Exhibit 1. This shows the domestic supply and demand curves for a good for which the country has a comparative advantage. Without trade the country produces Q_{BT} at a price of P_{BT}. Trade takes place at the world price of P_{AT}.

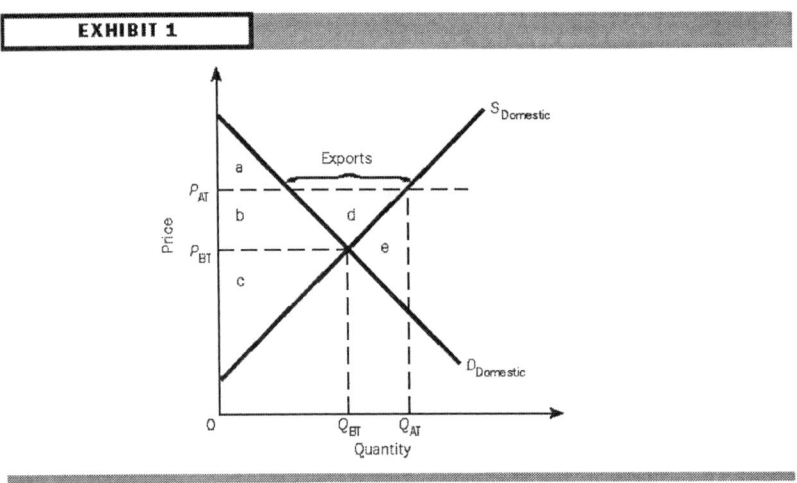

2. Trade reduces consumer surplus by an amount equal to the area
    A) a.
    B) b.
    C) c.
    D) d.

3. With trade, producer surplus increases by an amount equal to
    A) d.
    B) d + e.
    C) b + c + d.
    D) b + d.

4. Export trade will increase this country's domestic wealth because
    A) consumer surplus increases by more than producer surplus by an amount equal to e.
    B) consumer surplus increases by more than producer surplus by an amount equal to d.
    C) producer surplus increases by more than consumer surplus by an amount equal to e.
    D) producer surplus increases by more than consumer surplus by an amount equal to d.

IV   APPLICATION AND DISCUSSION

1. To protect its domestic apple industry, Botswana has for many years prevented international trade in apples. Exhibit 2 represents the Botswana domestic market for apples. P_{BT} is the current price and P_{AT} is the world price.

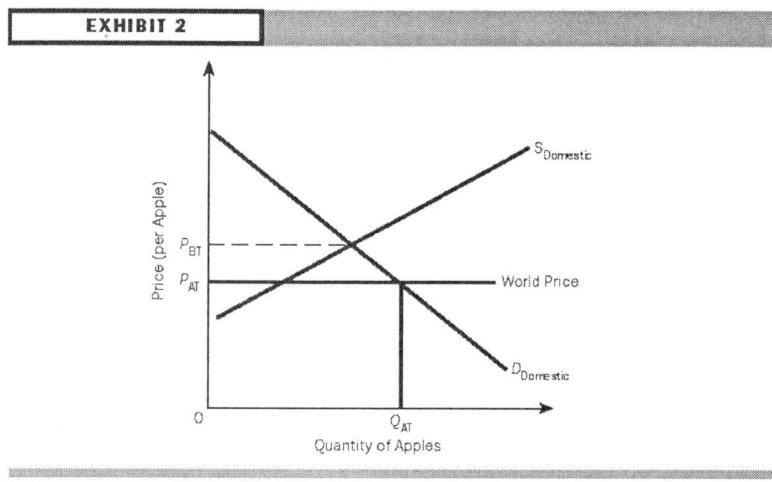

EXHIBIT 2

A) If the government allows world trade in apples, what will happen to the price of apples in Botswana? Why?

B) Indicate the amount of apples domestic producers produce after there is trade in apples as Q_{DT}. How many apples are imported?

C) Trade in imports causes producer surplus to be reduced by the amount b. Show b on the graph.

D) The gains from trade equal the amount increased consumer surplus exceeds the loss in producer surplus. Show this gain, g, on the graph.

E) Explain why consumers in Botswana would still be better off if they were required to compensate producers for their lost producer surplus.

SECTION 17.4
TARIFFS, IMPORT QUOTAS, AND SUBSIDIES

KEY POINTS

- A **tariff** is a tax on imported goods. Tariffs are usually relatively small revenue producers that retard the expansion of trade. They bring about higher prices and revenues to domestic producers, lower sales and revenues to foreign producers, and higher prices to domestic consumers. The gains to producers are more than offset by the losses to consumers.

- With import tariffs, the domestic price of goods is greater than the world price. At the new price, the domestic quantity demanded is lower and the quantity supplied domestically is greater, reducing the quantity of imported goods. While domestic producers do gain more sales and producer surplus at the expense of foreign producers, and the government gains from tariff revenue, consumers lose more in consumer surplus than producers and the government gain from the tariff.

- One argument for tariffs is that tariff protection is necessary temporarily to allow a new industry to more quickly reach a scale of operation at which economies of scale and production efficiencies can be realized. This argument has many problems. How do you identify "infant industries" that genuinely have potential economies of scale and will become quickly efficient with protection? Moreover, would it not be wise to make massive loans to the industry in such a case, allowing it to instantly begin large-scale production rather than slowly and at the expense of consumers with a protective tariff? Finally, the history of infant industry tariffs suggests that the tariffs often linger long after the industry is mature and no longer in "need" of protection.

- Tariffs can lead to increased output and employment and reduced unemployment in domestic industries where tariffs were imposed. Yet the overall employment effects of a tariff imposition are not likely to be positive. Not only might the imposition of a tariff lead to retaliatory tariffs by other countries, but domestic employment would likely suffer outside the industry gaining the tariff protection. If new tariffs lead to restrictions on imports, fewer dollars will be flowing overseas in payment for imports, which means that foreigners will have fewer dollars available to buy our exports. Other things equal, this will tend to reduce our exports, thus creating unemployment in the export industries.

- Sometimes it is argued that tariffs are a means of preventing a nation from becoming too dependent on foreign suppliers of goods vital to national security, but the national security argument is usually not valid. If a nation's own resources are depletable, tariff-imposed reliance on domestic supplies will hasten depletion of domestic reserves. From a defense standpoint, it makes more sense to use foreign supplies in peacetime and perhaps stockpile "insurance" supplies so that large domestic supplies would be available during wars.

- An **import quota** gives producers from another country a maximum number of units of the good in question that can be imported within any given time span.

- The case for quotas is probably even weaker than the case for tariffs. Like tariffs, quotas directly restrict imports, leading to reductions in trade and thus preventing nations from fully realizing their comparative advantage. But tariffs at least use the price system as the basis of restricting trade, while quotas do not. Further, unlike with a tariff, the U.S. government does not collect any revenue as a result of the import quota.

- Nations have also devised still other, more subtle means to restrict international trade. Examples include product standards ostensibly designed to protect consumers against inferior, unsafe, dangerous, or polluting merchandise, which, in effect, are sometimes a means to restrict foreign competition.

- Except in rather unusual circumstances, the arguments for tariffs and import quotas are rather suspect. They exist because of producers' lobbying efforts to gain profits from government protection called **rent seeking.** Because these resources could have produced something instead of being spent on lobbying efforts, the measured deadweight loss from tariffs and quotas will likely understate the true deadweight loss to society.

- Working in the opposite direction, governments sometimes try to encourage exports by subsidizing producers. With a subsidy, revenue is given to producers for each exported unit of output, stimulating exports. While not a barrier to trade like tariffs and quotas, subsidies can also distort trade patterns, leading to ones that are inefficient.

- With subsidies, producers export goods not because their costs are lower than that of a foreign competitor, but because their costs have been artificially reduced by government action transferring income from taxpayers to the exporter. The actual costs of production are not reduced by the subsidy—society has the same opportunity costs as before. A nation's taxpayers end up subsidizing the output of producers who, relative to producers in other countries, are inefficient. The nation, then, exports products in which it does not have a comparative advantage. Gains from trade in terms of world output are eliminated or reduced by such subsidies.

I **REVIEW**

A tariff is a(n) _____ on imported goods.

Tariffs are used today to _____ domestic industry from foreign competition.

Chapter 17: International Trade

A tariff is a(n) _____ on imported goods. Tariffs result in _____ prices to domestic producers and _____ sales and revenues to foreign producers.

Domestic producers gain from tariff protection, but domestic consumers lose _____ than producers gain.

The _____ industry argument in support of tariffs argues that tariff protection helps new industries reach the scale of operation at which they can be efficient.

Because tariffs increase domestic production they are often supported as a mechanism for reducing _____ in protected industries.

However, employment in other industries may suffer if exports are reduced because of _____ by other countries. Export industries may also suffer because with a reduction in foreign imports, other countries will have _____ dollars to purchase our exports.

Tariffs are also supported for national security reasons. They can be used to limit our _____ on foreign producers for those goods vital to our national security.

A tariff on a good will create _____ for producers and _____ for consumers. Even when losses exceed the benefits, a tariff may be adopted, because producers are a more effective _____ group for a tariff than consumer groups who lobby against tariffs.

An import _____ limits international trade by defining a maximum number of units of a good that can be imported in a time period. Unlike tariffs, governments do not collect any _____ with a quota.

Import quotas make domestic producers _____ off, but make domestic consumers _____ off.

Governments may also try to encourage exports by _____ producers. With subsidies, producers export goods, not because their costs are relatively _____ than other countries, but because their costs have been _____ lowered by transferring income from _____ to exporters.

II   TRUE/FALSE

_____1. Import quotas generate more government revenue than a tariff that is designed to realize the same level of imports.

_____2. Export subsidies can be used to change a country's comparative advantage.

_____3. If it can be shown that a tariff on steel imports will increase employment in the steel industry, we can be sure the effect of the tariff on U.S. employment will be positive.

III   MULTIPLE CHOICE

1. Which of the following is *not* a result we would expect from a tariff on leather shoes?
    A) The price of leather shoes in the United States would increase.
    B) The amount of shoes imported into the United States would decline.
    C) Fewer pairs of shoes would be sold in the United States.
    D) Domestic producers would sell fewer shoes at the higher prices.

2. Tariffs result in a decrease in consumer surplus because
    A) the price and quantity consumed of the protected good increase.
    B) the price and quantity consumed of the protected good decrease.
    C) the price of the protected good increases and quantity consumed decreases.
    D) the price of the protected good decreases and quantity consumed increases.

Answer questions 3 through 5 by referring to Exhibit 3. This graph shows the domestic market for sweaters for which this country has a comparative disadvantage. With the adoption of a tariff, the price of purchasing imports increases by the amount of the tariff. P_0 is the original domestic price.

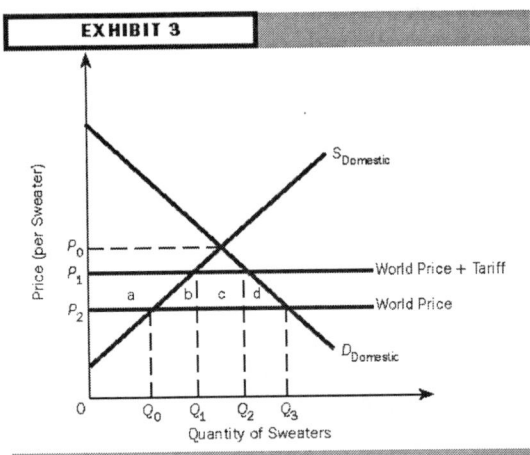

3. After the tariff on sweaters in imposed, the domestic price of sweaters will be
    A) P_0.
    B) P_1.
    C) P_2.
    D) zero because sweaters will no longer be imported.

4. The tariff on sweaters reduces consumer surplus by an amount equal to the area
    A) a.
    B) a + b.
    C) a + b + c.
    D) a + b + c + d.

5. The net loss in welfare caused by imposing the tariff is an amount equal to what area in the exhibit?
    A) a + c
    B) b + c
    C) b + d
    D) b + c + d

IV   APPLICATION AND DISCUSSION

1. When the United States, Canada, and Mexico created the North American Free Trade Agreement (NAFTA) in 1993, they began to lower tariffs and other trade barriers. Suppose tariffs had protected the U.S. maple syrup industry from lower cost Canadian producers.

    A) What would you expect to happen in the U.S. maple syrup market after the tariffs are removed?

    B) What would you say to critics that argue NAFTA is bad because it costs jobs in the maple syrup industry?

Questions

1. According to Jerry Lee, who has an absolute advantage in window washing and vacuuming?

2. How could you use the principle of comparative advantage to decide who does which household chores in the Lowell household?

CHAPTER 18
INTERNATIONAL FINANCE

SECTION 18.1 THE BALANCE OF PAYMENTS

SECTION 18.2 EXCHANGE RATES

SECTION 18.3 EQUILIBRIUM CHANGES IN THE FOREIGN EXCHANGE MARKET

SECTION 18.4 FLEXIBLE EXCHANGE RATES

SECTION 18.1
THE BALANCE OF PAYMENTS

KEY POINTS

- The record of all of the international financial transactions of a nation over a year is called the **balance of payments**. It records all the exchanges those in a nation engaged in that required an outflow of funds to other nations or an inflow of funds from other nations, and provides information about a nation's world trade position.

- The balance of payments is divided into three main sections: the current account, the capital account, and "statistical discrepancy."

- The **current account** is a record of a country's current imports and exports of goods and services.

- Because the United States gains claims over foreign buyers by obtaining foreign currency in exchange for the dollars needed to buy U.S. exports, all exports of U.S. goods abroad are considered a credit or plus item in the U.S. balance of payments. When a U.S. consumer buys an imported item, the reverse is true. U.S. imports are considered a debit item in the balance of payment because the dollars sold to buy the necessary foreign currency add to foreign claims against U.S. buyers.

- Imports and exports of goods are the largest component of the balance of payments. Nations also import and export services.

- Private and government grants and gifts to foreigners also count as a debit item in a country's balance of payments, and grants and gifts from foreigners count as a credit item.

- The balance on current account is the net amount of debits or credits after adding up all transactions of goods, services, and fund transfers. If the sum of credits exceeds the sum of debits, a nation is said to have a balance of payments surplus on current account. If debits exceed credits, it is running a balance of payments deficit on current account.

- The import/export goods relationship is often called the **balance of trade,** which is different from the balance on current account.

- A deficit on current account is settled by movements of financial, or capital, assets. A current account deficit is financed by a **capital account** surplus. The capital account records foreign purchases of assets in the U.S. and U.S. purchases of assets abroad.

- Due to the reciprocal aspect of trade, the balance of payments must balance so that credits and debits are equal; however, errors and omissions mean the official measures do not come out equal. The **statistical discrepancy** is included so that the official balance of payments do balance.

I   REVIEW

The record of all the international transactions of a nation over a year is called the balance of _____. The balance of payments is divided into three main sections: the _____ account, the _____ account, and the _____ _____.

The current account is made up of imports and _____ of goods and services. When a foreign buyer buys a good from a U.S. producer, the foreigner usually pays for the good in U.S. _____.

All exports of U.S. goods are considered _____ items in the U.S. balance of payments.

When a U.S. buyer buys an imported good the buyer usually pays in _____ currency. All imports of foreign goods are considered _____ items in the U.S. balance of payments.

When the United States gives foreign aid to another country or when private individuals send money to relatives in foreign countries, it is recorded as a _____ in the U.S. balance of payments.

The balance on current account is the net amount of credits and _____ after adding up all transactions of goods, services, investment income, and fund transfers.

Countries finance deficits in their current accounts by running _____ in their capital accounts.

II   TRUE/FALSE

_____1. In recent years, the United States has run persistent deficits in its balance on current account.

_____2. Another term for the balance on current account is "balance of trade."

_____3. If a country has a deficit in its current account, it must necessarily have a surplus in its capital account.

III   MULTIPLE CHOICE

1. Which of the following is a credit in the U.S. current account?
    A) A U.S. consumer buys a TV made in Malaysia.
    B) Singapore Airlines buys a jumbo jet made in the United States.
    C) British investors purchase U.S. government bonds.
    D) An American citizen flies to Lithuania on Lithuanian Airlines.

2. If consumers in Europe and Asia develop strong preferences for American goods, America's current account will
    A) not be affected because purchases of American goods by foreigners are recorded in the capital account.
    B) not be affected because purchases of American goods based on mere preferences are recorded under "statistical discrepancy."
    C) move toward surplus because purchases of American goods are recorded as credits on our current account.
    D) move toward deficit because purchases of American goods by foreigners are counted as debits in our current account.

IV   APPLICATION AND DISCUSSION

How are each of the following classified, as debits or credits, in the U.S. balance of payments accounts?

[insert 27.1]

	Credit	Debit

1. Americans buy autos from Japan.

2. American tourists travel to Japan.

3. Japanese consumers buy rice grown in the U.S.

4. United States gives foreign aid to Rwanda.

5. General Motors, a U.S. company, earns profits in France.

6. Royal Dutch Shell earns profits from its U.S. operations.

7. General Motors builds a new plant in Vietnam.

8. Japanese investors purchase U.S. government bonds.

SECTION 18.2
EXCHANGE RATES

KEY POINTS

- U.S. consumers must first exchange U.S. dollars for the seller's currency in order to pay for imported goods. Similarly, foreigners buying U.S. goods must sell their currencies to obtain U.S. dollars in order to pay for exported goods.

- The price of a unit of one foreign currency in terms of another is called the **exchange rate,** which can be expressed either as the number of units of currency A per unit of currency B or its reciprocal, the number of units of currency B per unit of currency A.

- Prices of goods in their own currencies combine with exchange rates to determine the domestic price of foreign goods. For instance, an increase in the euro–dollar exchange rate from $1 per euro to $2 per euro would increase the U.S. price of German goods, reducing the number of German goods that would be demanded in the United States.

- The demand for foreign currencies is a **derived demand** because it derives directly from the demand for foreign goods and services or for foreign capital. An increased demand for a currency will push up the exchange value of that currency relative to other currencies.

- Similarly, the supply of foreign currency is provided by foreigners who want to buy the exports of a particular nation. The more foreigners demand U.S. products, the more of their currencies they will supply in exchange for U.S. dollars.

- Just as in the product market, the supply of and demand for a foreign currency determine the equilibrium price (exchange rate) of that currency.

- The demand for a foreign currency is downward sloping because, as the price of the foreign currency falls relative to the dollar, foreign products become relatively more inexpensive to U.S. consumers, who therefore buy more foreign goods. To do so, the quantity of foreign currency demanded by U.S. consumers will increase to buy more goods.

- The supply curve of a foreign currency is upward sloping. In trade with Europe, as the price, or value, of the euro increases relative to the dollar, American products become relatively more inexpensive to European buyers and the quantity of dollars they will demand will increase. Europeans will, therefore, increase the quantity of euros supplied to the U.S. by buying more U.S. products.

- Equilibrium in the foreign exchange market is reached where the demand and supply curves for a given currency intersect.

I   REVIEW

When U.S. consumers buy goods from foreigners, the sellers of those goods want to be paid in their
_____ currency. As a result, U.S. importers must _____ foreign currency
with dollars in order to finance their purchases. Similarly, people in other countries buying goods made in America must
_____ their currencies to obtain U.S. dollars in order to pay for those goods.

The price of a unit of one foreign currency in terms of another is called the _____ rate.

The demand for foreign currencies is what economists call _____ demand. The more foreign goods
are demanded, the _____ of that foreign currency that will be needed to pay for those goods.
Increased demand for a currency will cause the exchange value of that currency to _____.

Foreign currency is supplied by foreigners who want to buy _____ of a particular nation. For
example, the more U.S. goods that foreigners demand, the _____ of their currency they will supply.

The equilibrium exchange rate for a currency is determined by the supply and _____ for that currency in the foreign exchange market.

II   TRUE/FALSE

_____1. The exchange value of the dollar, in terms of foreign currency, is established by the U.S. government.

_____2. If the euro becomes relatively more expensive in terms of dollars, Americans will buy fewer European goods.

III   MULTIPLE CHOICE

1. If the exchange rate between the dollar and the euro changes from $1 = 1 euro to $2 = 1 euro, European goods will become
    A) less expensive for Americans and imports of European goods to the United States will rise.
    B) less expensive for Americans and imports of European goods to the United States will fall.
    C) more expensive for Americans and imports of European goods to the United States will rise.
    D) more expensive for Americans and imports of European goods to the United States will fall.

2. Which of the following would result in an increase in the dollar price of a Japanese Yen?
    A) An increase in the Japanese supply of Yen.
    B) An increase in the Japanese demand for dollars.
    C) A decrease in the U.S. demand for Japanese Yen.
    D) A decrease in the Japanese supply of Yen.

IV   APPLICATION AND DISCUSSION

1. Which of the following parties would be pleased by an *increase* in the value of the U.S. dollar in relation to the euro?
    A) American farmers
    B) Americans planning to take trips to Europe
    C) American producers of manufactured exports like airplanes and tractors
    D) Europeans who consume lots of American products
    E) Americans who enjoy French cheese

2. Which of the following parties would be pleased by a *decrease* in the value of the dollar in relation to the Japanese yen?
    A) American farmers
    B) Americans planning to visit Tokyo
    C) General Motors stockholders
    D) Japanese students planning to attend American colleges and universities
    E) Japanese hotel owners

SECTION 18.3

EQUILIBRIUM CHANGES IN THE FOREIGN EXCHANGE MARKET

KEY POINTS

- Any force that shifts either the demand for or supply of a currency will shift the equilibrium in the foreign exchange market, leading to a new exchange rate. An increased demand for euros will result in a higher equilibrium price (exchange value) for euros, while a decreased demand for euros will result in a lower equilibrium price (exchange value) for euros.

- Changes in a currency's exchange rate can be caused by changes in tastes for goods, changes in income, changes in relative real interest rates, changes in relative inflation rates, and speculation.

- Because the demand for foreign currencies is derived from the demand for foreign goods, any change in the demand for foreign goods will shift the demand curve for foreign currency in the same direction. For instance, an increase in tastes for European goods in the United States would increase the demand for Euros, increasing the equilibrium price (exchange value) of Euros; a decrease in tastes for European goods in the United States would decrease the demand for Euros, decreasing the equilibrium price (exchange value) of Euros.

- An increase in incomes in the United States would increase the amount of European imports purchased by Americans, which would increase the demand for euros, resulting in a higher exchange rate for euros. A decrease in incomes in the U.S. would decrease the amount of European imports purchased by Americans, which would decrease the demand for euros, resulting in a lower exchange rate for euros.

- A decrease in U.S. tariffs on European goods would tend to have the same effect as an increase in U.S. incomes, by making imports more affordable, increasing the U.S. demand for European goods and increasing the exchange rate for euros.

- If interest rates in the United States were to increase relative to European interest rates, other things equal, the rate of return on U.S. investments would increase relative to that on European investments, increasing European's demand for U.S. investments. Therefore, it would increase the supply of euros to obtain the added dollars to buy added U.S. investments. At the same time, U.S. investors would also shift their investments away from Europe, decreasing their demand for euros. The combination of the increased supply of euros and the decreased demand for euros will lead to a new lower exchange rate for euros.

- If Europe experienced a higher inflation rate than the United States, European products would become more expensive to U.S. consumers, decreasing the quantity of European goods demanded by Americans and, therefore, decreasing the demand for euros. U.S. products would become less expensive to European consumers, increasing the quantity of U.S. goods demanded by Europeans and, therefore, increasing the supply of euros. The combination of the increased supply of euros and the decreased demand for euros will lead to a new lower exchange rate for euros.

- If currency speculators believe that the United States was going to experience more rapid inflation in the future than Japan, they will believe that the value of the dollar will soon be falling as a result. That will increase the demand for yen, so the yen will appreciate relative to the dollar. The opposite will occur if speculators expect less rapid inflation in the United States.

| I | REVIEW |

Any force that shifts either the demand for or supply of a currency will shift the _____ in the foreign exchange market, leading to a new _____ rate.

Chapter 18: International Finance

Factors that shift the demand for and supply of a currency include changes in _____ for goods and services, changes in _____, changes in real _____ rates, and changes in relative _____ rates.

If incomes increase in the United States, Americans will buy _____ goods, including European goods. This increase in demand for foreign goods will cause an _____ in the demand for euros.

If incomes decrease in the United States, Americans will buy _____ goods, including European goods. This decrease in demand for foreign goods will cause a _____ in the demand for euros.

If interest rates in the United States increase relative to those in Europe, other things equal, the rate of return on U.S. investments will _____ relative to that on European investments. European investors seeking higher rates of return will _____ dollars with euros.

If interest rates in the United States decrease relative to those in Europe, investors will _____ dollars and _____ euros in order to make European investments.

If the rate of inflation is higher in Europe than in the United States, European products will become _____ expensive to U.S. consumers. Americans will _____ the quantity of European goods they demand and their demand for euros will _____. At the same time, the higher rate of European inflation will make U.S. goods relatively _____ expensive to Europeans. This will lead Europeans to _____ the quantity of U.S. goods demanded and lead to an _____ in the supply of euros.

Overall, the result of the higher rate of European inflation will be a new, _____ equilibrium price for the euro.

If speculators believe that the price of a country's currency is going to rise they will buy _____ of that currency.

II   TRUE/FALSE

_____1. The equilibrium exchange rate of the dollar seldom changes.

_____2. If interest rates rise in the United States, relative to those in the rest of the world, the exchange value of the dollar will tend to appreciate.

_____3. Janelle, who lives in Dallas, has been saving for years in order to take a trip to Japan this summer. She should be happy if the dollar suddenly appreciates in value against the yen.

III   MULTIPLE CHOICE

1. An economic boom in the United States, which increases the incomes of Americans, will result in
   A) a decrease in the U.S. demand for goods, including foreign goods, and a decrease in the supply of dollars on the foreign exchange market.
   B) an increase in the U.S. demand for goods, including foreign goods, and an increase in the supply of dollars on the foreign exchange market.
   C) a decrease in the U.S. demand for goods, including foreign goods, and an increase in the supply of dollars on the foreign exchange market.
   D) an increase in the U.S. demand for goods, including foreign goods, and a decrease in the supply of dollars on the foreign exchange market.

2. If the exchange rate changes from 100 yen per dollar to 120 yen per dollar,
   A) the dollar has depreciated.
   B) the dollar has appreciated
   C) the yen has appreciated.
   D) None of the above will occur.

IV   APPLICATION AND DISCUSSION

What will happen to the supply of dollars, the demand for dollars, and the equilibrium exchange rate of the dollar in each of the following cases?

	Supply of Dollars	Demand for Dollars	Equilibrium Exchange Rate
1. Americans buy more European goods.			
2. Europeans invest in U.S. stock market.			
3. European tourists flock to the United States.			
4. Europeans buy U.S. government bonds.			
5. American tourists flock to Europe.			

SECTION 18.4
FLEXIBLE EXCHANGE RATES

KEY POINTS

- Since 1973, the world has essentially operated on a system of flexible exchange rates under which currency prices are allowed to fluctuate with changes in supply and demand, without governments stepping in to prevent those changes.

- Before 1973, governments operated under what was called the Bretton Woods **fixed exchange rate system,** in which they would maintain a stable currency exchange rate by buying or selling currencies or reserves to bring demand and supply for their currencies together at the fixed exchange rate.

- Governments are still sensitive to sharp changes in the exchange value of their currencies, and they do intervene from time to time to prop up exchange values considered to be too low or falling too rapidly or depress exchange values considered too high or rising too rapidly. Therefore, economists sometimes say the current exchange rate system is a "dirty float" system, where fluctuations in currency values are partly determined by market forces and partly determined by government intervention.

Chapter 18: International Finance

- When exchange rates change, they effect not only the currency market, but product markets as well. If the exchange value of the dollar relative to the yen or pound fell, it would increase the cost, and therefore decrease the volume of U.S. imports. It would also decrease the cost and lead to an increase in the volume of Japanese and British imports from the United States.

- Since the advent of flexible exchange rates, world trade has expanded.

- The most important advantage of the flexible rate system is that the recurrent crises that led to speculative rampages and major currency revaluations under the fixed Bretton Woods system, have significantly diminished. Today, exchange rates change almost constantly, but each change is much smaller in magnitude, with major changes typically occurring only over periods of months or years.

- Perhaps the most significant problem with fixed exchange rates is that they can result in currency shortages, just as domestic wage and price controls can lead to shortages.

- Under flexible exchange rates, an imbalance between debits and credits arising from shifts in currency demand and/or supply is accommodated by changes in currency prices rather than through the special financial borrowings or reserve movements necessary with fixed rates. In a pure flexible exchange-rate system, balance of payments deficits and surpluses tend to disappear.

- Flexible exchange rates also alleviate the need to use restrictive monetary and/or fiscal policy to end a currency imbalance, while maintaining fixed exchange rates, imposing less of a constraint on countries' internal macroeconomic policies.

- Flexible exchange rates have not been universally endorsed. Traditionally, the major objection to flexible exchange rates was that the resulting currency fluctuations introduce considerable uncertainty into international trade, potentially reducing the volume of trade and reducing the gains from international specialization.

- Flexible rate proponents have given three answers:

  1) the empirical evidence points to faster growth of international trade after the adoption of flexible exchange rates;

  2) one can, in effect, buy insurance against exchange rate risk through the forward or futures market in currencies; and

  3) the alleged certainty of currency prices under Bretton Woods was fictitious because countries could, at a whim, drastically revalue their currencies.

- A second, more valid, criticism of flexible exchange rates is that they can contribute to inflationary pressures by reducing the discipline the fixed-rate approach provided governments to constrain their domestic prices because lower domestic prices increase the attractiveness of their exported goods. Yet this criticism is not so clear given the inflationary potential in sudden substantial currency devaluations under the Bretton Woods system. Flexible exchange rate advocates argue that flexible exchange rates do not cause inflation; rather, it is caused by the expansionary macroeconomic policies of governments and central banks.

I   REVIEW

Since 1973 the world has essentially operated on a system of _____ exchange rates. Governments, however, sometimes _____ in foreign exchange markets in order to prop up an exchange rate that they consider too _____ or to depress an exchange rate they consider to be too _____.

Prior to 1973, the world operated on a system of _____ exchange rates called the Bretton Woods system.

When exchange rates change they affect not only the currency market but the _____ markets as well. For example, if the dollar increases in value relative to other currencies, the relative prices of foreign goods for Americans will _____. Foreigners will find that the stronger dollar makes U.S. products _____ expensive for them.

Since the advent of flexible exchange rates, world trade has not only continued, but _____.

Changes in exchange rates occur _____ often under a flexible-rate system than they do under a fixed-rate system, but the changes are much _____ than the drastic, overnight revaluations of currencies under the fixed-rate system.

Under a fixed-rate system, as the supply and demand for currencies _____, currency prices are not allowed to shift to a new equilibrium, leading to surpluses and _____ of currencies.

One major argument against flexible exchange rates is that they cause _____ and may lead to a decrease in the level of world trade.

Another argument against flexible rates is that they may allow governments to pursue expansionary fiscal and monetary policies that may lead to _____.

II   TRUE/FALSE

_____ 1. The world economy currently operates under a system in which the exchange values of nations' currencies are fixed by an international organization.

_____ 2. Under the current exchange rate system, governments sometimes intervene in the foreign exchange market in order to alter the exchange value of currencies.

III   MULTIPLE CHOICE

1. Under a system of flexible exchange rates, a decrease in the demand for a country's currency on the foreign exchange market will
   A) cause the country's currency to depreciate in value.
   B) cause the country's currency to appreciate in value.
   C) make the country's goods more expensive to foreigners.
   D) make foreign goods less expensive to the country's citizens.

2. Critics of flexible exchange rates argue that flexible rates
   A) reduce uncertainty in international trade.
   B) automatically create an equilibrium price for each currency in the foreign exchange market.
   C) make nations more constrained in carrying out internal macroeconomic policies.
   D) increase uncertainty in international trade.

3. Critics of fixed exchange rates argue that fixed rates
   A) reduce uncertainty in international trade.
   B) result in currency shortages just as wage and price controls lead to shortages in markets for goods and services.
   C) make nations less constrained in carrying out internal macroeconomic policies.
   D) lead to constant, day-to-day changes in the exchange values of currencies.

IV   APPLICATION AND DISCUSSION

What affect would a sudden shift by the Fed to a more expansionary monetary policy have on the exchange value of the dollar and on America's balance on current account?

Questions

1. Why is the value of the yen important to the Lowells?

2. What kinds of things could have happened to have caused the dollar to double in value against the yen?

ANSWER KEY

CHAPTER 1 THE ROLE AND METHOD OF ECONOMICS

Section 1.1 Economics: A Brief Introduction

I	Review

A student of economics learns that much of life involves making a <u>choice</u> between conflicting wants in a world of scarcity. Students develop an economic way of <u>thinking</u> about their options, which is a valuable problem-solving tool.

<u>Economics</u> is defined, as the study of the allocation of our <u>limited</u> resources to satisfy our unlimited wants.

The factors like machinery, labor, water, and land, that are used to make goods and services are called <u>resources</u>.

The problem of <u>scarcity</u> results because our wants are greater than the goods and services our resources can produce.

We are forced to make <u>choices</u> about the best use of our limited resources. The cost of choosing to use a resource one way is the lost <u>opportunity</u> to use the resource in another way.

Making costly choices about the use of scarce resources is known as the <u>economic</u> problem.

II	True/False

1. True. City budget decisions are choices about the use of scarce resources.

2. False. Resources are those things used to make goods and services; they include factories, machinery, and tools that are man-made.

3. True. Scarcity means we can think of many uses for our limited resources, so we have to choose the best use.

4. False. The cost of using a resource, like a truck, is the lost opportunity to produce other goods and services we value. For example, the trucks could be used to haul bats and balls.

5. False. Economics can help us understand a wide variety of problems involving scarce resources, such as the use of time, family decisions, and the allocation of government funds.

6. True. Time is a scarce resource and you have made a decision to use it in a particular way.

III	Multiple Choice

1. The answer is C. Resources are things used to produce goods and services. Toys are consumed. Rubber trees, paint sprayers, and hammers are used to produce other goods and services.

2. The answer is C. Resources are scarce, so we must choose how to use them. The cost of our choice is the loss of the opportunity to use the resource in other ways.

3. The answer is B. An economic problem exists whenever we make choices about the use of scarce resources. We have only a limited amount of time.

4. The answer is D. Every choice we make involves a trade-off. When we use resources one way, we can't use them in any other way. We trade off one use for the other. Answer D is the only answer that does not involve a choice. Winning the lottery may reflect past choices and require future choices about the use of your money. When you win you make no choice, you have been chosen.

ANSWER KEY

1. One of the most important resources used raising children has historically been the mother's time. As opportunities for women to hold jobs, start businesses, and participate in political life increase, the cost of using women's time for raising children increases. As the cost rises, fewer children are born.

2. A problem is an economic problem when scarce resources force people to make a costly choice. The decision to go on a date is an economic decision because you give up the time to do other things when you choose to go on a date. The cost of going on a date with one person also involves giving up the opportunity to go with someone else. Basketball coaches have a limited number of scholarships to award. To use this scarce resource on a point guard has a cost, the lost opportunity to offer the scholarship to a center or forward. Finally, the decision to admit one student usually means that some other student will be denied admission to the university. Universities have limited capacity in classrooms and dorms, and admissions policy are the rules schools use to allocate these scarce resources. Admissions policy is usually set to ensure that the students who get into the university are the ones most likely to succeed.

3. The definition must recognize the central parts of the economist's point of view: resources are scarce; scarcity forces us to make choices; and the cost of these choices is the lost opportunities.

Section 1.2 Economics as a Science

I   Review

Like other social sciences, the central concern of economics is <u>human behavior</u>. It is the social science that studies people's <u>choices.</u>

Of the two main branches of economics, <u>macroeconomics</u> examines the effects of human behavior on the total economy, while <u>microeconomics</u> deals with human behavior in smaller units like the household or the firm. Economic problems affecting the whole of society such as inflation and unemployment are topics of <u>macroeconomics</u>. Microeconomics examines the choice making behavior of firms and households and their interaction in <u>markets</u>.

II   True/False

1. False. All social sciences are interested in human behavior, so they often examine the same questions from their particular perspectives.

2. True. Microeconomics is the branch of economics that attempts to understand the decision-making behavior of small units like firms and households within the economy. Economists try to understand the factors that determine the number of avocados that farmers choose to produce and the amount consumers choose to buy.

3. False. The analysis of the small units of the economy helps us to understand the behavior of the aggregate economy, and macroeconomic events like recessions affect households and firms. Both branches are concerned with the determinants and results of human interaction.

4. False. Inflation is an increase in the general price level. It affects the total or aggregate economy. It is a subject of macroeconomics.

III   Multiple Choice

1. The answer is D. Social science examines human behavior. While some biologists study the human body, their interest is in the way the body works, not the way humans behave and interact with others.

2. The answer is C. Microeconomics is the study of individual decision making units such as firms and households. Studies A, B, and D focus on macroeconomic problems.

3. The answer is C. The Archer's choice of vacation spots is based on tradition. Economics teaches us to think about the alternatives in terms of the costs and benefits associated with each. In each of the other answers the decision is made only after considering the costs and benefits.

ANSWER KEY

4. The answer is A. Economics is concerned with reaching eneralizations about human behavior. Economists are attempting to identify and describe the factors that affect most of the people most of the time. Economics attempts to understand and to predict the average behavior of groups of individuals.

5. The answer is C. Unemployment and its consequences are the topics of study of many different sciences. Unemployment can be study by macroeconomics, microeconomics, as well as other social sciences, like anthropology. The consequences of unemployment can also be studies by physical sciences, like biology and health sciences. While these physical sciences may share a subject with economics and the other social sciences, they are not social sciences since they do not study human behavior.

IV   Application and Discussion

1. Identify which of the following headlines represents a microeconomic topic and which is a macroeconomic topic.

Topic	Micro	Macro
A. "U.S. Unemployment Rate Reaches Historic Lows"		X
B. "General Motors Closes Auto Plant in St. Louis"	X	
C. "OPEC Action Results in a General Increase in Prices"		X
D. "Companies Cut the Cost of Health Care for Employees"	X	
E. "Lawmakers Worry about the Possibility of a US Recession"		X
F. "Colorado Rockies Make Outfielder Highest Paid Ballplayer"	X	

Macroeconomics examines economic problems that influence the whole economy. The focus is on aggregate or total economic activity. Headlines A, C, and E reflect the overall health of the economy. Microeconomics explains the actions of smaller units. The focus is on the decision-making behavior of firms and households. Headlines B, D, and F reflect the actions of firms.

Section 1.3 Economic Behavior

I   Review

Economists assume that people act as if they were motivated by self-interest. Since people are also assumed to respond to changes in predictable ways, self-interest is a good predictor of behavior.
Self-interest motivates people to produce more and may also encourage benevolence. Pursuing self-interest is not the same as being selfish.
Choices will have both positive and negative consequences. Economists believe that it is rational for people to consider the consequences of their actions before they make a decision.

II   True/False

1. False. Economists assume that people act out of self-interest and that they consider the consequences of their actions. If someone commits a crime, economists assume that the criminal decided that the expected benefits exceed the expected costs.
2. False. Economists are famous for their assumption that people are motivated by self-interest. A person's self-interest, however, may include concern for his family, community, and others.
3. False. Economists assume that individuals try to anticipate the likely consequences of their behavior or actions. This does not mean that individuals will always make right choices, but they at least thought about the possible consequences.
4. False. Economists assume that individuals act as if they are motivated by self-interest and respond in predictable ways to changing circumstances.

ANSWER KEY

5. False. Self-interest can include benevolence. Self-interest is not the same as selfishness. Most people consider providing for their family part of their self-interest. If the health and welfare of other people is important for our own happiness, self-interested actions may be those that allow us to do the most for others.

6. True. Economists believe that it is rational for a person to anticipate the likely consequences of their actions. We may not know the outcome of any action with certainty, but we consider the likely benefits and cost when making decisions. Chandler certainly doesn't behave in this rational way.

III   Multiple Choice

1. The answer is D. Economists observe the behavior of large groups of people, like consumers in the United States, and make predictions about how they will respond to certain events, especially changes in economic incentives like prices.

2. The answer is C. Anyone who invites a bull into his china shop certainly seems oblivious to the consequences, although it is possible that Mr. Haviland either knows that "Tornado" is a pussycat or he wants to collect insurance. Economists, who assume that behavior is rational, would expect an unseen motive on Mr. Haviland's part.

3. The answer is D. As Adam Smith, the "father" of economics has stated, "It is not from the benevolence of the butcher, the baker, or the brewer that we expect our dinner, but from their regard to their own interest."

4. The answer is D. The new contract changes the rewards of Bobby's actions. His rewards are greater for completions, so he will change his behavior to increase the number of completions he makes by throwing short passes. He will continue to train because being in shape will help his performance. But the change in the circumstances of his contract will give him the incentive to choose short passes more often than either the run or long passes.

IV   Application and Discussion

1. Of course, it is up to you to decide on this one. Economists, however, believe that their predictions gain accuracy if they assume that people act out of self-interest and usually don't use the terms "self-interest" and "selfishness" interchangeably. While some self-interested people cheat, self-interest can also lead to honesty. Most successful businesses find it to be in their interest to treat customers fairly. Businesses that have reputations as cheaters don't find many customers.

Section 1.4 Economic Theory

I   Review

A <u>theory</u> is an explanation that is supported by the facts of the real world. Economic theories are propositions used to <u>explain</u> and <u>predict</u> human behavior in different circumstances.

Economic theories cannot account for every event; to be useful theories must <u>abstract</u> or focus on only the essential factors.

A <u>hypothesis</u> is a prediction about how people will behave in certain economic circumstances and can be tested to see how well the prediction fits the <u>facts</u>.

Economists engage in <u>empirical</u> analysis to test hypotheses by seeing if they are consistent with the real world observations.

II   True/False

1. False. An economic theory abstracts from the complexities of the real world to better understand economic behavior. We expect a good theory to explain and predict well, not provide a complete description of the world.

2. True. Economic theories are statements about patterns of human behavior that are expected to take place under certain circumstances. Good theories should explain and predict well. In a situation, the idea that incentives matter can be used to predict what will happen when incentives change in a certain way.

3. False. A hypothesis is a testable proposal that makes a prediction about behavior in response to certain changed conditions. While this statement predicts behavior, it is not testable since we can't live on Mars.

4. True. A hypothesis is a testable proposal about behavior. A hypothesis can only be stated as a theory if it has been tested against the facts of the real world and shown to be a good predictor of behavior. A hypothesis that is not supported by the facts sends the economist "back to the drawing board" to find a new explanation.

5. False. Hypotheses are testable proposals that make a prediction about behavior. A hypothesis is not a theory; a hypothesis must be tested by comparing its predictions to the real behavior. Following an untested story about stock market behavior is a risky strategy.

III   Multiple Choice

1. The answer is B. Making a hypothesis about behavior is the first step in developing a theory. A hypothesis is a testable proposal that makes a prediction about behavior in response to changes. Once a hypothesis can be shown to predict what actually happened, it can be restated as an economic theory.

2. The answer is C. A good theory should help us explain and predict human behavior. Marion's proposition is a good theory if it can be shown to explain the facts of the real world and is useful in predicting the way people behave under different circumstances.

3. The answer is D. Economic theories cannot realistically include every event that has ever occurred. To learn anything about the real world we have to abstract from its complexities. We often decide to set aside information and isolate only the important relationships to learn more about the world. Trying to incorporate too much information will simply confuse us.

4. The answer is D. The scientific method starts with a hypothesis, a testable proposal that makes a prediction about behavior. This hypothesis is tested against the facts; economists ask whether the prediction of the hypothesis fit the historic facts. If the facts support the hypothesis, the hypothesis can be restated as a theory. If they facts don't support the hypothesis, the economist needs to develop a new hypothesis.

IV   Application and Discussion

1. A hypothesis should be simple because we need to abstract from the real world's complexity. It should be a proposal that makes some type of prediction. Finally, a hypothesis should be testable. Your hypothesis might be generated from a number of sources such as your reading, your observations of the world, or your explorations of similar or related issues. Examples of hypotheses include "Women's wages are lower because they work fewer hours per week" or "Women have lower wages because they have on average less education that men."

2. The data support the second hypothesis better than the first. The number of days with polluted air generally increases with the population. The five cities with the most days "with polluted air" are large places. The first hypothesis does not seem to be supported by the data. El Paso, Texas, was the hottest place on our list and had relatively few polluted days. The causes of air pollution are complex and many things affect the level of pollution in a city. In our limited world of seven cities, the second hypothesis is supported by the facts, and we could make a theoretical statement that air pollution will increase in general as population increases.

Section 1.5 Problems to Avoid in Scientific Thinking

I   Review

The Latin expression for "let everything else be equal" is *ceteris paribus*.

Without a theory of <u>causation</u>, scientists cannot understand the complexity that occurs in the real world.

In seeking to find causes for events, people sometimes mistake <u>correlation</u> for causation.

If someone observes that new car sales and auto accidents rise at the same time and concludes that new car sales cause auto accidents, they are mistaking <u>correlation</u> for causation.

ANSWER KEY

When someone assumes that what is true of an individual is also true of a group, they are committing the fallacy of <u>composition</u>.

II   True/False

1. False. This phrase, often-used by economists, means "holding other things equal" or "let everything else be equal."

2. True. Scientists in laboratories do this all the time. For economists dealing with human behavior in a dynamic world where many variables change all the time, this is a big problem.

3. False. Two things may occur together, without one necessarily causing the other. Just because MTV was introduced in 1982 doesn't mean it caused the 1982 recession or vice versa.

4. True. An individual may be able to attract attention by painting their house with black and pink stripes, but if everyone in the subdivision does it, no one attracts special attention.

III   Multiple Choice

1. The answer is B. The scientist would hold all the variables except alcohol consumption constant in order to isolate the effect of the alcohol on longevity.

2. The answer is C. Just because tall people play basketball doesn't mean that playing basketball causes people to become taller.

3. The answer is A. Just because these two phenomena are associated there is no reason to expect a causal relationship

4. The answer is D. What is true for one team is not necessarily good for the group. One team can gain a competitive advantage b y p aying m ore a nd h iring b etter p layers; m aybe t hey can win the World Series. But if all other teams expand their payrolls to compete, they all simply end up with higher labor costs. The only parties who are better off are the players!

IV   Application and Discussion

1. This is a case of mistaking correlation for causality. People in Wisconsin tended to live long lives and since cancer is a disease of middle and old age, it was a more frequent cause of death in Wisconsin than in other states. An area low in cancer deaths is likely to be an area of poor health where inhabitants die young. (Cited in Martin Gardner, *Fads and Fallacies in the Name of Science,* Dover Publications, 1957, p. 341.)

Section 1.6 Positive and Normative Analysis

I   Review

When economists study h uman b ehavior t hey e mphasize h ow p eople b ehave n ot h ow t hey s hould b ehave. T his o bjective approach is called <u>positive</u> analysis.

When economists comment on the desirability of particular actions they are making <u>normative</u> statements. Normative statements involve judgements about what <u>ought</u> to happen.

It is especially important to be able to <u>distinguish</u> between normative and positive analysis when policy considerations contain both. The majority of <u>disagreements</u> among economists involve normative issues.

A second important reason economists disagree is disagreement on the <u>validity</u> of the economic <u>theories</u> in a particular policy application.

ANSWER KEY

II   True/False

1. False. This is a positive statement. It is a proposition about how people will behave and it can be tested. A normative statement might be "The tax on cigarettes should be increased because people should smoke less." This describes an opinion about how people ought to behave.

2. True. Economists have opinions and make judgments. Normative statements reflect their opinions about economic policy.

3. False. As in all sciences, economists often disagree about economic policy matters. There are two main reasons for this disagreement. Differences may be a matter of opinion or values, economists may disagree about what ought to happen. Economists may also disagree about the legitimacy of specific theoretical explanations of behavior that are important for a policy question.

4. True. The first statement is a positive statement while the second is a normative statement. We expect more disagreement over matters of opinion or normative statements.

5. False. Economists are scientists seeking the truth about the way people behave. As scientists, economists try to promote an objective, value-free approach to the study of economic behavior. When an econ professor states her opinions, she is not teaching economics.

III   Multiple Choice

1. The answer is A. The value of preserving small farms is a matter of opinion, a normative statement. The other statements are propositions about how the world works that can be tested, positive statements.

2. The answer is B. You could test this hypothesis against the facts of the world by comparing the IQs of people who watch different amounts of television.

3. The answer is C. Positive analysis of proposed policy change will provide decision makers with an understanding of the effects associated with a policy change. Normative statements reflect the weights and values the speaker gives to these changes. These values reflect one person's opinions and will differ across people.

4. The answer is D. Economists, like all scientists, disagree over policy issues and theories. The text offers two general reasons economists disagree. Difference in values or beliefs (normative issues) is the most important reason for disagreement. Disagreement over the validity of particular theories is also important.

IV   Application and Discussion

1. This is a normative statement because it is a matter of opinion. Unless you held this opinion or respected the speaker, this normative statement would not cause you to support a zero tolerance standard for air pollution. To add to the debate positive statements about the effect of such standards could be tested; these statements should most importantly reflect the changes in the costs and benefits of adopting the more extreme standards. For example, "imposing zero pollution standards will significantly reduce the industrial output of the U.S. economy" and "the reduction in health problems resulting from the imposition of zero pollution standards will provide the benefits of significant reduction in health care costs."

ANSWER KEY

CHAPTER 2 THE ECONOMIC WAY OF THINKING

Section 2.1 Idea 1: Scarcity

I   Review
_____

Scarcity is the problem that exists because we have limited resources and unlimited wants for goods and services.

The physical and mental labor expended by people in the production of goods and services is called labor.

Natural resources like trees, water and minerals, that are used in production are classified as land resources.

Resources like tools, office buildings, and factories are called capital, while people who make the risky decisions about what goods to produce and how to produce them are called entrepreneurs.

Items that we value or desire are called goods, while intangible acts for which people are willing to pay are called services.

Because no one can have all the goods and services they desire, everyone, even the very rich, faces the common problem of scarcity.

Overtime the resources available to individuals and societies may increase, but scarcity will not be eliminated because our wants will continue to increase.

II   True/False
_____

1. False. A nation's wealth increases as its resources increase but new goods and services are also introduced. As a nation grows richer, both wants and resources increase leaving us with the problem of scarcity.

2. False. Just like nations, individuals find that as their resources increase so do their wants. Wealth provides no cure for the condition of scarcity.

3. True. The problem of rising expectations means that people can always think of more and more ways to use any increase in resources produced by new technology.

4. False. Harriet must choose among many worthy charities when she gives away her riches. She faces a scarcity problem because there are many more deserving activities than she could support.

III   Multiple Choice
_____

1. The answer is D. Whenever a person has to make a choice about the use of resources, they face the problem of scarcity.

2. The answer is C. Invention and innovation would reduce the problem of scarcity if it only increased the goods and services our resources could produce, but it also increases our wants by introducing new goods and services. As long as wants exceed the resources available to satisfy them, the problem of scarcity exists.

3. The answer is A. The reduction in travel cost caused by the jet introduced the possibility of worldwide travel to visit interesting and beautiful places.

4. The answer is A. As societies get more resources, they find more wants. Historically, solving pollution problems and preserving the environment become more important as country's income rises. This is another example of wants staying ahead of resources.

5. The answer is C. Tangible goods are things we can see, hold, taste, or smell. Automobiles, bouquets of flowers and bags of potato chips are tangible goods. A haircut is a service like medical care and legal services.

IV   Application and Discussion
_____

ANSWER KEY

1. Being poor means that you have access to few resources, which limits the goods and services you consume. Scarcity means you don't have enough resources to do everything you want to do, so you have to make choices. Everyone experiences scarcity because we can always think of more things that we want than we can produce with our resources.

2. The car freed Americans to travel and helped to create the tourism business. New wants included motels, resorts, and theme parks. The increased importance of auto and truck transportation also created the desire for more and better roads and highways. Finally the car allowed people to live farther from where they worked; people wanted more land and newer houses.

Section 2.2 Idea 2: Opportunity Cost

I   Review

Economics is the study of the <u>choices</u> we make among our <u>unlimited</u> wants and desires and our <u>limited</u> resources.

The highest, or best, foregone opportunity resulting from a decision is called the <u>opportunity</u> cost of that decision. The expression "There's no such thing as a free <u>lunch</u>," is often used to express the relationship between scarcity and opportunity cost.

II   True/False

1. True. The problem of scarcity requires us to choose which wants we should satisfy with our limited resources.

2. True. The opportunity cost of attending college includes foregone income plus other things like the cost of books and tuition.

3. False. The opportunity cost of an action includes the time, money, and other things that are given up because of that action.

4. False. Because taxpayers give up money they could have used to buy other goods and services in order to pay for teachers salaries, books, and school construction, public education is not free. The resources used to provide public education have opportunity costs.

5. True. Even though the price is the same, one person may have to give up more than the other in order to eat the dinner. For example, one person's time may be worth more than the other's, or one person may value the things she has to give up in order to buy the dinner more highly than the other.

III   Multiple Choice

1. The answer is A. Economics is the study of how people and societies choose to allocate scarce resources to satisfy unlimited wants.

2. The answer is B. The opportunity cost of an action is the value of the highest valued alternative that is foregone.

3. The answer is C. The opportunity cost includes everything you give up to train—not just the cost of equipment, but the value of everything else sacrificed for the training like going to the movies, sleeping, etc.

4. The answer is D. In other words, scarcity necessitates giving up one thing to have another.

IV   Application and Discussion

1. Since Sarah's time is probably worth more during school (it would cost part of her salary), the opportunity cost of the trip is higher in February than in July.

2. No. First of all, McDonald's uses scarce resources to produce the burger, so it's not "free" to them. Secondly, if people value their time at all, ten minutes standing in line to get the burger carries an opportunity cost equal to whatever else they could have done with the ten minutes. Also included is the opportunity cost of driving to McDonald's to get the "free" Big Mac.

ANSWER KEY

Section 2.3 Idea 3: Marginal Thinking

I   Review

People rarely make "all or nothing" choices. Most choices involve changes from the status quo or <u>marginal</u> changes.

The positive results of these additional changes are called marginal <u>benefits</u> and the negative results are marginal <u>costs</u>.

When people make choices for which the expected marginal benefits exceed the marginal costs of the change, they are following the rule of <u>rational</u> choice.

The benefits and costs of many choices occur in the future. We can't know future outcomes for certain because the world is <u>uncertain</u>. People make choices they can only compare what they think is likely to happen, so they compare the <u>expected</u> marginal benefits and costs.

II   True/False

1. False. Marginal choices concern decisions that focus on additional changes. The marginal choice would be whether to go to Tuscaloosa one more time.

2. True. The rule of rational choice states that people act rationally when they make decisions for which the marginal benefits are greater than the marginal costs.

3. True. The expected cost of robbery depends on the penalty and the chance of being caught. By increasing the police patrols the city will increase the chance robbers will be caught.

4. False. Increasing wilderness areas has real benefits but it also has costs. The costs include loss of land for housing and farms. At some point the marginal benefits of additional wilderness will be less than the marginal costs.

III   Multiple Choice

1. The answer is C. Following the rule of rational choice, you compare the marginal benefits and costs of increasing your study time. The high benefits associated with doing well on this exam increase the likelihood of studying more for this exam. The low marginal benefits in A probably don't encourage increased study time; marginal costs increase in B; and the information in D doesn't effect either benefits or costs on the margin.

2. The answer is D. Marginal thinking deals with making relatively small changes to the status quo. Becoming a vegetarian is an all or nothing type of choice. Increasing the amount of vegetables you eat or reducing the amount of meat are marginal decisions.

3. The answer is A. Your friend will make jaywalking decisions by comparing the expected benefits and costs each time she has the opportunity. As her time becomes more valuable, the benefits of saving time crossing the street will increase, causing her to jaywalk more often. Answers B, C, and D increase the expected marginal costs of jaywalking.

4. The answer is C. The price of Bill's airline ticket is certain. Bill is uncertain about the weather, hotel neighbors, and his health. All of these will affect the benefits he receives from his trip.

5. The answer is D. We should do something to make the air cleaner only if the expected marginal benefits of doing so are greater than the expected marginal costs.

IV   Application and Discussion

1. The benefits of going to the movie include the happiness you receive from being entertained and the social interaction with friends. These are uncertain because they depend on the quality of the move and your companionship. Costs include the price of the movie ticket and the value of the time you give up to go to the movie. Uncertainty also affects your costs since you do not know for certain what you would get out of your alternative use of your time.

2. As long as a person follows the rule of rational choice, they will always make decisions were they expect to gain more in benefits than they have to give up in costs. They will always be better off in this case. If a person's expectations about benefits or costs are wrong, their decisions may make them worse off.

Section 2.4 Idea 4: Incentives Matter

I   Review

According to economists, rational people react to changes in expected marginal <u>costs</u> and expected marginal <u>benefits</u>. If a rational person engages in criminal activity the perceived benefits of criminal activity must be greater than the perceived <u>costs</u>.

Economics expect that harsher penalties for criminal activity will <u>reduce</u> the amount of crime.

Positive incentives are things that either <u>increase</u> benefits or reduce costs.

Negative incentives are things that <u>reduce</u> benefits or increase costs.

Since economists believe that people respond to incentives they would predict that couples would choose to have <u>fewer</u> children if the government imposed a tax on each baby born.

Economics would predict a(n) <u>decrease</u> in the amount of cheating that takes place in schools if penalties on cheating were harsher.

II   True/False

1. True. That people respond in predictable ways to changes in incentives is one of the basic postulates of economics.

2. False. Economists believe that people commit crimes because they view the benefits of criminal activity to be greater than the costs.

3. False. A tax on bicycles would be an example of a negative incentive, since it would increase the costs of owning a bike.

4. False. A tax deduction increases the benefit of having a child and is thus a positive incentive.

5. True. Since people respond to incentives, and the death penalty increases the likely costs of drug trafficking, the frequency of this activity is reduced by the harsh penalty.

6. False. According to the survey cited in the text, 94 percent of students who cheat never get caught.

7. True. The level at which a driver is legally drunk in the United States is at 0.08 percent alcohol, while in Norway the limit is 0.05 percent.

III   Multiple Choice

1. The answer is C. More generous unemployment benefits reduce the cost of remaining unemployed and are therefore a positive incentive for people to remain unemployed longer.

2. The answer is C. The offer of a free laptop is a positive incentive since it increases the benefits of doing well on the exam. All the other examples are negative incentives.

3. The answer is B. A fine is negative incentive since it increases the cost of a certain behavior. The other examples are positive incentives.

4. The answer is D. The tax probably provides more anti-smoking incentive than the other alternatives. Studies by economists support the notion that taxes that make cigarettes more expensive result in less teen smoking.

ANSWER KEY

IV   Application and Discussion

1. An organ market that provided cash rewards would likely increase the supply of available organs, especially if people from poor countries were allowed to participate. It would also allow people in dire need of a particular organ to go into the market and purchase it rather than put their name on a waiting list. Many people, however, feel that a person's body parts have a special status and should not be offered for sale. Some people worry that only the rich would get organs in a market while others fear that a market would result in people being murdered for their valuable organs. They prefer the current system where only donated organs are accepted, and are allocated by physicians according to need.

Section 2.5 Idea 5: Specialization and Trade

I   Review

When people <u>specialize</u> they dedicate their resources to one primary activity.

Specialization allows people to make the most out of their limited resources by lowering the <u>opportunity</u> cost of producing goods and services. When a person, region, or country can produce a good at a lower opportunity costs they have a <u>comparative</u> advantage in the production of it.

When we specialize we rely on others to produce most of the goods and services we consume, so <u>trade</u> is important for specialization to succeed.

Trade allows people, regions, and countries to increase their <u>wealth</u> by concentrating on the production of goods and services at which they are relatively better.

II   True/False

1. False. In a trading situation, the country with the lowest opportunity costs has the comparative advantage.

2. False. While Stan can paint the house in less time than the average painter can, the value of his time is high. Stan's opportunity cost of painting the house is higher than painters who take longer, because he could earn more using the time in medicine.

3. False. We all specialize to some extent. Teachers, mechanics, farmers, and lawyers all concentrate on one job and rely on others to provide the goods and services we want.

4. True. Labor can be trained on very specific jobs. Capital equipment can be design for specialized functions. Productivity is increased because both labor and capital is better at performing these specialized tasks.

5. True. Trade allows countries to specialize in the goods and services they are relatively best at producing. If countries specialize and produce the goods and services for which they have they lowest opportunity cost, more goods and services can be produced from the countries' resources.

6. False. It is relatively more costly to grow coffee in the United States than in Brazil. We would use more resources to produce coffee. We are better off using United States resources in more productive activities and trading with Brazil.

III   Multiple Choice

1. The answer is C. Individuals, regions, and countries choose to specialize in that activity they have the lowest opportunity cost in. The Candlestick maker gives up less or has the lowest cost by giving up careers as a Butcher or Baker than she would not being a Candlestick maker.

2. The answer is B. Axel has a comparative advantage in auto mechanics. Axel's opportunity cost of cutting the lawn is higher than it is for the person he hires.

ANSWER KEY

3. The answer is D. Firms gain through the specialization of jobs because the cost of producing falls when workers learn their jobs better, spend less time starting and stopping to change tasks, and work in jobs they are best at. Specialization does not allow workers to learn all of the jobs in the factory.

4. The answer is A. Trade allows countries to specialize in the production of the goods and services in which they have a comparative advantage. When all countries shift production to the goods for which they have the lowest opportunity cost, the same resources will produce more goods and services.

5. The answer is D. Specialization is decided by opportunity costs, not the absolute cost of the materials used to produce the good. While the South might have used fewer resources to grow food than the West, the real cost would have been the valuable lost cotton production.

6. The answer is B. Sergei has a comparative advantage in playing hockey. While he might take less time to sew clothes, the value of his time is great. The cost to Sergei is greater than if he were to buy his clothes from someone else.

IV   Application and Discussion

1. Of course answers to this question will vary. If you live in Nebraska, your answer might be corn; in Alaska, it might be oil and fish; in Hawaii, it might be tourism or macadamia nuts.

2. Denying trade possibilities also eliminates the possibility of specialization. In autarky, a country must produce everything it consumes. Scarce resources will be wasted producing goods with a higher opportunity costs. Trading would allow the country to produce more with the same resources.

3. The opportunity cost of growing soybeans is the lost value because Fran can't grow corn for $60. The opportunity cost of growing corn is the lost opportunity to grow and sell soybeans, which equals $75. Fran should specialize in soybeans, which is the crop with the lowest opportunity cost. For each acre of corn Fran converts to soybeans, she will gain $15.

Section 2.6 Idea 6: Market Prices Coordinate Economic Activity

I   Review

In a market economy most of the resources are owned by private individuals and firms.

The market system provides a way for millions of producers and consumers to allocate scarce resources. Individuals indicate their wants and desires through their actions and inactions in the marketplace. Market prices serve as the language of the market.

Market prices communicate important information to buyers and sellers. This communication results in a shifting of resources from uses that are less valued to those that are more valued.

Government policies that set prices above or below what they would be in a free market are called price controls.

When the market mechanism fails to allocate resources efficiently it is called market failure. For example, lack of competition in a market can lead to higher prices and reduced product quality.

A question of special concern is whether or not the market economy provides a fair distribution of income.

II   True/False

1. False. In a market economy most of the resources are owned by private parties.

2. False. Physical violence has been used since the beginning of time to gain control of scarce resources.

3. True. Since the collapse of the Soviet Union, which relied on government control to allocate resources, the market has emerged as the predominant form of economic organization.

251

ANSWER KEY

4. False. Market prices communicate information about the relative value of products to both buyers and sellers.

5. False. Price controls interrupt communication between buyer and sellers.

6. True. Since minimum wage laws raise wages above market levels, they discourage employers from hiring unskilled teens, while at the same time increasing the number of teens looking for work.

7. True. Pollution and lack of competition are examples of market failure.

III   Multiple Choice

1. The answer is D. Sexton and other economists liken the signals that prices send to consumers and suppliers to language.

2. The answer is C. An increase in prices means that oranges have become more scarce and therefore more valuable than before.

3. The answer is A. As the book says, price controls strip the market price of its meaning for consumers and suppliers. Using the language metaphor, market prices tell the truth, while price controls lie.

4. The answer is C. As the book says, minimum wage laws have two effects on teenage employment. The higher wage (1) makes teens want to work more, but (2) discourages employers from hiring.

5. The answer is D. Air pollution, which imposes costs on others not connected with producing or consuming a particular good, is a symptom of market failure.

IV   Application and Discussion

1. A) People who see an energetic and loveable Jack Russell Terrier in a popular TV series want Jack Russell Terriers as pets.

   Price of Jack Russell Terriers __X__ Rises _____ Falls

   B)   Aging retirees flock to Tampa, Florida to live.

   Price of housing in Tampa   __X__ Rises _____ Falls

   C) Weather-related crop failures in Colombia and Costa Rica reduce coffee supplies.

   Price of Coffee   __X__ Rises _____ Falls

   D) Sugar cane fields in Hawaii and Louisiana are replaced with housing.

   Price of sugar   __X__ Rises _____ Falls

   E) More and more students graduate from U.S. medical schools.

   Wages of U.S. doctors   _____ Rises __X__ Falls

   F) Americans are driving more and they are driving bigger, gas-guzzling cars like sports utility vehicles.

   Price of gasoline   __X__ Rises _____ Falls

2. A, B, and C would cause increases in the value and prices of potatoes. A reduction in the prices of potato substitutes would make them more attractive and reduce the value and price of potatoes.

252

ANSWER KEY

CHAPTER 3 SCARCITY, TRADE-OFFS, AND ECONOMIC GROWTH

Section 3.1 The Three Economic Questions Every Society Faces

I   Review

Scarcity forces all societies from the richest to the poorest to answer three fundamental questions.

   1) <u>What</u> do we produce?

   2) <u>How</u> do we produce these goods and services?

   3) For <u>whom</u> do we produce the goods and services?

In market economies, individuals control the production decisions by "voting" with their <u>dollars</u> for the goods and services they want. This consumer control is called consumer <u>sovereignty</u>.

Societies organize in two major ways to answer these economic questions. Economies are called <u>command</u> economies when government officials make decisions in a highly centralized system.

When many individual producers and consumers make economic decisions in a decentralized manner the economy is a <u>market</u> economy.

Since there are several ways to produce any good or service, all economies must decide <u>how</u> to produce the goods and services they want. If an economy uses lots of labor to produce goods and services, economists would say production is <u>labor</u> intensive.

Countries tend to use production processes that conserve its relatively <u>scarce</u> resources and use more of their relatively <u>abundant</u> resources.

"Who gets what?" is an economic questions that <u>scarcity</u> forces all societies to answer. This question is about the <u>distribution</u> of output.

In a market economy, the amount of output any one person can secure depends on their <u>income</u>, which depends on the amount and quality of scarce <u>resources</u> they control.

II   True/False

1. False. The decision our society makes about what goods and services to produce is difficult to make because we have to choose among a wide variety of known wants. We have to choose because our resources are scarce.

2. False. In a market economy, consumers decide what goods and services are produced by voting with their dollars. If a manufacturer produces a good that no one wants, they will not be rewarded for producing it, and so will stop its production. The power of consumers to decide what is produced in a market economy is called consumer sovereignty.

3. True. In high wage countries, capital-intensive production methods tend to be used in order to economize on relatively expensive labor resources.

4. False. Because of scarcity there will not be enough goods and services to go around, so societies need to find a way to decide who gets the goods and services that are produced.

5. False. LeBron James has a very high income. The typical college student has a low income. James can consume more because his higher income allows him to buy more of the goods and services produced each year.

253

ANSWER KEY

1. The answer is A. Economic decisions in a command economy are made by government officials in a central planning organization. Individual consumers and producers make economic decisions in a market economy. As economies go through the transition from command to market, we would expect the decisions of individual consumers and producers to replace those made by officials of central government organizations.

2. The answer is A. In a market economy, production decisions are controlled by the consumer. Consumer sovereignty is the concept that consumers' decisions about how to spend their money determine what goods and services are produced. Consumers are already getting what they think is best for them. Barry's list would impose a command economy on consumers.

3. The answer is C. A fishing boat is an example of a man-made resource that is used to produce final goods.

4. The answer is B. For every good and service we produce, there is more than one method of production. We can use capital intensive or labor-intensive production techniques. For example, we can build houses out of wood or brick with lots of labor or lots of machines. We can build sprawling homes on large plots of land or three story homes on less land.

5. The answer is D. In a market economy, a person's claim on the economy's goods and services depends on their income. The greater a person's income, the more goods and services they can consume.

IV   Application and Discussion

1. Hollywood will probably make more movies like *Titanic* because of consumer sovereignty. Consumers, "voting" with their dollars have shown they want movies like *Titanic*. Since movie studios are in the business to make money, not simply movies, they will produce what the consumers want, not what the critics like.

2. The relevant question here is how to produce household goods and services like meals and laundry services. Since in most homes women do most of the housework, an increase in their earnings and job opportunities outside the home raises the opportunity cost of their time. Such an increase in the cost of labor would likely cause households to economize on labor and substitute capital, in the form of household appliances.

Section 3.2 The Circular Flow Model

I   REVIEW

Households make payments to firms for goods and services in the product market. Money flows to the firms in exchange for the goods and services that flow to households.

Firms buy inputs from households in the factor market. Firms use households' labor, land, capital, and entrepreneurship to produce goods and services.

Money flows from the firms to the households as compensation for the use of these inputs. The households receive payments in the form of wages, rent, interest, and profit.

The simple circular flow model illustrates the continuous flow of payments, income, inputs, and goods and services between households and firms. This model shows how product and factor markets are interrelated.

ANSWER KEY

1. False. Money moves in the opposite direction as the flow of goods and services. Money is a payment for these products. Money is exchanged for goods and services in the product market.

2. True. The factor market is where households sell the resources they own to firms for wages, interest, rent, and profits.

3. True. The money paid by firms in exchange for the use of the households' resources is the households' money income.

III   Multiple Choice

1. The answer is B. The money household receives as income from firms is used to buy the goods and services produced by the firms. In the circular flow model the money flows from firms to households to firms in the form of spending in the product and factor markets.

2. The answer is B. Households buy goods and services in the product market. Households spend their income in the product market. This spending becomes the revenue of the firms selling the products.

3. The answer is C. Wages, interest, rent, and profit are forms of payment households receive from firms for the use of their labor, land, capital and entrepreneurship.

IV.   APPLICATION AND DISCUSSION

Identify the appropriate market where each of the following transactions takes place by placing an X in the appropriate box.

Transaction	Factor Market	Product Market
Billy buys a sofa from Home Time Furniture for his new home.		X
Home Time Furniture pays its manager her weekly salary.	X	
The manager buys dinner at Billy's Café.		X
After he pays all of his employees their wages and pays his other bills, the owner of Billy's Café takes his profit.	X	

Furniture is a good purchased in the product market from firms. Labor is a resource that households sell to firms in the factor market. Restaurant food is a good purchased by consumers in the product market. Finally, Billy's entrepreneurial resource is paid a profit, which is the amount left over after all his other costs have been paid. This takes place in the factor market. These few transactions trace the circular flow of money between households and firms in the factor and product markets.

Section 3.3 The Production Possibilities Curve

I   Review

The problem of making choices regarding what to produce and in what quantities can be illustrated with a production possibilities curve.

ANSWER KEY

Most economies have resources that are <u>idle</u> for at least some period of time.

Efficiency requires society to use its resources to the fullest extent and get the <u>greatest</u> output from its scarce resources.

If an economy is operating at a point off and below its production possibilities curve, it means that resources are not being utilized <u>efficiently</u>.

When a production possibilities curve is bowed outward from the origin it is because of the law of <u>increasing</u> opportunity cost.

II   True/False

1. False. It represents the potential total output combinations of two goods for an economy with given amounts of land, labor, capital, and entrepreneurship.

2. True. Since a production possibilities curve represents the total output combinations of two goods for an economy, using one to represent South Korea's total output combinations of rice and soybeans would be appropriate.

3. True. All resources are not alike. A good fisherman may be a lousy boat builder.

4. False. Factories are capital resources. Idle factories represent "unemployed" capital.

5. True. Efficiency requires society to use its resources to the fullest extent possible.

III   Multiple Choice

1. The answer is A. Point A represents 500 million bushels of rice, as shown on the vertical axis, and 350 million bushels of soybeans, as shown on the horizontal axis.

2. The answer is A. Point A represents an economy producing bananas but no coffee.

3. The answer is D. At point E the economy is off its production possibilities curve and operating at less than full potential.

4. The answer is C. As the economy moves from A to D, the quantity of bananas that must be given up in order to get another unit of coffee increases.

5. The answer is B. When resources are unemployed they can't be used to produce goods and services.

6. The answer is D. All of the concepts, except economic growth, are illustrated by the production possibilities curve. Scarcity requires that we choose how to allocate scarce resources between the production of two goods; opportunity cost is shown by the fact that we have to give up guns in order to have more butter, and increasing opportunity costs is shown as the economy gets less butter each time it gives up an equal number of guns. Economic growth, a long-term increase in total output, is not illustrated.

IV   Application and Discussion

1. Upon entry into the war, the United States would move from point A toward the production of military goods, as in the movement to point B. After the war the economy moves back to point A. [Exh0301ans]

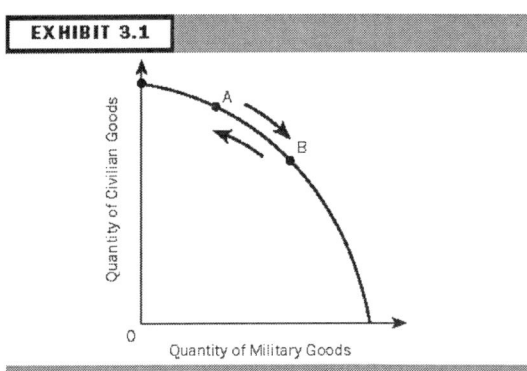

EXHIBIT 3.1

Quantity of Civilian Goods

A

B

O   Quantity of Military Goods

2. A. Unemployed Labor

    B. Unemployed Capital

    C. Unemployed Labor

    D. Unemployed Land

3. As you learned in Chapter 1, people respond to incentives. If government policies do not provide proper incentives to entrepreneurs so they can make profits and control their property, they may well sit on the sidelines and become idle.

Section 3.4 Economic Growth and the Production Possibilities Curve

I   Review

A country's economic growth depends on the <u>sacrifices</u> made today. To grow we have to give up <u>consumer</u> goods and produce more <u>capital</u> goods.

An increase in an economy's capital stock will allow it to increase its future <u>productive</u> capacity and consume more in the future. The effect of the increase in a country's capital stock is represented by a(n) <u>outward</u> shift in its production possibilities curve.

Investment can be more than building new physical capital stock. Upgrading the <u>skills</u> and <u>knowledge</u> of a country's workforce has a similar effect on economic growth.

While today's sacrifices allow a country to produce more in the future, growth will not eliminate scarcity. Even with more resources countries must still make <u>choices</u> among the ways these resources will be used.

II   True/False

1. False. Countries choose to grow. Economic growth requires that countries make sacrifices today to increase their future p roductive c apacity. E conomic g rowth r equires t hat c ountries g ive u p c onsumption g oods t oday i n o rder to increase their production of capital goods.

2. False. While the expansion of a country's productive capacity provides benefits, economic growth has costs. The costs of economic growth are the current sacrifices necessary for growth. The essential question countries must ask is whether the increased consumption allowed by economic growth is worth the current sacrifices. Pursuit of economic growth is only good for a country if the benefits are greater than the costs.

ANSWER KEY

3. False. While happy workers may be important to a country's economic performance, growth requires that sacrifices be made. A society must produce fewer consumer goods than possible in order to produce more capital goods. Capital goods are a resource used to produce other goods and services. To increase capital and its ability to produce more goods and services in the future, a country must sacrifice some consumption today.

4. True. The production possibilities curve represents the possible bundles of goods and services a country can produce with its available resources. As the resources available to the country increase or technological progress provides better ways of using these resources, the possible bundles of goods and services expands. This expansion is represented by a rightward shift in the production possibilities curve.

5. False. Scarcity is not a problem of poverty. Affluent societies also face the problem of scarcity. As long as there are a number of uses for any resource, people will have to make choices. Scarcity exists as long as you have to give up one thing to get more of something else.

III   Multiple Choice

1. The answer is C. Investment in human capital includes all investments that improve the productivity of the population. Upgrading skills and knowledge through training and education are human capital investments. Investment in improving the health of the population can also be a human capital investment if it increases the average productivity of the population. Chile has invested in capital goods.

2. The answer is B. To expand its ability to produce goods and services, a country must increase the resources it has available. In order to increase a country's capital stock, the country must reduce its production of consumption goods unless it receives a gift of capital from another country. Many foreign aid programs of the United States and other rich nations transfer capital goods to less developed countries.

3. The answer is C. Growth occurs when the economy is able to produce more. Growth may result because the economy is more efficient (A to C) or because of new technologies or the addition of more resources (C to D and B to D). Movements along the production possibilities curve (C to B) represent a change in the way resources are used but not an expansion of productive capacity.

IV   Application and Discussion

1.   Economic growth depends on a country's willingness to sacrifice current consumption and invest in capital goods or in human capital. Expanding the country's capital stock or improving the quality of its labor force allows it to produce more goods and services. Economic growth occurs when a country expands its productive capacity. A country will fail to grow if it chooses not to sacrifice because it cares a lot about current consumption (C) or if its sacrificed consumption is spent in other countries (A) and on goods other than capital goods (E). A country may also have such a low income that the sacrifices of giving up consumption are too great (B). Growth will also be limited if a country does not invest in human capital   (D).

CHAPTER 4 SUPPLY AND DEMAND

Section 4.1 Markets

I   Review

A <u>market</u> is the process of buyers and sellers exchanging goods.

The term "market" is hard to define because an incredible variety of <u>exchange</u> arrangements exist in the world.

For some goods, like housing and cement, markets are numerous but <u>geographically</u> limited. For other goods, like gold and automobiles, markets are <u>global</u>.

The <u>buyers</u> determine the demand side of the market, while <u>sellers</u> determine the supply side.

A <u>competitive</u> market is one characterized by lots of buyers and sellers and in which no single buyer or seller can influence the market price.

II   True/False

1. True. A bookstore, like any retail establishment, is a place where buyers and sellers come together to trade.

2. True. The doctor's office is a place where sellers of medical services (doctors and nurses) meet buyers of medical services (patients).

3. False. A market, as stated in the book is "the process of buyers and sellers exchanging goods and services." eBay, for example, isn't a place, but it helps bring buyers and sellers together.

4. False. Fans are consumers of baseball services. They are on the demand side of the market. The sellers of baseball, the teams, players, and TV and radio stations, etc. are on the supply side of the market.

III   Multiple Choice

1. The answer is C. A factory is a place where goods are produced, whereas a market is a place where buyers and sellers come together.

2. The answer is A. As the text says, when transportation costs are high relative to the selling price, as in the case of concrete, markets are numerous and geographically isolated. Goods will be produced close to the point of sale.

3. The answer is C. The market for autos is global. Cars made in the United States (or Japan or Germany or anywhere else for that matter) are sold all over the world.

IV   Application and Discussion

1. The market is global. Manufacturers sell to dealers throughout the world. Transport costs are low relative to the costs of a laptop computer. Middlepeople make information about prices and quality easily available.

Section 4.2 Demand

I   Review

According to the law of demand, other things being equal, the quantity of a good or service demanded goes up when its price goes <u>down</u>. The primary reason for the inverse relationship between price and quantity demanded is the substitution effect.

ANSWER KEY

A(n) <u>individual</u> demand curve is a graphical representation of the relationship between the price of a good and the <u>quantity</u> demanded. The horizontal summing of the demand curves of all the buyers in the market is called the <u>market</u> demand curve.

II   True/False

1. False. According to the law of demand, price and quantity demanded move in opposite directions.

2. True. The relationship described by the law of demand is an inverse, or negative, relationship. As price goes down, consumption goes up.

3. False. As the book points out, demand is an actual willingness to pay.

4. False. As the book points out, "need" is a fuzzy concept that is a poor guide to analyzing behavior.

5. False. An individual's demand schedule shows the amounts that a person will actually be willing to buy at various prices.

6. True. A demand curve shows graphically the various amounts that someone will buy at various prices.

7. True. As it says in the text, the market demand curve is created by summing horizontally the individual demand curves.

III   Multiple Choice

1. The answer is B. The law of demand describes an inverse relationship between price and quantity demanded; as one goes up, the other goes down.

2. The answer is C. The relationship is inverse because price and quantity move in opposite directions.

3. The answer is C. The law of demand says that all other things constant, a decrease in the price of the product will result in an increase in the quantity purchased.

4. The answer is A. When economists use the term *ceteris paribus,* we recognize that although many things affect our consumption, we are focusing on the effect of price.

5. The answer is A. An individual demand schedule shows the different amounts of a product that a person would be willing to buy at various prices in a particular time interval.

6. The answer is C. The market demand curve is derived by adding the various amounts that all the demanders in the market will be willing to buy at various prices.

7. The answer is D. Because a demand curve describes a negative relationship between two variables, price and quantity demanded it slopes down and to the right.

IV   Application and Discussion

1. Holding other variables such as incomes and tastes constant, land in rural Minnesota must be less expensive than land in New York. Sid's behavior is in accordance with the law of demand, which describes an inverse relationship between price and quantity demanded.

2. See Exhibit 4.1.

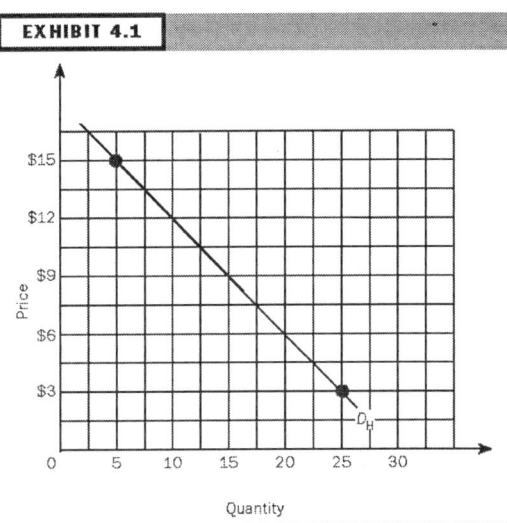

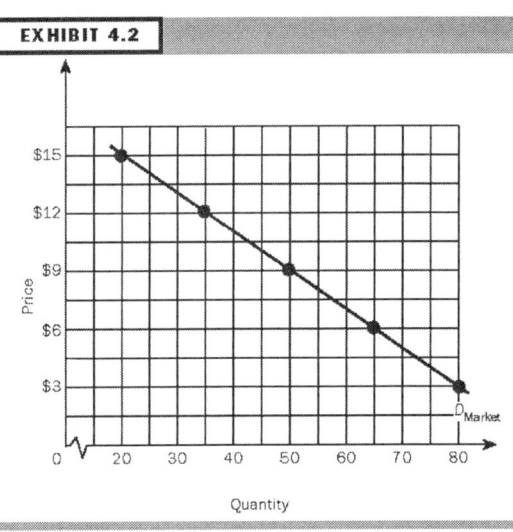

3. See Exhibit 4.2.

Price (dollars per ounce)	Quantity Demanded (ounces per week)							
	Hillary	Barbara	Nancy	Market				
$15					5	0	15	20
12	10	5	20	35				
9	15	10	25	50				
6	20	15	30	65				
3	25	20	35	80				

Section 4.3 Shifts in the Demand Curve

I   Review

A change in a good's price leads to a change in <u>quantity</u> demanded, while a change in one of the <u>determinants</u> of demand will lead to a shift in the entire demand curve.

Determinants of demand are called demand <u>shifters</u> and they lead to a change in <u>demand</u>. Some possible demand shifters are: the prices of closely <u>related</u> goods; income; number of <u>buyers</u>; <u>tastes</u> of buyers; and <u>expectations</u> of buyers.

ANSWER KEY

Two goods are substitutes if an increase in the price of one good causes an <u>increase</u> in the demand for the other. Two goods are complements if an increase in the price of one good causes a <u>decrease</u> in the demand for the other.

As their incomes rise, consumers generally buy <u>more</u> of most goods. When higher income leads to an increase in demand for a good the good is called a <u>normal</u> good. If higher income leads to a reduction in demand for a good, it is called an <u>inferior</u> good.

The vital statistics of the potential consumer population, including size, income, and age characteristics, are referred to as the <u>demographics</u> of a product.

When demand changes with changes in fashion, the cause of the change is referred to as a change in <u>tastes</u>.

<u>Expectations</u> about the future, such as fear of shortages or concern over future price rises may affect consumer <u>demand</u>.

If the price of a good changes it leads to a change in quantity <u>demanded</u>, but if one of the other factors influencing consumer behavior changes it leads to a change in <u>demand</u>.

II   True/False

1. False. A change in a good's price leads to a change in quantity demanded. A change in demand results from a change in one of the variables that shift the demand curve, such as consumers incomes or tastes.

2. True. If the price of a good falls, it becomes cheaper relative to its substitutes, so people will buy more of it and less of the substitute goods.

3. True. Because CDs and tapes are substitutes, consumers will buy CDs rather than tapes when CD prices fall.

4. False. An increase in the price of a complement like hot dogs, will decrease the demand for a product like mustard. Higher hot dog prices mean that people will buy fewer hot dogs. Hence, they will consume less mustard on their dogs.

5. True. According to the law of demand, more tennis racquets will be sold at lower prices. Because racquets and balls are complements, people will buy more tennis balls.

6. False. As incomes rise, the demand for normal goods rises.

7. True. Inferior goods are goods whose demand falls as income rises.

8. False. Demographic changes, like changes in the average age of the population, do affect demand, but we would expect to see the demand for other products like orthopedic shoes and medical services to increase as the population ages.

III   Multiple Choice

1. The answer is A. A change in a good's price leads to a change in quantity demanded, or a movement along a given demand curve, while a change in one of the variables leads to a change in demand, or a shift in the demand curve.

2. The answer is C. A change in the price of the product causes a change in quantity demanded but does not cause a change in demand.

3. The answer is B. If people think that they can become better-looking by eating jelly beans, they will buy more at each and every price and the demand curve will shift to the right.

4. The answer is D. If the demand for a good goes down when consumers' incomes increase, it is an inferior good.

5. The answer is B. If higher incomes lead to an increase in the demand for a good, the good is a normal good.

ANSWER KEY

6. The answer is C. An increase in the number of newborns will likely cause the demand for disposable diapers to go up. It is a change in demographics, or number of demanders.

7. The answer is D. An increase in the own-price of a good or service results in a decrease in quantity demanded, or a movement up along the demand curve.

8. The answer is B. Smokers in Alaska stocked up because of an expected increase in cigarette prices.

IV   Discussion and Application

1. A. The price of chicken falls.
        Determinant: Price of substitute [Exh un0401ans]

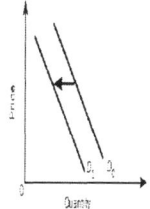

   B. The price of hamburger buns doubles.
       Determinant variable: <u>Price of complement</u>

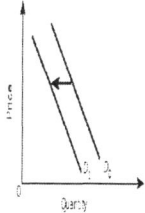

   C. Scientists find that eating hamburger prolongs life.
       Determinant variable: <u>Tastes</u>

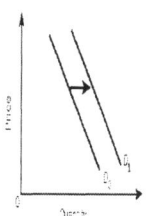

   D. The population of Hilo doubles.
       Determinant variable: <u>Number of consumers</u>

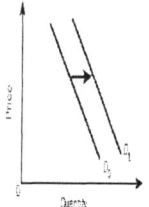

2. A. The price of Fords plummets!
        Determinant variable: <u>Price of substitutes</u>

    B. Consumers believe that the price of Chevrolets will rise next year.
        Determinants variable: <u>Expectations</u>

    C. The incomes of Americans rise.
        Determinants variable: <u>Income</u>

    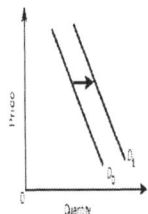

    D. The price of gasoline falls dramatically.
        Determinants variable: <u>Price of complements</u>

    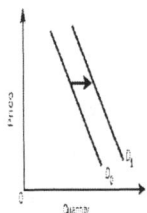

3. A. Point B represents an increase in quantity demanded.

    B. Point E represents an increase in demand.

    C. Point F represents a decrease in demand.

    D. Point C represents a decrease in quantity demanded.

ANSWER KEY

Section 4.4 Supply

I   Review

The answer to the questions, "What do we produce and in what quantities?" depends on the interaction of both <u>buyers</u> and <u>sellers</u>.

The law of supply states that, other things being equal, quantity supplied varies <u>directly</u> with price.

A producer requires a higher price to produce additional units of the good because of the law of <u>increasing</u> opportunity costs.

The individual supply curve is <u>upward</u> sloping as you move from left to right.

Adding the amount each individual producer would supply at each price will give us the <u>market</u> supply curve.

II   True/False

1. False. Market outcomes depend on understanding both the demand and supply sides of the market.

2. False. When two variables are directly related, like price and quantity supplied, they move in the same direction.

3. True. Producers usually use the most efficient, lowest-opportunity-cost resources first when they produce a good.

4. True. The supply curve shows how much a producer would produce at any price. The law of supply states that an increase in price is necessary for more to be produced.

5. True. A change in the quantity supplied describes the response of producers to changes in the good's price. A change in one of the SPENT factors causes a change in supply.

III   Multiple Choice

1. The answer is A. The result depends on the decisions of both buyers and sellers.

2. The answer is C. The law of supply says that there is a direct relationship between price and quantity supplied.

3. The answer is A. According to the law of supply, as prices fall, so does the amount any producer would produce.

4. The answer is A. Because it is more costly to produce wheat in these fields, Jones would only do it if the price of wheat increased to cover his costs.

5. The answer is B. The market supply curve is found by adding the amount produced at each price for every firm in the market.

IV   Application and Discussion

1. The opportunity costs of production are higher at the second field. Felix would spend more time traveling to the second field, consume more gasoline, use extra time and energy to clear the rocks from the field, and probably use more fertilizer. Felix would have to give up more to produce from the second field.

2. The market price of wheat would have to rise for Felix to have the incentive to produce from the second field. Because costs are higher in the second field, Felix must receive a higher price to compensate him for his higher costs.

3. See Exhibit 4.3.

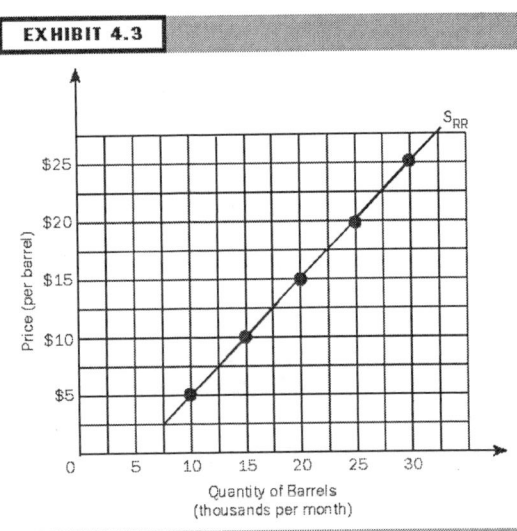

EXHIBIT 4.3

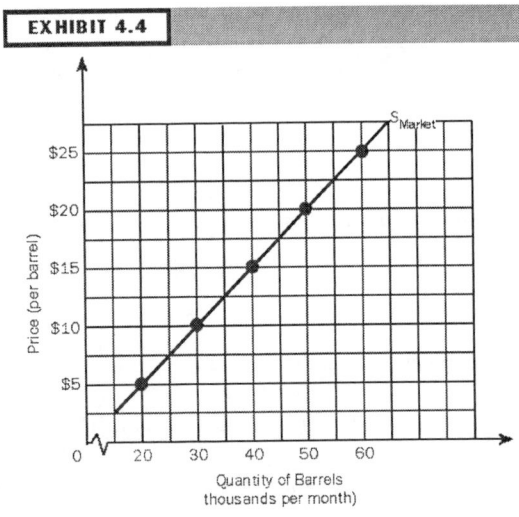

EXHIBIT 4.4

4. See Exhibit 4.4.

Quantity Supplied (barrels per month)

Price (dollars per barrel)	Rolling Rock	Armadillo	Pecos	Market
$ 5	10,000	8,000	2,000	20,000
10	15,000	10,000	5,000	30,000
15	20,000	12,000	8,000	40,000
20	25,000	14,000	11,000	50,000
25	30,000	16,000	14,000	60,000

Section 4.5 Shifts In The Supply Curve

I   Review

When other factors remain the same, price change results in a movement along the supply curve; this is called a change in quantity supplied. When the other important factors that affect supplier behavior change, the entire supply curve shifts; this is called a change in supply.

ANSWER KEY

Labor, materials, and energy are examples of supplier <u>inputs</u>. Higher input prices increase the <u>costs</u> of production and shift the supply curve to the left. Lower input prices <u>lower</u> the costs of production and shift the supply curve to the <u>right</u>.

When two goods can be produced using the same resources they are called <u>substitutes</u> in production. Producers tend to substitute the production of <u>more</u> profitable goods for that of <u>less</u> profitable goods.

If suppliers expect the price of a good will be higher in the future, they will sell <u>less</u> now so that they will have <u>more</u> to sell in the future. If they expect prices to fall in the future they will supply <u>more</u> now rather than wait for their goods to be worth less.

An increase in the number of suppliers leads to an <u>increase</u> in supply, while a decrease in the number of suppliers will lead to a <u>decrease</u> in supply.

Improvements in <u>technology</u> lead to lower costs and increase in supply.

Government regulations that increase production costs cause <u>decreases</u> in the supply of goods.

Weather can also affect the supply of certain goods, especially <u>agricultural</u> products.

If the price of a good changes it will lead to a change in the <u>quantity</u> supplied. If one of the determinants of supply, such as supplier input prices or technology changes, it will lead to a change in <u>supply</u> and to a shift in the <u>supply</u> curve.

II   True/False

1. False. Timber is an input in lumber production. When the price of an input increases, production becomes more costly and the supply decreases.

2. True. When the price of a good falls, producers shift resources from producing it to producing more of its now relatively more profitable substitute in production.

3. False. If Midge expects future prices to be higher, she will sell less today and reduce current supply.

4. False. The relevant supply curve is the market supply curve; including more firms will increase the amount offered for sale at any given price and increase supply.

5. False. Improved technology lowers the cost of production, which increases supply.

6. True. Government actions such as taxes and tampering will make it more costly to produce the product and will shift the supply curve to the left.

III   Multiple Choice

1. The answer is C. This represents an increase in the number of firms in the market, which results in an increase in supply.

2. The answer is A. A change in the quantity supplied describes movement along the supply curve, while a change in supply represents a shift in the supply curve.

3. The answer is C. A change in the price of the product, *ceteris paribus,* will cause a movement along the supply curve, or a change in the quantity supplied.

4. The answer is B. El Niño is an example of one of the four Ts. Bad weather conditions reduce the supply of certain products.

5. The answer is C. Decreased taxes will lower the cost of production and cause supply to increase. All of the other changes will increase production costs and shift the supply curve to the left.

6. The answer is B. This represents a decrease in the number of sellers and results in a decrease in supply.

7. The answer is A. When the price of a supplier's inputs falls, supply will increase.

IV   Application and Discussion

1. A. Tomato prices skyrocket!
        Determinant: <u>Supplier input prices</u>

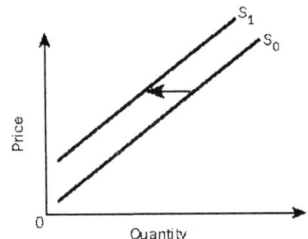

    B. Congress places a 20 percent tax on salsa.
        Determinant: <u>Taxes and subsidies</u>

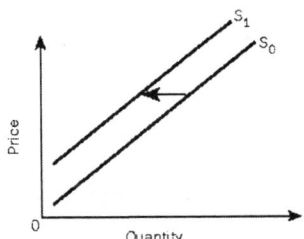

    C. Ed Scissorhands introduces a new, faster vegetable chopper.
        Determinant: <u>Technology</u>

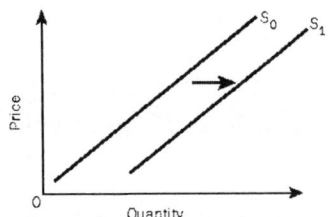

ANSWER KEY

D. Elton John, Madonna, and Paul Newman each introduce new brands of salsa.
    Determinant: <u>Number of suppliers</u>

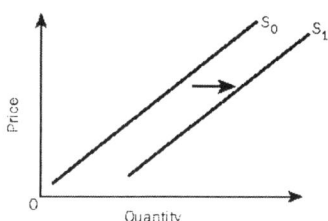

2. A. Freezing temperatures wipe out half of Brazil's coffee crop.
        Determinant: <u>Weather</u>

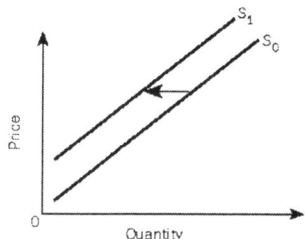

    B. Wages of coffee workers in Latin America rise as unionization efforts succeed.
        Determinant: <u>Supplier input prices</u>

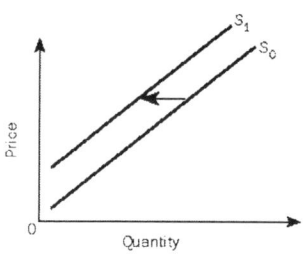

    C. Indonesia offers big subsidies to its coffee producers.
        Determinant: <u>Taxes and subsidies</u>

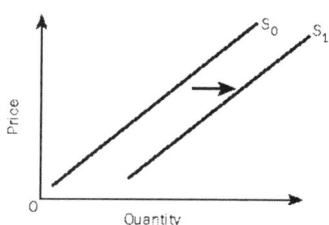

    D. Genetic engineering produces a super coffee bean that grows faster and needs less care.
        Determinant: <u>Technology</u>

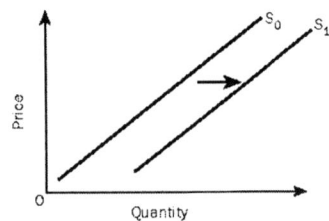

E. Coffee suppliers expect prices to be higher in the future.
   Determinant: <u>Expectations</u>

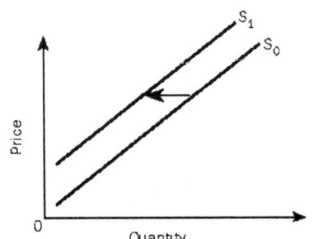

3. A. Point B represents an increase in quantity supplied.

   B. Point C represents an increase in supply.

   C. Point D represents a decrease in quantity supplied.

   D. Point E represents a decrease in supply.

CHAPTER 5 BRINGING SUPPLY AND DEMAND TOGETHER

Section 5.1 Market Equilibrium Price and Quantity

I   Review

The price at the intersection of the market demand curve and the market supply curve is call the <u>equilibrium</u> price.

If the price of a good or service is below the equilibrium price, a <u>shortage</u> will result.

If the price is above equilibrium, a <u>surplus</u> will result.

If there is a shortage of a good, the price of that good will <u>rise.</u> If there is a surplus of a good, the price will <u>fall</u>.

II   True/False

1. False. Although prices tend toward equilibrium, the actual price may be higher or lower than the equilibrium price. If so, the result will be a shortage or a surplus.

2. True. When a market is in equilibrium, the quantity demanded is equal to the quantity supplied.

3. True. Shortages cause prices to go up.

4. False. It's just the opposite. A surplus exists when quantity demanded is less than quantity supplied.

5. False. The surplus, like any surplus, will put downward pressure on prices.

III   Multiple Choice

EXHIBIT 4.5

Price	Quantity Demanded	Quantity Supplied
$6	700 cans	100 cans
7	600	200
8	500	300
9	400	400
10	300	500

1. The answer is D. The equilibrium price is $9.00, where the quantity demanded equals quantity supplied at 400 cans.

2. The answer is B. At $7.00 the quantity demanded is 600 cans but the quantity supplied is only 200. Hence there is a shortage of 400 cans.

3. The answer is B. At a price of $10.00, the quantity supplied exceeds the quantity demanded by 200 cans.

4. The answer is A. At $5.00 the quantity supplied will exceed the quantity demanded, which means a surplus exists.

5. The answer is C. The market is in equilibrium where the demand and supply curves intersect, which is where quantity demanded equals quantity supplied.

6. The answer is C. At $2.00 the quantity demanded exceeds the quantity supplied, which means a shortage would occur. The shortage would tend to drive donut prices up.

IV   Application and Discussion

The Deputy Commissioner may be correct. Fewer young people may want to be lifeguards now than in the past. An economist, however, knows that shortages are caused by prices that are below equilibrium. Since the quantity of lifeguards demanded in New York exceeds the supply, it would seem that wages are too low. An economist would advise the city to raise lifeguards' wages in order to eliminate the shortage.

Section 5.2 Changes in Equilibrium Price and Quantity

I   Review

A shift in either the supply or demand curves for a good will result in a change in its <u>equilibrium</u> price and quantity.

An increase in the demand for a good or service is represented by a shift of the demand curve to the <u>right</u> and results in an <u>increase</u> in the equilibrium price and quantity.

If the supply curve does not change, an increase in demand causes a <u>movement</u> along the supply curve and an increase in the <u>quantity</u> of the good supplied.

A(n) <u>decrease</u> in the supply of a good or service is represented by a shift in the supply curve to the left. If demand does not change, the decrease in supply will cause a decrease in the quantity <u>demanded</u> of the good and an <u>increase</u> in the equilibrium price.

If supply increases at the same time that demand decreases, equilibrium price will <u>fall</u> while the change in quantity will be <u>indeterminant</u>.

If both supply and demand increase, the equilibrium quantity will <u>rise</u>, while the change in equilibrium price will be <u>indeterminant</u>.

An increase in either demand or supply is shown by shifting the curve to the <u>right</u>. A decrease in either demand or supply is shown by shifting the curve to the <u>left</u>.

II   True/False

1. True. With an increase in demand for bing cherries, people will want to buy more cherries at every price, including the original equilibrium price. The quantity people want to buy at $1 will now be greater than the quantity people want to sell at this price. This excess quantity demanded is a shortage.

2. False. Compact disc players and compact discs are complementary goods. As the price of a complement falls the demand for the related good increases. An increase in demand, *ceteris paribus,* causing an increase in the equilibrium price and quantity of the good.

3. False. An increase in the number of chicken farmers represents an increase in the number of suppliers. An increase in the number of suppliers causes an increase in supply and shifts the supply curve to the right. When supply increases, *ceteris paribus,* the equilibrium price of the product will decrease, not increase.

4. True. At the equilibrium price, the quantity of the good people want to buy equals the quantity people want to sell. Either a decrease in demand or an increase in supply will result in the quantity of the good people want to buy falling below the quantity people want to sell creating a surplus.

5. True. This new information will give people one more reason to appreciate chocolate and will result in a change in their taste for chocolate. At all prices people will want to buy more chocolate so demand will increase. An increase in demand results in an increase in the quantity supplied and more chocolate will be consumed.

6. False. Both an increase in demand and a decrease in supply would tend to raise the price of apples. When they occur together, the equilibrium price will rise.

ANSWER KEY

7. True. The population decrease means less demand for housing, while the additional construction means an increase in supply. These two factors would result in a excess supply of housing and falling prices.

8. False. When there are simultaneous shifts in both curves we can only determine which way one of the variables will go. The direction of the other, either price or quantity, will be indeterminate.

III   Multiple Choice

1. The answer is A. Troy changes peoples' tastes, a determinant of demand. The increased demand results in an excess quantity demanded at the original equilibrium price. In order to secure ostrich meat consumers will raise the price. The increased price will encourage producers to increase the quantity supplied and consumers to reduce the quantity demanded until a new equilibrium price is reached. The new equilibrium will be at a higher price and a larger quantity.

2. The answer is B. The wage increase increases the price of inputs used to produce Broadway shows. This results in a shift to the left of the supply curve. A decline in the quantity supplied at each price will cause prices to rise and the quantity of shows produced to decline.

3. The answer is B. The medical news will change consumers' taste for chickens so they like it more. This will cause an increase in the amount of chicken consumers want to buy at every price or a shift to the right of the demand curve. This shift will result in a shortage at the original price and an increase in the price consumers offer. The increased price will encourage farmers to increase the quantity of chicken supplied. Farmers will move along their supply curve in response to the price increase.

4. The answer is A. Technological change is one of the determinants of supply. New technology causes the supply curve to shift to the right. The new equilibrium will be at a lower price and a greater quantity of beef sold.

5. The answer is C. There is no reason that a shift to the right of the gasoline demand curve will cause a similar shift to the right of the supply curve. The increase in demand will cause a shortage at $1.19 and an increase in the price consumers are willing to pay for gasoline. The increased price will result in producers increasing the quantity of gasoline they produce or moving along their supply curve.

6. The answer is B. The increase in the demand for plywood resulting from the hurricane means that at every price consumers want to buy more plywood. At the pre-hurricane equilibrium price, the quantity demanded would exceed the quantity supplied. There would be a shortage of plywood.

7. The answer is B. Of the possibilities listed, only an increase in the demand for wheat, represented by a rightward shift in the demand curve, would cause the price to increase.

8. The answer is D. Of the choices listed only a simultaneous decrease in demand and increase in supply would cause the price to drop.

9. The answer is D. We can only predict that the quantity bought and sold (the equilibrium quantity) will rise. In order to predict which way price would go, we would have to have information about how much demand and supply actually changed.

10. The answer is A. For a simultaneous increase in supply and demand to lower price, the supply curve would have to shift to the right more than the demand curve. It's just like the example of VCRs in the textbook.

IV   Application and Discussion

1. Show the effects of the changes listed below on the relevant supply and demand curves.

    Label the new equilibrium price, $P1$, and the new equilibrium quantity, $Q1$.

273

ANSWER KEY

A. An increase in the price of hot dogs on the hamburger market.

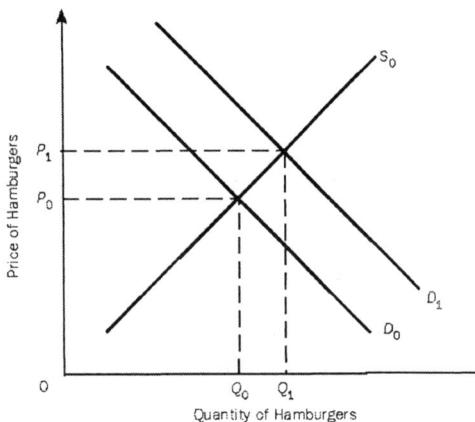

B. A decrease in the number of taxicab companies in New York City on cab trips.

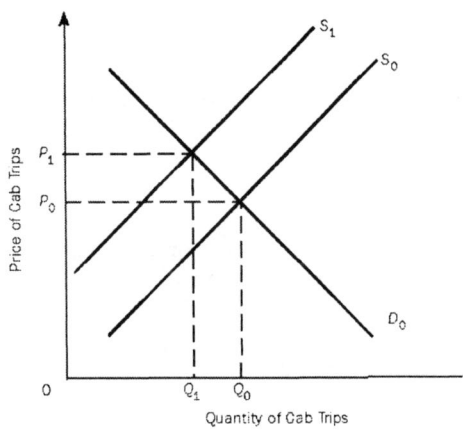

C. El Niño rain storms destroy the broccoli crop in two California counties.

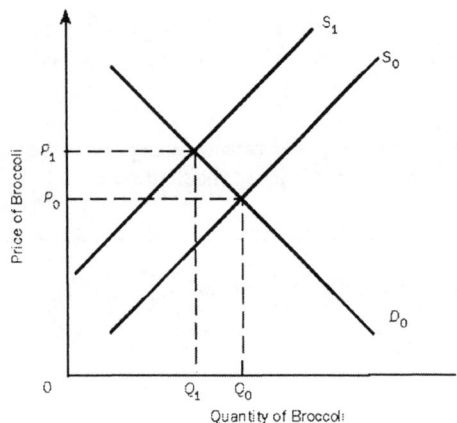

274

ANSWER KEY

2. A. simultaneous increases in supply and demand, with a large increase in supply and a small increase in demand.

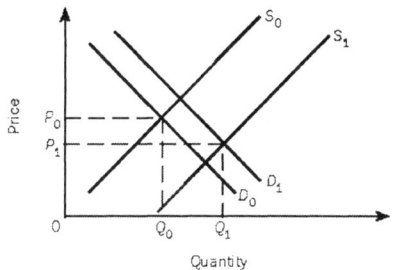

B. simultaneous increases in supply and demand, with a small increase in supply and a large increase in demand.

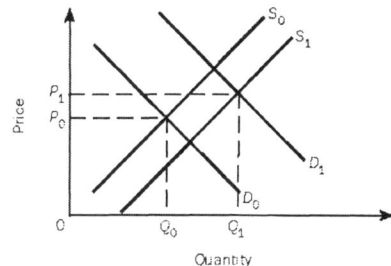

C. simultaneous decreases in supply and demand, with a large decrease in supply and a small decrease in demand.

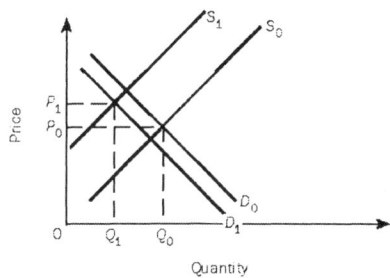

D. simultaneous decrease in supply and demand, with a small decrease in supply and a large decrease in demand.

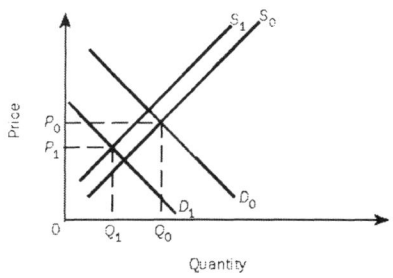

Section 5.3 Price Controls

I   Review

Price controls involve the use of government power to impose <u>nonequilibrium</u> prices.

ANSWER KEY

A maximum price imposed by government is called a <u>ceiling</u> price. A minimum price is called a price <u>floor</u>.

Rent controls are laws that set rental prices <u>below</u> the equilibrium price.

Rent controls have several effects. First, people living in rent-controlled apartments are <u>reluctant</u> to move; second, the incentive to build new rental housing is <u>reduced</u>; third, the stock of rental housing tends to <u>deteriorate</u> over time; and fourth, rent control promotes <u>discrimination</u> against people that landlords deem undesirable.

Minimum wage laws set wages for unskilled workers <u>above</u> the equilibrium wage. Minimum wage laws result in a(n) <u>decrease</u> in the quantity of labor demanded and a(n) <u>increase</u> in the quantity of labor supplied. Minimum wage laws may also result in a <u>reduction</u> of fringe benefits to employees.

II   True/False

1. False. Price controls are used to establish prices that are either above or below equilibrium.

2. False. Price ceilings are prices that are set below equilibrium by law.

3. True. Price floors are minimum prices, set above equilibrium. It is illegal to charge a price lower than the floor price.

4. True. Rent controls, like those in Berkeley, set maximum rental prices below equilibrium.

5. True. Price floors fix prices above equilibrium, where the quantity supplied is greater than the quantity demanded, which means a surplus.

III   Multiple Choice

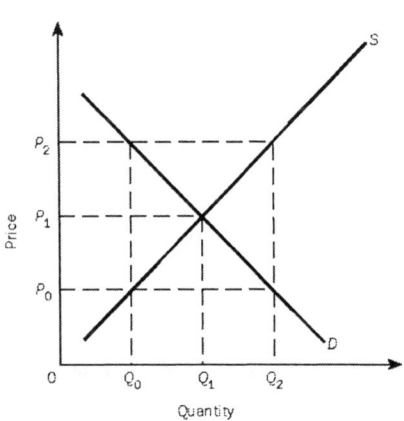

1. The answer is B. The equilibrium price is $P1$, where the demand and supply curves intersect.

2. The answer is C. A price ceiling at $P0$ will result in a quantity demanded of $Q2$ and a quantity supplied of $Q0$. Hence there will be a shortage in the amount $Q2 - Q0$.

3. The answer is A. A price floor at $P2$ will mean quantity supplied of $Q2$ but a quantity demanded of only $Q0$. Hence a surplus of $Q2 - Q0$ will result.

4. The answer is D. Rent controls don't increase tenant turnover. In fact tenants move less often because they want to hang onto their rent-controlled units.

ANSWER KEY

5. The answer is C. An increase in the federal minimum wage is likely to increase the quantity of labor supplied, decrease the quantity demanded and result in an increase in teen unemployment. It is *not* likely to reduce teen unemployment.

IV   Application and Discussion

The $2.00 price ceiling will likely result in a shortage of movie tickets. At the new, lower price, quantity demanded will rise. People will want more tickets at $2.00 then they did at $10.00. Assuming that the equilibrium price is somewhere around $10.00, the ceiling will cause the quantity of tickets sold to decline. Some theaters may reduce their hours of operation and some may even go out of business. Some theaters may stop showing first-run movies. Theater owners will certainly suffer. While some movie-goers may benefit from lower prices, they may also have to stand in long lines to buy tickets. They may also see a reduction in the quality of movies offered by theaters.

CHAPTER 6 ELASTICITIES

Section 6.1 Price Elasticity of Demand

I   Review
_____

The price elasticity of demand measures the <u>responsiveness</u> of quantity demanded to changes in the price.

Price elasticity of demand is defined as the <u>percentage</u> change in quantity demanded divided by the <u>percentage</u> change in price.

Demand is <u>elastic</u> when the quantity demanded is very responsive to changes in price. In this case the price elasticity is <u>greater</u> than one and the percentage change in quantity is <u>greater</u> than the percentage change in price.

When demand is inelastic, the price elasticity is <u>less</u> than one and the quantity demanded is <u>not</u> very responsive to price changes.

If the demand is perfectly <u>inelastic</u>, consumers will buy the same amount regardless of the price.

Demand for a good will be more elastic the greater is the number of close <u>substitutes</u> available for the good. Elasticity of demand will also be greater for goods that take up a <u>larger</u> proportion of a household's budget.

The price elasticity of demand will be greater the <u>longer</u> the time period consumers have to adjust to price changes.

II   True/False
_____

1. False. The price elasticity of demand does measures the responsiveness of changes in quantity demanded to changes in price or movement along a demand curve. Elasticity is measured as the percentage change in quantity divided by the percentage change in price. Using percentage eliminates problems caused by different units of measurement and allows us to compare elasticity of demand across goods and services.

2. True. E-mail is a substitute for regular postal service; a person can send a letter or an email message. With the widespread use of this good substitute the demand for postal services has become more elastic.

3. True. The price elasticity of demand is the percentage change in quantity, six percent, divided by the percentage change in price, ten percent. The demand is inelastic since the price elasticity (.6) is less than one. For inelastic demand the percentage change in quantity is less than the percentage change in price.

4. False. Cars are expensive goods and car payments are likely to be a relatively large part of a household's budget. Auto wax is an insignificant component of most households' budgets. The impact of a change in the price of auto wax on a consumer's budget is likely to be much smaller than the impact of the same percentage change in the price of a car. Consumers will respond less to price changes for auto wax than for automobiles, so the demand will be relatively less elastic for auto wax than for automobiles.

III   Multiple Choice
_____

1   The answer is A. The percentage change in the quantity of steel demanded is much greater than the percentage change in the price. The price elasticity of demand is greater than one. The demand facing Marge and Al is elastic.

2. The answer is C. The price elasticity of demand is calculated by dividing the percentage change in quantity demanded by the percentage change in price. For the Up and Down Co. this is 3, 15 divided by 5.

3. The answer is B. The demand is inelastic. A change in price produces very little change in the quantity demanded. This is most likely because there are few good substitutes for heroin once someone is addicted.

ANSWER KEY

4. The answer is A. The demand over a longer period of time is more elastic than over the shorter period because consumers have more time to adjust to the price change. When demand is relatively more elastic the change in quantity demanded will be relatively larger for a given percentage change in price.

IV   Application and Discussion

	More Substitutes	Greater Share of Budget	More Time
1. Cars or <u>Chevrolets</u>	X		
2. Salt or <u>Housing</u>		X	
3. <u>New York Mets</u> or Cleveland Indians	X		
4. Natural Gas this month or <u>over the year</u>			X

The price elasticity of demand for a product will increase the more and better substitutes are available. Chevrolets have more substitutes than cars in general since any other brand is a good substitute. There are more, good substitutes for the Mets than the Indians because the Mets share a market with the Yankees. Natural gas has a more price elastic demand in the long run since this gives consumers time to adjust their habits and complementary capital to any change. Finally, the price elasticity of demand for housing will be greater than for salt because of the large role housing plays in the household budget.

Section 6.2 Total Revenue and Price Elasticity of Demand

I   Review

Total revenue is equal to the price of a good times the <u>quantity</u> of the good sold.

If the demand for a good is elastic, total revenues will <u>rise</u> as price declines. On the other hand, if the demand for a good is inelastic, total revenues will <u>fall</u> as the price declines.

If the demand for wheat is inelastic, farmers will become <u>better</u> off as a result of a reduction in the supply of wheat.

The steeper one demand curve is relative to another, the more <u>inelastic</u> it is relative to the other, although the elasticity of demand <u>varies</u> along a linear demand curve.

As you move along a linear demand curve from a high price to a low price, the demand changes from relatively <u>elastic</u> at high prices to relatively <u>inelastic</u> at low prices.

II   True/False

1. True. total revenue is equal to price times quantity sold, in this case $3.60 301005 $360.

2. True. When price and total revenue move in opposite directions, demand is elastic.

3. False. When demand is elastic price and total revenue vary inversely. For example when price goes up, total revenue goes down.

III   Multiple Choice

1. The answer is A. Total revenue goes up because you gain revenue by selling *lots* more units as price declines. The percentage increase in quantity demanded is large while the percentage decrease in price is relatively small.

2. The answer is C. Total revenues rise as price goes up because the seller gains more from the price increase than she does from the relatively small decrease in quantity demanded.

3. The answer is A. At $4 their total revenue is $200 ($4 x 50 videos = $200). When they lower the price to $3, total revenue is $300 ($3 x 100 videos = $300). So as price falls from $4 to $3, total revenue goes from $200 to $300 per week.

4. The answer is B. Between $2 and $1, price and total revenue move in <u>opposite</u> directions. Therefore demand is inelastic. At $2, for example, they rent 150 videos and total revenue is $300. As you can see, if they lower the price to $1, they rent 200 videos and total revenue goes down to $200.

IV   Application and Discussion

1. Lastic actually gave Wayne good advice. If the demand facing the Gotham City hotel is inelastic, then raising prices will increase total revenue, even if it reduces the number of guests. Lastic assumed that the demand facing the Gotham City Hotel was inelastic. There are three reasons for this assessment. First, since there are no other first class hotels in Gotham, there are few good substitutes for the services provided by the hotel. The fewer the available substitutes the more inelastic the demand elasticity. Second, hotel expenditures are probably a small part of budgets of people who stay in first class hotels, and the elasticity of demand will be less the less important an item in a household's budget. Finally, it takes time for people to adjust their behavior, especially if they are traveling to Gotham City. In the short run, demand will be relatively inelastic.

Section 6.3 Price Elasticity of Supply

I   Review

The price elasticity of <u>supply</u> is defined as the percentage change in the quantity supplied divided by the percentage change in the price. It measures how <u>responsive</u> the quantity sellers are willing to sell is to changes in price.

When supply is perfectly <u>inelastic,</u> a change in the price will not change the amount supplied. When supply is perfectly <u>elastic,</u> no goods will be sold below a certain price, but at higher prices, as much as buyers want will be supplied.

Supply is more elastic in the <u>long</u> run than in the <u>short</u> run.

The relative supply and demand elasticities determine the <u>distribution</u> of the burden of a tax imposed on a good or service. If the demand is relatively <u>more</u> elastic than supply, the producer pays the greater proportion of the tax. If demand is relatively <u>less</u> elastic than supply, the consumer pays the greater proportion of the tax.

II   True/False

1. False. The price elasticity of supply is usually greater in the long run. It takes producers time to adjust to price changes just like consumers. In the short run expanding output may require expensive changes. Given time firms can adjust production schedules and add machinery which allows them to produce more at lower prices.

2. The answer is false. The price in the two markets depends on the interaction of demand and supply. The Price elasticity of supply only describes how the amount sellers are willing to sell responds to price changes. All we know is that California electricity suppliers are less responsive than suppliers in New York; with a given increase in price California will see a smaller percentage increase in quantity supply than New York.

3. The answer is true. When supply is perfectly inelastic, the same amount will be supplied no matter what the price.

III   Multiple Choice

1. The answer is B. The price elasticity of supply measures the responsiveness of the quantity supplied to a change in price. An increase in the price elasticity of supply will result in a greater percentage increase in supply from any given percentage increase in price.

2. The answer is C. The two extremes of the range of price elasticity of supply are perfectly elastic supply and perfectly inelastic supply. When supply is perfectly inelastic there is no change in quantity supplied in response to the price.

3. The answer is B. The price elasticity of supply equals the percent change in the quantity supplied divided by the percent change in the price. In this case the percent change in quantity is 23 and the percent change in price in 10, so the price elasticity is 23/10 or 2.3.

ANSWER KEY

4. The answer is B. The elasticity of demand and supply will affect the share of a sales tax paid by consumers in the form of higher price and producers in the form of lower revenue per unit. The distribution of this burden will depend on the relative elasticity of supply and demand. If demand is relatively more elastic than supply, the producer will pay the largest portion of the tax. In this case the demand becomes more elastic relative to supply and the proportion of the tax paid by producers will increase.

IV   Application and Discussion

When demand is less elastic than supply, the tax burden falls primarily on consumers. When demand is more elastic than supply, the tax burden falls primarily on producers.

The tax burden of a tax on food would fall primarily on consumers while the tax burden of a tax on basketball tickets would fall primarily on producers.

Section 6.4 Other Types of Elasticities

I   Review

The cross elasticity of demand measures the effect on the quantity demanded of one good of a change in the price of <u>another</u> good. It is equal to the percentage change in the quantity demanded of one good at a given <u>price</u> divided by the percentage change in the price of a second good.

The <u>direction</u> as well as the magnitude of the change is measured by the cross elasticity.

In general, a positive cross elasticity means the two goods are <u>substitutes</u> and a negative cross price elasticity means the two goods are <u>complements.</u>

An elasticity that measures the percentage change in the quantity demanded of a good, ceteris paribus, given a one-percent change in income is called the <u>income</u> elasticity of demand.

The good is a normal good when demand and income move in the <u>same</u> direction and it will have a positive income elasticity. If the income elasticity of demand is negative, the good is an <u>inferior</u> good.

II   True/False

1. False. Cars made by Ford and Toyota are substitutes. The cross elasticity of demand between substitute goods will be positive. As the price of Fords rises people will, at a given price, increase their demand for Toyotas.

2. False. Inferior goods have a negative income elasticity. Income and quantity demanded for inferior goods move in the opposite direction. Per capita bus travel should decline as incomes increase. Of course, this assumes that other important determinants of demand and supply remain constant.

3. False. The income elasticity of demand measures the responsiveness of quantity demanded to a change in income, *ceteris paribus*. The elasticity is estimated by dividing the percentage change in quantity demanded by the percentage change in income. In the melon case the income elasticity equals one.

4. The answer is true. An income elasticity of less than one means that the percentage increase in expenditure on food will be less than the percentage increase in income. As a result, the share of income spent on food will decline as a country's income increases.

III   Multiple Choice

1. The answer is D. The income elasticity of demand is calculated by dividing the percentage change in quantity by the percentage change in income. The calculation assumes that price and the other factors that affect demand do not change.

2. The answer is A. When the quantity demanded of one good and the price of another good move in opposite direction the cross elasticity will be negative and the goods are substitutes.

ANSWER KEY

3. The answer is C. When the income elasticity of demand is negative the good is inferior. In Anchorage the probability of owning a mobile home declines as a household's income rises.

4. The answer is B. The cross price elasticity of demand can be used to identify substitutes and complements when they may not be obvious. When the cross price elasticity of demand is positive the goods are substitutes. In this case, they are substitutes because an increase in the price of gasoline causes a consumer to substitute frozen food for trips to the store to buy fresh food.

IV   Application and Discussion

1. The income elasticity of demand equals (the percentage change in the quantity demanded)/ (the percentage change in incomes). The percentage change in quantity demanded over the period equals (19.5-20)/[20+19.5]/2) = -.025. The income elasticity of demand for rail travel equals (-.025)/(.13) = -.19

2. The cross price elasticity equals (percentage change in quantity demanded)/ (percentage change in the price of air travel). The percentage change in quantity demanded equals (19-17.5)/([19 +17.5]/2) = .082. The cross price elasticity of demand for rail travel equals (.082)/(.075) = 1.09.

3. The positive cross price elasticity shows us that air travel and rail travel are substitute goods. The negative income elasticity shows us that rail travel is a inferior good.

282

CHAPTER 7 MARKET EFFICIENCY AND WELFARE

Section 7.1 Consumer Surplus and Producer Surplus

I   Review

The difference between what a consumer *actually* pays for a good and what they are *willing* to pay is called consumer <u>surplus</u>.

A consumer's willingness to pay <u>declines</u> for each additional unit of the good he consumes. Earlier units purchased add <u>more</u> to consumer surplus than later ones.

When price falls, consumer surplus increases because you buy <u>more</u> of the good and because you get <u>more</u> consumer surplus from those units you would have purchased at the original price.

As the price of a product falls, the consumer surplus derived from consumption of the product <u>increases</u>.

The difference between the price a seller is paid for a good and her cost of providing it is <u>producer</u> surplus.

The welfare gain from trade of a product equals the <u>sum</u> of the consumer surplus and the producer surplus created by each unit traded. Both buyer and seller are <u>better</u> <u>off</u> from each of the units traded than they would have been without trade.

Once the equilibrium output is reached, all <u>mutually</u> <u>beneficial</u> trade opportunities between suppliers and demanders will have taken place.

A deadweight loss is a reduction in total surplus that results from the <u>misallocation</u> of resources.

II   True/False

1. False. The prices consumers *actually* pay are often less than they would be *willing* to pay, yielding them a consumer surplus.

2. True. The consumer surplus is the monetary difference between what a consumer is willing to pay and what he is actually required to pay. In this case, it's the difference between the $30 Choon is willing to pay and the $20 he actually pays, or $10.

3. True. Producer surplus is the difference between the price the producer receives for a unit of his product and the cost of producing it. When the cost of electricity production increases, utility producer surplus may fall for two potential reasons. First, producers may sell fewer units of electricity and lose the producer surplus on those units. Second, the high costs reduce the producer surplus on the units they continue to produce.

III   Multiple Choice

1. The answer is B. Because of the law of diminishing marginal utility, the marginal willingness to pay for the extra apple is less than that of previous apples. Since the price that Roy actually has to pay for apples has fallen, however, his consumer surplus is larger.

2. The answer is C. His consumer surplus, if the price is P0, is equal to the area above the price and below the demand curve or the area, a.

3. The answer is B. As the price falls from P0 to P1, Carmine's consumer surplus is the area above P1, but below the demand curve. Thus he *gains* an amount equal to (b + c).

4. The answer is C. The mutually beneficial gains from trade equal the sum of producer and consumer surplus. While trade might create greater surplus from one group or the other, both producers and consumers will gain as long as they receive positive surplus.

ANSWER KEY

IV   Application and Discussion

A)   Steve is willing to pay $4.50 for one bag of potato chips.

B)   Steve is willing to pay $4.00 for a second bag of potato chips.

C)   Steve's consumer surplus is $5.00 when he buys five bags. He gets a $2.00 surplus on the first bag, $1.50 on the second, $1.00 on the third, and $.50 on the fourth. At $2.50 per bag he gets no consumer surplus on the fifth bag.

D)   Steve's total willingness to pay when he buys 5 bags is $17.50. He is willing to pay $4.50 for the first bag, $4.00 for the second, $3.50 for the third, $3.00 from the fourth, and $2.50 for the fifth bag.

Section 7.2 The Welfare Effects of Taxes and Subsidies

I   Review

The efficient output occurs at the market-clearing price, which is where the sum of consumer and producer surplus is <u>maximized</u>. Economists refer to the gains and losses associated with government intervention in the economy as <u>welfare</u> effects.

The net loss in consumer and producer surplus from government intervention in the economy is called a <u>deadweight</u> loss. This loss results because government intervention distorts market <u>incentives</u>, like price.

Taxes result in consumers buying <u>less</u> because they pay a higher price and suppliers selling less because they receive a <u>lower</u> price. The net loss results because the <u>efficient</u> output is not produced.

The size of the deadweight loss from a tax on a good depends on the <u>price elasticities</u> of supply and demand.

The deadweight loss from a price ceiling results from production that is <u>less</u> than the efficient output. The loss from a price floor results from consumers buying <u>less</u> than the efficient output and producers producing <u>more</u>.

II   True/False

1. False. The lower the elasticity of either supply or demand, the smaller will be the deadweight loss from a tax. The deadweight loss results from the tax-induced changed in the amount of the good produced. The less elastic either supply or demand the smaller is the change in output from the efficient amount.

2. False. The visitor tax will be partly paid by the producers of tourist services, like tour operators, fishing guides, and waitresses. The distribution of the loss will depend on the elasticities of supply and demand. If the supply curves is less than perfectly elastic, any reduction in output will result in a loss of producer as well as consumer surplus.

3. True. Price celings prevent the price from rising to the market clearing level. There would still be mutually beneficial gains from increasing the amount of housing provided. There is a loss of consumer and producer surplus from producing "too little" housing.

4. False. Deadweight loss imposes real cost on society. We give up the welfare measured by lost consumer and producer surplus. We also use our scarce resources inefficiently. It is a deadweight loss because we give something up and receive nothing in return.

III   Multiple Choice

1   The answer is B. The deadweight loss from a tax increase results because output falls below its efficient level. When demand is perfectly inelastic, the change in price will not result in a change in the amount consumed or produced. The price consumers pay will increase and consumer surplus will fall by the amount of the tax revenue, but there will be no deadweight loss.

ANSWER KEY

2. The answer is B. The deadweight loss that results from taxes designed to raise the same revenue will be greater the more elastic the demand for the product. We might expect the demand for used cars would be relatively elastic since new cars are very good substitutes. The demand for cigarettes would be inelastic for smokers since there are few god substitutes for those with the smoking habit. Since salt and matches are a small part of most households' budgets, the demand for each of these products is also relatively inelastic.

3. The answer is C. With this scheme, the consumer is doubly affected suffering both a reduction in consumer surplus and paying increased taxes to buy the surplus cheese. Producers gain because they receive a higher price then they would without government interference and they produce more.

IV APPLICATION AND DISCUSSION

A. The consumers lose consumer surplus equal to area B, since they consume less electricity. They gain surplus equal to C.

B. The producers lose producer surplus equal to areas C + D. Since they produce less and receive a lower price for electricity.

C. California's total loss is the sum of the producer and consumer loss or the area B + D since the amount produced is less than the competitive equilibrium E_0.

D. California's brownouts are another way of saying that there were shortages that arose from the price being below P_0. The brownouts reflect the shortage, E_D minus E_S.

E. Allowing the market to set the price P_0 would increase the total surplus by B + D. However, consumer surplus may actually fall if area B was less than area C. With market set prices producers would receive the surplus C and consumers would gain surplus B.

CHAPTER 8 MARKET FAILURE AND PUBLIC CHOICE

Section 8.1 Market Failure and Externalities

I   Review

When the costs or benefits of an activity impact people outside the market mechanism, economists say an <u>externality</u> exists.

If production or exchange harms outside parties it is called a(n) <u>negative</u> externality. If production or exchange benefits outside parties it is called a(n) <u>positive</u> externality.

Air pollution is an example of a(n) <u>negative</u> externality.

If the education of a person benefits not only that person, but others as well, economists say that education generates <u>positive</u> externalities.

When producers are unable to collect payments from all those who benefit from a good, the market has a tendency to produce too <u>little</u> of the good.

When producers shift the costs of producing a good onto others who are not involved in production or consumption of the good, the market tends to produce too <u>much</u> of the good.

II   True/False

1. False. Litter, like other forms of pollution, is an example of a negative externality.

2. False. Negative externalities like pollution are created by people responding to certain incentives. Economists believe that if you reduce the incentive to pollute you will reduce pollution.

3. True. Few people consistently enjoy the smell of smoke from other peoples' cigarettes. Cigarette smoke imposes costs on people not directly involved in the production or consumption of that good.

4. True. Pleasant aromas from plants in neighbors' yards are positive externalities. They are benefits that you don't have to pay for.

5. False. If producers can lower their own costs by shifting some onto others, they are likely to produce *too much* fertilizer.

6. True. Markets by themselves, tend to underproduce goods that yield positive externalities. Hence, a subsidy that results in more production can improve efficiency.

III   Multiple Choice

1. The answer is C. Vinnie is shifting some of the costs of his drum-playing onto Mae. Noise pollution is a negative externality.

2. The answer is B. When firms can shift some of their costs to others who are not directly involved in production or consumption of the good output will be *higher* than it would be if producers paid all the costs.

3. The answer is B. Carl is providing neighbors with a positive externality. They can enjoy looking at his new, beautified yard and the value of their own property may rise as well since property in a nice neighborhood is worth more than property in a run-down neighborhood.

4. The answer is B. If the Mayor thinks education merits more public money he must believe that taxpayers in general, not only those whose children are in school, benefit from education. In economic parlance, he probably believes that education yields positive externalities.

ANSWER KEY

5. The answer is D. Taxes, prohibitions against pollution, and mandatory cleanup would help correct a negative externality like pollution. Subsidies would result in more pollution rather than less.

6. The answer is A. If government wants to promote any activity it should _not_ tax it.

IV   Application and Discussion

Since honey bees pollinate apple trees and help increase apple production, the apiaries would provide a positive externality to apple growers and strengthen the local economy. Thus, the Mayor's proposal might have some merit. Since land has many uses, however, there is an opportunity cost involved in giving the land to beekeepers. to fully evaluate the proposal all of the benefits of the proposal have to be weighed against all of the costs.

Section 8.2 Public Goods

I   Review

A good that is yours and yours alone is called a _private_ good. Goods, that are both not rival and not excludable are called _public_ goods.

Someone who receives benefits that they don't pay for is called a _free_ rider.

Because non-payers can't be excluded from consumption and because of the free rider problem, the market tends to produce too _few_ public goods.

II   True/False

1. True. Since consumption of national defense is nonrivalrous and since it is difficult to exclude those who don't pay for it, national defense is a good example of a public good.

2. False. Any vehicle is a private good. Nonpayers can be excluded from owning one and one person's use of the vehicle precludes another's use.

3. False. The status of the owner has nothing to do with whether a good is private or public.

4. False. The market actually tends to underproduce public goods and governments often try to do things that encourage additional production.

III   Multiple Choice

1. The answer is A. Crystal is a free rider. She gets the benefit of the show without paying.

2. The answer is B. Radio programs are not excludable because anyone who owns a radio and is within the broadcast range of the radio station can listen. It is impossible to charge listeners and exclude those who don't pay.

3. The answer is C. A public good is both nonrival in consumption (everyone can consume it simultaneously) and nonexclusive (it is hard to exclude people who don't pay for it).

4. The answer is A. Where free-riding is possible producers can't collect fees from consumers. Hence goods are underproduced and overconsumed.

IV   Application and Discussion

GOOD	NONRIVAL CONSUMPTION	NONEX- CLUSIVE	PRIVATE GOOD	PUBLIC GOOD
1. Hot Dogs	NO	NO	X	
2. Cable TV	YES	NO	X	
3. Broadcast TV	YES	YES		X
4. Automobiles	NO	NO	X	
5. National Defense	YES	YES		X

ANSWER KEY

6. Pollution Control	YES	YES		X
7. Parking in a Parking Structure	NO	NO	X	
8. A Sunset	YES	YES		X
9. Admission to a Theme Park	NO	NO	X	

Section 8.3 Imperfect Information

I   Review

Since information is scarce like other goods, people will stop searching for it when the <u>costs</u> of obtaining additional information outweighs the <u>benefits</u> they expect to gain from it.

Government often acts to reduce <u>information</u> costs for consumers.

Occupational <u>licensing</u> laws are intended to insure consumers that certain standards will be met by providers of goods and services.

Occupational licensing laws often restrict the <u>supply</u> of services and lead to <u>higher</u> prices to consumers.

Governmental information policies can actually reduce efficiency when the costs of providing the information exceed the <u>benefits</u> of the information.

Asymmetric <u>information</u> exists when one party to a trade has better information than the other. In the used car market this may result in "<u>bad</u> cars driving good cars from the market."

Obtaining a college degree may be considered a form of <u>signaling</u> behavior that indicates intelligence and perseverance.

<u>Moral</u> hazard is an information problem in the insurance market that results from the high cost of monitoring the insured. Insurance against risks changes a person's <u>incentive</u> to take precautions against risk.

II   True/False

1. False. A rational person will gather information only as long as the extra benefit of gathering the information is greater than the extra costs.

2. True. The government supplies lots of information about the characteristics of a wide variety of goods and services. The more information consumers have the better their decisions will be.

3. True. The federal government requires those warnings that contain some information about the effects of smoking.

4. True. This is an example of moral hazard. The Park Service guarantee is like an insurance policy. Climbers know they will be rescued, so this changes their incentives. The expected cost of being less cautious is reduced by the Park Service policy.

5. False. Signaling behavior, like a college degree, neat appearance, and punctuality when arriving for a job interview, can be indicators of future productivity and job performance.

III   Multiple Choice

1. The answer is D. Elimination of the licensing requirement will increase the supply of taxis and lower fares.

2. The answer is C. You can have too much information. If people go to great time and expense to gather information that has little value they will make themselves worse off.

3. The answer is C. There is little, if any, criticism regarding the governments role in warning consumers about possible dangers involved in using certain products like insecticides or flammable materials.

288

ANSWER KEY

4. The answer is C. Economist think that "one bad apple spoils the bunch" is a saying about the problems of asymmetric information. Consumers are not willing to pay more for an apple than they expect it to be worth. If there were a good chance they would get a bad apple, they would offer no more than what they would pay for a bad apple. If the amount they would pay for a bad apple were less than the cost of producing a good apple, good apple growers would be driven from the business.

IV   Application and Discussion

The exam, its cost, and the waiting period likely decreases the supply of veterinarians. The time and expense of the exam may discourage some foreigners from even applying. The rationale for the exam is that it improves quality and informs consumers that veterinarians, wherever they are trained, are competent. Another motive for the exam may be that is protects existing veterinarians from competition.

Section 8.4 Public Choice

I   Review

The application of economic principles to politics is called public <u>choice</u> theory.

Economists assume that people are influenced by self-<u>interest</u> in both the private and public arenas.

In the public sector the presence of <u>scarcity</u> forces politicians and voters to make choices.

Unlike the private sector, choices made in the public sector by majority rule break the individual-consumption- <u>payment</u> link. When the majority decides what to purchase, individuals pay for goods through higher <u>taxes</u>, independent of the value they attach to the goods.

II   TRUE/FALSE

1. False. Public choice theory is the study of how people make decisions in the public or political arena.

2. False. They assume that politicians and voters are motivated by self-interest, just like individuals in the private market.

3. True. Individual consumers make private sector decisions. The only information required is how the individual values the good. If he values it more than the cost he will make an efficient purchase, since benefits outweigh costs. In the public sector decisions often affect many people. Efficient decisions would require that information from everyone affecting be collected in a way that would result in their telling the truth about how they value the good. The more people involved the greater is the collection costs.

III   Multiple Choice

1. The answer is C. Both public choice theorists and economists who study market behavior assume that people are motivated by self-interest.

2. The answer is A. The new approach forces consumers to pay a given amount for goods they may not like. Consumers no longer are able to make decisions that reflect their comparison of the value they attach to the goods with the price they have to pay. Consumers no longer make the choice based on comparing the cost to them and the benefits they receive. As with public sector decisions, this approach breaks the link between consumption and payment for the consumer.

3. The answer is A. According to Roger G. Noll an economist at the Brookings Institution they provide no significant benefits. Any small benefits they may generate are swamped by their costs.

4. The answer is D. For most people, the costs of becoming politically informed are substantial, while the personal benefits are negligible.

289

ANSWER KEY

Individual	Incentive
1) Grocery Shopper	c) low food prices
2) U.S. Senator	a) re-election
3) Business Owner	d) high profits
4) U.S. Federal Agency Director	e) a bigger budget
5) Factory Worker	b) a higher salary
6) Voter	f) more government services

ANSWER KEY

CHAPTER 9 CONSUMER CHOICE

Section 9.1 Consumer Behavior

I   Review

The assumption that individuals act to advance their goals is known as the rule of <u>rational</u> choice.

A <u>util</u> is a hypothetical unit of satisfaction derived from consumption.

Economist believe that it is <u>impossible</u> to make interpersonal utility comparisons.

The total amount of satisfaction derived from the consumption of a certain number of units of a good is called <u>total</u> utility.

The <u>marginal</u> utility is the additional satisfaction generated by the last unit of a good consumed.

The law of diminishing marginal utility states that the incremental satisfaction from the consumption of additional units of a good <u>declines</u> as consumption increases.

II   True/False

1. False. In economics we assume that whatever people do is done with a purpose.

2. False. A util is equivalent to one unit of satisfaction. A consumer may get more or less than one util of satisfaction from consuming an extra unit of a good.

3. True. Economists don't think it is possible to make interpersonal utility comparisons.

4. True. This is the famous law of diminishing marginal utility.

III   Multiple Choice

1. The answer is A. Marginal utility is the extra utility someone gets by consuming an extra unit of a good.

2. The answer is D. The marginal utility of each successive fry goes down, but her total utility continues to rise.

3. The answer is C. Economists don't believe it is possible to compare the relative enjoyment of different individuals.

4. The answer is A. Victor would eat only bananas. Since they are his favorite food they give him more utility than anything else *and* his enjoyment grows with each successive banana.

IV   Application and Discussion

1.

Escargot Per Day	Total Utility	Marginal Utility
1	10	10
2	18	8
3	24	6
4	28	4
5	30	2
6	30	0

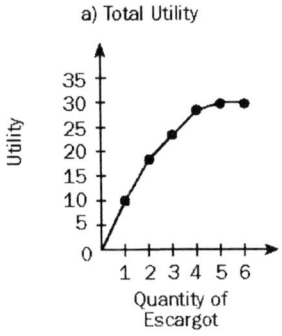

a) Total Utility

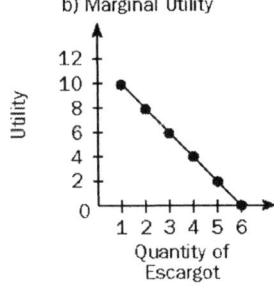

b) Marginal Utility

2.

Section 9.2 The Consumer's Choice

I   Review

A rational consumer will avoid purchases of one good if there are other goods that give greater <u>satisfaction</u> for the amount spent.

The additional satisfaction or marginal utility of a good <u>declines</u> as more of it is consumed.

When a consumer acquires the bundle of goods that maximizes her utility or happiness, she is at a point of consumer <u>equilibrium.</u>

When people have spent their <u>income</u> on goods and services so that the marginal utility they receive per <u>dollar</u> spent is the same for every good, they have reached consumer equilibrium.

When the price of a good falls, consumers buy <u>more</u> of it because the marginal utility per dollar spent for the good <u>increases.</u> As they buy more the marginal utility per dollar spent <u>falls</u> and a new equilibrium is reached.

The law of demand reflects consumer equilibrium where goods are subject to the law of <u>diminishing</u> marginal utility.

II   True/False

1. False. Consumer equilibrium is reached when there is no way a consumer, given their income, could make themselves happier. Grete has an opportunity to change the way she spends her income and make herself happier. She is not at a point of consumer equilibrium.

ANSWER KEY

2. True. Franco is rational. By shifting his purchases from ravioli to chili he is making himself happier. When Franco spends less on ravioli he gives up the marginal utility he would get from the third can, but when he spends more on chili he gets the marginal utility from the fourth can of chili. He will only make himself happier if the marginal utility he gains exceeds what he is giving up.

3. False. Consumers can increase the utility they receive from a fixed income by reallocating their spending as long as the marginal utility per dollar spent differs among goods. While Malcolm receives the same marginal utility from each good, the marginal utility he receives from the last dollar spent on soup is greater. Malcolm can make himself happier by spending more on soup and less on books.

4. False. The law of diminishing marginal utility supports the law of demand. Since marginal utility falls with increased consumption, when the price of a good falls consumers reach a new equilibrium at a lower level of marginal utility.

III   Multiple Choice

1. The answer is C. The consumer has reached the point of consumer equilibrium when the utility maximizing amount of each good has been purchased. Given their income the consumers cannot make themselves happier than they do consuming this combination of goods and services.

2. The answer is C. When consumers reach consumer equilibrium and maximize their utility they allocate their income so that the marginal utility per dollar spent on each good and service is the same. If Juanita has reached consumer equilibrium, the marginal utility per dollar of the last hot dog and hamburger she buys must be the same. Since hamburgers cost more the marginal utility the last one provides must be greater than the marginal utility provided by the last hotdog.

3. The answer is B. As long as the marginal utility per dollar spent on two goods differs, consumers can increase their utility by reallocating their income. In this case Werner should have spent less on rides and more on hot dogs. If he spent one dollar less on rides he would have reduced his utility by 20 but when he spent that dollar on one more hot dog he would have increased his utility by 40 for a net gain in utility of 20 utils.

IV   Application and Discussion

Consumers allocate their incomes across goods and services by comparing the marginal utility per dollar spent for all goods and services. When the price of goods and services change consumers will seek a new consumer equilibrium by changing the way they spend their income. As the price of goods falls consumers will buy more since the marginal utility per dollar spent will rise; consumers will reduce the amount they buy of goods which experience a price increase. The assumptions behind the CPI are unrealistic since consumers will respond to price changes by changing the bundle of goods and services they buy. The CPI will most likely over-estimate the effect of price changes since consumers reduce the importance in their spending of more expensive goods and increase the importance of less expensive goods in response to price changes.

CHAPTER 10 PRODUCTION AND COSTS

Section 10.1 Profits: Total Revenue Minus Total Costs

I   Review

When economists explain the behavior of firms they assume the firm's ultimate goal is to maximize <u>profits</u>, which is the difference between the <u>revenue</u> the firm earns and its <u>costs.</u>

There are two types of costs. <u>Explicit</u> costs are measured by the money payments for resources. The opportunity costs of using the resources owned by the firm are <u>implicit</u> costs; these are costs even though no <u>money</u> is spent.

<u>Accounting</u> profits are the difference between total revenue and explicit costs.

<u>Economic</u> profits will be less than accounting profits because they include as a cost the opportunity cost of the firm's resources or its implicit costs.

A <u>zero</u> economic profit means that the firm's revenue is just sufficient to cover its total opportunity costs. Even with a zero economic profit the firm's owners would be <u>compensated</u> for the time and money they put in to the business.

When costs have been incurred and cannot be recovered they are called <u>sunk</u> costs. These costs are <u>irrelevant</u> to any future decisions since they will not be changed by any decision.

II   True/False

1. False. Eddy's time at the firm has an opportunity cost. During the time he was working on mousetraps Eddy could have been practicing law. The money he could have earned as a lawyer, the alternative earnings that are foregone, are implicit costs of mousetrap production.

2. True. Profits are calculated by subtracting total costs from total revenue. When the electric bill is added to her other costs, Carrie's costs will be higher so her estimate of profits will be lower.

3. False. Accounting profits will always be greater than or equal to economic profits. Accounting profits equal total revenues minus total explicit or monetary costs. Because economic profits also subtract any implicit costs from accounting profits, economic profits can never be greater than accounting profits.

4. False. Hank's time has an opportunity cost. He could be working somewhere else. Hank may also use other resources that he owns in the business. If the implicit cost of using his time and other resources is greater than $20,000 per year, staying in the towing business is irrational. When economic profits are negative the rational move would be to leave the business.

III   Multiple Choice

1. The answer is C. The development costs are expenditures that the company cannot recover, and they will not be affected by any production decision. They are sunk costs. Sunk costs are irrelevant to any production decision.

2. The answer is D. Economic profit is the difference between total revenue and total cost. P.C. has total monthly revenue of $900. Brown's explicit costs of $350 per month for jars and labor, so his accounting profit ($900 minus $350) is $550. He also has implicit costs of $400 per month for his land and his labor, so his economic profit equals $900 minus $750 or $150.

3. The answer is C. All of the deposits over the year equal LaTisha's total revenue. The sum of the year's checks equals the company's total explicit costs. The difference between the two is the year's accounting profits. Money payments do not include the implicit costs of the firm so the change in the balance is not economic profits.

Fishermen may not have to pay their relatives to work as crew but that does not mean this strategy has no cost. Employing relatives reduces the fisherman's explicit cost because crew salaries are reduced. However, this strategy will only reduce total costs if relatives have no alternative ways to use their time. Implicit costs will increase if the relatives have other uses of their time. Employing relatives might increase accounting profits but it may not increase economic profits.

Section 10.2 The Production in the Short Run

I   Review

To produce a certain level of <u>output</u> a firm must use <u>inputs</u> in certain combinations.

The period of time that is too short for the firm to change the amount of some input is called the <u>short</u> run. Inputs that cannot be varied during this time period are called <u>fixed</u> inputs.

The long run is the period of time in which all inputs are <u>variable</u> inputs. The actual time in this period <u>varies</u> from industry to industry.

The maximum amount of product a firm can produce with a given combination of inputs is determined by the existing <u>technology</u> and described by firm's <u>production</u> function.

The total amount of a firm's output is called its total <u>product</u>. The <u>marginal</u> product is the amount total product changes when one input is increased by a small amount.

Diminishing <u>marginal</u> product states that in the <u>short</u> run, when some input is fixed, increasing the amount of the <u>variable</u> input will add to total product but after some point marginal product will decline.

II   True/False

1. True. Jed and Ellie May are operating in the short run since an important input, oil wells, is available to them in a fixed amount. The short run is the period of time when an important input is fixed.

2. False. The trucks are fixed inputs and Beth's short run output decisions must reflect the fact that she can't change the number of trucks she has to work with. But Beth can vary the number of driver hours she uses and the amount of gasoline. Drivers and gasoline are variable inputs. Beth can increase production by using more drivers and more gasoline and driving each truck more hours.

3. True. A firm's production function describes the maximum amount of output that can be produced with any given combination of inputs. The assembly line allowed workers to gain skills through specialization and reduce the time wasted moving between cars. The assembly line was new technology for the auto industry, which changed the production function.

III   Multiple Choice

1. The answer is B. The length of the short run is determined by the time it takes to change the amount of a particular input a firm has to work with. For most firms the time it takes to expand or reduce their capital input will determine the short run. When capital has a long life it takes time to change the amount. When capital is specialized it takes time to produce. These vary from firm to firm.

2. The answer is D. Diminishing marginal product states that in the short run as the amount of the variable input (labor) is increased, a point is ultimately reached where the additions to output decline. When Cal reaches the point of diminishing marginal product output will increase by smaller amounts for each worker or each $70 he spends. This will only change when Cal has time to expand his capital.

3. The answer is C. Diminishing marginal product occurs with the third worker. Starting with worker number three the marginal product of each additional person hired is less than the marginal product of the previous worker.

4. The answer is B. Diminishing marginal product occurs because we are applying more and more of a variable input (cooks) to a fixed input (the kitchen). As we add more cooks after some point they begin to crowd the fixed input. Crowding limits the opportunities for expanding output.

IV   Application and Discussion

A)   See Exhibit 10.1.

EXHIBIT 8.1

With 3 Machines:			With 4 Machines:		
Labor	Total Product (Hats)	Marginal Product (Hats)	Labor	Total Product (Hats)	Marginal Product (Hats)
1 day	8	8	1 day	9	9
2 days	18	10	2 days	20	11
3 days	30	12	3 days	35	15
4 days	45	15	4 days	55	20
5 days	57	12	5 days	76	21
6 days	67	10	6 days	88	12
7 days	72	5	7 days	95	7

B)   The point of diminishing marginal product is at 5 worker days with three machines and six worker days with four machines.

C)   Crowding occurs later with more machines.

Section 10.3 Costs in the Short Run

I   Review

In the short run, a firm's <u>fixed</u> costs are those expenses that are not affected by the level of output.

Those costs that change as the level of output changes are called <u>variable</u> costs.

<u>Total</u> costs are the sum of the firm's fixed and variable costs.

Average total, fixed, and variable costs present the firm's costs on a per <u>unit</u> of output basis.

The change in the firm's total costs that results from an increase in output by one unit is the <u>marginal</u> cost. This is another way to look at the firm's variable costs.

As a firm increases its output, its fixed costs become a <u>smaller</u> share of total costs and its average fixed costs <u>decline</u>.

Marginal costs equal average variable and average total costs at their <u>minimum</u> points. When marginal costs are above average variable and average total costs these costs <u>increase</u>.

ANSWER KEY

II   True/False

1. False. Her total monthly variable costs are $140. Her $750 rent is a fixed costs, since the amount she pays is set by a lease and will not change as her output changes. If she does more work than usual she will have to hire more secretarial services and these costs will increase.

2. False. Total fixed costs will remain constant but as Tremaine sells more lumber these costs will be spread over more units of output so per unit or average fixed costs will fall.

3. True. Marginal costs describe the change in a firm's variable costs as output increases by one unit. Average variable costs describes the per unit variable costs.

4. False. Average total costs are the sum of the firm's average variable and average fixed costs. Average variable costs can never be greater than average total costs.

III   Multiple Choice

1. The answer is B. The question Roger should ask is whether or not one more fight will make him better off. The relevant cost is marginal costs which tells him how his costs will change with one more fight. He wants to know whether his costs will increase by as much as the $6500 he will earn from the fight.

2. The answer is A. When marginal costs equal average cost, average cost is neither rising nor falling. It is a minimum.

3. The answer is A. The per unit fixed costs fall as output expands.

4. The answer is D. Marginal costs describe the change in variable costs with an increase in output and cross the average variable and total costs curves at their lowest points.

5. The answer is B. The average variable cost curve describes the per unit variable costs associated with a given level of output. Total variable costs expand with output.

6. The answer is C. The average total cost equals total costs divided by output.

IV   Application and Discussion

See Exhibit 10.2.

EXHIBIT 8.2							
Total Product (Magnets)	Total Fixed Costs	Total Variable Costs	Total Costs	Average Fixed Costs	Average Variable Costs	Average Total Costs	Marginal Costs
1	$100	$30	$130	$100	$30	$130	$30
2	$100	$50	$150	$50	25	$75	20
3	$100	$60	$160	$33.33	20	$53.33	$10
4	$100	$64	$164	$25	16	$41	$4
5	$100	$90	$190	$20	18	$38	$26
6	$100	$126	$226	$16.67	21	$37.67	$36
7	$100	$168	$268	$14.29	24	$38.29	$42
8	$100	218	318	$12.50	27.25	$39.75	$50

Section 10.4 The Shape of the Short-Run Cost Curves

I   Review

The average total cost curve is roughly "U" shaped.

Average total costs initially fall with increased production in the short run because average fixed costs fall rapidly at small amounts of production.

As production increases marginal costs rise since more variable input has to be used to increase output by the same amount.

Diminishing marginal product is the reason average total costs rise in the short run.

When marginal product is rising, marginal costs are falling. When marginal product is falling, marginal costs are rising.

When marginal costs exceed average costs, average costs are rising. When marginal costs are below average costs, average costs are falling.

II   True/False

1. False. Most average total and variable cost curves resemble the letter "U". Initially falling over a range of output but eventually increasing as output increases.

2. True. In the short run the primary reason average costs increase is diminishing marginal product. Diminishing marginal product says additional variable inputs add less and less to output. Since more of the input is used to produce one more unit of output, the cost of producing additional units of the good increases. If diminishing marginal product did not hold incremental costs would not rise.

3. True. The last quiz is Sara's marginal quiz. If the marginal score exceeds the average the average will be raised by it, as in this case. If the marginal score were less, the average would fall. This arithmetic also explains the relation between average and marginal costs.

4. False. Initially, average total costs will fall as output increases, because average fixed costs decrease as fixed costs are spread over more units of output. Fixed costs for most firms are a relatively large share of total costs at small levels of production and changes in per unit fixed costs dominate average total costs.

III   Multiple Choice

1. The answer is D. Average total costs equal the sum of average fixed and average variable costs. Initially fixed costs are a large proportion of the total. As output expands total fixed costs are constant and are spread over an increasing number of bricks. The decrease in per unit fixed costs usually outweighs any increase in average variable costs.

ANSWER KEY

2. The answer is A. In the region of diminishing marginal product an increase in output will result in falling marginal product and increasing marginal costs. It takes increasing amounts of the variable input to produce one more unit of output so the marginal costs will increase.

3. The answer is C. Whenever marginal cost is greater than average total costs, average total costs will rise. Whenever marginal cost is below average total costs, average total costs will fall. This is a result of the arithmetic relation between averages and marginal.

IV   Application and Discussion

1. The marginal product of the 51st worker is 200 vests per month. The marginal cost equals $8 ($1600/200) Average variable costs will rise because average cost is $6.67 when 12,000 vests are produced ($1600 x 50/12,000). Average costs will rise when marginal costs is greater than the average.

2. Marginal cost rises because marginal product is falling.

Section 10.5 Cost Curves: Short Run Versus Long Run

I   Review

In the long run firms can <u>substitute</u> capital for labor if that will reduce the cost of producing a given amount of output.

The effects of diminishing marginal product are reduced in the long run because the firm can <u>vary</u> all of its inputs.

In the long run, average costs associated with expanding output are <u>lower</u> than in the short run because of the greater <u>flexibility</u> firms have in choosing inputs.

In the long run, firms experience <u>economies</u> of scale when increased output results in declining per unit costs.

When per unit costs increase with output firms experience <u>diseconomies</u> of scale.

In the long run firms can often expand output and keep average costs the same. This is the range of <u>constant</u> returns to scale.

When economies of scale are exhausted firms are producing at the minimum <u>efficient</u> scale in the long run.

II   True/False

1. True. In the long run no inputs are fixed. Edith's remodeling will increase the capital she uses. She is substituting capital for labor. The increased flexibility of the long run allows her to produce at lower average total costs.

2. False. The firm is in the range of constant returns to scale when output can be increased with no change in per unit costs. Diseconomies of scale occurs when increased output results in an increase in per unit costs.

III   Multiple Choice

1. The answer is D. Factories are examples of capital, and it takes a long time to change the level of this type of capital. In the short run a firm will produce a given level of output using its fixed number of factories and labor. It may be possible in the long run for the firm to use more capital and fewer workers and reduce the average cost of producing a given amount of output.

2. The answer is B. The fee will be a cost of doing business that Max must pay. Since it does not vary with the production, it will only affect fixed costs in the short run. It will also affect the cost of production in the long run, since it must be paid to produce.

3. The answer is C. The efficient scale of production is the scale at which long-run average costs are at their lowest.

4. The answer is B. While B is not the lowest possible average cost in the long run, it is the lowest that can be achieved with the fixed input available to the firm in the short run.

5. The answer is B. At output level D average costs rise with increased output.

IV   Application and Discussion

Mrs. Bill is assuming that Buffalo Bill is at home in the range of economies of scale. If this were the case increasing his output would lower average total costs. She also recognizes that Bill is operating in the short run and that given time he can reduce his per unit costs by substituting capital (chip machines) for labor. These changes may lower average total costs below the price Bill receives for his chips.

CHAPTER 11 PERFECT COMPETITION

Chapter 11.1 The Four Market Structures

I   Review
___

Economists have identified four different market structures; these are <u>perfect competition</u>, <u>monopoly</u>, <u>oligopoly</u>, and <u>monopolistic competition</u>.

Perfect competition is one market type that is characterized by (1) <u>many</u> buyers and sellers, (2) selling a <u>homogeneous</u> product, and (3) <u>easy</u> market entry and exit.

Firms in this type of market produce homogenous products or products that are <u>identical</u>.

In a perfectly competitive market there are so many buyers and sellers that each feels they have little <u>control</u> over the prices. Firms in this type of market are price <u>takers</u> and take the market price as given.

In a perfectly competitive industry it is fairly easy for entrepreneurs to become suppliers of a product because there are no significant <u>barriers</u> to entry or exit.

II   True/False
___

1. True. Firms produce a homogenous product when they produce identical or standardized products. Production of identical products is one characteristic of firms in a perfectly competitive market.

2. False. The hot dog business in Coney Island is not a perfectly competitive market because there is a significant barrier to entry. The city will not allow more than five firms so others who wish to pursue the rewards of the hot dog business are not allowed in the market. To be a perfectly competitive market an industry must have all three characteristics.

3. False. In a perfectly competitive market with standardized products, like eggs, producers are price takers. If Farmer Brown raises his price above the market price, his customers will simply buy from someone else. Other farmer's eggs are perfect substitutes for Farmer Brown's and, in a perfectly competitive industry, there are many other sellers.

III   Multiple Choice
___

1. The answer is D. The many sellers in a perfectly competitive industry provide buyers with alternatives. If one seller raises her price, buyers simply buy from one of the other sellers of the identical product.

2. The answer is C. Labor is a cost of production that all firms in business must pay. While it will affect the profitability in the industry, it won't stop firms from entering if the industry offers profits. Limited information, government regulation, and high entry costs are all barriers to entry.

3. The answer is D. Oligopoly is an industry structure where there are few firms. While each firm has a significant share of the market, they compete because they produce products that are similar or identical. The limited number of firms means each firm is conscious of their rivals' actions.

IV   Application and Discussion
___

See Exhibit 11.1

ANSWER KEY

Industry	Many Firms and Buyers	Identical Products	Ease of Entry and Exit	Perfectly Competitive Market?
New York taxi business: City issues a limited number of permits.	X	X		no
Commercial aircraft industry: The costs of starting such a business are significant.		X		no
Window washing business: Low cost of entry and limited specialized training.	X	X	X	yes
Fast-food business: Restaurant chains produce meals that are distinct.	X		X	no
Broccoli farming: There are many producers of broccoli, which requires no special growing conditions.	X	X	X	yes

EXHIBIT 9.1

Section 11.2 An Individual Price Taker's Demand Curve

I   Review

Firms in a perfectly competitive industry sell at the market-determined price, so they are price <u>takers</u>.

If a perfectly competitive firm charged a higher then market price, buyers would purchase the product from <u>other</u> sellers.

A seller is such a <u>small</u> fraction of the market they can place as much of their product as they want on the market with no effect on the market price. They have no reason to <u>lower</u> their price below the market price since they can sell all they want.

The demand facing the perfectly competitive seller is <u>perfectly</u> elastic.

Changes in the market demand for a firm's product will change the <u>position</u> of the firm's demand curve.

Price changes provide sellers with current <u>information</u> about market demand and supply conditions. Sellers alter their <u>production</u> decisions in response to the price signals.

II   True/False

1. False. When a firm's demand curve is perfectly elastic all of its customers would buy from other producers if it raised its price above the market price. There are many firms selling perfect substitutes at the market price.

2. False. Brooke is in a perfectly competitive industry. She knows she can sell as much as she wants at the market price, so she has nothing to gain by lowering her price.

3. True. Changing market demand and supply conditions determine the changes in the market price. The entrepreneur only needs to know is how these changes affect his firm, and this effect occurs through changes in the price.

III   Multiple Choice

1. The answer is C. The firm's perfectly elastic demand curve will be at the market clearing price of $5.

2. The answer is B. When changes in the market demand or supply conditions change the market price firms will face a new demand at the new price.

3. The answer is D. Changing tastes may not be news but the outward shift in the market demand curve will cause the price of apples to rise. In a perfectly competitive industry the rising prices provide all of the information Johnny and Granny need. They will now face a new perfectly elastic demand curve at the new higher market price.

302

ANSWER KEY

Farms can be thought of as perfectly competitive businesses, which produce products that are very close to perfect substitutes. For example, one farmer's eggs are very good substitutes for any other eggs. Any advertising for eggs will increase the market demand for all farmers' eggs. All farms will benefit since the market price will rise. In this situation no single farm has an incentive to invest in advertising since the price they can charge will increase and they will benefit from the advertising of others.

Section 11.3 Profit Maximization

I   Review

The objective of a firm is to maximize <u>profits</u>, the difference between total revenue and total costs.

The firm wants to produce the amount of output that <u>maximizes</u> the difference between total revenue and total costs.

Total revenue equals the product price times the <u>quantity</u> of output sold.

Average revenue is total revenue <u>divided</u> by quantity. It is equal to the <u>price</u> of the product in perfect competition.

The additional revenue from producing and selling one more unit of output is <u>marginal</u> revenue. In a perfectly competitive firm, it also equals the price and average revenue.

As long as marginal revenue is greater than marginal costs, revenues increase by more than costs when output increases so profits <u>increase</u>.

The output level where marginal revenue <u>equals</u> marginal costs is the output where the difference between total revenue and total costs is greatest or where profits are maximized.

II   TRUE/FALSE

1. True. Marginal revenue is the change in total revenue that results from selling one more unit of output. Average revenue equals total revenue divided by quantity. However, for a perfectly competitive firm marginal revenue equals average revenue since both equal price.

2. False. Bob and Lou want to maximize their profits. They should continue to add concerts as long as the marginal costs are less than $4,500, their marginal revenue. Even though marginal costs increase, Bob and Lou can continue to increase profits as long as marginal costs are less than marginal revenue.

3. True. Total revenue equals the price times the quantity sold. If we assume all the horses shooed had four hoofs, Francis shooed 400 hooves at $35 apiece for total revenue of $14,000.

III   Multiple Choice

1. The answer is C. The profit maximizing output is six cabbages where marginal cost is equal to marginal revenue. Mr. MacGregor should increase cabbage production as long as the marginal revenue exceeds the marginal cost. This is true for less than six cabbages. MacGregor will maximize profits by reducing output if marginal cost is greater than marginal revenue. This is true for more than six cabbages.

2. The answer is A. Average revenue is found by dividing total revenue by quantity sold. For perfectly competitive firms average revenue equals the price.

3. The answer is B. A firm in a perfectly competitive industry can sell as much as they want at the market-clearing price. Since they are a small fraction of the market their sales will not affect the market price. Each additional unit sold adds an amount equal to the price to their revenue, so marginal revenue always equals price.

ANSWER KEY

1.

Quantity	Price	Total Revenue	Marginal Revenue	Marginal Cost	Total Profit
10	$12	$120	$12	$8	$25
11	12	132	12	9	28
12	12	144	12	11	29
13	12	156	12	12	29
14	12	168	12	14	27

2. Marginal   revenue   equals   marginal   costs   at   the profit-maximizing output of 13 units. Even though the firm does not increase profits on the 13th unit it will still produce since its is covering its costs, so the entrepreneur is earning an amount equal to his opportunity costs.

3. At a price of $9 the profit-maximizing output would be 11 units where price equals marginal cost. If the firm produced 12 units profits would fall by $2 (marginal cost minus marginal revenue).

Section 11.4 Short-Run Profits and Losses

I   Review

The firm can make economic profits, suffer economic losses, or make zero profits at the profit-maximizing level of output.

The profit-maximizing output is where price equals marginal cost. At this output a firm will make an economic profit if total revenue is greater than total cost.

At this output a firm will suffer an economic loss if total revenue is less than total cost.

If total revenue equals total cost at this output, the firm earns zero economic profit. Entrepreneurs are covering their implicit and explicit costs. They produce since they are doing as well as they could anywhere else.

In the short run the firm will continue to produce when it suffers an economic loss as long as price is greater than average variable costs. It reduces its loss by producing since it can use the excess to cover some of its fixed costs.

A firm will shut down in the short run if price is less than average variable cost, since it will lose more than its fixed cost by producing.

The short-run supply curve of an individual competitive seller is that portion of the marginal cost curve that lies above the minimum of the average variable cost curve.

The short-run market supply curve for a competitive industry is the horizontal summation of the individual firms' supply curves.

II   True/False

1. False. In the short run a firm will only produce this level of output if the price it receives is greater than its average variable costs. If price is less than average variable costs, the firm will lose less money by shutting down.

2. True. Marge and Al are experiencing an economic loss of about $43. Economic profit equals total revenue (750 times $1= $750) minus total costs (750 times $.59 plus $350= $792.50) or -$42.50. Since the profit is negative, it is an economic loss.

3. False. Production even with losses is a rational decision if production reduces the size of the firm's loss. If price is greater than the firm's average variable cost at the profit maximizing output, the firm will cover all of its variable costs and have revenue left over to apply to its fixed costs. In this case, the firm will lose more by shutting down than by producing.

ANSWER KEY

1. The answer is D. Zero economic profit means that the firm's total cost just equals its total revenue. Revenue covers both explicit and implicit costs. The entrepreneur's implicit costs include the opportunity cost of using her resources or their value in their next best alternative use. Since the entrepreneur is covering her opportunity cost, she could make no better use of the resources she owns.

2. The answer is A. The firm will not produce. At the output where price equals marginal cost, price is less than average variable cost.

3. The answer is B. The firm will produce as long as it can cover its average variable costs. At prices below P1 the firm will shut down since it cannot cover its variable costs.

4. The answer is C. In the short run, Loren will produce abalone as long as he covers his variable cost even though he doesn't earn enough to cover his boat payment. Since Loren produces at $2.50, this price is greater than his average variable cost. Firms shutdown when the price is less than average variable cost. Since he shuts down at a price of $2, this price is less than his average variable cost.

IV   Application and Discussion

When average total cost is $3, profit will be total revenue (1000 times $5= $5000) minus total costs (1000 times $3= $3000) or $2000. When average total cost is $6, profit will be total revenue (1000 times $5= $5000) minus total costs (1000 times $6= $6000) or -$1000. A firm will make a profit if it makes a profit on each unit it sells. It will make a loss if it loses money on each unit it sells.

Section 11.5 Long-Run Equilibrium

I   Review

Positive economic profits in a perfectly competitive industry are signals that <u>attract</u> additional resources to the industry in the long run.

As more firms enter the industry the market supply will <u>increase</u> and the market supply curve will shift to the <u>right</u>. The impact of this shift is a <u>decline</u> in the equilibrium price of the product.

As the product price falls, the economic profit earned by firms in the industry will <u>decline</u>. New firms will stop entering the industry only when firms in the industry are earning <u>zero</u> economic profits.

When firms in an industry suffer economic <u>loss</u>, resources will leave the industry causing market supply to decline and prices to <u>rise</u>. Firms will stop leaving the industry when no firm earns an economic <u>loss</u>.

Zero economic profit is an <u>equilibrium</u> situation in the long run because there is neither a signal for firms to leave nor enter the industry.

Long-run equilibrium results in each firm producing at its <u>lowest</u> average total costs, the point where price equals marginal costs and average total costs.

II   TRUE/FALSE

1. True. Firms enter an industry with economic profits because they can earn more than they could earn in their next best alternative. However, the increased competition causes prices to fall and economic profits to go to zero. Consumers benefit from competition, because it results in goods being produced at the most efficient, lowest cost scale.

ANSWER KEY

2. False. Economic profits are a signal that attracts resources to an industry. In the poinsettia industry economic profits will result in an increase in the market supply as old firms add resources and new firms enter. If demand does not change, the equilibrium price will fall as supply increases.

3. False. Johnny may be disappointed that he is not making economic profits, but he has no better place to use his resources. When economic profits are zero Johnny is covering his implicit cost, so he is earning as much with his resources in the video business as he would in any other business.

III   Multiple Choice

1. The answer is C. As firms leave an industry where they earn an economic loss, prices will rise. As long as prices are below average total cost at the profit maximizing output, economic losses will occur and firms will continue to leave the industry.

2. The answer is A. Initially an increase in demand will cause the equilibrium price to rise and firms in the industry will experience economic profits. This will attract more firms, increasing supply, and lowering price. Entry will stop when price falls to the point where economic profits are zero. If costs conditions do not change this will be the old equilibrium price.

3. The answer is B. Economic loss is also a signal. It tells entrepreneurs that there are other, better ways to use their resources. Since Larry isn't covering his implicit costs in the golf club business, he should move his resources to uses with where they have greater value.

IV   Application and Discussion

Entrepreneurs see an industry with economic profits as a place to maximize their gain. They move resources to a use that earns more than their opportunity cost. These actions increase market supply and lower equilibrium price, a result that makes consumers better off. Eventually entry will continue until economic profits are eliminated. At this point firms will be producing where average total costs are the lowest. In a society of scarce resources producing at this efficient scale is good for all of us since it gives society the goods using the fewest resources. Consumers are also able to buy the good at a price equal to this minimum average total cost. Firms seeking to make the largest economic profit end up providing goods in the lowest cost way.

Section 11.6 Long-Run Supply

I   Review

When the output of an entire industry changes there is a likelihood that <u>costs</u> will be affected.

As the industry output increases, the industry's <u>demand</u> for the inputs it uses will also increase.

If the industry uses a significant share of any particular input, this increased demand will cause input prices to <u>rise</u> or the quality of the input to <u>decline</u>.

In a(n) <u>increasing</u>-cost industry, the cost curves of the individual firms shift up as the industry output increases because input prices <u>rise</u> or input quality <u>declines</u>.

When an industry's use of inputs is a relatively <u>small</u> share of the total available, the increased demand that results from expanding output will have little effect on input prices.

In a(n) <u>constant</u>-cost industry, the cost curves of the individual firms will not change as the industry output increases since input prices will not be effected by the change.

In a constant-cost industry, increased demand will result in a new equilibrium at the <u>initial</u> equilibrium price. The long run supply curve will be <u>perfectly</u> elastic at a price equal to the minimum average total cost of production.

ANSWER KEY

In an increasing-cost industry, increased demand will result in a new equilibrium at a <u>higher</u> price than the original equilibrium. The long run supply curve will have a <u>positive</u> slope, since increasing output results in higher costs.

The long-run supply curve will be <u>more</u> elastic than the short-run supply curve in a competitive industry because firms can enter and exit.

At the competitive industry equilibrium resources are used <u>efficiently</u>.

II   True/False

1. True. Since the industry uses a significant share of this input and it takes time to increase the supply, any increase in demand will result in an increase in the price of the input. As the industry expands output, the price of pilots will increase, which will also result in an increase in each firm's cost of production.

2. False. The wedding business is a constant cost industry. Increased demand will cause prices to rise in the short run, but the economic profits created by the price increase will result in new firms entering lowering prices back to the long run equilibrium or original price.

III   Multiple Choice

1. The answer is D. A constant cost industry can expand its output and use of inputs with little effect on price. If the supply of the input was perfectly inelastic, any increase in use would result in an increase in the price of the input. This would cause costs to rise for firms in the industry.

2. The answer is A. The price in the long run must eliminate economic profits and clear the market. Given the new demand and new costs, $P1$ is the price and $Q1$ the output on the long run supply curve.

IV   Application and Discussion

Industry	Input Market	Increasing or Constant Costs?
Major League Baseball	Uses the majority of pitchers. As the number of pitchers used increases, the quality declines.	Increasing costs since more teams will bid up the price of good pitchers and reduce the quality of the average pitcher.
Fast Food Restaurants	Uses a relatively small share of land and unskilled labor in most cities.	Constant cost since expansion of output will not significantly increase the price of these unspecialized inputs.
Trucking Industry	Uses a large portion of the trained and experienced drivers, especially long-distance drivers.	Increasing costs since industry expansion will put upward pressure on the wages offered these trained workers.

CHAPTER 12 MONOPOLY

Section 12.1 Monopoly: The Price Maker

I   Review

A pure monopoly exists when there is only <u>one</u> seller of a product, which has no available close <u>substitute</u>.

Examples of pure monopoly are <u>hard</u> to find because most goods have some available <u>substitute</u>.

<u>Barriers</u> to entry are necessary for a monopoly to persist.

Government's award of franchise, occupational licenses, and patents for new inventions are examples of <u>legal</u> barriers to entry.

A <u>natural</u> monopoly exists when economies of scale give one firm a cost advantage over production by a number of firms. Government may grant these firms <u>monopoly</u> rights and erect another barrier to entry.

One firm's control of the <u>supply</u> of an important input to production, such as DeBeers control over diamonds, provides another a barrier to entry.

II   True/False

1. False. A pure monopoly exists when there is one seller of a product that has no good close substitutes. Regular sized bagels are good substitutes for Betty's big bagels.

2. True. A natural monopoly exists when one firm can supply a market with a product at lower per unit costs than two or more firms could. The existence of significant economies of scale results in average costs declining over the whole range of the market. If competition replaces the water monopoly each firm would produce less and the per unit water costs would rise since they would lose some of the advantages of scale economies.

III   Multiple Choice

1. The answer is C. Pure monopolies are rare because there are usually goods and services that, while not perfect substitutes, are close substitutes. Answers A, B, and D are examples of services that provide substitutes for the postal service in sending information. The economic profits earned by monopolies provide entrepreneurs with the incentive to figure out ways around the monopolist barrier to entry.

2. The answer is D. A pure monopoly is a single producer of a product with no close substitute. The monopolist depends on a barrier to entry to keep competition away. Only the town's water utility has a significant barrier to entry, a legal limit to competition. All the other businesses have no significant barriers to firms producing close substitutes.

IV   Application and Discussion

See Exhibit 12.1.

ANSWER KEY

Monopoly case:	Government patents or license	Ownership of essential resource	Large entry costs
In the 1940s, Aluminum Company of America owns all of the world's known bauxite deposits.	☐	☒	☐
Local cable TV company has the only government issued license to supply services in the area.	☒	☐	☐
The pharmaceutical company, MAXCO, invented and patented a new baldness drug.	☒	☐	☐
In the 1950s, AT&T provided long-distance telephone service by stringing millions of miles of copper wiring across the United States.	☐	☐	☒

Section 12.2 Demand and Marginal Revenue in Monopoly

I Review

The <u>market</u> demand curve is the demand curve of the monopoly firm.

The firm faces a <u>downward</u> sloping demand curve. The monopolist can increase price by <u>lowering</u> output. <u>Increasing</u> output will cause price to fall.

To sell more the monopolist must lower his price to <u>all</u> customers. The <u>increased</u> revenue from selling one more unit is offset by the <u>decreased</u> revenue from the lower price, the monopolist's marginal revenue is <u>less</u> than price. The marginal revenue curve lies <u>below</u> the demand curve.

Monopolist will always produce where marginal revenue is <u>positive</u> and this is on the <u>elastic</u> portion of his demand curve.

II True/False

1. False. A monopolist faces the market demand curve, which is downward sloping. To sell more, the monopolist has to lower their price. Watts UP cannot set a price and sell as much as they want.

2. True. The monopolist like all producers wants to produce where revenue increases with production or where marginal revenue is positive. When price falls revenue increases when demand is elastic but decreases when it is inelastic. Marginal revenue is negative along the inelastic portion of the demand curve.

3. False. The industry or market demand curve in a pure monopoly is also the firm's demand curve. The firm will sell the same amount as the market demands at any given price.

III Multiple Choice

1. The answer is C. The marginal revenue is the change in total revenue that results from selling one more unit of the product. For a monopolist like Joan, selling more affects revenue in two ways. First, the additional cubic foot sold increases revenue by the price, $1.09. Second, lowering the price by one cent lowers the revenue earned on the initial 100 cubic feet by $1.00 ($.01 times 100 cubic feet). Joan's marginal revenue is $.09 ($1.09 minus $1), which is less than the price.

2. The answer is B. If a perfectly competitive firm raises its price above the market price, customers will buy from the other producers of the product. These firms must take the market price as given. Since no one produces close substitutes for the product of a monopoly, the monopolist can raise its price without losing all of its customers. The monopolist is a price maker seeking the profit maximizing price.

ANSWER KEY

3. The answer is B. As owners of the only drag strip for hundreds of miles Billy and Bob have some monopoly power because they control an input important to the production of the drag races. When total revenue moves in the same direction as price, demand is inelastic. Monopolists, like Billy and Bob, would never operate for long on the inelastic portion of the demand curve, since by raising price they can increase revenue. The marginal revenue at this point is negative.

IV Application and Discussion

Quantity	Price	Total Revenue	Marginal Revenue	Elastic or Inelastic?
30	$3.65	$109.62		
31	3.58	110.92	$1.30	Elastic
32	3.50	112.06	1.14	Elastic
33	3.43	113.06	1.00	Elastic
34	3.35	113.90	0.84	Elastic
35	3.27	114.59	0.69	Elastic
36	3.20	115.13	0.54	Elastic
37	3.12	115.51	0.38	Elastic
38	3.05	115.75	0.24	Elastic
39	2.97	115.83	0.08	Elastic
40	2.89	115.76	(0.07)	Inelastic
41	2.82	115.54	(0.22)	Inelastic
42	2.74	115.16	(0.38)	Inelastic
43	2.67	114.64	(0.52)	Inelastic
44	2.59	113.96	(0.68)	Inelastic
45	2.51	113.13	(0.83)	Inelastic
46	2.44	112.15	(0.98)	Inelastic
47	2.36	111.01	(1.14)	Inelastic
48	2.29	109.73	(1.28)	Inelastic
49	2.21	108.29	(1.44)	Inelastic
50	2.13	106.70	(1.59)	Inelastic

A) At first marginal revenue increases as the price declines. After the price falls to $2.89, marginal revenue falls as price declines. Marginal revenue is always below the price.

B) Marginal revenue falls as the price declines when the demand is inelastic, so the demand becomes inelastic below a price of $2.89.

C) Mobile Phones of Mobile will increase the number of substitutes for Mobile Phone long distance service. An increase in the number of substitutes will increase the elasticity of the demand facing Mobile Phone.

Section 12.3 The Monopolist's Equilibrium

I REVIEW

The monopolist, like the perfect competitor, maximizes profits by producing the output where marginal revenue equals marginal costs.

The monopolist's equilibrium output level determines the price it will charge. The monopolist will charge the maximum price consumers are willing to pay for the equilibrium output.

The monopolist's total profit at the equilibrium output equals the difference between the price times output and average total costs times output.

In perfectly competitive industries, economic profits will be eliminated in the long run by competition. Monopolists can earn profits in the long run because barriers to entry keep competitors out of the market.

Monopolies have gone out of business. Being a sole provider does not mean consumers will <u>demand</u> your product. Monopolies can suffer loses when average revenue is <u>less</u> than average total costs at its equilibrium output.

Patents and copyrights are forms of <u>monopoly</u> power granted by government. The patent holder has the <u>exclusive</u> right to make a product for twenty years. Patents give producers the <u>incentive</u> to undertake the expensive research effort required to develop new products.

II   True/False

1. False. Both monopolies and perfectly competitive firms follow the same profit-maximizing rule: Produce where marginal revenue equals marginal costs. The main difference is that marginal revenue equals price for a competitive firm but is less than price for a monopolist.

2. True. Unlike perfectly competitive firms, monopolists can earn profits in the long run. Barriers to entry keep competitors from the industry. Dwayne has a patent that is a barrier to entry since no one else can copy his drain design.

3. False. Monopolists charge a price that is greater than marginal costs because that is the price which consumers are willing to pay. This is the price at which the quantity demanded equals the monopolist's equilibrium output.

III   Multiple Choice

1. The answer is B. Monopolists produce where MR = MC.

2. The answer is A. Monopolists restrict or constrain supply. A price set equal to marginal cost would result in excess demand. Consumers would bid the price up to P3 where the excess demand is eliminated at the monopolist's equilibrium output.

3. The answer is C. The firm's per unit profit is the difference between the price it charges or its average revenue and its average total costs.

IV   Application and Discussion

1. See Exhibit 12.2.

EXHIBIT 12.2

Quantity (gallons)	Price (per gallon)	Total Revenue	Marginal Revenue	Marginal Costs	Average Total Costs	Profit
100	$1.28	$128		$0.15	$1.252	$2.80
101	$1.27	128.27	$0.27	$0.18	$1.241	2.93
102	$1.26	128.52	0.25	$0.21	$1.231	2.96
103	$1.25	128.75	0.23	$0.23	$1.231	2.99
104	$1.24	128.96	0.21	$0.26	$1.212	2.91

2. Profits are greatest at 103 gallons where marginal revenue equals marginal costs.

3. The tax is a fixed cost. Since it does not affect the marginal cost the level of output would remain the same as long as the firm produced. The firm would lose $100.01 by producing ($103 – 2.99). The firm would stay in operation in the short run because it loses less than the $103 it would by going out of business.

Section 12.4 Monopoly and Welfare Loss

I   Review

A monopoly will result in a <u>lower</u> output and a <u>higher</u> price than would exist if the industry were organized under perfect competition. This is the main objection economists have to monopoly.

ANSWER KEY

Monopolists produce where <u>price</u> is greater than marginal cost. This means monopolists do not produce <u>enough</u> of the product. A welfare loss results because the monopolist stops producing even though the value to society of the last unit produced is <u>greater</u> than its cost.

Critics argue that monopoly is bad because it results in market <u>inefficiencies</u>. Another criticism is economic power and that monopolists have no incentive to <u>innovate</u>. On the other hand, others argue many important <u>innovating</u> firms have been monopolists.

Some dispute the notion that monopoly retards innovation. Many important <u>innovators</u>, like AT&T and IBM, have been near-monopolists. To expand profits, monopolists may innovate to <u>lower</u> costs, expand revenues, or <u>preserve</u> their monopoly power.

II   True/False

1. False. Consumers lose from monopolies in two ways. First, monopolists charge higher prices, which reduce consumers' surplus but shows up as increased monopoly profits. Second, since a monopolist produces less than a competitive industry would consumers lose the consumer surplus they would have gained on the lost output. The welfare loss to society as a whole results from the reduction in the amount produced.

2. True. As a monopolist, Rita will change the amount she produces and price she charges. The profit-maximizing amount for a monopolist is less than the perfectly competitive industry will produce. Since she produces less, she can charge more for the beets. Monopolists produce less and charge more than would be the case under competitive conditions.

3. False. While there have been examples of monopolies, like the US railroad industry, that had strong monopoly power and did not spend much on research and development, there have also been many cases of firms with monopoly power that were important innovators. AT&T, Bell Labs, Microsoft, IBM, Xerox, and Polaroid are all examples cited in the book.

III   Multiple Choice

1. The answer is B. In each of these cases firms had significant monopoly power. Except for the railroad industry, these firms produced important innovations even though they had strong market power.

2. The answer is B. The welfare loss represents a loss in efficiency. When the price consumers are willing to pay is greater than the marginal cost of producing a good, society is better off if its resources are used to produce more of the good. Consumers value the good more than the next best use of the resources used to produce it. Monopolists don't let this production take place.

3. The answer is D. Monopolists produce the amount where marginal revenue equals the marginal cost. At this amount price is greater than marginal costs. Price tells us how much consumers value one more unit of the good (what they are willing to give up) and marginal cost tells us what society would have to give up to get one more unit of the good. At the monopolist result people would be willing to pay more than it costs to produce more of the good, but the monopolist refuses to expand production. This is the source of the inefficiency of monopoly.

IV   Application and Discussion

1. Consumers suffer a cost because monopolists produce less and charge a higher price than a competitive industry. Consumers' loss equals their lost consumer surplus. Only part of this loss shows up as monopolist profits. The consumer surplus lost because of the monopolist's reduced production is not recovered as profits. The consumers' loss is greater than the monopolist's profit.

2. The government could buy the patent rights for an amount equal to the monopolists profits, since the monopolist could do no better than this by producing. The competitive industry would produce more goods at lower prices. The consumer would gain consumer surplus equal to the monopoly profits because of the price decline. This would compensate them for the cost of purchasing the patent. The consumer would also gain consumer surplus because more of the product would be produced.

ANSWER KEY

Section 12.5 Monopoly Policy

I   Review
___

Two approaches government has taken to dealing with monopoly are <u>antitrust</u> policies and <u>regulation</u>.

<u>Antitrust</u> policies make monopolies illegal and impose costs on monopolists. These policies attack restrictions placed on price <u>competition</u> like limits to advertising in industries or firms collectively setting prices.

To achieve the <u>efficiency</u> of large scale privately, owned natural monopolies, government regulates <u>pricing</u> and other monopoly practices of these firms.

Allocative <u>efficiency</u> occurs when firms produce the amount of the good for which the <u>value</u> consumers receive from the last unit just equals the opportunity <u>cost</u> of producing it. This occurs where <u>price</u> equals marginal cost.

Without regulation a natural monopoly will <u>produce</u> where marginal revenue equals marginal costs and earn an economic profit. This is not a point of <u>allocative</u> efficiency.

When a firm produces an output where average costs are falling, marginal cost is <u>below</u> average total costs. At the equilibrium output if regulators set price equal to marginal cost, the monopolist would suffer <u>losses</u> since price will be less than average total cost.

A regulatory compromise is <u>average</u> cost pricing. Prices are set so that average revenue will just equal average costs or where the demand curve crosses the average total cost curve.

Average cost pricing sets price so that economic profits are <u>zero</u> but allows firms to earn a <u>normal</u> rate of return.

One problem with implementing average cost pricing is the difficulty of calculating the <u>fair</u> rate of return.

Another problem is average cost pricing gives monopolist no <u>incentive</u> to reduce costs. The price will be set so that a firm earns a normal rate of return <u>independent</u> of costs.

A final problem with average cost pricing is that rates are set in a <u>political</u> arena so the outcome reflects the power of <u>special</u> interest groups.

II   True/False
___

1. False. A natural monopolist would not produce the efficient level of output, where price equals marginal cost. Since average costs are falling at the efficient output, a natural monopolist would lose money because price would be less than average cost. A monopolist maximizes profit by producing where marginal revenue equals marginal cost.

2. True. Competition in an industry with the characteristics of a natural monopoly may increase the average cost of production. Government may allow a firm to operate as a monopolist to gain the efficiency of large-scale production. In exchange government regulates the behavior of these firms so they do not act like monopolists.

3. False. Antitrust policy has the goal of eliminating monopolies by making them illegal. These policies attempt to control the size of businesses, encourage price competition, and eliminate barriers to entry. Regulation of firms often allows the existence of monopolies but controls the firm's output and pricing decisions so they do not act like a monopolist.

III   Multiple Choice
___

1. The answer is D. The most efficient level of output is where price equals marginal cost. Unfortunately at this output the natural monopolist would suffer losses since price is less than average total cost.

313

2. The answer is B. The monopolist maximizes profits by producing where marginal revenue equals marginal cost and charging the price consumers will pay for this output.

3. The answer is C. The regulators want to limit monopoly profits to the fair rate of return but keep firms from suffering loses. Average cost pricing sets the regulated price equal to the average cost of production.

4. The answer is B. Antitrust policy attempts to increase price competition among firms. Advertising prices makes information about prices easy to acquire and allows consumers to 'shop around' for the best deal. Association restriction on price advertising makes it harder for consumers to shop and reduces competition.

5. The answer is D. Average cost pricing is a compromise between the monopolist profit maximizing price and the efficient, but loss producing, price. Average cost pricing is difficult to implement because it is made in a political environment and costs and values are not easily known. Average cost pricing provides no incentive for firms to be efficient in production since it allows them to earn a fair rate of return independent of their cost.

IV   Application and Discussion

One reason for the change might be changes in technology, which eliminate the advantages of scale. One firm may no longer be able to produce the product at lower per unit costs than two or more firms may. The inefficiencies of a regulated monopoly may also result in competition being a more efficient organization. Regulated monopolies suffer three types of inefficiencies. First, they produce less than the output at which allocative efficiency is reached. Second, there is no incentive for the firm to produce in the least cost way. Finally, if special interest dominate decision-making efficiency is only an accidental outcome. Since a competitive environment would not suffer these inefficiencies, competition may be more efficient even with the loss of scale if these other losses are significant.

Section 12.6 Price Discrimination and Peak Load Pricing

I   Review

Price <u>discrimination</u> occurs when producers charge different customers different prices for the same good or service.

Producers' motive for price discrimination is <u>profit</u> maximization.

Even though the marginal cost is the same, producers charge different prices to groups of consumers who differ in the <u>demand</u> for the product.

Price discrimination is possible only with <u>monopoly</u> or where members of a small group of firms follow identical pricing policies. Competitors would <u>undercut</u> the high prices charged to certain groups.

Price discriminating monopolists must also prevent <u>resale</u> of the product by the group that is charged the lower price.

A firm that perfectly price discriminates sets the price for each unit at the <u>maximum</u> amount customers will pay.

Perfect price discrimination results in a monopoly producing an <u>efficient</u> level of output.

Higher peak load prices leads to greater efficiency because they reflect higher <u>marginal</u> <u>costs</u> of production.

II   True/False

1. False. Price discrimination occurs because monopolists want to increase their profits. By increasing the price charged to different groups of consumers total revenue and profits increase.

ANSWER KEY

2. True. Airlines price discriminate on the basis of time. Tickets purchased weeks in advance of the flight sell for less than tickets purchased near the date of the flight. This is often discrimination against business travelers with last minute travel needs. People buying tickets in advance could profitably resell their tickets to business travelers. Airlines work to prevent easy reselling. Requiring a picture ID for security reasons makes it easy to prevent resale of tickets.

3. False. The tomato industry is competitive with many producers producing goods that are perfect substitutes. If he attempts to raise the price he charges men, other producers will take away these customers. To price discriminate the producer must have monopoly power.

4. False. Monopolist who price discriminate leave no surplus for the consumer. Compared to the competitive result the consumer is worse off.

III   Multiple Choice

1. The answer is C. Price discrimination occurs when a firm charges different prices to customers even though the cost of providing the good is the same to all customers. A firm must be a monopolist and prevent resale. Demand must also differ among the firm's customers.

2. The answer is D. Monopolists wish to maximize their profits. Charging higher prices to customers with less elastic demand will increase their profits.

3. The answer is C. With peak load pricing consumers have an incentive to give their appliances a rest when the price is higher and use them when the price is lower.

IV   Application and Discussion

1. Demand would be greater during the morning and afternoon rush hour periods when commuters drive into work and back home.

2. The bridge authority might have to add toll collectors, bridge wear and tear, and people to direct traffic. The biggest cost would be paid by the commuters who spend more time sitting in traffic; these are cost of congestion.

3. A higher rush hour toll would provide an incentive for some bridge users to adjust their schedules to use the bridge in less congested times. People not traveling for work would travel at other times. Some commuters might also be able to adjust their work schedules to come into St. Louis to avoid rush hour. This would reduce the rush hour congestion.

CHAPTER 13 MONOPOLISTIC COMPETITION AND OLIGOPOLY

Chapter 13.1 Monopolistic Competition

I   Review

Monopolistic competition is similar to both <u>monopoly</u> and perfect competition. As in monopoly, firms have some control over market <u>price</u>, but as in perfect competition, they face <u>competition</u> from many other sellers.

Due to the free entry of new firms, long-run economic profits in monopolistic competition are <u>zero</u>.

Firms in monopolistic competition produce products that are <u>differentiated</u> from those produced by other firms in the industry.

In monopolistic competition, firms use <u>brand</u> names to gain some degree of control over price.

The theory of monopolistic competition is based on three characteristics: (1) product <u>differentiation</u>, (2) many <u>sellers</u>, and (3) free <u>entry</u>.

Product differentiation is the accentuation of <u>unique</u> product qualities to develop a product identity.

II   True/False

1. True. Monopolistic competition exhibits elements of both.

2. False. Ease of entry of new firms makes it impossible for monopolistically competitive firms to earn economic profits in the long run.

3. True. Product differentiation and brand names make demand for unique products more inelastic and allow firms to increase profits by raising prices.

4. False. Although firms in perfect competition sell identical products and charge identical prices, firms in monopolistic competition can charge different prices due to product differentiation.

III   Multiple Choice

1. The answer is B. Differences in quantities offered for sale does not differentiate a product as do physical differences, service differences, and differences in location.

2. The answer is D. Ease of entry by new firms is a characteristic of both monopolistic competition and pure competition.

3. The answer is C. Ease of entry assures that new entrants will generate competition that reduces long-run economic profit to zero.

IV   Application and Discussion

1. Fast-food restaurant.s Physical differences are probably most important. Big Macs, Whoppers, tacos, and various sorts of pizza all rely on physical differences to attract customers. Location of restaurants is important as well.

2. Espresso shops/carts. A convenient location is very important, although service is considered an important aspect by many espresso drinkers.

3. Hair stylists. Service is number one, but location is important as well. How far are you willing to drive to get a great cut or perm?

4. Soft drinks. Physical qualities, including taste and the look of the container are most important although location is important too. Coca-Cola gained market leadership years ago by making Coke available everywhere—at movie theaters, lunch counters, and in ubiquitous vending machines.

5. Wine Physical differences and prestige are most important. Physical differences are probably the most important.

Section 13.2 Price and Output Determination in Monopolistic Competition

I   Review

Monopolistic competitive sellers are price <u>searchers</u> like monopolists, and they do not regard price as given by the market. Because products in the industry are slightly different, each firm faces a(n) <u>negatively</u> sloping-demand curve.

In the short run, equilibrium output is determined where marginal revenue equals marginal <u>cost</u>. The price is set equal to the <u>maximum</u> the consumer will pay for this amount.

When price is greater than average total costs, the monopolistic competitive firm will make an economic <u>profit</u>. .

Barriers to entry do not protect monopolistic competitive firms in the <u>long</u> run. Economic profits will <u>attract</u> new firms to the industry. Similarly, firms will leave when there are economic <u>losses</u>.

As new firms enter an industry, the demand curve of existing firms will shift to the <u>left</u>. Entry will continue until there are <u>zero</u> economic p rofits o r p rice j ust e quals a verage t otal c ost. T his i s t he p oint w here t he d emand c urve f or the typical firm is <u>tangent</u> to the long run average total cost curve.

When there are economic losses, firms will leave the industry and the demand curve of remaining firms will shift to the <u>right</u>. Firms will exit the industry until the economic loss is <u>eliminated</u>.

Long-run equilibrium in a monopolistic competitive industry occurs when there are <u>zero</u> economic profits or losses, so there is no incentive for firms to <u>enter</u> or <u>exit</u> the industry.

II   True/False

1. False. Frank's choice of output reflects the monopolistic character of the industry. Since Frank's shop is slightly different from others, he faces a negatively sloped demand curve. The firm chooses the profit maximizing output like a monopolist, producing where marginal revenue equals marginal cost and sets a price greater than marginal revenue.

2. True. Firms choose to produce the output at which marginal revenue equals marginal cost.

III   Multiple Choice

1. The answer is D. A monopolistic competitor will operate in the short run as long as she earns more than the average variable cost. In this case, if she suffers a loss, it is less than the fixed costs. If by operating Maria lost more than her fixed cost, she would shut down the bakery.

2. The answer is C. Claire cannot count on earning these economic profits in the long run. A monopolistic competitive firm may earn economic profits in the short run. However, profits will attract new firms to the industry, which will decrease the demand facing the firm and reduce economic profits. Eventually entry of competitors will eliminate the restaurant's profits.

3. The answer is B. Long-run equilibrium occurs when no economic profits or losses occur. This occurs where the demand curve is tangent to the average total cost curve.

ANSWER KEY

4. The answer is D. A monopolistic competitive firm will act like a monopoly or a perfectly competitive firm and shut down when price is less than average variable cost at the profit maximizing output. Price is always less than average variable cost along D₃.

IV   Application and Discussion

Both types of firms operate in industries with many other sellers and with no real barriers to entry and exit. They follow similar rules when choosing the level of output. Both types of firms also will experience zero economic profits in the long run.

In the short run, monopolistic competitors and perfectly competitive firms follow similar rules for choosing the profit maximizing output. They produce where marginal revenue equals marginal cost. Monopolistic competitors will produce less than perfectly competitive firms will, because the relation between price and marginal revenue differs between these types of firms. Since firms that are monopolistic competitors face a negatively sloped demand curve, they are price makers and price is greater than marginal revenue. They produce an output less than the output where price equals marginal cost. A perfectly competitive firm will produce where price equals marginal cost since they are price takers.

In the long run, entry will force both types of firms to the output where economic profits are equal to zero, which occurs where the demand curves are tangent to the average total cost curve. Because the monopolistic competitor faces a negatively sloped demand curve, this point will be at a level of output less than the perfect competitor.

Section 13.3 Monopolistic Competition versus Perfect Competition

I   Review

Because it faces competition, a monopolistically competitive firm has a <u>downward</u>-sloping demand curve that tends to be more <u>elastic</u> than the demand curve for a monopolist.

Even in the long run, monopolistically competitive firms do not operate at levels that permit the full realization of <u>economies</u> of scale.

Unlike a perfectly competitive firm in long-run equilibrium, a monopolistically competitive firm will produce with <u>excess</u> capacity. The firm could lower average costs by increasing output but this would reduce <u>profits</u>.

In monopolistic competition there is a tendency toward too <u>many</u> firms in the industry. Monopolistically competitive industries will not reach <u>productive</u> efficiency since in long run equilibrium firms in the industry do not produce at the <u>lowest</u> per unit cost.

In monopolistic competition, firms operate where price is <u>greater</u> than marginal cost which means that consumers are willing to pay <u>more</u> for the product than it costs society to produce it. In this case, the firm fails to reach <u>allocative</u> efficiency.

Although average costs and prices are higher under monopolistic competition than they are under perfect competition society gets a benefit from monopolistic competition in the form of <u>differentiated</u> products.

II   TRUE/FALSE

1. False. A monopolistic competitor's demand curve is relatively more *elastic* than a monopolist's due to the existence of a greater number of substitute products.

2. True. Monopolistic competitors stop producing before they fully realize economies of scale—before they reach the low points on their long-run average total cost curves.

3. True. In monopolistic competition, firms fail to achieve productive and allocative efficiency but, in return, we get a *variety* of restaurants, clothing, hair salons, etc.

ANSWER KEY

1. The answer is C. Productive efficiency is reached when a firm produces at the lowest cost possible—the low point on its long-run average total cost curve. Because they have downward-sloping demand curves, firms in monopolistic competition produce at a point to the left of that lowest point.

2. The answer is B. In monopolistic competition firms produce where price is *greater* than marginal cost. Firms achieve allocative efficiency only when price *equals* marginal cost.

3. The answer is B. Under monopolistic competition, firms stop producing before costs are at their lowest, and charge prices that are higher than marginal costs. In perfect competition, firms produce where their costs are lowest and charge prices that are equal to marginal cost.

IV   Application and Discussion

Perfect Competition	Monopolistic Competition
Standardized Product	Differentiated Product
Allocative Efficiency	Downward-Sloping Demand Curve
Productive Efficiency	Excess Capacity
Horizontal Demand Curve	
No Control Over Price	

Section 13.4 Advertising

I   Review

Advertising is an important type of <u>non-price</u> competition that firms use to <u>increase</u> the demand for their products.

Advertising may not only increase the demand facing a firm, it may also make the demand facing the firm more <u>inelastic</u> if it convinces buyers the product is truly different. A more inelastic demand curve means price changes will have relatively <u>smaller</u> effects on the quantity demanded of the product.

Critics of advertising assert that it <u>raises</u> average total costs while manipulating consumer's tastes. However, if people are <u>rational</u>, this argument loses some of its force.

When advertising is used in industries with significant economies of <u>scale,</u> per-unit costs may decline by more than per-unit advertising costs.

An important function of advertising is to lower the cost of acquiring <u>information</u> about the availability of substitutes and the <u>prices</u> of products.

By making information about substitutes and prices less costly to acquire, advertising will increase the <u>competition</u> in industries, which is good for consumers.

II   True/False

1. True. If advertising increases the demand for a firm's product and the number of units sold, the existence of economies of scale will reduce the per unit production costs. This production cost reduction may be large enough to compensate for the extra cost of advertising. Advertising cost may also be subject to economies of scale and decline with an increase in output.

2. False. If we assume that people are rational, consumers will make sure the benefits of a purchase will be greater than the costs. They are unlikely to be influenced by such claims.

ANSWER KEY

1. The answer is C. Rolf produces a service that many others produce. The only way he can reduce the elasticity of demand facing his firm is to convince some consumers that other chiropractors do not produce services that are perfect substitutes for his services. By using advertising to reduce the number of good substitutes for his product, he will reduce the elasticity of demand for his product.

2. The answer is A. The cost of acquiring information about prices may keep some consumers from switching to other firms when a producer raises its price. Advertising lowers the cost of acquiring information about prices. When prices are well known, buyers will always buy similar products from the lowest priced seller. It is the willingness and ability of consumers to abandon high priced producers that make suppliers in a competitive industry price-takers.

IV   Application and Discussion

Producers use advertising to increase the demand for their products and reduce the elasticity of the demand facing their firm. They do this to increase their profits. If all firms advertise, the results are often not those anticipated by the firm. Advertising by firms will make consumers more aware of the prices charged by other firms and the availability of substitutes for the goods and services they buy. This type of information will increase the elasticity of demand facing firms as well as making the industry more competitive. Advertising may result in lower prices and more output and lower profits.

Section 13.5 Oligopoly

I   Review

Oligopolies exist when only a <u>few</u> firms control all or most of the production and sale of a product.

In oligopoly, products may be either homogeneous or <u>differentiated</u>.

In oligopoly, <u>barriers</u> to entry are often very high, preventing competing firms from entering the market.

In oligopoly, firms can earn long-run <u>economic</u> profits.

Oligopoly is characterized by mutual <u>interdependence</u> among firms. Oligopolists must <u>strategize</u> because the number of firms in the industry is so small that changes in one firm's price of output will affect the sales of competing firms.

In oligopoly, barriers to entry in the form of large start-up costs, economies of scale, or <u>patents</u> are usually present.

The economy of large-scale production <u>discourages</u> new firms from entering a market because high initial average total costs impose heavy losses on new entrants.

Mutual interdependence means that no firm knows with <u>certainty</u> what its demand curve looks like. The demand curve and the profit maximizing price and output will depend on how others <u>react</u> to the firm's policies.

II   True/False

1. False. Under oligopoly, relatively few firms produce most of the output. Each individual firm produces a substantial share of total output.

2. True. In the auto industry a few large firms—GM, Ford, Chrysler, Toyota, and Honda—produce most of the output. Each firm shapes its policies with an eye on what the others do, and there are high start-up costs and significant economies of scale in production.

3. False. Under both perfect competition and monopolistic competition firms cannot earn economic profits in the long run. Under oligopoly, however, they can. The reason is that high barriers to entry keep competitors out.

ANSWER KEY

III   Multiple Choice

1. The answer is C. Oligopoly is characterized by high barriers to entry. It is difficult for new competitors to enter.

2. The answer is A. Oligopoly is the result of the existence of barriers to entry—primarily economies of scale that make it hard for small firms to compete.

3. The answer is A. In oligopolies, firms are mutually interdependent. That is, they constantly observe and anticipate the moves of their rivals.

IV   Application and Discussion

Perfect Competition	Oligopoly
many small firms	mutual interdependence
allocative efficiency	downward-sloping demand curve
productive efficiency	high barriers to entry
horizontal demand curve	few large firms
no control over price	large economies of scale

Section 13.6 Collusion and Cartels

I   Review

Because they are mutually interdependent, oligopolists are tempted to get together and agree to act jointly or to <u>collude</u> in order to reduce uncertainty and raise profits.

Collusion has the same effects that monopoly does; goods that are priced too <u>high</u> and outputs that are too <u>low</u>.

International agreements between firms regarding sales, pricing, and other decisions are called <u>cartels</u> agreements.

Although collusive oligopolies may be profitable for participants they are often short-lived because firms have a great temptation to <u>cheat</u> on their fellow colluders.

II   True/False

1. True. In each case goods are both overpriced and underproduced and firms earn economic profits.

2. False. Collusion makes firms' demand curves more inelastic. By colluding, each firm can reduce the number of customers it loses when it raises prices.

3. False. Most collusive monopolies are short-lived. Not only are they illegal and thus subject to prosecution, but they often break down because one or more participating firms cheats on the others.

III   Multiple Choice

1. The answer is D. Collusive oligopolies often fall apart because someone thinks that they can do better by cheating—by undercutting other firms prices, for example.

2. The answer is B. Joint profit maximization requires the determination of price on the basis of the market demand for the product and the summation of marginal costs of the various firms.

IV   Application and Discussion

1.   If the Canadian and Russian mines provide a significant share of the world's supply, increasing the supply will result in the price of diamonds falling. This will be the result of the breakdown of the cartel.

ANSWER KEY

2.   CSO will no longer be willing to advertise to increase the demand for diamonds in general. This type of advertising might only sell more Canadian or Russian diamonds and generate no profit for CSO. If CSO continues to advertise diamonds they will try to distinguish the diamonds they are selling. They might try to establish a brand to differentiate their product from the others.

Section 13.7 Other Oligopoly Models

I   Review

Prices in some oligopolistic industries tend to be stable or <u>rigid</u>. One explanation of this is the <u>kinked</u> demand model.

This model recognizes a firm's demand curve is <u>dependent</u> on the actions and reactions of competing firms. The kinked demand curve is a result of the greater tendency of competitors to follow a firm's price <u>reductions</u> than price increases. Demand is very <u>elastic</u> above an established price but relatively <u>inelastic</u> below this price. One consequence of this is that firms are <u>slow</u> to adjust price in response to cost changes.

In oligopoly, an understanding may develop under which one large firm will play the role of price <u>leader</u>, sending signals to competitors that they have changed their prices.

Competitors that go along with the pricing decisions of a price leader are called price <u>followers</u>.

Collusive behavior is no guarantee of economic profits in the <u>long</u> run.

Without <u>barriers</u> to entry, new firms will be attracted by the economic profits earned when firms act to maximize joint profits.

New firms will lower <u>prices</u> and break down existing pricing agreements. Price competition will result in prices approaching the level of average total <u>costs</u>.

Oligopolists may charge a price lower than the profit maximizing price to <u>discourage</u> new firms from entering the market. This strategy will be effective when new firms face <u>higher</u> costs than firms in the industry do.

II   True/False

1.   False. A successful cartel restricts supply so that member firms earn monopoly profits. At the cartel price, consumers only want to buy the amount the cartel is selling. New firms will need to lower prices to break into the market. Firms in the cartel will experience a loss of sales unless they lower their prices. The price war that results may eliminate the economic profits earned by diamond firms if prices fall to average total costs.

2.   False. Unless there are significant barriers to entry, the economic profits will attract competitors to the industry. Competitors will bid down the price of moon travel to sell their products. The new competition may result in prices falling and economic profits being eliminated.

III   Multiple Choice

1.   The answer is C. Firms in an oligopoly may collude and earn economic profits in the short run, but they need a barrier to entry to maintain these profits in the long run. Setting a price below the profit maximizing price makes entry by new firms less attractive; it also reduces the profits earned by the existing firms. Lowering prices works as a barrier only if existing firms have lower costs than potential entrants.

2.   The answer is C. If competitors fail to follow a firm's price increase they will take away business and the firm that raised its price will experience dramatic loss of sales. Since other firms provide lower cost substitutes small price increases will result in a relatively large declines in quantity demanded from the firm making demand very elastic. When the firm tries to capture market share by lowering prices, competitors are more likely to respond by lowering their own prices. In this case no customers switch and the only gain in sales is from the increase in quantity demanded for the industry. Since the quantity demanded from the firm will not change much, demand will be relatively inelastic.

3. The answer is A. Oligopolies earn excess profits by following a joint profit maximization strategy like price leadership. If these US industries were successful at earning excess profits, they would have to maintain a barrier to entry to maintain them. Domestic competition might have been limited because of significant economies of scale, but foreign firms were already producing for large markets. Import restrictions were needed to prevent newcomers in the market that would breakdown price agreements and cause profits to fall through price competition.

4. The answer is C. Dominator, Inc. is a price leader, because it initiated price changes that are followed by other firms in the industry.

IV   Application and Discussion

Information	Anti-Competitive Strategy	Competitive Response
1. Large unrecoverable start up costs for new airlines.	X	
2. Many airlines serve the airport.		X
3. Dominant airline drops price below average variable cost.	X	
4. There is excess capacity on the dominant airline flights before the new airline enters the market.		X

When there are significant start-up costs for a new airline, predatory pricing will let new airlines know they will lose this money when they leave the market. This will limit the number of competitors willing to enter. When there are many airlines serving a market, this is most likely a competitive strategy since lowering the price will not gain one airline significant monopoly power. If the dominant airline loses more than its fixed costs, it is probably an anti-competitive move because they believe they can recover these costs by charging monopoly prices in the future. Finally, when an airline has excess capacity, they can offer these seats for very low fares since the cost is close to zero.

Section 13.8 Game Theory and Strategic Behavior

I   Review

An approach to oligopoly that focuses on the tendency of firms to act in ways that minimize damage from opponents is called game theory.

Games can either be cooperative or noncooperative and the primary difference between them is the existence of contracts.

In game theory, a strategy that will be optimal no matter what your opponent does is called a dominant strategy.

The Prisoners' Dilemma is a famous game that has a dominant strategy and demonstrates the basic problem confronting noncolluding monopolists.

Firms in oligopoly often behave like the prisoners in the Prisoners' Dilemma because they carefully anticipate the moves of their rivals in a(n) uncertain environment.

At a(n) Nash equilibrium, each player in a game is said to be doing as well as he can given the actions of his competitor.

II   True/False

1. False. A dominant strategy is one that is optimal regardless of the opponent's actions. This will not always be the case.

2. False. In the Prisoners' Dilemma, the two prisoners cannot make contracts or otherwise communicate with each other. Hence it is a noncooperative game.

ANSWER KEY

III   Multiple Choice

1. The answer is C. The main difference is that in cooperative games players can talk and set binding contracts. Because antitrust laws forbid firms to collude most strategic behavior by firms is noncooperative.

2. The answer is D. Economists believe that oligopolists are extremely sensitive to the moves that their competitors are likely to make.

3. The answer is C. They act like players in a poker game who make decisions on the basis of what other players have done or might do.

IV   Application and Discussion

A)   Yes. Carmella's dominant strategy is to implement a frequent flyer program. If Duke implements one too, Carmella is better off ($20,000 profit compared to $10,000). If Duke doesn't implement one, Carmella is still better off if she does ($30,000 profit compared to $15,000). No matter what Duke does Carmella is better off with a frequent flyer program.

B)   No. Duke has no dominant strategy. If Carmella initiates a frequent flyer program, Duke is better off having one also ($50,000 profit compared to $40,000). But, if Carmella doesn't initiate a program, Duke is better off *not* having one as well ($45,000 profit compared to $25,000).

C)   Since she has a domiant strategy, you should advise her to go ahead and add the program.

D)   Since Duke has no dominant strategy, it would be best for him to wait and see what Carmella does. If Carmella initiates a program, Duke should have one too, but if she doesn't, Duke is better off not having a program.

ANSWER KEY

Chapter 14 Supply and Demand in Input Markets

Section 14.1 Input Markets

I   Review

The three major categories of productive resources are land, labor, and <u>capital</u>. <u>Entrepreneurs</u> employ these resources for production.

The prices and quantities of productive resources are determined by the forces of supply and <u>demand</u>.

In the market for productive resources, the buyer's cost is the seller's <u>income</u>.

An important thing to remember is that the demand for productive resources is <u>derived</u> from the demand for the goods and services that those resources produce.

II   True/False

1. True. The salaries of college professors, like the wages of factory workers or the pay of professional athletes, are determined by the interaction of supply and demand. That's why some professors, in fields like engineering and finance, make more than professors of English or physical education. The demand for professors in some fields is greater, relative to the supply, than others.

2. False. The demand for auto workers, like the demand for other productive resources, is derived from the demand for the output they produce. Higher demand for autos means higher demand for auto workers.

III   Multiple Choice

1. The answer is D. The terms "productive resource" and "factor of production" are used interchangeably. "Input" is also used to describe "productive resources."

2. The answer is C. The demand for natural gas is a derived demand. People don't want natural gas to consume but to use as an input in the production of some important good. In this case the good is electricity, which Californians need to run their air conditioners. As the demand for electricity increases, producers will demand more natural gas to produce the electricity.

IV   Application and Discussion

Business supported liberal immigration because it meant more labor supply, lower labor prices, and higher profits. Unions wanted to restrict immigration in order to reduce labor supply and raise wages.

Section 14.2 Supply and Demand in the Labor Market

I   Review

In making hiring decisions, firms are guided by their desire to maximize <u>profits.</u>

The additional revenue a firm obtains from hiring one more unit of input is called the <u>marginal</u> revenue product.

The marginal <u>resource</u> cost is the amount the extra unit of an input increases the firm's total costs.

A firm will hire one more unit of labor as long as that labor's marginal revenue product <u>exceeds</u> the marginal resource cost. If the marginal resource cost of the labor is <u>greater</u> than the marginal revenue product, hiring the labor will be unprofitable.

The <u>demand</u> curve for labor is the same as the marginal revenue product.

ANSWER KEY

The marginal revenue product for a firm in a competitive industry is equal to the <u>marginal</u> product multiplied by the price of the output.

Thre is a <u>negative</u> relation between the wage and the quantity of labor demanded.

The demand curve for labor is downward sloping because of the law of <u>diminishing</u> marginal product. This law states that as more labor is added to some fixed amount of another input, output <u>increases</u> but by diminishing amounts.

The marginal revenue product declines as more labor is added to a fixed input because the marginal <u>product</u> of labor declines.

Profits are maximized if the firm hires only to the point where the marginal <u>resource</u> cost equals the marginal <u>revenue</u> product.

The intersection of market demand and market supply determines the <u>market</u> wage rate.

The <u>market</u> supply of labor shows how much work effort people collectively are willing and able to supply to the market. There is a <u>positive</u> relationship between wage level and the quantity of labor supplied.

For an individual, wage increases have two conflicting effects. The <u>substitution</u> effect of a wage increase increases the cost of leisure, so people consume <u>less</u> leisure and work more. The <u>income</u> effect of a wage increase increases a person's income, so people buy more leisure and work <u>less</u>.

II   True/False

1. False. Marginal resource cost is the amount an extra unit of labor adds to the firm's total costs. When Al hires a day of labor his costs increase by the wages plus his contribution to the worker compensation fund or by $27.75.

2. True. Margie wants to maximize profits. Gail's marginal revenue product, which is the amount revenue increases, is $700. Gail's marginal resource cost, which is the amount cost increase, is $500. Hiring Gail will increase profits by the difference between marginal revenue product and marginal resource cost or $200.

3. False. The demand curve for labor is downward sloping because of the law of diminishing marginal product. Even if all workers were of the same quality, their additional contribution to revenue would decline as more workers were hired because each worker would have smaller amounts of fixed input to use. The marginal revenue product of workers is the firm's labor demand curve.

4. False. The slope of the individual's supply curve will depend on the relative size of the income and substitution effects. If the income effect of a wage increase is greater than the substitution effect, individuals will consume more leisure as the wage rate increases and reduce the amount of labor they supply.

III   Multiple Choice

1. The answer is B. As a competitor in the labor market, Ernie is a price or wage taker. He employs such a small share of the total labor in the market that his actions will not affect the price. He can hire all the labor he wants at the market wage. However, no one will work for Ernie if he pays less than the market wage since there are other firms hiring at the market wage.

2. The answer is C. The marginal revenue product curve is the demand curve for labor. When the wage is the marginal resource cost, firms will hire labor up to the point where the marginal revenue product equals the wage rate. When the wage rate changes, the profit maximizing quantity of labor will also change. The marginal revenue product curve tells us how much labor a firm would hire at each wage rate.

3. The answer is D. The marginal revenue product is equal to the product price multiplied by the marginal product of labor. As more labor is hired, the marginal product of labor declines resulting in the decline in marginal revenue product. The demand curve for labor is the marginal revenue product curve, so the declining marginal product also explains the negative slope of the labor demand curve.

ANSWER KEY

IV   Application and Discussion

1. Relative earnings in the various occupations are determined by the supply and demand in each. Earnings reflect the marginal revenue product of the last person hired. The salaries of athletes could be higher because people are willing to pay more for to watch sports than to enjoy the services of engineers, nurses, and construction workers. They could also be higher because the supply of labor to sports teams is relatively less than the supply to the other careers. This may be because it is less expensive to train engineers, nurses, and construction workers than to produce athletes of professional caliber or because of the importance of natural abilities in professional sports.

2.

Event	Change in Marginal Revenue Product	Change in Marginal Factor Cost	Change in Earnings
A. Baseball Players: Television networks begin to broadcast major league baseball games.	+	0	+
B. Football Players: New technology allows new football stadiums to be built twice as big as they currently are.	+	0	+
C. Hockey Players: Teams begin to recruit European hockey stars to play in the NHL.	0	–	–
D. Nurses: The time to earn a standard degree in Nursing is increased by one and one-half years	0	+	+

Section 14.3 Labor Market Equilibrium

I   Review

The wage in the labor market is established where the quantity of labor demanded is equal to the quantity of labor <u>supplied</u>.

If, at the prevailing wage, the quantity of labor supplied exceeds the quantity of labor demanded, wages will tend to <u>fall</u>.

If the quantity of labor supplied is less than the quantity of labor demanded, wages will tend to <u>rise</u>.

An increase in labor productivity will <u>increase</u> the marginal product of labor and shift the demand curve for labor to the <u>right</u>. If labor productivity falls, the demand curve for labor will shift to the <u>left</u>.

The greater the demand for a firm's product, the <u>greater</u> the firms demand for labor will be.

An increase in labor demand will shift the demand curve for labor to the <u>right</u>, while a decrease in labor demand will shift the demand curve for labor to the <u>left</u>.

If new workers enter the labor force, the labor supply curve will shift to the <u>right</u>.

If people become willing to work fewer hours at a given wage, the labor supply curve will shift <u>left</u>.

Increases in income from sources other than employment can cause the labor supply curve to move <u>left</u>.

If the amenities associated with work improve, the supply of labor is likely to <u>increase</u>.

An increase in labor supply shifts the supply curve to the <u>right</u>, while a decrease in labor supply shifts the curve to the <u>left</u>.

ANSWER KEY

1. True. Wages are determined by the forces of supply and demand, just like the prices of oranges and haircuts.

2. False. A shortage, where the quantity demanded exceeds the quantity supplied, will put upward pressure on wages.

3. False. Mindy's inheritance if invested well will increase the yearly income she receives without working. Nonwage income is one of the factors that cause an individual labor supply curve to shift. Increases in nonwage income will decrease individual labor supply.

III   Multiple Choice

1. The answer is B. Since the demand for labor is derived from the demand for the output produced by that labor, increased demand for housing would cause the demand for carpenters to increase.

2. The answer is A. At W_e the market is in equilibrium, with the quantity supplied being equal to the quantity demanded.

3. The answer is C. At W_0 or any other wage rate below W_e, the quantity of labor demanded will exceed the quantity supplied and there will be a shortage of labor.

4. The answer is B. At W_1, or any other wage above W_e, there will be a surplus of labor, since the quantity supplied will be greater than the quantity demanded.

IV   Application and Discussion

1. Immigration increases dramatically.

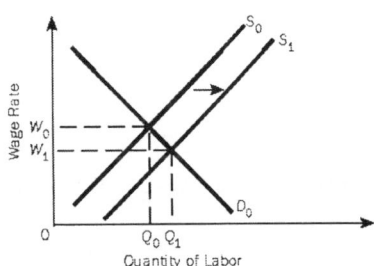

2. Demand for U.S. manufactured goods declines.

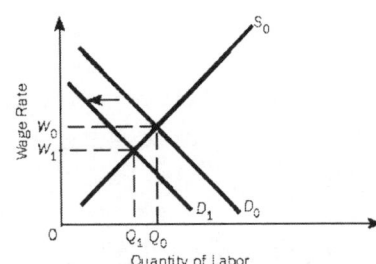

3. New computerized technology increases productivity of U.S. factory workers.

328

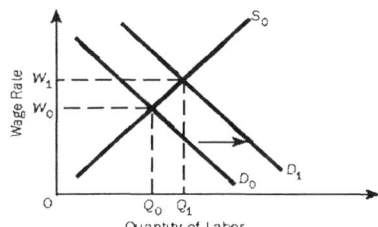

4. U.S. factory owners increase job amenities for workers.

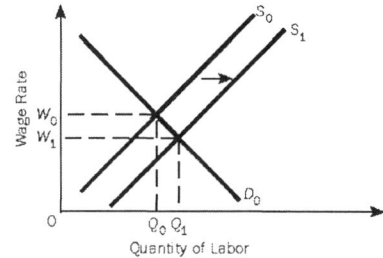

5. U.S. workers want more time off work to spend with their families.

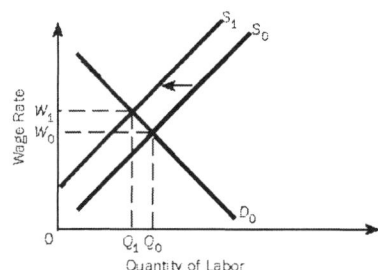

Section 14.4 Labor Productivity and Standard of Living

I. REVIEW

From the 1940s to the mid-1970s real wages in the United States <u>rose</u> an average of about three percent per year.

Since 1950, the supply of most forms of labor in the United States has <u>increased</u>, causing the supply curve for labor to shift to the <u>right</u>.

During the same time, the demand for most forms of labor has <u>increased</u> even more than supply, causing real wage to <u>rise</u>.

Compared to the 1950–1970 period, the growth of labor productivity from 1970 to present has been <u>slower</u>.

Reasons for the reduction in the rate of worker productivity since the 1970s include a <u>slowdown</u> in capital formation, an <u>increase</u> in labor supply, and an <u>increase</u> in the proportion of workers in the service sector.

ANSWER KEY

II   True/False

1. True. When the demand for anything, including teachers, increases faster than supply, its price will rise.

2. False. A decrease in the supply of programmers shifts the supply curve for programmers to the left and results in higher wages.

3. False. An economy's real wage will be determined by the supply and demand for labor. An increase in the supply of labor without a change in demand will result in a decline in the real wage. However the demand for labor may also increases, because of increased capital formation, technology progress, or improved worker skills. If demand increases relatively more than supply real wages will increase.

III   Multiple Choice

1. The answer is B. The demand for labor increased faster than the supply, reflecting a rising marginal productivity of labor.

2. The answer is D. Increased labor supply does not increase worker productivity.

IV   Application and Discussion

Change in the Economic Environment	Change in the Demand for Labor	Change in the Supply of Labor	Change in the Real Wage
1. Increased corporate invest ment in efficiency enhancing equipment and computer software	+	0	+
2. Increased immigration of working-age population	0	+	–
3. Introduction of biotechnology innovations to agriculture	+	0	+
4. Increases in the rate of college graduate in the workforce	+	0	+
5. Laws that require companies to limit overtime work	0	–	+

Three changes affect the demand side of the labor market. Increase investment (1), improved technology (3), and smarter workers (4) all increase the marginal revenue product of workers. Two of these changes affect the supply side of the labor market. Increased immigration (2) will increase supply while adopting laws on overtime work (5) will restrict the potential labor supplied by the US population.

Section 14.5 Labor Unions

I   Review

When workers act collectively as a <u>union</u>, they have more <u>bargaining</u> power with the employer than they would individually.

The two primary objectives of labor unions are to increase members' <u>wages</u> and <u>improve</u> working conditions.

ANSWER KEY

As a proportion of the workforce, union membership has <u>declined</u> since 1947. However, union efforts have been successful in the <u>public</u> sector.

When unions successfully raise wage rates in the unionized sector, the downward sloping demand curve for labor means that <u>less</u> labor will be hired in this sector. Workers released from the unionized firms will <u>increase</u> the supply of labor to the non-unionized sector causing wages to <u>fall</u>.

Freeman and Medoff argue that unions increase worker productivity by reducing the number of <u>resignations</u> and <u>improving</u> worker morale. However, the evidence, which suggests that unions tend to <u>lower</u> the profitability of firms, weakens this argument.

II   True/False

1. True. Freeman and Medoff argue that unions increase productivity by reducing the number of quits a firm experiences and improving morale. The main way unions do this is by providing workers with an effective way to communicate their grievances.

2. False. The primary objectives of a union are to increase the wages and improve the working conditions of union members. If these objectives are achieved, the number of jobs will be reduced unless other conditions change in the industry.

3. False. A wage increase in the unionized sector of the unskilled labor market will result in a decrease in the number of workers employed in this sector since firms have negatively sloped demand curves for labor. These workers will seek employment in the non-unionized part of this market, which will increase supply and lower wages for non-unionized workers.

4. True. One reason for unions is to strengthen the bargaining position of workers. Without a union, employers can simply replace a worker with a grievance or a worker who demands more pay with another worker. Unions limit competition between workers.

III   Multiple Choice

1. The answer is D. Unions give workers greater collective bargaining power. This is more important in large firms where workers are distant from managers, which is not the case in many service industries. Collective bargaining is also more useful for grievances and objectives that workers hold in common. When jobs and tasks are varied there will be less use for collective bargaining.

2. The answer is C. By contract the union is able to set the wage above the market clearing wage in the union sector. Because firms in this sector face a negatively sloped demand curve, they will reduce the number of workers they hire. These workers will try to find work in the non-union sector, which will increase supply and lower the wage rate in this part of the industry.

3. The answer is A. If unions had no effect on productivity, we would expect that wage and work condition concessions won by unions would lower a firm's profits. Productivity increases would reduce a firm's costs and compensate for the higher wages in unionized firms. Profits should be higher if unions improved productivity. Preliminary evidence suggests that unions lower firms' profits, which provides little support for the argument that unions raise productivity.

IV   Application and Discussion

1. Wages will rise above the minimum in the unionized part of the low wage sector resulting in jobs being reduced. The workers who lose their jobs in the union sector will increase the supply of workers in the non-union part of the low pay labor market. The increased supply will not force wages lower in the sector because wages are set by law. The effect of the unionization will be increased unemployment among the low wage workers.

Section 14.6 The Markets for Land and Capital

I   Review

The three productive <u>factors</u> are labor, land, and capital.

The price of using land is determined by the <u>supply</u> and demand for land.

The <u>demand</u> for land is the marginal revenue product of land.

The supply of land can be thought of as fixed or perfectly <u>inelastic</u>. In this case, the price of land will be determined by changes in the <u>demand</u> for land. Economic <u>rent</u> is the price paid to any factor that has a fixed supply.

In the market for land, an increase in the prices of the commodities that are produced with land will <u>increase</u> the demand for land and the <u>rental</u> price of land.

Differences between the types of land and other resources result in variations in resource productivity. This results in variations in <u>compensation</u>.

People who receive their income because of a distinct, unique skill, or talent are collecting economic <u>rent</u> since their labor represents a resource whose supply is perfectly inelastic. <u>Stars</u> in various fields earn high salaries because there is a great demand for their services and their unique talents are in limited supply.

Economic rent represents a payment that the resource owner receives above its <u>opportunity</u> cost.

Capital can be <u>leased</u> or borrowed for a stipulated period of time. The cost of borrowing these factors is the <u>rental</u> price.

When entrepreneurs buy capital, they often borrow funds. The price of these borrowed funds is the <u>interest</u> rate. The yearly interest cost of borrowing an amount of money equals the interest rate <u>times</u> the loan amount. The cost of buying capital will <u>increase</u> when the interest rate rises and decline when the interest rate <u>falls</u>.

The interest rate is determined by the <u>intersection</u> of the supply and demand for capital. The demand curve for capital is downward sloping reflecting the decline in the marginal revenue <u>product</u> of capital as more is used.

Resource markets are <u>interconnected</u>. Changes in the price of one resource may result in the increased demand for other if they are <u>substitutes</u>.

II   True/False

1. False. The amount of land available may not be affected by price but the interaction of supply and demands determine the rental price of land. Changes in the demand for land will result in changes in its price.

2. True. The change in Asian demand for oranges will cause orange prices to fall. The demand for farmland reflects land's marginal revenue product. The demand for orange land will decline because the output of each acre of land will produce less revenue because of the lower price of oranges.

3. False. The markets for land, labor, and capital are interconnected. Producers might substitute capital for the more expensive labor, and increase the demand for capital.

ANSWER KEY

III   Multiple Choice

1. The answer is A. Economic rent is the payment of any resource above its opportunity costs, which is the minimum amount necessary to supply the resource. Smith would work for a minimum of $300,000 a year anything above this is economic rent.

2. The answer is B. When a resource is available in inelastic supply the price it receives is determined by the demand for the resource. Harrison Ford's marginal revenue product determines the demand for his services. Harrison Ford and stars in other areas are paid their marginal revenue products.

3. The answer is B. Entrepreneurs buy additional capital as long as its marginal revenue product exceeds its marginal resource cost. In this case the yearly rental price of capital is $5,000 (50% * $10,000). Because they don't borrow the money to buy the machine, we know they don't expect the machines marginal revenue product to cover this cost.

4. The answer is C. The demand for capital reflects its marginal revenue product. As an entrepreneur increases the amount of capital she uses with all other factors fixed, the law of diminishing marginal product predicts that output will increase at a declining rate or that the marginal product of capital will decline. As the marginal product declines, the marginal revenue product will also decline.

IV   Application and Discussion

Given the growth of government in the twentieth century a single tax on land would probably not supply all of the needed revenue for government. However an additional benefit of George's plan remains; a tax on economic rent would result in little change in resource use or little distortion to the economy. Economic rent is a payment to a resource above the minimum you would have to pay to have the resource supplied. If you taxed away the entire rent, the owners of resources in fixed supply would still put them to use. We would expect no change in the supply of land or movie actors or athletes, since they would still earn their opportunity costs.

CHAPTER 15 INCOME DISTRIBUTION, POVERTY, AND HEALTHCARE

Section 15.1 Income Distribution

I   Review

The proportion of income received by the top 5 percent of Americans <u>declined</u> after 1935, but has gone <u>up</u> since the 1980s.

Since the 1980s, the share of measured income received by the lowest fifth of families has <u>fallen</u>.

At any moment in time, middle-aged persons tend to have <u>higher</u> incomes than younger or older persons.

Demographic trends like an <u>increase</u> in the number of divorced couples and an <u>increase</u> in the number of two-income families have caused the measured distribution of income to appear more unequal.

It has been argued that state-subsidized higher education has benefited the <u>rich</u> and middle-income groups more than the <u>poor</u>.

On the other hand, government programs like food stamps and school lunch programs benefit the <u>poor</u> rather than the <u>rich</u>.

If we consider age distribution, institutional factors, and in-kind transfers, the actual distribution of income in America is more <u>equal</u> than it appears.

Generational studies suggest there is considerable income <u>mobility</u> between generations. In addition, most Americans experience significant year to year <u>fluctuations</u> in their economic well being.

Productivity and income are <u>positively</u> related.

Income inequality is <u>greater</u> in the United States and Great Britain than in Sweden and Japan.

The greatest disparities in income are found in <u>low</u>-income countries like Mexico and India.

Income inequality within nations is far <u>less</u> than income inequality among nations.

II   True/False

1. True. Attitudes toward work affect peoples' incomes. People who work intensely for long hours tend to earn more than people who choose to work less and spend more time pursuing leisure activities.

2. False. Tanya is likely to earn more since her job is more dangerous. Differences in the danger or unpleasantness of jobs contributes to differences in pay.

3. False. According to research cited in the text, the majority of people in the bottom quintile move up to another quintile within a decade or less.

III   Multiple Choice

1. The answer is B. Middle-aged people earn higher incomes because they are at their peak level of productivity. They have had time to get both skills and experience and are still physically able. Middle-aged people also participate in the labor force to a greater extent than either the very young or the very old.

2. The answer is D. Actually, the proportion of women in the labor force has risen over the past 40 years. All of the other three phenomena have contributed to greater measured income inequality.

ANSWER KEY

3. The answer is C. Subsidies to airports are likely to help the rich by making air travel easier and cheaper since the rich fly more often than the poor.

IV   Application and Discussion

See Exhibit 15.1.

EXHIBIT 15.1

	2001 Median Hourly Earnings	Explanation
Engineers	$29.33	The most likely factor is differences in education and training. Engineers generally need college while farm workers don't need much education.
Farm Workers	$8.56	
Police Officers and Detectives	$20.17	Job preferences are important here. Police work is more dangerous than cooking. Police probably have more education and training too, although some cooks are highly trained.
Cooks	$9.24	
Engineers	$29.33	Difference can probably be attributed to differences in skills and human capital. Engineers have more specialized training.
Police Offices	$20.17	
Surgeons	$65.89	Skills and human capital. Surgeons have considerably more training and education.
Medical and Clinical Lab Technicians	$14.52	
Computer Programmers	$30.23	Skills and human capital. Programmers need more training than sales workers.
Sales Workers, Retail	$10.06	
Bus drivers	$14.15	Bus drivers may make more because the work is more dangerous. However, the pay of waiters and waitresses may be higher than reported if they don't tell the IRS about all of their tips!
Waiters and Waitresses	$7.36	

Section 15.2 The Pros and Cons of Income Equality

I   Review

Political and social changes in the last century have worked to <u>reduce</u> income inequality.

However, it is impossible to prove that one income distribution is <u>better</u> than another, because it is impossible to <u>compare</u> the welfare of one person with another.

The principle of <u>diminishing</u> marginal utility can be used to support policies that redistribute income. This principle suggests that increases in income will generate <u>less</u> additional happiness the higher the level of income.

If people have similar <u>preferences</u> for income, the <u>decrease</u> in utility that results from taking a given amount of income from high-income groups will be less than the <u>increased</u> utility which results from giving this income to low-income groups.

The <u>assumption</u> that individuals have similar preferences is critical for this argument, since we cannot make utility <u>comparisons</u> among individuals.

One argument against policies to redistribute income is that it is not <u>fair</u> to take income from one group and give it to another.

ANSWER KEY

II   True/False

1. True. The principle of diminishing marginal utility states that an equal increase in income will increase total utility by smaller amounts the greater a person's income. If tastes are the same for everyone in Stepford, an equal change of income will have a greater effect on the happiness of poorer citizens. The transfer described above will increase total utility. Of course, this depends on the critical assumption that tastes are the same.

2. False. A nation's welfare might be thought of as the sum of the citizens' happiness. Since we can't compare the welfare of individuals we can't say for certain whether such moves will make the nation better off.

3. False. Robin Hood's redistribution techniques might be considered fair if we view the rich in medieval England as crooks. In this case, Robin was robbing from the robbers. Independent of equity, his efforts might not have been good for the poor in the long run if the rich were investors. The rich by investing would have increased England's output resulting in more income to share. The poor might have seen their incomes grow even if their share of income stayed the same. If Robin's actions discouraged investment, the poor might have been worse off in the long run.

III   Multiple Choice

1. The answer is D. It is safe to assume that diminishing marginal utility holds for everyone so that more income will result in smaller increases in happiness. If people's tastes were exactly alike, we could describe the effect on societies total utility. When tastes are not the same for everyone in a society, we have no way of knowing whether the reduced happiness the rich suffer is greater than or less than the increased happiness of the poor.

2. The answer is C. Economic growth and income redistribution are often conflicting goals. Income is transferred from the rich to the poor by taxing the rich. These taxes reduce the incentive the rich have to work, so labor is reduced. Taxes also reduce the incentive the rich have to invest in capital formation. Growth is diminished since less labor and capital is used in production.

IV   Application and Discussion

1. The mayor's plan may make the income distribution in Surf City more even, but the policy doesn't seem fair. It is not fair to take the income from hard working people like Bob and give it to people who choose not to work. The surfers may be poor because they choose to consume leisure rather than work. An even distribution of income is not necessarily fair.

Section 15.3 The Economics of Discrimination

I   Review

When someone is denied employment on the basis of some noneconomic factor like race, religion, or gender, it is called job-entry discrimination.

When some workers are paid lower wages than others because of something other than productivity differences, it is called wage discrimination.

Women earn less than men in most job categories and white men earn more than black men.

White males in general have acquired more years of schooling than black males.

Merely demonstrating that wages are lower for blacks and females does not in itself prove wage discrimination.

Several scholars have developed statistical models that argue that a great deal of the earnings differentials across the sexes and races can be explained by differences in productivity.

The primary means used to address economic discrimination in the United States is affirmative action programs, in which employers are encouraged to hire more minority group workers in occupations where those groups are under-represented.

ANSWER KEY

II   True/False

1. False. There are reasons other than discrimination that can explain the preponderance of female nurses, including the fact that nursing simply appeals more to women than to men.

2. False. Wage discrimination exists only if the differential is based on something other than productivity differences.

3. True. The more education a person has, the higher his or her income will be. College graduates, for example, earn significantly more than high school graduates.

III   Multiple Choice

1. The answer is B. When a worker is denied employment on the basis of some non-economic factor like sex, it is called job-entry discrimination.

2. The answer is D. This is the only statement that does not reflect the "environmental explanation," i.e. that past discrimination's perverse influences on the environment of women and non-whites has caused them to have an inferior endowment of human capital so that even in the absence of discrimination, their earnings are lower.

3. The answer is C. Since discrimination limits the potential job opportunities for women sailors, the market wage for these sailors is lower than it is for men sailors. The nondiscriminating firm (Captain Bob) can hire the unfavored but equally competent women sailors and have a cost advantage over those firms that discriminate (Captain Ahab). Captain Bob will be able to undercut Ahab's prices and perhaps sink his business.

IV   Application and Discussion

Explaining the Change in Women's Relative Earnings

A) Skills and Human Capital:

Women may be investing more in education and training now than they did in the past. Certainly there has been a dramatic increase, over the past 25 years, in the number of women earning college degrees in high-paying areas like accounting, medicine, law, and economics. Women may be gaining experience and there may also be more women entertainers and others who have special skills that are in demand.

B) Worker Preferences:

Women may be working more hours per year than they used to, placing more emphasis on work, and working more intensely.

C) Job Preferences:

Women may be engaging in riskier work like law enforcement, dirtier work like trash collection, or working more frequently in other types of unpleasant work. They may also be engaged more in work that requires sacrifices like working at night or being on the road for long periods of time.

Section 15.4 Poverty

I   Review

The poverty rate in the United States is defined as the proportion of the population who fail to earn a minimum absolute income standard.

The income standard varies with family size.

Poverty rates in the United States have generally fallen since the 1960s. However, during recessions as unemployment increases, the poverty rate also tends to rise.

Unless lower income groups do not share at all in the rising income, one cure for poverty as defined by the absolute income criterion is economic <u>growth</u>.

An alternative definition of poverty compares incomes between people and considers a person poor if their income is low <u>relative</u> to others is the same geographical area.

Poverty defined using relative income cannot be eliminated by economic <u>growth</u>, only by income <u>redistribution</u>.

Government uses taxes, transfer payments, and subsidies to <u>redistribute</u> income.

II   True/False

1. False. This poverty index provides an absolute measure of poverty. The income defined by this approach is that which allows a family to purchase an adequate standard of living. The minimum income varies by family size and, over time, with changes in the cost of living.

2. True. The Transferians use a relative measure of poverty. Even with significant economic growth there will be families with less than the average income. Rose's only option would be to impose a policy to completely equalize incomes.

3. False. Social Security and Medicare redistribute income from the young to the old. One does not have to be poor to receive these transfers.

III   Multiple Choice

1. The answer is B. Absolute measures of poverty reflect the income required to meet some minimum adequate standard of living. Providing the goods and service to meet this minimum standard directly to the poor should reduce the income standard required to meet this standard of living.

2. The answer is D. Relative poverty cannot be eliminated by economic growth or by policies that increase the human capital of the smartest students. Relative poverty is based on comparisons of income among groups in a country. Only redistribution of income that moves everyone closer to the country's average income will reduce relative poverty.

IV   Application and Discussion

1.

Change in Economic Environment	Change in Relative Poverty	Change in Absolute Poverty
With no changes in income, the cost of food and housing increases by 25 percent.	0	+
The stock market booms and the 45 percent of Americans who have invested in the market experience significant income gains.	+	0
Government transfer and tax programs reduce the difference between the highest and lowest incomes in the United States.	–	–
The economy grows by 6 percent during the year.	0	–

Section 15.5 Healthcare

I   Review

Healthcare involves the utilization of <u>scarce</u> resources; resources used for healthcare can't be used to produce other goods and services. Decisions about the allocation of scarce resources to healthcare uses are <u>complex</u> because of the ethical and equity considerations.

ANSWER KEY

The United States spends <u>more</u> money per capita on healthcare than other industrialized nations. The United States also spends a larger share of its <u>GDP</u> and this share has been increasing since 1960.

Healthcare can be thought of as a type of <u>human</u> capital investment increasing the quality and quantity of labor.

The demand for medical services in the United States has increased because our real income has increased and healthcare services are <u>normal</u> goods. The demand has also increased as a result of the <u>aging</u> of the United States population, since the elderly consume a <u>disproportionate</u> share of healthcare services.

Most consumers in the United States do not pay the <u>full</u> cost of healthcare because of third-party payers, such as insurance companies. <u>Employers</u> provide the majority of this insurance coverage. Insurance lowers the cost consumers pay for using healthcare services and <u>increases</u> the expenditure on healthcare services. Insurance creates a <u>moral</u> hazard by lowering the cost of risky behavior; it may increase this behavior that requires more healthcare services.

Health maintenance organizations combine the provision and the <u>financing</u> of healthcare. HMOs attempt to control the <u>cost</u> of healthcare by attempting to control a patient's choice of treatment options.

Innovations in the healthcare industry may <u>raise</u> as well as lower costs by introducing treatment options where none had been available.

Healthcare markets are <u>imperfectly</u> competitive because of the existence of barriers to entry that may be justified as ways to protect the patient from inferior quality. Economies of <u>scale</u> in healthcare provision may also create "natural monopolies" in some areas. Costs will be <u>higher</u> because of the lack of competition.

In situations where prices are controlled, such as in the Canadian healthcare sector, there will be <u>shortages</u>.

II   True/False

1. False. Insurance reduces the cost of buying a unit of healthcare. The reduction in per unit cost will result in consumers increasing the amount of healthcare they purchase. Insurance may also encourage consumers to pursue more risky behavior, because it reduces the cost of risky behavior. Both of these changes will increase the amount spent on healthcare.

2. True. 'Incentives matter' for doctors as well as everyone else. When doctors are paid on a fee for service basis their incomes increase the more services consumers purchase. They have an incentive to err on the side of recommending too many tests, procedures, and treatments. When doctors are paid a salary, like in HMO's, they have no incentive to prescribe more services.

3. False. There are two costs involved with organ transplants. One cost is the cost of the actual transplant, which includes the cost of the surgery and care. These are probably lower because patients do not have to pay for the organs. The second type of costs is the costs involved with waiting for a transplant organ that results from zero prices. These costs involve the cost of care while waiting, the lost productivity from people out of the work force, and the loss of life. While establishing a market in transplant organs may seem gruesome, increasing the price paid may encourage more people to become donors and result in a reduction of the excess demand.

III   Multiple Choice

1. The answer is D. A voluntary health insurance plan is likely to attract a relatively high proportion of the chronically ill. Since it is expensive to tell who these people are, the companies will not expect the high costs associated with having a higher than average enrollment of the chronically ill. The insurance companies will be required to raise their rates. As the rates rise the healthy population will drop out of the plan.

2. The answer is A. Certain innovations reduce the cost of good health. Cholesterol reducing drugs save on surgical and hospital costs by providing a less expensive substitute. Insurance, rising incomes, and aging population all increase the demand for healthcare services and the total amount spend on healthcare.

3. The answer is A. Occupational licensing is justified as a way of reducing the information cost patients would face to find a quality provider without it. However, these test are a type of barrier to entry that makes it harder for competitors to enter. They will decrease supply by increasing the cost of entry into the medical market. This will raise the price of medical services.

IV   Application and Discussion

A) *Employers introduce "Wellness Programs" that compensate employees for adopting healthy lifestyles.*

This would probably reduce the expenditure on healthcare by changing the incentives on healthy behavior. This increases the benefits of healthy behavior so people would be more likely to choose healthy living and possibly reduce their need for healthcare. This would counter the effect of the moral hazard of health insurance.

B) *Insurance companies change the way they reimburse dentists, paying them by the cavity filled instead of by the visit.*

By changing the incentives facing dentists, the per cavity payment would probably increase the number of cavities filled and reduce the time per office visit. While this might reduce the cost of dental services by allowing one dentist to see more customers, it might, in the long run, increase expenditures if necessary preventative measures were avoided.

C) *Instead of paying a portion of the fee for medical service, insurance companies pay a set amount for each type of illness or procedure, which is independent of the actual amount the consumer pays.*

This would be like car insurance; consumers would be able to keep the difference between the actual cost of the treatment and the insurance payment. Consumer would have an incentive to seek the lowest cost provider or the lowest cost alternative treatment. The effect would be to reduce the expenditures on healthcare.

D) *State's abandon laws that mandate the treatments that any employer's health insurance must include.*

This would lower the cost of insurance, which would increase the number of insured individuals. Once insured, the new insurees would increase their consumption of healthcare services. However, the consumption of those healthcare services that were previously mandated is likely to decrease. Therefore, the overall effect on healthcare costs is ambiguous.

E) *Congress eliminates patent protection on new medicines so that companies do not have a monopoly on the drugs they develop.*

In the short run this would reduce the price consumers would pay for particular medicines since it would allow more competition. It would change the incentives that drug companies have to invest in the development of new medicines. Since the introduction of medicines as substitute for more expensive treatments is one way of reducing healthcare expenditures, the long-run consequences would probably be to increase these expenditures.

ANSWER KEY

MODULE 16 THE ENVIRONMENT

Section 16.1 Negative Externalities and Pollution

I   Review

When people other than those making the demand and supply decisions share the benefits or costs of an activity, an <u>externality</u> occurs.

A <u>negative</u> externality occurs when a decision imposes costs on people other than those making the decisions about production or consumption.

The costs that accrue to the total population are called <u>social</u> costs. Those costs that are incurred by the producer or consumer who makes the decision are called <u>private</u> costs.

When a negative externality exists, social costs are <u>greater</u> than private costs.

The amount of a good or service producers choose to produce reflects <u>supply</u> and demand. When there are only negative externalities, the demand curve represents the marginal social <u>benefits</u> of the good while the supply curve represents the marginal <u>private</u> costs.

For society, the optimal level of output occurs where the marginal social cost <u>equals</u> the marginal social benefits for the last unit produced.

When there are negative externalities in the production of a good, output will be <u>greater</u> than and price will be <u>less</u> than the optimal level.

One reason the extent of any negative externality is difficult to measure is that certain external costs may be <u>nonpecuniary</u> and not involve money.

II   True/False

1. False. Mac is producing the profit-maximizing amount of pork on his farm. It will only be optimal from society's point of view if there are no negative externalities. If the smell from Mac's hogs imposes costs on others, Mac will be producing too much pork when he produces where price equals marginal private cost.

2. True. The airport noise is a negative externality. The noise cost was imposed on Paul, and he should be compensated for suffering it. Polly chose to move into the noisy neighborhood. Lower housing prices was probably one of the things that attracted her to the neighborhood. Housing prices are lower because the noise reduces demand for this housing. The lower housing prices compensate Polly for suffering the noise.

3. False. Che will likely ignore the external costs he imposes on the tea room. Any costs an entrepreneur can avoid will increase their profits. Che is in business to maximize his profits.

III   Multiple Choice

1. The answer is C. Once the external costs are internalized, the firm's private marginal costs will increase. The firm's decisions will reflect these higher costs. At the previous output, marginal private costs will now be greater than the price. The firm will increase profits by reducing the amount of the good it produces.

2. The answer is D. Private costs are those costs that the producer pays. In Adam's case, this is the cost of labor and utilities. The social cost includes all of the costs society pays. The social costs of a rib dinner includes Adam's private cost of $6.33 plus the external cost of $.45, which others pay. The total social cost is $6.78.

3. The answer is D. Nonpecuniary costs are costs where there is no money outlay. Not all external costs are nonpecuniary; the medical costs and repainting costs are external costs, but in each case there is a money outlay. The reduced utility that results from the smell of the steel mill and is experienced by neighbors is a nonpecuniary external cost.

IV   Application and Discussion

See Exhibit 16.1 with answers.

EXHIBIT 16.1

Action	Affected Group	External Cost
A mother reads a Dr. Seuss book to her children in a doctor's waiting room.	The other patients in the waiting room	The mother's voice and the rhymes of the book disturb or distract others doing different activities.
An entrepreneur opens a flavored popcorn stand next to an espresso cart. (Hint: The popcorn smells of the various flavors.)	Owners of the espresso cart	The popcorn smells detract from the taste of the coffee in the shop and reduce the shop's sales.
A church decides to celebrate the holiday by playing Christmas music on its external speakers twenty-four hours a day.	The neighbors of the church	Christmas music may be nice, but any music 24 hours a day will reduce the utility and maybe the sleep of the neighbors.
Your neighbor plants fifteen large deciduous trees right on the border between your house and hers. (Hint: Think of the Fall.)	You	In the Fall when these trees lose their leaves, some will blow on your lawn. You will suffer the costs of raking these leaves.

Section 16.2 Public Policy and the Environment

I   Review

To be effective, compliance standards, such as those established by the Environmental Protection Agency (EPA), must result in _less_ pollution than would exist in the absence of those standards.

Compliance standards have led to a _reduction_ in some types of pollution.

In a world of scarcity, society must incur _costs_ in order to have the benefits of a cleaner environment.

People with different preferences and situations are likely to have _different_ ideas about the costs and _benefits_ of pollution abatement.

Because of the principles of diminishing marginal utility and increasing marginal cost, the benefits of further expenditures on pollution control will, sooner or later, fall _below_ the added costs to society imposed by stricter controls.

One means of solving problems posed by the existence of negative externalities is for government to create incentives for firms to _internalize_ the costs resulting from their activities.

When pollution taxes are imposed on activities that cause pollution, the amount of pollution caused by those activities goes _down_.

Rights that allow the holder to discharge a specific amount of pollution are called transferable _pollution_ rights.

Transferable pollution rights give firms an incentive to lower their levels of pollution because they can _sell_ their permits if they don't use them. The market will allocate these rights among firms so that those firms with the _lowest_ clean up costs are doing most of the cleaning up. Placing market prices on the right to pollute also give firms an incentive to invest in new _technologies_.

ANSWER KEY

The i deal p ollution c ontrol policy would do three things: 1) achieve the <u>efficient</u> level of pollution, 2) achieve pollution reduction at the <u>least</u> cost, and 3) motivate advances in pollution clean up <u>technology</u>.

II   True/False

1. True. If compliance standards are too strict, the costs to society of attaining them may be higher than the benefits society gets from the reduced level of pollution that results.

2. False. Firms that can lower their emissions at the lowest costs will do so and trade their pollution rights to firms that have high costs of reducing pollution.

III   Multiple Choice

1. The answer is B. The EPA's job is to enforce standards for environmental pollution such as the maximum amount of hydrocarbons that autos can emit per mile.

2. The answer is C. The optimal amount of pollution control exists when the marginal costs of control equal the marginal benefits. For society as a whole, continuing pollution control when the costs to society are greater than the benefits is inefficient.

3. The answer is D. Taxes raise production costs, leading to reduced output and higher prices—just as in the example of the pollution tax on steel given in the text.

4. The answer is C. A system of transferable pollution rights does not require polluters to reduce pollution no matter what the cost. They can keep polluting if they are willing to buy pollution rights from others who in turn must reduce pollution.

IV   Application and Discussion

See Exhibit 16.2.

ANSWER KEY

EXHIBIT 16.2		
Initiative	Negative Externality Involved	Policy Type
1. Alaska levies a $1 per pack state tax on cigarettes.	Second-hand cigarette smoke. (Although the primary goal may be to discourage smokers themselves from consuming cigarettes.)	Pollution Tax
2. The Federal Government makes it illegal to smoke inside a federal building.	Second-hand cigarette smoke.	Compliance Standard
3. The 1990 Clean Air Act allocates transferable rights to emit sulphur dioxide to U.S. electrical utilities.	Air pollution. (Sulfur dioxide is a prime cause of "acid rain.")	Transferable Pollution Rights
4. Residents of Singapore face stiff fines if they spit on the sidewalk.	Saliva in a public place. Germs.	Compliance Standard
5. The Environmental Protection Agency requires new automobiles to pass tests that show that their emissions do not exceed specified limits.	Air Pollution	Compliance Standard
6. Germany taxes industrial plants according to how much air and water pollution they cause. The more pollution, the higher the tax.	Air and water pollution	Pollution Tax

Section 16.3 Property Rights

I   Review

The problem of externalities can be examined as a question of <u>property</u> rights. Solutions to externality problems involve questions of how to <u>alter</u> existing property rights.

Because solutions to externality problems involve the evaluation of the legal arrangements of property rights, this is one area where <u>law</u> and economics merge.

The <u>Coase</u> Theorem states that if the benefits of some action exceed the costs there is some potential transaction that would make someone better off and no one worse off. As long as ownership or property rights are well defined, there would be <u>no</u> externality problem.

If the polluter owns the right to pollute and the benefits of cleaning up the pollution are <u>greater</u> than the costs, those who suffer from the pollution could pay the polluter's clean-up costs and all would be better off.

If those who suffer from the pollution owned the right to pollute and the benefits from pollution exceed the costs, they could make the polluter <u>compensate</u> them for their suffering and all would be better off.

<u>Transaction</u> costs are the cost of negotiating and executing an exchange. They do not include the cost of the good or service purchased.

The ability of voluntary exchange to limit externality problems depends on the existence of <u>low</u> transaction costs. Transaction costs <u>increase</u> as the number of participants in the exchange increases.

There are three reasons voluntary exchange and private negotiations have not been used to address pollution problems. First, <u>property</u> rights in environmental resources are ambiguous. Second, transaction costs are usually <u>high</u> because of the number of people and firms involved. Finally, the market is likely to <u>fail</u>, because people cannot be excluded from enjoying the benefits of improved air and water quality.

ANSWER KEY

1. True. Zoning laws designate the types of uses for which land in specific locations can be used. These laws limit the right of landowners to use their land in any way they wish. Zoning laws have redefined property rights to limit neighborhood externalities.

2. False. Transaction costs must be low for well-defined property rights to internalize externalities.

3. True. The use of voluntary exchange and private negotiation to restrict pollution problems is limited by three factors. The difficulty of defining property rights to the air, the high transaction costs that result from the large number of people involved, and the inability to make people pay for the benefits they receive all restrict the ability of private negotiation to limit pollution problems.

III   Multiple Choice

1. The answer is C. If the ranch has the property right to its skies, the Air Force will have to compensate it for the cost imposed on the Yippy I-O for the exercises. The ranch would not have to compensate the Air Force for moving; the Air Force would move if the cost of moving were less than the cost of compensating the ranch. In answers A, B, and D the Air Force pays to either compensate for the loss or limit the loss.

2. The answer is A. For externalities to be internalized through private negotiation, transaction costs must be low. The more people affected by the actions, the greater are the transaction costs. In answers B, C, and D there are many people involved and the high transaction costs are likely to limit role of private negotiation. Transaction costs are likely to be low in A since only two people are involved.

3. The answer is C. While light bulbs are a common household product, they are not a common good. Ownership of light bulbs is well defined. Deer, air, and tuna (in the ocean, not in the can) are owned by all of us.

IV   APPLICATION AND DISCUSSION

A) If Dr. Dan owned the rights, he could charge the Rock Island for his loss of business. The Rock Island would be willing to pay up to $50/per train to use Dan's track, since that is their savings over the alternative. So they would send only three trains a week on the track and Dr. Dan would be compensated for the lost income.

B) If the Rock Island owned the rights, Dr. Dan would be willing to pay them to use the alternative track. The Rock Island would move the trains for $50; Dan would gladly pay the $50 per train to keep train trips down to three a week. His loss would be greater than $50 per train if the Rock Island used the track more than three times.

ANSWER KEY

CHAPTER 17 INTERNATIONAL TRADE

Section 17.1 The Growth in World Trade

I   Review

Although it varies from country to country, in a typical year about <u>15</u> percent of the world's output is traded in international markets. In 1998, about **12** percent of U.S. output was <u>exported</u>, and imports amounted to over <u>13</u> percent of GDP.

The United States has important trading relations with many countries, but our three most important partners are <u>Canada</u>, <u>Mexico</u>, and Japan.

II   True/False

1. True. As a percentage of our total imports, goods from Canada represented 19 percent of total goods imported. While goods from China constituted 8 percent.

2. False. Over time the importance of international trade to the U.S. has increased dramatically.

III   Multiple Choice

1. The answer is C. Canada is our most important trading partner. Closeness and similar cultures may explain the extent of our trade. Canada accounts for almost twice the value of U.S. exports in goods as our second most important trading partner, Japan. The value of our imports from Canada exceeds the value of Japanese imports by almost 36 percent. Changes to the trade environment in Canada will affect our economy.

2. The answer is A. Since 1940 international trade has become more important for the U.S. economy. Exports and imports have doubled as a percent of U.S. Gross Domestic Product. Both consumers and producers would be more aware of any reduction in their ability to trade with other countries.

IV   Application and Discussion

For the world as a whole total exports have to equal total imports, since one country's exports are another country's imports, Consequently, if total exports are $6.7 trillion, total imports must also equal $6.7 trillion.

Section 17.2 Comparative Advantage and Gains from Trade

I   Review

We know trade is economically <u>beneficial</u> because it exists. Since trade is <u>voluntary</u> and people <u>maximize</u> utility, participants must expect trade to make them better off.

David Ricardo developed the explanation of the mutual <u>benefits</u> of trade. His theory is the Principle of <u>Comparative</u> Advantage.

The Principle of Comparative Advantage states that a nation can gain from trade by <u>specializing</u> in the production of those goods it can produce at a <u>lower</u> opportunity cost than other countries. This principle also applies to regions and individuals.

A country has a(n) <u>absolute</u> advantage in producing a good when it uses fewer resources to produce a given level of output. A country may have a comparative advantage in a good without having an absolute advantage when the production of the good has <u>lower</u> opportunity costs than its trading partner.

By specializing in the production of goods and services for which they have the lowest opportunity cost, trading partners can produce <u>more</u> of all of the goods they trade. <u>Differences</u> in opportunity costs between trading partners provide the <u>incentive</u> to gain from specialization and trade.

ANSWER KEY

II   True/False

1. True. We know voluntary trade makes people better because individuals are utility maximizers. Trade allows people and nations to specialize in the production of the goods and services they are relatively best at producing. This allows trading partners to produce more of the traded goods.

2. False. History has shown that as the economy of a country grows, self-sufficiency declines and specialization increases. Trade between individuals and countries is necessary once specialization occurs in production.

3. False. The United States has an absolute advantage in the production of shirts. If the United States also has an absolute advantage in the production of potatoes, Malawi may have a comparative advantage in shirt production. Comparative advantage is based on a country's relative opportunity costs. The United States may have to give up more potatoes to produce one more shirt than Malawi does.

III   MULTIPLE CHOICE

1. The answer is D. The opportunity cost of a bottle of wine is the water you have to give up to produce the wine. In the time it takes a worker to produce one bottle of wine (1/500 of a person year) they could produce two bottles of sparkling water ([1/500]31000).

2. The answer is B. Singapore has an absolute advantage in both the production of rice and shirts since one worker can produce more of each product in a year. Bangladesh has a comparative advantage in the production of rice, since the opportunity cost of rice production is lower. To produce six more pounds of rice would require the resources that could produce only two shirts in Bangladesh, while in Singapore it would use the resources that could produce three shirts.

IV   Application and Discussion

A. Fill in the following table assuming that they *each* spend four hours a day fishing and four hours a day harvesting berries.

	Fish per day	Buckets of Berries per day
Bud	16 = (4 fish per hour 3 4 hours)	8 = (2 buckets per hour 3 4 hours)
Larry	8 = (2 fish per hour 3 4 hours)	8 = (2 bucket per hour 3 4 hours)
Total	24 fish	16 buckets of berries

B. Bud is better off because he has more of both fish and the same number of berries and works no more time than Larry. Bud has an absolute advantage in fish production.

C. Assume that Larry and Bud operate on straight-line production possibility curves.

	Opportunity Cost of a Bucket of Berries	Opportunity Cost of a Fish
Bud	2 fish	1/2 bucket of berries
Larry	1 fish	1 bucket of berries

D. Larry has a comparative advantage in berry production since he has the relatively lowest opportunity cost. Bud has a comparative advantage in fish production since his opportunity cost is lower.

ANSWER KEY

E. Larry can produce 16 buckets of berries in an eight hour day. Bud can produce 32 fish in an eight hour day. The gains from trade are the eight extra fish produced. Specialization in the activity in which Larry and Bud have the lowest opportunity cost allows them to increase the number of fish they produce with neither more time worked nor fewer berries consumed.

Section 17.3 Supply and Demand in International Trade

I   Review

The difference between what a consumer is willing to pay for a given amount of a good and what they have to pay is called consumer <u>surplus</u>. Consumers benefit from paying less than they would be willing to pay.

Producer <u>surplus</u> is the difference between the revenue the producer receives for selling a given amount of the good and the amount the producer is willing to accept. Producers benefit from receiving more than they would be willing to accept.

The demand curve represents the <u>maximum</u> prices consumers are willing and able to pay for different quantities of a good or service. The supply curve represents the <u>minimum</u> prices at which suppliers are willing to offer different quantities of the good or service.

As long as the maximum price the consumer is willing to pay <u>exceeds</u> the minimum price the supplier requires for one more unit of a good or service, there are mutually <u>beneficial</u> opportunities for trade.

When markets reach the <u>equilibrium</u> price, all the opportunities for mutually beneficial trade have taken place and the sum of consumer and producer surplus is <u>maximized</u>.

When a country trades with the rest of the world the price of the exported good is <u>higher</u> after trade than before. Domestic consumers <u>lose</u> from free trade because their consumer surplus is <u>reduced</u>. However, these losses are offset by the positive gains captured by domestic <u>producers</u>. On net, export trade <u>increases</u> domestic wealth.

When an economy trades with the rest of the world, the price of the imported good is <u>lower</u> after trade than before. Domestic consumers <u>gain</u> from free trade because their consumer surplus is <u>increased</u>. However, domestic producers lose because their producer surplus is <u>reduced</u>. On net, import trade <u>increases</u> domestic wealth since the gain to consumers <u>exceeds</u> the loss to producers.

II   True/False

1. False. For voluntary trade to take place *both* consumers and producers must benefit. Consumer surplus will be positive as long as the price consumers pay is no greater than the maximum they would be willing to pay. However, producers will not trade if that price is less than the minimum price they would be willing to accept, and producer surplus is negative. Voluntary trade will increase both consumer and producer surplus.

2. True. If the United States has a comparative advantage in farm products, we would expect that farm prices would increase with world trade and the U.S. farm industry producer surplus would increase. If the United States has a comparative disadvantage in cement production, we would expect cement prices would decline with world trade and the producer surplus in the U.S. cement industry would decrease. The domestic industries would be supporting their own self-interest with these opposing views on free trade.

3. False. Greece would have a comparative advantage if it could produce bananas at a relatively lower cost than other countries. The fact that other countries can sell bananas at a lower price than Greece suggests that Greece does not have the relatively lowest opportunity cost for banana production.

III   Multiple Choice

1. The answer is B. The producer surplus is the difference between the price the producer receives and the minimum price he would be willing to accept for a particular quantity of the product.

2. The answer is B. Consumer surplus is reduced because consumers pay a higher price, *P*AT, and consume a lower quantity of the good.

3. The answer is D. Producer surplus is increased because producers receive a higher price, *P*AT, after trade and produce a larger output, *Q*AT, of the good. A portion of the increased producer surplus equal to the area b is a transfer from consumers.

4. The answer is D. Export trade increases the producer surplus and reduces the consumer surplus generated in the country by the good. Net wealth increases though because the gain to producers exceeds the loss to consumers. In Exhibit 1 the area d represents the gains from trade.

IV   Application and Discussion

A) With international trade the Botswana price would fall to the world price. Once apples were available at the world price there would be no reason to pay more for apples.

B) Domestic production equals *Q*DT. Apple imports equal an amount (*Q*AT – *Q*DT).

C) See the modified Exhibit 26.1.

D) See the modified Exhibit 26.1.

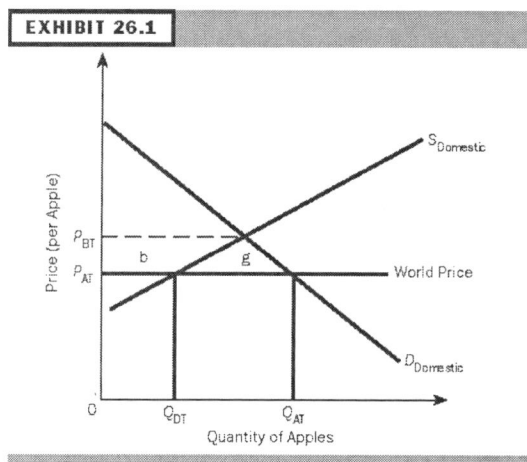

EXHIBIT 26.1

E) The increased consumer surplus equals a part, b, that is transferred from producers and a part, g, that results from the increased consumption. If consumers were required to compensate producers for their loss, they would give up b, but they would still receive increased consumer surplus equal to g.

Section 17.4 Tariffs, Import Quotas, and Subsidies

I   Review

A tariff is a(n) <u>tax</u> on imported goods.

Tariffs are used today to <u>protect</u> domestic industry from foreign competition.

A tariff is a <u>tax</u> on imported goods. Tariffs result in <u>higher</u> prices to domestic producers and <u>lower</u> sales and revenues to foreign producers.

ANSWER KEY

Domestic producers gain from tariff protection, but domestic consumers lose <u>more</u> than producers gain.

The <u>infant</u> industry argument in support of tariffs argues that tariff protection helps new industries reach the scale of operation at which they can be efficient.

Because tariffs increase domestic production, they are often supported as a mechanism for reducing <u>unemployment</u> in protected industries.

However, employment in other industries may suffer if exports are reduced because of <u>retaliation</u> by other countries. Export industries may also suffer because with a reduction in foreign imports, other countries will have <u>fewer</u> dollars to purchase our exports.

Tariffs are also supported for national security reasons. They can be used to limit our <u>dependence</u> on foreign producers for those goods vital to our national security.

A tariff on a good will create <u>benefits</u> for producers and <u>losses</u> for consumers. Even when losses exceed the benefits a tariff may be adopted, because producers are a more effective <u>lobbying</u> group for a tariff than consumer groups who lobby against tariffs.

An import <u>quota</u> limits international trade by defining a maximum number of units of a good that can be imported in a time period. Unlike tariffs, governments do not collect any <u>revenue</u> with a quota.

Import quotas make domestic producers <u>better</u> off, but make domestic consumers <u>worse</u> off.

Governments may also try to encourage exports by <u>subsidizing</u> producers. With subsidies producers export goods, not because their costs are relatively <u>lower</u> than other countries, but because their costs have been <u>artificially</u> lowered by transferring income from <u>taxpayers</u> to exporters.

II   True/False

1. False. A tariff is a tax, which increases the tax revenues of the country that imposes it. A quota limits the quantity of foreign goods entering a country but generates no tax revenue. Both tariffs and quotas result in higher domestic prices. The higher price paid for the import goes to the foreign producers under a quota.

2. False. Government subsidies can be used to lower the price at which a domestic producer can sell his product in other countries, but they do not change the cost of producing the good. Government subsidies shift part of the cost of producing export goods to taxpayers. Since export subsidies do not change the cost of production, they cannot change a country's comparative advantage. Such subsidies distort trade patterns and are inefficient.

3. False. Employment in other industries may suffer because of a tariff on steel. Jobs may be lost in the U.S. export sector because other countries may retaliate and impose tariffs on U.S. goods. Other countries may also import less because the U.S. tariff limits their ability to earn dollars. Finally, tariffs will raise the price of steel and make all goods for which steel is an input more expensive, which will result in reduced output and employment in these industries.

III   Multiple Choice

1. The answer is D. Domestic producers are willing to supply more shoes to the market at the higher domestic price.

2. The answer is C. Consumer surplus is reduced by a tariff because consumers buy less of the protected good and pay a higher price for it.

3. The answer is B. The price of imports with the tariff, $P1$, is still lower than the no tariff price of $P0$. Consumers will pay no more than the lower import price for sweaters.

4. The answer is D. Consumer surplus is reduced by a tariff because consumers buy fewer sweaters and pay a higher price for them.

ANSWER KEY

5. The answer is C. The net loss in welfare equals the reduced consumer surplus (the area a + b + c + d) minus the gain in producer surplus (the area a) and government revenues (the area c).

IV   Application and Discussion

A. When the tariff is removed we would expect 1) domestic maple syrup prices would fall; 2) domestic maple syrup production would decline; 3) total maple syrup consumption in the United States would increase; and 4) the amount of imported maple syrup would increase.

B. This is a sticky problem. If NAFTA did, in fact, result in a decrease in the U.S. production of maple syrup, U.S. jobs may be lost in that particular industry. However, with freer trade, it is likely that compensating increases in jobs in other industries will occur when Canada removes its tariff barriers, the United States will export more and this will create more jobs. Canadian maple syrup makers will also have more dollars to buy more U.S. goods. Even without the compensating job gains, removing the tariff on maple syrup is good policy because consumers would be able to compensate workers and producers from their increased consumer surplus and still be better off.

CHAPTER 18 INTERNATIONAL FINANCE

Section 18.1 The Balance of Payments

I   Review

The record of all the international transactions of a nation over a year is called the balance of <u>payments</u>. The balance of payments is divided into three main sections: the <u>current</u> account, the <u>capital</u> account, and the <u>statistical</u> <u>discrepancy</u>.

The current account is made up of imports and <u>exports</u> of goods and services. When a foreign buyer buys a good from a U.S. producer, the foreigner usually pays for the good in U.S. <u>dollars</u>.

All exports of U.S. goods are considered <u>credit</u> items in the U.S. balance of payments.

When a U.S. buyer buys an imported good the buyer usually pays in <u>foreign</u> currency. All imports of foreign goods are considered <u>debit</u> items in the U.S. balance of payments.

When the United States gives foreign aid to another country or when private individuals send money to relatives in foreign countries, it is recorded as a <u>debit</u> in the U.S. balance of payments.

The balance on current account is the net amount of credits and <u>debits</u> after adding up all transactions of goods, services, investment income, and fund transfers.

Countries finance deficits in their current accounts by running <u>surpluses</u> in their capital accounts.

II   True/False

1. True. We have run deficits in our balance on current account since the early 1980s.

2. False. "balance of trade" records imports and exports of goods and services. The current account balance also includes trade in services and transfers.

3. True. O verall t he d ebits i n the b alance o f p ayments e qual the c redits. If a nation buys more goods and services abroad t han it sells, so that debits exceed credits on current account, it must settle its debts by borrowing abroad. When financial capital flows in, it is counted as an offsetting credit on the capital account.

III   Multiple Choice

1. The answer is B. When Singapore Airlines buys an airplane made in the United States, its an export that counts as a credit to our current account. The British purchase of U.S. government bonds is also a credit, but it is a credit on our capital account.

2. The answer is C. When foreigners' tastes move in favor of American goods, they buy more from us and because our exports count as credits on current account, our balance on current account moves toward surplus.

IV   Application and Discussion

See Exhibit 18.1.

EXHIBIT 27.1

	Credit	Debit
1. Americans buy autos from Japan.	☐	☒
2. American tourists travel to Japan.	☐	☒
3. Japanese consumers buy rice grown in the United States.	☒	☐
4. United States gives foreign aid to Rwanda.	☐	☒
5. General Motors, a U.S. company, earns profits in France.	☒	☐
6. Royal Dutch Shell earns profits from its U.S. operations.	☐	☒
7. General Motors builds a new plant in Vietnam.	☐	☒
8. Japanese investors purchase U.S. government bonds.	☒	☐

1. Imports of goods are debits in the current account.

2. When American tourists travel to Japan, they buy foreign-produced services, including the use of hotels, sightseeing tours, etc. They are "importing" services; it is classified as a debit.

3. When we export rice to Japan, it's a credit on our current account.

4. Foreign aid creates a debit in the U.S. balance of payments because it gives foreigners added claims against the United States in the form of dollars.

5. General Motor's profits can be viewed as compensation for the use of capital services. Thus, the United States obtains claims on foreign countries just as it does when it exports goods, only in this case, a U.S. corporation is exporting capital services.

6. When a Dutch company earns profits from U.S. operations, it obtains compensation for the use of its capital services and the transaction is classified as a debit on the U.S. balance of payments.

7. When General Motors builds a plant abroad it is a capital outflow and classified as a debit on our capital account.

8. When foreign investors buy U.S. bonds it is a capital inflow and classified as a credit on our capital account.

Section 18.2 Exchange Rates

I   Review

When U.S. consumers buy goods from foreigners, the sellers of those goods want to be paid in their <u>domestic</u> currency. As a result, U.S. importers must <u>buy</u> foreign currency with dollars in order to finance their purchases. Similarly, people in other countries buying goods made in America must <u>sell</u> their currencies to obtain U.S. dollars in order to pay for those goods.

The price of a unit of one foreign currency in terms of another is called the <u>exchange</u> rate.

The demand for foreign currencies is what economists call <u>derived</u> demand. The more foreign goods are demanded, the <u>more</u> of that foreign currency that will be needed to pay for those goods. Increased demand for a currency will cause the exchange value of that currency to <u>rise</u>.

Foreign currency is supplied by foreigners who want to buy <u>exports</u> of a particular nation. For example, the more U.S. goods that foreigners demand, the <u>more</u> of their currency they will supply.

ANSWER KEY

The equilibrium exchange rate for a currency is determined by the supply and <u>demand</u> for that currency in the foreign exchange market.

II   True/False

1. False. The exchange value of the dollar is determined by the supply and demand for dollars on the foreign exchange market.

2. True. If it costs more dollars to buy a euro, it will become more expensive for Americans to buy European goods and they will buy fewer of those goods.

III   Multiple Choice

1. The answer is D. When Americans have to give up $2 to obtain a euro, rather than $1, it makes European goods more expensive. they will import fewer European goods.

2. The answer is D. The equilibrium dollar-yen exchange rate will increase when the supply of Yen decreases.

IV   Application and Discussion

1. Those who would be pleased by an appreciation of the dollar include (B) Americans planning to take trips to Europe, and (E) Americans who enjoy French cheese. An appreciation in the value of the dollar will make it less expensive for American tourists to travel in Europe, and it will make imported French cheese cheaper. Because an appreciation in the value of the dollar makes American goods more expensive to foreigners, the others won't like it.

2. Those who would be pleased by a depreciation in the value of the dollar include (A) American farmers, (C) General Motors stockholders, and (D) Japanese students planning to study in America. A depreciation in the value of the dollar makes American goods less expensive to Japanese consumers, or anyone else who holds yen. On the other hand, a depreciation in the dollar makes Japanese goods more expensive to Americans. American farmers will be pleased because their oranges, rice, wheat, and other products will become less expensive for Japanese consumers and those consumers will buy more U.S. agricultural products. GM stockholders will like it because a weaker dollar makes Toyotas, Hondas, and other Japanese vehicles more expensive. Japanese students like it because their yen will go farther in terms of what they can buy.

Section 18.3 Equilibrium Changes in the Foreign Exchange Market

I   Review

Any force that shifts either the demand for or supply of a currency will shift the <u>equilibrium</u> in the foreign exchange market, leading to a new <u>exchange</u> rate.

Factors that shift the demand for and supply of a currency include changes in <u>tastes</u> for goods and services, changes in <u>income</u>, changes in real <u>interest</u> rates, and changes in relative <u>inflation</u> rates.

If incomes increase in the United States, Americans will buy <u>more</u> goods, including European goods. This increase in demand for foreign goods will cause an <u>increase</u> in the demand for euros.

If incomes decrease in the United States, Americans will buy <u>fewer</u> goods, including European goods. This decrease in demand for foreign goods will cause a <u>decrease</u> in the demand for euros.

If interest rates in the United States increase relative to those in Europe, other things equal, the rate of return on U.S. investments will <u>increase</u> relative to that on European investments. European investors seeking higher rates of return will <u>buy</u> dollars with euros.

If interest rates in the United States decrease relative to those in Europe, investors will <u>sell</u> dollars and <u>buy</u> euros in order to make European investments.

ANSWER KEY

If the rate of inflation is higher in Europe than in the United States, European products will become <u>more</u> expensive to U.S. consumers. Americans will <u>decrease</u> the quantity of European goods they demand and their demand for euros will <u>decrease</u>. At the same time, the higher rate of European inflation will make U.S. goods relatively <u>less</u> expensive to Europeans. This will lead Europeans to <u>increase</u> the quantity of U.S. goods demanded and lead to an <u>increase</u> in the supply of euros.

Overall, the result of the higher rate of European inflation will be a new, <u>lower</u>, equilibrium price for the euro.

If speculators believe that the price of a country's currency is going to rise they will buy <u>more</u> of that currency.

II   True/False

1. False. The equilibrium exchange rate of currencies like the dollar, the yen, and the euro, change constantly as factors such as tastes, incomes, relative interest rates, and relative inflation rates change. Changes in the exchange value of the dollar are followed daily in the business section of your newspaper.

2. True. Higher U.S. interest rates will attract investors who will have to buy dollars with foreign currency in order to earn interest in the United States. The increased demand for dollars will cause the dollar to appreciate in value.

3. True. If the dollar appreciates it will buy more yen. Janelle can buy more goods and services in Japan with the dollars she has saved. For example, if the dollar goes from $1 = ¥100 to $1 = ¥150 she can buy ¥150 worth of goods and services with each dollar, whereas before she could buy only ¥100 worth of goods and services with each dollar.

III   Multiple Choice

1. The answer is B. If Americans' incomes rise, they will buy more goods, including those made in foreign countries. As they buy foreign goods, they supply dollars and demand foreign currencies, like yen and euros, on the foreign exchange market. The supply curve for dollars shifts to the right.

2. The answer is B. The dollar can now buy more yen and more Japanese goods. It has appreciated or become "stronger."

IV   Application and Discussion

See Exhibit 27.2

EXHIBIT 27.2			
	Supply of Dollars	**Demand for Dollars**	**Equilibrium Exchange Rate**
1. Americans buy more European goods.	increase	same	decrease
2. Europeans invest in U.S. stock market.	same	increase	increase
3. European tourists flock to the United States.	same	increase	increase
4. Europeans buy U.S. government bonds.	same	increase	increase
5. American tourists flock to Europe.	increase	same	decrease

1. When Americans buy European goods they supply dollars and demand Euros. The increases supply of dollars shifts the supply curve to the right and the equilibrium exchange rate for dollars decreases.

ANSWER KEY

2. When Europeans buy U.S. stocks, they must use their currency to buy dollars in order to make the investments. Europeans supply their currency and demand dollars. The increased demand for dollars causes the equilibrium exchange rate for dollars to rise.

3. When European tourists visit America they must convert their currency to dollars. Thus, they supply their currency and demand dollars, causing the equilibrium exchange rate of the dollar to rise.

4. When Europeans buy U.S. government bonds they must do so with dollars. To get the necessary dollars they supply their currency and demand dollars. The exchange value of the dollar rises.

5. When Americans visit Europe they need euros, pounds, and other European currency. They supply dollars and demand those foreign currencies. The increase in the supply of dollars pushes the equilibrium exchange rate of the dollar down.

Section 18.4 Flexible Exchange Rates

I   Review

Since 1973 the world has essentially operated on a system of <u>flexible</u> exchange rates. Governments, however, sometimes <u>intervene</u> in foreign exchange markets in order to prop up an exchange rate that they consider too <u>low</u> or to depress an exchange rate they consider to be too <u>high</u>.

Prior to 1973, the world operated on a system of <u>fixed</u> exchange rates called the Bretton Woods system.

When exchange rates change they affect not only the currency market but the <u>product</u> markets as well. For example, if the dollar increases in value relative to other currencies, the relative prices of foreign goods for Americans will <u>decrease</u>. Foreigners will find that the stronger dollar makes U.S. products <u>more</u> expensive for them.

Since the advent of flexible exchange rates, world trade has not only continued, but <u>expanded</u>.

Changes in exchange rates occur <u>more</u> often under a flexible-rate system than they do under a fixed-rate system, but the changes are much <u>smaller</u> than the drastic, overnight revaluations of currencies under the fixed-rate system.

Under a fixed-rate system, as the supply and demand for currencies <u>change</u>, currency prices are not allowed to shift to a new equilibrium, leading to surpluses and <u>shortages</u> of currencies.

One major argument against flexible exchange rates is that they cause <u>uncertainty</u> and may lead to a decrease in the level of world trade.

Another argument against flexible rates is that they may allow governments to pursue expansionary fiscal and monetary policies that may lead to <u>inflation</u>.

II   True/False

1. False. Since 1973 the world has operated under a system of flexible exchange rates under which exchange values are determined by the forces of supply and demand.

2. True. Governments intervene from time to time in order to prop up exchange rates that they consider to low, or to depress exchange rates that they consider to be too high.

III   Multiple Choice

1. The answer is A. A decrease in demand for the currency will cause the value of the currency to depreciate (i.e. one dollar will buy fewer Euros). The country's exports will become less expensive and foreign goods will become more expensive.

2. The answer is D. A major argument against flexible rates is that they create uncertainty.

ANSWER KEY

3. The answer is B. When currency rates are fixed, changes in supply and/or demand can lead to shortages or surpluses of currencies.

IV   APPLICATION

A shift toward more expansionary monetary policy by the Fed would cause the exchange value of the dollar to decrease (depreciate) and would tend to move America's balance of trade toward surplus. Expansionary monetary policy would lower U.S. interest rates, boost incomes temporarily, and tend to cause inflation. All of these will result in a new, lower exchange value for the dollar. The weaker dollar will make U.S. exports cheaper to the rest of the world, so that our exports will increase. In turn, foreign goods will cost more imports will decrease.